'This is a book for those who take children seriously. A wonderful, practical resource for those who want to nurture children to be disciples in their own right: to pray, to engage with Scripture, to contribute to worship, to play their part as children of God. A must-read for those who work and volu̶ ̶ ̶ ̶ ̶ ̶ ̶ ̶ ̶ ̶ ̶ ̶'

*The Most Revd J̶*

CH00920001

'*Diddy Disciples* approaches worship and storytelling with reverence and joy! Ch̶ learn from the liturgical intelligence, sensitivity and natural language of Sharo̶ An inspirational resource for all on the way of discipleship, including special at̶ baptism.'

*Dr Matthew Salisbury, National Liturgy and Worship, Church of England*

'*Diddy Disciples* is a flexible resource that acknowledges the importance and significance of enabling the youngest at church to engage in worship and begin a faith journey. The book not only offers ideas for a range of different settings and of personality and learning styles, but is also clearly built upon a theological and developmental understanding of children and faith. This is a resource that we will be using within our church setting, as we seek to engage and empower children from the youngest age in their understanding of God, faith, themselves and the world.'

*Steve Chalke, founder and leader, Oasis Global*

'Even though Jesus makes it clear that entering the kingdom of God requires us to become like children, real children are often neglected in the catechetical and formational life of the Church. *Diddy Disciples* puts that right! Here is a resource to help the children come to Jesus and grow as his disciples.'

*The Rt Revd Stephen Cottrell, Bishop of Chelmsford*

'*Diddy Disciples* is an invaluable blend of Sharon Moughtin-Mumby's reflective practice and contemporary thinking about childhood spirituality. The result is an exceptional and inspiring resource for churches working with the very youngest children. A powerful case for seeing why the very young deserve the very best, and this is a well-tested method for doing that.'

*Dr Rebecca Nye, Godly Play expert and researcher and consultant in children's spirituality*

'Wonderful! We have here a handling of Christian worship and the Bible that embodies a rich and creative imaginative seriousness, a sure understanding of theology and an experienced appreciation of the practicalities of working with young children. I haven't come across anything else nearly as good as this.'

*The Revd Professor Walter Moberly, Durham University*

'*Diddy Disciples* is aimed at pedagogy for children, but the author is mindful of Jesus' words, and what she has written is just as relevant for adult education and pedagogy as well. Sharon Moughtin-Mumby's book stresses that education is "not words alone", and that doesn't just apply to children. What she has produced gives due attention to what it is one is wanting to communicate. What she has given us is based on the importance of movement, repetition, attending to children's own voices and emotions, nurturing what's already there and offering children a space in church which is dedicated to their needs and gifts. We are all in her debt for this insightful mixture of information and method.'

*The Revd Professor Christopher Rowland*
*Emeritus Professor of Exegesis of Holy Scripture, University of Oxford*

'Sharon Moughtin-Mumby has accomplished something marvellously fresh, profound and practical with *Diddy Disciples*. There is a depth of biblical and liturgical understanding here which sets this resource apart, yet that understanding consistently serves the most kinetic and straight-out joyful set of Christian materials for children that one could hope to encounter. The rich array of options on offer within each unit and section means that it is all superbly flexible and adaptable for churches of different sizes, shapes and settings. I cannot recommend it highly enough.'

*The Revd Dr David Hilborn, Principal, St John's College, Nottingham*

'Thank God for Diddy Disciples, an excellent programme of Christ-centred discipleship for our children and youth. I commend this book to you, as a real hope to this and future generations.'

*The Rt Revd Dr Karowei Dorgu, Bishop of Woolwich, aka 'the Diddy bishop'*

'This is a must-have resource, bringing scholarship and imagination together. No one is excluded from the wonder of exploring the Bible!'

*The Rt Revd Dr Helen-Ann Hartley, Bishop of Waikato, New Zealand*

'I am really impressed with the *Diddy Disciples* resources – accessible, fun, interactive, inclusive and orthodox all at the same time, while introducing children to the profundity and life-giving nature of Jesus and his teaching . . . loving it!'

*The Rt Revd Dr Mike Harrison, Bishop of Dunwich*

'We all think we know that biblical scholarship and Sunday School teaching belong in different worlds. *Diddy Disciples* shows that we are wrong. Sharon Moughtin-Mumby brings the wisdom of a professional biblical scholar to the task of communicating the essence of the Bible to very young children, unveiling the depths of biblical stories for young disciples. Very user-friendly material from which adults can learn too.'

*The Revd John Barton, Emeritus Professor, University of Oxford*

'*Diddy Disciples* is brilliant: a rich resource for leaders, simple and accessible for young children, inviting them into a lifelong journey of faith. Highly commended.'

*The Rt Revd Dr Steven Croft, Bishop of Oxford*

'I'm excited by *Diddy Disciples*! It's a celebration of Psalm 8.2 and all that babies and toddlers bring to worship. Movement, stories, actions and songs combine in carefully crafted sessions to draw groups into a new way of worshipping that will enrich everyone involved. I can't wait to start using it.'

*The Revd Mary Hawes, National Children and Youth Adviser, The Church of England*

'When Jesus taught, he often used a language that was unafraid to hover rather than land. Through imaginative and playful provocation, he was opening up spaces for his listeners to move into. This is exactly what *Diddy Disciples* does. It takes for granted the fact that young children are intelligent and perceptive, and it therefore doesn't look down on them. Neither does it pretend that Christian faith is anything but a rich, complex and teasing migration towards the love and mystery of God, where questions can be as vital as insights. This is a liberating combination for everyone involved.'

*The Revd Canon Mark Oakley, Chancellor of St Paul's Cathedral*

'Diddy Disciples [the programme] is being taken up enthusiastically by a growing number of parishes in the Diocese of Southwark. Helping young children grow into the fullness of Christ through creative, age-appropriate engagement is a wonderful journey of adventure and discovery; and this book, which I gladly commend, will be an essential resource for anyone starting out on that path.'

*The Rt Revd Christopher Chessun, Bishop of Southwark*

'I am very happy to support [the] Diddy Disciples [programme]. I was particularly encouraged and impressed by the way in which the biblical approach is intelligent and searching, without being above the heads of those for whom it is intended, or condescending to them. Similarly, the programme is firmly connected with the liturgical life of the Church, and this is something that is particularly important in a time when there seems to be widespread enthusiasm for separating all-age worship from good liturgy.'

*The Most Revd Dr Richard Clarke, Archbishop of Armagh and Primate of All Ireland*

'This is a serious book: serious about children; serious about worship; serious about spirituality; serious about God. Sharon Moughtin-Mumby draws upon her own experience as a priest, a parent and a theologian, and on the time-honoured shape of the liturgy, to create patterns for worship that honour God, by enabling the tiniest worshippers to hear the word and respond in praise. She offers enchanting and creative resources that will help to build the Church.'

*Gill Ambrose, Consultant to the Liturgical Commission and Chair of Godly Play UK*

'Anyone involved in education would agree that the early years in a child's life are crucial for laying the foundations of learning. We so often underestimate children's abilities and needs. *Diddy Disciples* is the resource I have been waiting for: a superb treasure trove of meaningful, interesting and challenging activities for pre-school children in our churches. Whether at a weekday event or Sunday School, *Diddy Disciples* provides singing, texts and ideas that link with the Church's year and provide the building blocks for Christian education. This is an essential resource for every church school, parish and Christian nursery.

[The] Diddy Disciples [programme] has been road-tested in a real parish with real children. It demands nothing more than the resources available in any parish or setting. It is properly theological and completely age appropriate. If children are to experience proper faith development and to grow as disciples, it is just material like this that will give the resources needed. A lifetime of Christian discipleship is built on solid foundations. *Diddy Disciples* provides that resource.'

*Fr Richard Peers, Director of Education, Diocese of Liverpool*

**The Revd Dr Sharon Moughtin-Mumby** is the author of Diddy Disciples, which she set up at St Peter's, Walworth, South London, when her own wriggly children were three, three and two, and going to church with them felt impossible! Sharon is an Anglican priest and a respected Bible scholar with a strong interest in Bible translation, imagery, art and biblical languages. Before ordination, she was a tutor in Old Testament studies at Ripon College Cuddesdon, and taught Hebrew at the University of Oxford. She continues to have a passion for education, particularly during the formative early years of life, and loves exploring new, ancient and imaginative ways of engaging with the Bible and worshipping alongside young children.

# Diddy Disciples
## Book 2: January to August

Worship and storytelling resources for babies, toddlers and young children

Sharon Moughtin-Mumby

First published in Great Britain in 2017

Society for Promoting Christian Knowledge
36 Causton Street
London SW1P 4ST
www.spck.org.uk

There are supporting web resources at <**www.diddydisciples.org**>. The password for the website is **likeachild18**

*British Library Cataloguing-in-Publication Data*
A catalogue record for this book is available from the British Library

ISBN 978–0–281–07788–5
eBook ISBN 978–0–281–07789–2

Designed by Melissa Brunelli
Typeset by Fakenham Prepress Solutions, Fakenham, Norfolk NR21 8NN
First printed in Great Britain by Ashford Colour Press
Subsequently digitally reprinted in Great Britain

eBook by Fakenham Prepress Solutions, Fakenham, Norfolk NR21 8NN

Produced on paper from sustainable forests

*For my inspirational daughters, Joy, Anastasia and Zoe,*
*and my husband, colleague and friend, Andrew*

# CONTENTS

## Part 2: Additional information and resources

# ACKNOWLEDGEMENTS

Diddy Disciples would never have happened without the children of St Peter's, Walworth. As I said in Book 1, I've come to see the Diddy Disciples as a little editorial team, giving me helpful comments and suggestions as we've gone along! Thank you, little sisters and brothers: it's such a joy to worship with you and learn from you.

## Regular Diddy contributors from St Peter's Church

Aaron, Abbey, Abigail, Abu, Adammah, Aimee, Albert, Alex, Albert, Alfred, Alice, Amy, Anastasia, Anna, Ariyanna, Austin, Ava, Bernice, Bella, Cameron, Chelsea, Christian, Cleo, Daijuan, Decory, Daniel, Daniel, Deborah, Demari, Dickson, Eden, Efe, Elijah, Emerald, Emmanuel, Emmanuella, Eri, Ezra, Fire, Gavin, Geoffrey, Gladys, Golden, Gracie, Imani, Isaac, Isabella, Isla, James, Jayden, Jessica, Jo Jo, Joseph, Jovianni, Joy, Jude, Justin, Kaiden, Keisha, Khari, Latif, Latoya, Libby, Lily, Lorien, Louise, Lucas, Maryam, Mary, Maxwell, Micah, Michael, Miller, Mitchell, Mofiyin, Nancy, Naomi, Otter, Philip, Rachel, Richard, Russell, Ryan, Samson, Sasha, Sepphorah, Shemaiah, Shane, Shannon, Sophia, Susan, Temitope, Timi, Ximena, Zayden, Zoe, Zoe, Zoey.

## Diddy contributors and friends from St Peter's School

Aamilah, Aania, Abass, Abigail, Abu, Adiss, Adonia, Ainhoa, Akil, Alexandra, Alfie, Alicia, Alieu, Alisha, Amaya, Amelia, Amir, Amy, Andres, Aneesa, Ansel, Arielle, Ashleigh, Austin, Ayla-May, Biola, Brigitte, Chelsea, Christian, Cleo, Crystal, Daijuan, Daniel, Darcey, David, Deborah, Dickson, Divine, Dylan, Eden, Eleanor, Eleil, Elijah, Elissa, Eliza, Elizabeth, Emerald, Emil, Emmanuel, Emmanuelle, Enoch, Ephraim, Ethan, Fabrice, Fraser, Gavin, Grace, Harry, Ibrahim, Isab, Isabella, Isaiah, Jaida, Jake, James, Jasmine, Jeffrey, Jessica, Jhon, Joel, Joel, Joel, Josephine, Jovianni, Joyce, Jude, Julia, Juliet, Kai, Kayleigh, Keisha, King, Kofi, Kwabena, Kwaku, Kwame, Lateef, Leonard, Lily-Rose, Luke, Madox, Mahlon, Maisie, Maja, Ma'khadijah, Marlon, Mason, Michael, Michelle, Mitchell, Moremi, Muhammed, Mya, Nancy, Nathaniel, Osariemen, Pearl, Philip, Reggie, Rhys, Rosa, Rukaiya, Ryleigh, Samuel, Saoirse, Sarah, Selleh, Shalom, Soufriere, Stanley, Sultan, Susan, Victory, Ya-Kai, Ya-Sapor, Zayden, Zephaniah, Zoe, Zoe.

## The amazing Diddy illustrators from St Peter's Church and School

Abigail, Amelia, Amy, Anastasia, Bella, Christian, Daijuan, Darcey, Eden, Elijah, Gavin, Harry, Isabella, Isla, Jessica, Joy, Julia, Kayleigh, Lily, Marlon, Mya, Michael, Michelle, Mitchell, Nancy, Pearl, Philip, Samson, Samuel, Sarah, Sultan, Susan, Susannah, Zayden, Zoe, Zoey.

It's a special pleasure to thank the congregation, PCC, wardens, staff and clergy team of St Peter's, Walworth, once again for their support and all they contribute to the project. Particular thanks go to Gene, Kate, Doreen, Aisha, Dipo, Femi, Clare, Lucia, Lady, Laura, Chris, Ian, Theo, Eileen, Novelette, Donna, Robert, Beryl, Lahan, Mary, Catherine, Michael, Alan and Andrew. Thank you also to St Peter's School for making Tuesday Diddy Disciples in the sanctuary such a joy especially Laura, Debbie, Julie, Tracy, Sue, Deborah, Linda, Audrey, Marcia, Wendy, Charlie, Laura, Claudette and their head teacher, Anne-Marie Bahlol.

Huge thanks go to Christopher Chessun, Bishop of Southwark, the first bishop to preside at Diddy Disciples, for his unwavering support and encouragement. Thank you also to Bishop Karowei, Bishop of Woolwich, who to our great joy has named himself 'the Diddy Bishop', and Jane Steen, the first archdeacon to preside at Diddy Disciples. Book 2 was completed while I was scholar in residence at the Anglican Centre in Rome: thank you, Archbishop David Moxon, for the generosity of your welcome.

Thank you to all those involved in creating the Diddy Disciples website at <www.diddydisciples.org>, especially Gemma McGrillis from Whistle Graphics for her creativity and amazing patience, Femi Omole for some stunning photography and Alan Mumby for his experience and wisdom. Thank you also to the Woolwich Area in the Diocese of Southwark for funding the site and making it possible.

There are many others who contribute to the project behind the scenes. It's impossible to mention them all here, but special thanks go to Kate Penfold, Hugh Ridsdill-Smith, Niall Sloane, Daniel Trott, Michael Robinson,

Nick Shepherd, Richard Peers, Sam Wells, Alison Seaman, Mary Hawes, Mae Mouk, Alex Lawson, Sarah Strandoo, Beth Hayward, Ross Moughtin, Odette Penwarden and Charlotte Chappell.

Thank you to the team at SPCK for their guidance, experience and advice, especially Tracey Messenger, Juliet Trickey, Liz Jones, Olivia Carson and Rima Devereaux. I'm particularly grateful to Rima for her painstaking and patient work on both Books 1 and 2 and to Tracey for her advice and encouragement.

Finally, I would like to thank Andrew and my daughters for all they bring to Diddy Disciples as it grows bigger than we ever imagined. Andrew, Joy, Anastasia and Zoe, thank you!

# INTRODUCTION

Book 1 includes a thorough introduction for those interested in starting up a Diddy Disciples group. If you're using the material for the first time, our advice is to start there with the Introduction (pp. 3–22) and A Guide to the Building Blocks (pp. 217–32).

# Part 1
## The Diddy Disciples units
(January to August)

# UNIT 1
# JESUS, LIGHT OF THE WORLD! (EPIPHANY)

The Jesus, Light of the World! unit continues the Christmas celebrations of Jesus' birth and is designed for the Epiphany season (the weeks immediately after Christmas). Together with the John the Baptist unit that follows, this unit is designed to lead the children, week by week, from the joy of Christmas through to the wilderness, the quiet giving up of things in Lent and the journey to the cross.

Rather than leaving Christmas behind immediately, the children are invited to join the Magi (Wise Men/Three Kings) in reflecting on the gifts they'd like to bring to Baby Jesus now that all the excitement of the present-giving/receiving in homes is generally over. The unit culminates with the joyful presentation of Jesus at the Temple, where Simeon (like Zechariah before him) recognizes Jesus as the Light: this time the Light not just *dawning* in Israel (Luke 1.78) but *shining* through the whole world (Luke 2.32)!

'Extra' sessions are included for this unit, because the number of weeks between Christmas and the beginning of Lent changes yearly. We suggest that you look at how many weeks your groups will be meeting between Christmas and the beginning of Lent this year and construct your own timetable so that Jesus Gives Up Everything for Us (the final week of the John the Baptist unit) is held on the Sunday before Lent. Suggestions of how to fit the stories to the current year can be found on the Diddy Disciples website.

So your group can work out your timetable up to Lent more easily, the sessions from the next unit, John the Baptist, are as follows.

**John the Baptist (the weeks before Lent)**

* In years with very few Sundays between Christmas and Lent, your group may need to combine Weeks 1 and 2 of John the Baptist into a single week. The storytelling material in that unit sets out how to combine the stories.

Churches that follow the Revised Common Lectionary may notice that the baptism of Jesus (traditionally told during the Epiphany season) instead appears in the following unit (John the Baptist). In practice, we found the lectionary's move from Jesus being a baby (the Magi) to being an adult (baptism of Jesus) then back to being a baby (presentation of Jesus) was confusing for young children. We've therefore reordered these stories so that all the stories of Jesus as a baby/toddler are told together (though not necessarily chronologically).

## Section 1

# The Building Blocks: Jesus, Light of the World! unit

Pick and choose from these Building Blocks and their various options to build sessions for your group. Whatever choices you make, we suggest you keep to that pattern for the whole of the unit as this will open up opportunities for the children to participate fully and confidently during your time together.

> **Build your own Diddy Disciples session** (Book 1, p. 6) provides an overview of the Building Blocks and a short introduction to fitting them together, along with examples.
>
> **A Guide to the Building Blocks** (Book 1, pp. 217ff.) provides a step-by-step guide to each Building Block.

### Tip

Throughout this unit, you might like to use a doll to represent Baby Jesus, born at Christmas: lying in a manger or on white/gold cloth on a focal table.

## Welcome

→ **Guide: Book 1, p. 218**

*Welcome your group.*

Let's start by going around the circle
and saying our name out loud.
My name's _____.

*Go around the circle so that every adult and child has the chance to say his or her name (and introduce any dolls, teddies or toys). If any of the children don't want to say their name, or aren't able to, you (or a parent or carer) could say it for them and wave.*

It's time to sing our Welcome Song!

### Welcome Song: Option 1

→ **Song: 'The Diddy Disciples welcome song'. Words: © Sharon Moughtin-Mumby**
→ **Tune: 'Glory, glory, alleluia!' (traditional). For a taster see the Diddy Disciples website. For tips on teaching songs for the first time, see Book 1, p. 215.**

*Go around the circle the same way as above. See if you can remember each other's names and insert them into the song.*

**Welcome** *Name 1* **to St Peter's\***
**Welcome** *Name 2* **to St Peter's\***
**Welcome** *Name 3* **to St Peter's\***
**You are welcome in the name of the Lord!**

*\* Insert the name of your church or children's group, or sing 'our worship'.*

### Welcome Song: Option 2

→ **Song: 'You are welcome in the name of the Lord' (traditional)**
→ **Tune: traditional. For a taster see the Diddy Disciples website. For tips on teaching songs for the first time, see Book 1, p. 215.**

Let's wave with one hand. *Lead waving*

Then with our other hand. *Lead waving*

Then let's choose someone and show God's 'glory'!

*Move arms up and down in front of you with fingers wiggling, palms facing out, towards one person.*

And someone else! *Repeat*

Then let's wave with both hands all around the circle.

*Lead waving.*

We're ready to sing!

**You are welcome in the name of the Lord!**
*Wave with right hand to one person.*
**You are welcome in the name of the Lord!**
*Wave with left hand to another person.*
**I can see all over you, the glory of the Lord!**
*Move arms up and down in front of you with fingers wiggling,*
*palms facing out, towards one person and then another.*
**You are welcome in the name of the Lord!**
*Wave with both hands all around the circle.*

# Getting Ready to Worship

→ **Guide: Book 1, p. 218**

*Choose one of the following greetings according to which greeting is familiar in your church. (If your church uses a different greeting, you could use that here instead.)*

## Getting Ready to Worship: Option 1

→ Action: the sign of the cross. Words: © Sharon Moughtin-Mumby

*Invite the children to make the sign of the cross slowly with you. As the children become more confident, invite a child to lead the action as the whole group says the words and makes the sign of the cross.*

**In my head,** *touch head*
**in my heart,** *touch chest*
**and all around me,** *touch shoulders one by one*
**Jesus is here.** *open hands in front, facing upwards*

## Getting Ready to Worship: Option 2

→ Action: 'The Lord be with you' (open hands)

Let's start by clenching our hands together tightly.

*Lead children in clenching fists against your body to show a defensive posture.*

When we close ourselves up like this,
it's hard to let anyone into our heart.
It's hard even to let God into our heart!

When we get ready to worship,
we show that we're open to God and to each other.

*Open your hands out, facing up.*

Can you show me your open hands?
We're ready to let God and each other in!

The Lord be with you.
*Hold hands open to the children.*

**And also with you.**
*Invite the children to open their hands towards you.*

# Introducing the Unit

→ Guide: Book 1, p. 218

## Introducing the Unit: Option 1

At the moment, we're celebrating Baby Jesus,
born at Christmas.

Let's close our eyes and feel the dark.
Let's imagine Jesus shining like a tiny star in the sky.
Now let's imagine that light growing brighter and brighter and brighter . . .
until it fills the whole world!
So bright we can't even look at it!
Let's open our eyes again.

Baby Jesus, the Light of the World, is shining bright. *Jazz hands*
Let's show jazz hands for Jesus' light. *Jazz hands*

> *If your group used the 'Busy, busy, busy' Gathering Song in the previous unit (Book 1, p. 171)*
> Before Christmas, we were 'busy, busy, busy'
> getting ready for Jesus, Light of the World,
> to DAWN in the darkness. *Show the sun rising up and out with your arms*
>
> Jesus' light was just beginning to come up,
> like the sun in the morning.
> Now Jesus' light is shining BRIGHT! *Jazz hands*

It's time to celebrate!

## Introducing the Unit: Option 2

→ **Focus: the liturgical colours white and gold**

*Note for churches that use liturgical colours: the rule of thumb is that the season changes from Epiphany (white/gold) to Green Time (green) on the Sunday between 28 January and 3 February. After this date, change your colours to green and use Option 1 above instead.*

Who can tell us what colour season we're in now?
> *If appropriate:* You may have seen our colours in church.

White and gold are the colours of joy and celebration!

It's 'Epiphany'!

> *If appropriate:* Can you say 'Epiphany'?
> **Epiphany.**

In 'Epiphany' we celebrate Baby Jesus,
born at Christmas.

Let's close our eyes and feel the dark.
Let's imagine Jesus shining like a tiny star in the sky.
Now let's imagine that light growing brighter and brighter and brighter . . .
until it fills the whole world!
So bright we can't even look at it!
Let's open our eyes again.

Baby Jesus, the Light of the World, is
shining bright. *Jazz hands*
Let's show jazz hands for Jesus' light. *Jazz hands*

> *If your group used the 'Busy, busy, busy' Gathering Song in the previous unit (Book 1, p. 171)*
> Before Christmas, we were 'busy, busy, busy'

getting ready for Jesus, Light of the World,
to DAWN in the darkness. *Show the sun rising up and out with your arms*
Jesus' light was just beginning to come up,
like the sun in the morning.
Now Jesus' light is shining BRIGHT! *Jazz hands*

That's the message of Epiphany:
Jesus is the Light of the World shining! *Jazz hands*
It's time to celebrate!

# Gathering Song

→ **Guide: Book 1, p. 219**
→ **Song: 'We are waking in the light of God', based on 'We are marching in the light of God' (traditional)**
→ **Tune: traditional. For a taster see the Diddy Disciples website.**

> **Tip**
>
> If your group has imaginative aids, you may like to think about whether you want to use them for this song, which also works well with whole body movements. If you do use the aids, they can add a great flourish on the word 'Oh!' and we've found the children can be wonderfully inventive in finding actions that use the aids.

*If you're using imaginative aids, ask two or three children to give them out at this point. Then invite the children to warm up their imaginations by exploring actions for different kinds of activities: writing, eating, painting, washing, cooking, eating, playing, hiding, brushing teeth, etc.* 'Can you show me . . . writing!' *etc.*

Our song [for Epiphany] is all about Jesus' light shining.
It's about how everything we do is in 'the light of God'.

We started off our day in bed.
So let's start our song fast asleep in bed.
Who can show me fast asleep!
*Lead the children in showing fast asleep.*

Morning! It's time to wake up!
Let's stretch up high with our arms.
*Lead the children in stretching and waking.*
When we wake up, we wake up in the light of God!

Now let's eat our breakfast.
Maybe we had toast or cereal or something else . . .
Let's eat our breakfast together now.
*Lead the children in miming eating their breakfast.*

Let's sing 'We are waking in the light of God'. *Stretching action*
Then halfway through, let's change to
'We are eating'. *Eating breakfast action*

> *Either:*
> And when we sing 'oh!' *jazz hands*
> let's show Jesus' light shining all around us with jazz hands.
> *Lead the children in jazz hands.*

> *Or (if you're using imaginative aids):*
> And when we sing 'oh!' *fireworks action (aids moving very fast above head)*
> let's show Jesus' light SPARKLING like fireworks all around us. *Fireworks action*

*This song is so repetitive it doesn't need to be taught line by line. Instead, start singing with the actions and the children and the rest of the group will gradually begin to join in. Some of the group may already know the traditional version of the song.*

Let's start off asleep . . . Ssssssssh!
*Lead the children in miming sleeping.*
Time to wake up!

**We are waking** *stretching action* **in the light of God,**
**we are waking** *stretching action* **in the light of God!**
**We are waking** *stretching action* **in the light of God,**
**we are waking** *stretching action* **in the light of God!**
*Interrupt the song:* Breakfast time!
**We are eating,** *eating action* **we are eating, oh!** *Jazz hands*
**We are eating** *eating action* **in the light of God!**
**We are eating,** *eating action* **we are eating, oh!** *Jazz hands*
**We are eating** *eating action* **in the light of God!**

I wonder what else we'll do today?
*Invite two different children to make two different suggestions together with an action. (We change actions halfway through the song.) If the group is part of a playschool/nursery/school you could also ask one of the teaching staff what the children will be doing that day to help make connections between this time of worship and the rest of each child's day.*

> *Example: the children might suggest counting and playing.*
> Let's start by *painting* in the light of God.
> Can you show me painting?
> *Lead the group in following the suggested action for painting.*

> Then let's *play* in the light of God!
> Can you show me an action for playing?
> *Lead the group in following the suggested action for painting.*
> Let's go!

> *Lead the children in continuing painting as you sing.*
> **We are painting in the light of God,**
> **we are painting in the light of God!**
> **We are painting in the light of God,**
> **we are painting in the light of God!**
> *Interrupt singing:* Playtime!
> *Lead the children in their chosen playing action as they sing.*
> **We are playing, we are playing, oh!** *Jazz hands or fireworks action*
> **We are playing in the light of God!**
> **We are playing, we are playing, oh!** *Jazz hands or fireworks action*

**We are playing in the light of God!**
*Depending on your group, you may like to repeat with two new actions.*

*Actions we have used at St Peter's, Walworth, include:*
**We are** *learning* **in the light of God!** *Action for phonics sound of the week*
**We are** *singing* **in the light of God!** *Conducting action*
**We are** *jumping* **in the light of God!** *Jumping up and down*
**We are** *counting* **in the light of God!** *Counting on fingers*
**We are** *praying* **in the light of God!** *Hands together*
**We are** *brushing* **in the light of God!** *Mime brushing teeth*
**We are** *walking* **in the light of God!** *Walking on the spot*
**We are** *climbing* **in the light of God!** *Mime climbing a tree*
**We are** *reading* **in the light of God!** *Mime reading a book*
**We are** *cooking* **in the light of God!** *Mime stirring*
*Encourage the children to make their own suggestions. Everything we do is in the light of God!*

*When it comes to the final time that you'll sing the song:*
My goodness! We've done a lot today!
Who's feeling tired?
Let's rest.
*Raise arms and wiggle fingers, slowly bringing arms downwards to show a resting action.*

Can you show me resting? *Resting action*
And now sleeping . . . *Rest head to one side on joined hands*
It might be dark outside when we go to bed,
but let's remember Jesus' light is still shining in us.

So let's rest in the light of God. *Resting action*
Then let's sleep . . . *Sleeping action*

*Sing quietly:*
**We are resting in the light of God,** *resting action*
**we are resting in the light of God!** *Resting action*
**We are resting in the light of God,** *resting action*
**we are resting in the light of God!** *Resting action*
*Interrupt:* Sleepy time! Ssssh!
*Lead the children in settling down to sleep.*
**We are sleeping, we are sleeping, ssssh!**
**We are sleeping in the light of God!**
**We are sleeping, we are sleeping, ssssh!**
**We are sleeping in the light of God!**

Jesus is the Light of the World!
We'll be doing lots of things today.
Let's remember [the message of Epiphany]
Jesus' light is shining whatever we do.

# Getting Ready for Bible Storytelling

→ **Guide: Book 1, p. 220**

## Getting Ready for Bible Storytelling: Option 1

→ **Action: opening your group's box and naming this week's object**
→ **Guide: Book 1, p. 221**

*See the beginning of the weekly storytelling material for ideas of items to place in your box. Invite one of the children to open the box.*

What's in the box? *Ask the child to respond*

## Getting Ready for Bible Storytelling: Option 2

→ Song: 'Jesus, open up my eyes'. Words: © Sharon Moughtin-Mumby
→ Tune: 'Michael, row the boat ashore' (traditional). For the music see p. 359, or for a taster see the Diddy Disciples website. For tips on teaching songs for the first time, see Book 1, p. 215.

It's time to tell our Bible story.
Let's get ready!

Let's take our thumb *lead children in showing thumb*
and draw our cross on our eyes, *draw cross*
and our lips, *draw cross*
and our heart. *Draw cross*
Let's ask Jesus to help us get ready to listen out for God!

**Jesus, open up my eyes. Alleluia!**
*Trace a cross between your eyes.*
**Jesus, open up my lips. Alleluia!**
*Trace a cross on your lips.*
**Jesus, open up my heart. Alleluia!**
*Trace a cross on your heart.*
**Jesus, help me hear your voice. Alleluia!**
*Cup your hands behind your ears.*

# Interactive Bible Storytelling

→ **Guide: Book 1, p. 221**

*See the Bible Storytelling material in Section 2 of this unit.*

# Saying Sorry to God

→ **Guide: Book 1, p. 223**

*Invite the children to sit in a circle for a moment of quiet.*

Jesus is the Light of the World!
Jesus wants us to be like little lights, too.
It's time to say sorry for the times when we haven't
shone like little lights in the world.
For the times we've made the world
feel dark to other people instead.
It's time to sing our Sorry Song.

## Saying Sorry to God: Option 1

→ Song: 'The Diddy Disciples sorry song'. Words: © Sharon Moughtin-Mumby
→ Tune: © Sharon Moughtin-Mumby. For the music see p. 356, or for a taster see the Diddy Disciples website. For a description of the 'I'm Sorry' and 'New Start' signs, see p. 355 or the website. For tips on teaching songs for the first time, see Book 1, p. 215.

Let's put our hands on our head.
I wonder if there's anything we've thought this week
that we wish we hadn't thought?

*Lead the children in placing your hands on head, singing:*
**With my hands on my head,**
**I remember the things I've thought today,**
**I remember the things I wish I'd thought a different way.**

**I'm sorry, I'm sorry,** *Diddy Disciples 'I'm Sorry' sign twice (see p. 355)*
**I wish I could start again.** *Diddy Disciples 'New Start' sign (see p. 355)*

**I'm sorry, I'm sorry,** *'I'm Sorry' sign twice*
**I wish I could start again.** *'New Start' sign*

Let's put our hands by our mouths.
I wonder if there's anything we've said this week
that we wish we hadn't said?

*With hands by mouth, singing:*
**With my hands by my mouth,**
**I remember the things I've said today,**
**I remember the things I wish I'd said a different way.**

**I'm sorry, I'm sorry,** *'I'm Sorry' sign twice*
**I wish I could start again.** *'New Start' sign*
**I'm sorry, I'm sorry,** *'I'm Sorry' sign twice*
**I wish I could start again.** *'New Start' sign*

Let's cross our hands on our chest.
I wonder if there's anything we've done this week
that we wish we hadn't done?

*With hands crossed on chest, singing:*
**With my hands on my chest,**
**I remember the things I've done today,**
**I remember the things I wish I'd done a different way.**

**I'm sorry, I'm sorry,** *'I'm Sorry' sign twice*
**I wish I could start again.** *'New Start' sign*
**I'm sorry, I'm sorry,** *'I'm Sorry' sign twice*
**I wish I could start again.** *'New Start' sign*

*Continue with a Saying Sorry Action or move straight to God Gives Us a New Start, below.*

## Saying Sorry to God: Option 2

→ Song: 'We need a new start'. Words: © Sharon Moughtin-Mumby
→ Tune: 'Molly Malone' (traditional). For the music see p. 356, or for a taster see the Diddy Disciples website. For tips on
  teaching songs for the first time, see Book 1, p. 215. For a description of the 'I'm Sorry' and 'New Start' signs, see p. 355 or
  the website.

> **Tip**
>
> This song can be sung using 'we're sorry' as indicated, or as 'I'm sorry', adapting the material accordingly.

Let's put our hands on our head.
I wonder if there's anything we've thought this week
that we wish we hadn't thought?

*Lead the children in placing your hands on head, singing:*
**For the things we have thou-ght**
**that we wish we'd not thou-ght,**
**we're sor-ry, we're sor-ry,** *Diddy Disciples 'I'm Sorry' sign twice (see p. 355)*
**we need a new start.** *Diddy Disciples 'New Start' sign (see p. 355)*

Let's put our hands by our mouths.
I wonder if there's anything we've said this week
that we wish we hadn't said?

*With hands by mouth, singing:.*
**For the things we have sa-id**
**that we wish we'd not sa-id,**

**we're sor-ry, we're sor-ry,** *'I'm Sorry' sign twice*
**we need a new start.** *'New Start' sign*

Let's cross our hands on our chest.
I wonder if there's anything we've done this week
that we wish we hadn't done?

*With hands crossed on chest, singing:*
**For the things we have do-ne**
**that we wish we'd not do-ne,**
**we're sor-ry, we're sor-ry,** *'I'm Sorry' sign twice*
**we need a new start.** *'New Start' sign*

*Continue with a Saying Sorry Action or move straight to God Gives Us a New Start, below.*

# Saying Sorry Action

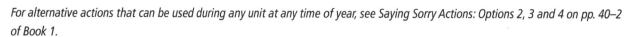

→ **Guide: Book 1, p. 223**

*For alternative actions that can be used during any unit at any time of year, see Saying Sorry Actions: Options 2, 3 and 4 on pp. 40–2 of Book 1.*

## Saying Sorry Action: Option 1

→ **Action: placing hands over eyes then removing them**

Let's put our hands on our eyes.
*Lead the children in placing hands over eyes.*

When we do something that makes God sad
or other people sad,
it can make us feel sad and dark inside.

When we say sorry, we ask God
to shine like a light in the dark.
Let's imagine Jesus, Light of the World,
shining bright inside us!

Let's take our hands off our eyes.
Now we can see what we've done wrong.
We can see that God gives us a new start too!

> *Either:*
> After 3, let's shout, 'God gives us a new start!'
> **1, 2, 3 . . . God gives us a new start!**
>
> *Or: choose one of the God Gives Us a New Start options from pp. 15–16.*

## Saying Sorry Action: Option 2

→ **Action: shining a torch on the group, passing around a battery tealight or lighting a real candle (out of reach)**

*Ask an adult to turn off the lights in the room.*
When we do something that makes God sad
or other people sad,
it can make us feel sad and dark inside.

When we say sorry,
we ask God to shine like a light in the dark.

*Turn on a torch or a battery tealight, or light a candle in a safe place.*
We can see what we've done wrong,
but we can see that we have a new start too!

*Go around the circle and shine the torch on each child and adult, pass the battery tealight around or point to the candle.*

*As you do so, either invite the children to go around the circle and say together:* **Name, God gives you a new start!**

*Or, if you're using a real candle or are in a large group, ask the children, after 3, to say, 'God gives us a new start!'*
**1, 2, 3 . . . God gives us a new start!**

## Saying Sorry Action: Option 3

→ **Action: placing a battery tealight/star on a [white/gold] cloth in the centre of the circle**

The Good News is:
God always wants to give us a new start!

*Show the children the candles/stars. If you're using battery tealights, ask an adult or child to turn off the lights in the room. We ask an adult to light the battery tealights in advance as we've found younger children can be distracted by attempts to light the tealights themselves.*

When we do something that makes God sad
or other people sad,
it can make us feel sad and dark inside.

When we say sorry,
we ask God to shine like a light in the dark in us.

I'm going to ask *Name* and *Name*
to bring around these candles/stars now.
If you like, you can take one
and let God's light shine on you.

*While the candles/stars are taken around, lead the group in either:*
*Option 1: singing the 'I'm Sorry' refrain, or*
*Option 2: humming the first two lines of the 'We need a new start' song followed by singing the refrain 'We're sorry, we're sorry. We need a new start'.*

*When the group is ready:*
The Good News is:
God is always ready to give us a new start!
God's light is shining on and in us!

*If you've turned the lights off in the room:*
Let's turn our lights back on!

Let's hold our lights high!
After 3, let's say: 'God gives us a new start!'
**1, 2, 3: God gives us a new start!**

Let's promise to use our new start
to shine like lights in the world this week.
Let's give our candles to God
and promise to share God's love with each other.

*Invite the children to place their tealight/star on a [gold/white] cloth in the centre of the circle as the group sings one of the following songs, or another that the children are familiar with.*

*Either:*
→ **Song: 'We are loving in the light of God'**, based on 'We are marching in the light of God' (traditional)
→ **Tune: 'We are marching in the light of God'** (traditional)

**We are loving in the light of God,**
**we are loving in the light of God!**
**We are loving in the light of God,**
**we are loving in the light of God!**
**We are loving, we are loving, oh!** *Jazz hands*

**We are loving in the light of God!**
**We are loving, we are loving, oh!** *Jazz hands*
**We are loving in the light of God!**

*Or:*
→ Song: 'This little light of mine' (traditional)
→ Tune: traditional. For a taster see the Diddy Disciples website. For tips on teaching songs for the first time, see Book 1, p. 215.

**This little light of mine, I'm gonna let it shine!**
**This little light of mine, I'm gonna let it shine!**
**This little light of mine, I'm gonna let it shine!**
**Let it shine, let it shine, let it shine.**

*Or:*
→ Song: 'God loves to give me a new start!' Words: © Sharon Moughtin-Mumby
→ Tune: 'Give me oil in my lamp' (traditional). For the music see p. 357, or for a taster see the Diddy Disciples website

**[Yes, my] God loves to give me a new start!** *Trace a smile/cross on own forehead*
**How amazing God's love for me!** *Cross hands on chest*
**[Yes, my] God loves to give me a new start!** *Trace a smile/cross on own forehead*
**How amazing is God's love for me!** *Cross hands on chest*

**Sing hosanna! Sing hosanna!** *Wave hands in the air*
**Sing hosanna to the King of Kings!** *Wave hands in the air followed by crown on head*
**Sing hosanna! Sing hosanna!** *Wave hands in the air*
**Sing hosanna to the King!** *Wave hands in the air followed by crown on head*

## Saying Sorry Action: Option 4

→ **Action: placing a battery tealight or paper star on a piece of dark fabric, with a focus on giving other people a new start too**

*Show the children one or more baskets/trays with stars or lit battery tealights. We ask an adult to light the battery tealights in advance as we've found younger children can be distracted by attempts to light the tealights themselves.*

> *If you're using battery tealights:*
> Let's turn the lights off
> for a moment and look at these candles.
> *Ask an adult or child to turn off the lights.*

When we do things that make God or other people feel sad
everything can feel dark and lonely.

The Good News is that Jesus is the Light of the World.
Jesus can shine in any dark place.

In a moment, *Name* and *Name* are going to bring around these candles/stars.
If you like, you could take one
and hold it gently in your hands like this.
*Model to the children holding their tealight/star.*
Imagine Jesus' love shining on you.

> *If you've turned the lights off:*
> We're going to sing
> as we wait in the dark for Jesus,
> Light of the World, to come to us.

*While the candles/stars are taken around, lead the group in either:*
*Option 1: singing the 'I'm sorry' refrain, or*
*Option 2: humming the first two lines of the 'We need a new start' song followed by singing the refrain 'We're sorry, we're sorry. We need a new start'.*

*When the group is ready:*
God gives us a new start!
Let's hold our candle/star high!
*Joyfully, lead the children in holding your candle/star high.*

But there are other people
feeling like they're in a dark place.
Let's ask God to help us give other people a new start, too.

*Lay a dark piece of fabric in the centre of the circle.*
If you like, you can put your candle here
and promise to give other people a new start this week,
especially when they've made us feel cross or sad.
When we give other people new starts
It can fill dark places like this with light!

*Lead the children in singing/humming again as the candles are placed. Some groups may like to ask two children to take two trays covered with dark fabric opposite ways around the circle to collect the candles. The trays can then be placed in the centre of the circle.*

*When the group is ready:*
After 3, let's say, 'God gives us a new start!'
**1, 2, 3 . . . God gives us a new start!**
Let's use our new start to share God's love this week!

# God Gives Us a New Start

→ **Guide: Book 1, p. 225**

*Every time of Saying Sorry should end by assuring the children that God gives them a new start. Most Diddy Disciples Saying Sorry Actions already include this promise of a new start. If they don't – or if you've created your own Saying Sorry Action – you should choose from one of the following New Start options, or create your own assurance of forgiveness. You could also choose to move straight from the Sorry Song to God's promise of a new start, without any Saying Sorry Action.*

## New Start Action: Option 1

→ **Action: tracing a cross/smile on each other's forehead**

The Good News is:
God always wants to give us a new start!

Let's turn to the person next to us
and show that God gives us a new start.
Let's take our thumb/finger *Show thumb/finger*
and draw a cross/smile on that person's forehead *Draw a cross/smile in the air*

> *If your group is drawing a smile, add:*
> to show that God is very happy with us!

Let's say, 'God gives you a new start!'
Then let the other person give you a new start, too!

*When the group has finished showing each other God's new starts:*
Let's use our new start to share God's love this week!

## New Start Action: Option 2

→ **Action: standing up and hugging each other**

The Good News is:
God always wants to give us a new start!

Let's help someone next to us stand up from the floor.
Then let that person help you stand up too!
*Lead the children in helping each other stand up.*

Then let's give each other a hug and say:
'God gives you a new start!'

*When the group has finished showing each other God's new starts:*
Let's use our new start to share God's love this week!

## New Start Action: Option 3

→ **Song: 'God loves to give me a new start!' Words: © Sharon Moughtin-Mumby**
→ **Tune: 'Give me oil in my lamp' (traditional). For the music see p. 357, or for a taster see the Diddy Disciples website. For tips on teaching songs for the first time, see Book 1, p. 215.**

The Good News is:
God always wants to give us a new start!
Let's sing our New Start song together.

**[Yes, my] God loves to give me a new start!** *Trace a smile/cross on own forehead*
**How amazing is God's love for me!** *Cross hands on chest*
**[Yes, my] God loves to give me a new start!** *Trace a smile/cross on own forehead*
**How amazing is God's love for me!**

**Sing hosanna! Sing hosanna!** *Wave hands in the air*
**Sing hosanna to the King of Kings!** *Wave hands in the air followed by crown on head*
**Sing hosanna! Sing hosanna!** *Wave hands in the air*
**Sing hosanna to the King!** *Wave hands in the air followed by crown on head*

# Introduction to Prayers

It's time to bring our prayers to Jesus, Light of the World.

# Prayers for Other People

→ **Guide: Book 1, p. 223 and p. 225**

*Invite the children to sit in a circle in a moment of quiet.*
Let's imagine holding our prayer gently,
*hands together gently in traditional prayer gesture, but cupped so you can imagine a prayer inside*
and then let it go up in prayer to God.
*Hands opened upwards to God*

> *If you're using Option 1:*
> Jesus, *hands together, cupped*
> hear our prayer. *Hands opened upwards to God*
> Let's pray . . .

## Prayers for Other People: Option 1

→ **Song: 'Jesus, hear our prayer!' Words: © Sharon Moughtin-Mumby**
→ **Tune: 'Brown girl in the ring' (traditional). For the music see p. 358, or for a taster see the Diddy Disciples website. For tips on teaching songs for the first time, see Book 1, p. 215. For similar words designed to fit with the alternative tune 'He's got the whole world in his hands', see p. 359.**

| For the world: | Jesus, hear our prayer! |
|---|---|
| *Make a circle shape* | *Open hands upwards to God* |
| **For the Church:** | **Jesus, hear our prayer!** |
| *Praying hands* | *Open hands upwards to God* |

| | |
|---|---|
| **For our place, *Walworth*\*:** | Jesus, hear our prayer! |
| *Hands down moving out in* | *Open hands upwards to God* |
| *a semi-circle to show the land around us* | |
| **Lord Jesus, hear our prayer. Amen.** | |
| *Open hands upwards to God* | |

\* *Insert local area/school/church/community/parish.*

| | |
|---|---|
| **For the sick and lonely:** | Jesus, hear our prayer! |
| *Fingers showing tears falling* | *Open hands upwards to God* |
| *down cheeks* | |
| **For our friends and family:** | Jesus, hear our prayer! |
| *Arms around yourself* | *Open hands upwards to God* |
| **For ourselves:** | Jesus, hear our prayer! |
| *Both hands on heart* | *Open hands upwards to God* |
| **Lord Jesus, hear our prayer. Amen.** | |
| *Open hands upwards to God* | |

Let's close our eyes for a moment.
I wonder if there's someone special
you'd like to pray for?
Let's imagine that person now.

Now, let's imagine Jesus coming to them.
Does Jesus say anything?
Does Jesus do anything?

Let's open our eyes.

*Continue with one of the Prayer Action options outlined below. Once the Prayer Action has been completed, you may like to use the following verse, to close this time of prayer.*

| | |
|---|---|
| **Take our prayers:** | Jesus, hear our prayer! |
| *Hands together gently* | *Open hands upwards to God* |
| **Make them holy:** | Jesus, hear our prayer! |
| *Hands together gently* | *Open hands upwards to God* |
| **Make them beautiful:** | Jesus, hear our prayer! |
| *Hands together gently* | *Open hands upwards to God* |
| **Lord Jesus, hear our prayer! Amen.** | |
| *Hands together gently, then open hands upwards to God* | |

## Prayers for Other People: Option 2

→ Song: 'The Diddy Disciples little prayers song'. Words: © Sharon Moughtin-Mumby
→ Tune: 'Frère Jacques' (traditional). For the music see p. 356, or for a taster see the Diddy Disciples website. For tips on teaching songs for the first time, see Book 1, p. 215.

*These prayers are especially suited to churches that prefer less traditional prayer forms.*
> *Either: choose what you'd like the group to pray for before the session.*
> *Or: ask the children at this point if there is anything or anyone that they'd like to pray for. Ask them or others to suggest actions.*

*You will need two different 'thank you' suggestions and two different 'hear our prayer' suggestions. Try to encourage at least one prayer for other people outside the group.*

*Invite the children to sing after you, repeating your words and their actions. Sometimes it might be almost impossible to fit the child's own words in! It's really valuable to do this where possible, resisting the urge to try and 'neaten' their suggestions.*

For *our foo-ood,*
**For *our foo-ood,***
Thank you, God!
**Thank you, God!**

Fo-r *our teachers*,
**Fo-r *our teachers*,**
Thank you, God!
**Thank you, God!**

For *Nancy's Nanny*,
**For *Nancy's Nanny*,**
Hear our prayer!
**Hear our prayer!**

For *people with no homes*,
**For *people with no homes*,**
Hear our prayer!
**Hear our prayer!**

*Having sung your prayers, you could insert a Prayer Action, repeat the process or move straight on to close with the following (or other words that remain the same each week).*

| For today, | *Point hands down for 'now'* |
|---|---|
| **For today,** | *Point hands down for 'now'* |
| Thank you, God! | *Open hands upwards to God or hands together in prayer* |
| **Thank you, God!** | *Open hands upwards to God or hands together in prayer* |
| Fo-r your love, | *Cross hands on chest* |
| **Fo-r your love,** | *Cross hands on chest* |
| Thank you, God! | *Open hands upwards to God or hands together in prayer* |
| **Thank you, God!** | *Open hands upwards to God or hands together in prayer* |

# Prayer Actions

→ **Guide: Book 1, p. 225**

*Continue with one of the Prayer Action options outlined below, or you can use the Prayer Actions: Options 2 and 3 in Book 1, pp. 47–8, at any time of year.*

> ## Tip
>
> Some of these Prayer Actions are similar to the options for the Getting Ready for Baby Jesus (Advent) unit, but with slightly different words as we give the children the opportunity to strengthen and deepen their understanding of Jesus as the Light of the World.

## Prayer Action: Option 1

→ **Action: placing battery tealights or star/sun shapes with a Baby Jesus doll, lying in a manger or on white/gold cloth on your focal table**

*Show the children one or more baskets/trays with lit battery tealights. We ask an adult to light the battery tealights in advance as we've found younger children can be distracted by attempts to light the tealights themselves.*

> *If you're using battery tealights:*
> Now as we pray, we're going to turn the lights off
> for a moment and look at these candles.
> *Ask an adult or child to turn off the lights.*

Jesus is the Light of the World!
In a moment, *Name* and *Name*
are going to bring around these candles/stars/suns.

If you like, you could take one
and hold it up like this *hold the candle/star/sun high above your head*

to show that Jesus, Light of the World, is here!
Imagine Jesus' love shining on you
and on a special person you're praying for.

*Hum the tune together, with 'Jesus, hear our prayer' as a refrain until all the children and adults who wish to take tealights/stars/ suns have done so.*

Jesus is the Light of the World!
Our prayers can be part of sharing Jesus' light.
We're going to sing again.
If you like, you can give your candle/star/sun to Baby Jesus.
Let's promise to shine with God's love in the world.

*Lead the children in singing again until all the children and adults who wish to place their tealights have done so. End this time of prayer with the final verse from the Prayer Song you've chosen.*

## Prayer Action: Option 2

→ **Action: placing battery tealights or star/sun shapes around a lit globe**

*At St Peter's, Walworth, we've used a globe that can be lit up to show Jesus, Light of the World. In our space, it's possible to plug the globe in from the focal table with the cable stowed safely away. If you'd like to use an electric globe, think through how this might work safely in your setting with curious young children present. We encourage the children to explore the globe along with an adult afterwards, if they like.*

*Show the children the lit globe on the focal table.*

This is a 'globe', showing the world.
We live here. *Point to where you live on the globe*
But people live all over the world. *Point all around the globe*

> *If your church or group has a connection with people elsewhere in the world, you could briefly show the children this place here.*
> *Example:* This is Zimbabwe, our link diocese in Africa.
> *Point to Zimbabwe.*
> Our friends from Zimbabwe live here.

Jesus is the Light of the World!
Look at the light lighting this globe up from the inside.

*Show the children one or more baskets/trays with lit candles/stars/suns. We ask an adult to light the battery tealights in advance as we've found younger children can be distracted by attempts to light the tealights themselves.*

In a moment, *Name* and *Name*
are going to bring around these candles/stars/suns.
If you like, you could take one
and hold it up high. *Model holding one up high*

Let's ask God to help us
be part of shining Jesus' light in the world.

*Hum the tune together, with 'Jesus, hear our prayer' as a refrain until all the children and adults who wish to take tealights/stars/ suns have done so.*

Jesus is the Light of the World!
When we pray, we can be part of shining Jesus' light!

Let's sing again.
If you like, you can come and put your little light around the world.
Let's ask God to see our candle/sun/star
as a prayer for a special person and for the world.

*Lead the children in singing again as they place their candles around the globe on a focal table. We've found that asking the children to do this in age groups helps. End this time of prayer with the final verse from the Prayer Song you've chosen.*

## Prayer Action: Option 3

→ **Action: placing battery tealights or star/sun shapes on a map of the world**

*At St Peter's, Walworth, we've used a map jigsaw (that the children can also explore afterwards). At other times, we've used a laminated world map that shows the world in its proper proportions.*
*Place a map of the world in the centre of the circle. If your group is using a doll to represent Baby Jesus, you might like to place Jesus at the head of the map in the manger or on the cloth.*

This is a map of the world.
Jesus is the Light of the World!

*Show the group one or more baskets/trays with lit candles/stars/suns. We ask an adult to light the battery tealights in advance as we've found younger children can be distracted by attempts to light the tealights themselves.*

In a moment, *Name* and *Name*
are going to bring around these candles.
If you like, you could take one.
Let's ask God to help us be part
of shining Jesus' light in the world.

*Hum the tune together, with 'Jesus, hear our prayer' or 'Hear our prayer' as a refrain until all the children and adults who wish to take tealights have done so.*

> *If appropriate*
> At the moment, there's fighting in the world
> Here and here. *Place candles*
> *Name the countries or areas if appropriate.*

> There's been *an earthquake [or other disaster]*
> here. *Place candles*
> There are people who *[e.g. have no homes]* here. *Place candles*
> There are people who need our prayers all over the world.

Let's sing again.
If you want to, you can put your little light anywhere you like on our map.
Let's be part of bringing Jesus' light to the world.

*Lead the children in singing again as they place their candles on the map. We've found that asking the children to do this in age groups helps, as the older children tend to be more intent on finding a location than the others. Some groups may like to ask two children to carry the map around the circle on a tray so the children can place their stars from where they are sitting. The map can then be placed in the centre of the circle. End this time of prayer with the final verse from the Prayer Song you've chosen.*

## Prayer Action: Option 4

→ **Action: placing stars on a dark piece of fabric**

*Lay a dark piece of fabric in the centre of the circle. Show the group one or more baskets/trays filled with stars.*

Jesus is the Light of the World!
In a moment, *Name* and *Name*
are going to bring around these stars.
If you like, you could take a star
and hold it up high like this. *Model holding the star high*

Imagine Jesus' love shining on you
and on the special person you are praying for
like a star shines in the night sky.

*Hum the tune together, with 'Jesus, hear our prayer' or 'Hear our prayer' as a refrain until all the children and adults who wish to take stars have done so.*

Let's give our star prayers to God as we sing.

*Lead the children in singing again as they place their stars on the dark piece of fabric. Some groups may like to take one or more trays covered with a dark cloth around the circle so the children can place their stars from where they are sitting. These trays can then be placed in the centre of the circle. End this time of prayer with the final verse from the Prayer Song you've chosen.*

## Prayer Action: Option 5

→ **Action: making 'twinkle' hand actions in a circle around a Baby Jesus doll, lying in a manger or on white/gold cloth**

*Place Baby Jesus in the centre of the circle in his manger or on the cloth.*
Jesus is the Light of the World!
Our prayers can be part of sharing Jesus' light.
Let's make 'twinkle, twinkle stars'
with our hands in the air
and show them to Baby Jesus.
*Lead children in opening and closing hands*
*to make 'twinkle, twinkle stars'.*

We're going to sing the end of our song now.
As we sing, let's show our 'twinkle, twinkle stars' for Baby Jesus.
Let's ask God to hear our stars as prayers.
Let's ask God to help us be part
of Jesus' light, shining in the world.

*Lead the children in singing the final verse from the Prayer Song you've chosen as you make 'twinkle, twinkle' signs in the air.*

# Thank You, God

→ **Guide: Book 1, p. 227**

## Thank You, God: Option 1

→ **Song: 'My hands were made for love'. Words: © Sharon Moughtin-Mumby**
→ **Tune: 'Hickory, dickory, dock' (traditional). For the music see p. 360, or for a taster see the Diddy Disciples website. For tips on teaching songs for the first time, see Book 1, p. 215.**

*Invite the children to sit in a circle for a moment of quiet.*
It's time to remember all the things we've done this week.
It's time to say 'thank you' to God
for when we've been part of showing God's love.

Let's wiggle our fingers!
I wonder when you've shown love
with your hands this week?

*Wiggle fingers as you sing.*
**My hands were made for love!**
**My hands were made for love!**
**Thank you for the love they've shown.**
**My hands were made for love!**

Let's wiggle our feet!
I wonder when you've shown love
with your feet this week?

*Wiggle feet as you sing.*
**My feet were made for love!**
**My feet were made for love!**

**Thank you for the love they've shown.**
**My feet were made for love!**

Let's put our hands gently on our neck.
Let's sing 'Ahhh!'
**Ahhhhh!**
Can you feel your throat vibrating and dancing with your voice?
I wonder when you've shown love
with your voice this week?

*Hold neck and feel your voice 'dancing' as you sing.*
**My voice was made for love!**
**My voice was made for love!**
**Thank you for the love it's shown.**
**My voice was made for love!**

## Thank you, God: Option 2

→ **Song: 'For the love we've shown'. Words: © Sharon Moughtin-Mumby**
→ **Tune: 'All through the night' (traditional). For the music see p. 357, or for a taster see the Diddy Disciples website. For tips on teaching songs for the first time, see Book 1, p. 215.**

*Most suitable for use with children over the age of four.*

*Invite the children to sit in a circle for a moment of quiet.*
It's time to remember all the things we've done this week.
It's time to say 'thank you'
for when we've been part of showing God's love.

> *Either:* Let's wiggle our fingers.
> *Or:* Let's hold up our hands.

I wonder when you've shown love
with your hands this week?

> *Either:* Let's wiggle our feet.
> *Or:* Let's show our feet.

I wonder when you've shown love
with your feet this week?

Let's put our hands gently on our neck.
Let's sing 'Ahhh!'
**Ahhhhh!**
Can you feel your neck vibrating and dancing with your voice?
I wonder when you've shown love
with your voice this week?

Let's sing our 'thank you' song to God
For the times we've been part of sharing God's love.

**For the love we've shown with our hands,**
*Hold hands up or wiggle fingers.*
**Thank you, God!**
**For the love we've shown with our feet,**
*Point to feet or wiggle feet.*
**Thank you, God!**
**When we love all those around us,**
*Cross hands on chest.*
**It's the same as loving Jesus!**
**For the love we've shown with our voice,**
*Hands on neck or point to singing mouth.*
**Thank you, God!**

# Creative Response

→ Guide: Book 1, p. 228

*See the Creative Responses in Section 3 of this unit.*

# Sharing God's Peace

→ Guide: Book 1, p. 231

*This Building Block is particularly designed for children's groups that join the adult congregation to share communion but can also be used to end any session or Service of the Word.*

## Sharing God's Peace: Option 1

→ Song: 'I've got peace like a river' (traditional), Isaiah 66.12, NIV
→ Tune: traditional. For a taster see the Diddy Disciples website. For tips on teaching songs for the first time, see Book 1, p. 215.

> *Either: hold one end of the peace cloth (Book 1, p. 231) and ask one of the older children or an adult to hold the other end. Start singing the Peace Song. As the children begin to gather, invite them to join in holding a small section of the cloth, raising and lowering it so it 'flows' like a river as you sing together.*

> *Or: invite the children to sit in a circle in the worship space. Start singing the Peace Song. As the children begin to gather, invite them to join in raising and lowering their hands like the waters of a flowing river.*

I've got peace like a river,
I've got peace like a river,
I've got peace like a river in my soul.
I've got peace like a river,
I've got peace like a river,
I've got peace like a river in my soul.

*If your group is about to rejoin the adults for communion: when all the children are gathered, continue with the words of the Peace, below.*

## Sharing God's Peace: Option 2

→ Song: 'Peace is flowing like a river' (traditional), Isaiah 66.12, NIV
→ Tune: traditional. For a taster see the Diddy Disciples website. For tips on teaching songs for the first time, see Book 1, p. 215.

> *Either: hold one end of the peace cloth (Book 1, p. 231) and ask one of the older children or an adult to hold the other end. Start singing the Peace Song. As the children begin to gather, invite them to join in holding a small section of the cloth, raising and lowering it so it 'flows' like a river as you sing together.*

> *Or: invite the children to sit in a circle in the worship space. Start singing the Peace Song. As the children begin to gather, invite them to join in raising and lowering their hands like the waters of a flowing river.*

Peace is flowing like a river,
flowing out through you and me.
Spreading out into the desert,
setting all the captives free.

*If your group is about to rejoin the adults for communion: when all the children are gathered, continue with the words of the Peace, below.*

## Sharing God's Peace: Option 3

→ Song: 'I've got peace in my fingers'. Words: © 1995 Susan Salidor ASCAP
→ Tune: © 1995 Susan Salidor ASCAP
→ The words and music can be found on the album *Little Voices in My Head* by Susan Salidor © 2003 Peach Head. They can also be found on iTunes or YouTube, or at <www.susansalidor.com>. For tips on teaching songs for the first time, see Book 1, p. 215.

*If your group is about to rejoin the adults for communion: when all the children are gathered, continue with the words of the Peace, below.*

# The Peace

→ 2 Thessalonians 3.16; 1 Peter 5.14

*Once you have finished singing . . .*

The peace of the Lord be always with you.
*Hold hands open to the children.*
**And also with you.**

*Invite the children to open their hands towards you.*
Let's shake hands or hug each other
and say, 'Peace be with you' *or whatever is said on sharing the Peace in your church*
as a sign of God's peace.

*Lead the children in giving and receiving the Peace. Immediately following this, at St Peter's, Walworth, we lead the children back to join the rest of the congregation to continue our worship with the Eucharistic Prayer.*

# Taking God's Love into the World

→ **Guide: Book 1, p. 232**
→ **Song: 'This little light of mine' (traditional)**
→ **Tune: traditional. For a taster see the Diddy Disciples website. For tips on teaching songs for the first time, see Book 1, p. 215.**

*This Building Block is particularly designed for standalone groups or groups that are held during a Service of the Word. Alternatively, you could use one of the Peace Songs above to end your worship.*

Our time together is coming to an end.
*Invite the children to sit in a circle for a moment of quiet.*
God has lit a little light of love inside all of us.
*Trace a circle on your heart.*
Let's make our finger into a candle.
*Bring your finger from your heart and hold it out.*

Let's be God and light our little light of love together, after 3.
*Lead the children in lighting their finger candle by striking an imaginary match in the air on 3 and pretending to light your finger.*
**1, 2, 3 . . . Tssss!**
Let's imagine God's love shining and dancing like light in us.

*Wave your finger in front of you.*
**This little light of mine, I'm gonna let it shine!**
**This little light of mine, I'm gonna let it shine!**
**This little light of mine, I'm gonna let it shine!**
**Let it shine, let it shine, let it shine!**

*Blow on your finger as if blowing out a candle on 'puff'. Then hold it up high.*
**Won't let no one *puff* it out! I'm gonna let it shine!**
**Won't let no one *puff* it out! I'm gonna let it shine!**
**Won't let no one *puff* it out! I'm gonna let it shine!**
**Let it shine, let it shine, let it shine!**

*Hold your finger behind a cupped hand, then take your cupped hand away
to reveal the 'candle' and hold it high!*
**Hide it under a bushel? No! I'm gonna let it shine!**
**Hide it under a bushel? No! I'm gonna let it shine!**
**Hide it under a bushel? No! I'm gonna let it shine!**
**Let it shine, let it shine, let it shine!**

*Lead the children in placing your finger back on your heart.*
Now let's put our little light of love
back in our hearts, where it belongs.

Let's remember to let our little light shine
in all our playing and working today . . .

*If you're building a Service of the Word and this is your final Building Block, you may like to close with a familiar blessing, the Peace and/or one of the following.*

> *Either:*    Praise the Lord! *Both hands to self*
> **Alleluia!** *Both arms upwards in 'V' shape*

> *Or:*    Let us bless the Lord. *Both hands to self*
> **Thanks be to God.** *Both arms upwards in 'V' shape*

> *Or:*    And all the people said . . . *Both hands to self*
> **Amen!** *Both arms upwards in 'V' shape*

*The first few times you introduce this call-and-response, you may find it helpful to say, for example:*

Now it's 'my turn' *point to self*, 'your turn' *leader's hands out to group*.
When I say, 'Praise the Lord' *both hands to self*,
you say, 'Alleluia!' *Both arms upwards in 'V' shape*

Praise the Lord! *Both hands to self*
**Alleluia!** *Both arms upwards in 'V' shape*
*Repeat.*

## Section 2

# The Bible Storytelling material: Jesus, Light of the World! unit

> **Tip**
>
> The length of this unit changes each year as Lent can start earlier or later. See p. 3 for advice on working out which Bible stories to tell in which week. Suggestions of how to fit the stories to the current year can be found on the Diddy Disciples website.

## Week 1: The Magi's Journey

→ **Matthew 2.1–2**
→ **Song: 'Follow the star to Bethlehem'. Words: © Sharon Moughtin-Mumby**
→ **Tune: 'Here we go round the mulberry bush' (traditional). For a taster see the Diddy Disciples website.**

Let's fol-low, fol-low, fol-low the star, fol-low the star, fol-low the star. Let's
fol-low, fol-low, fol-low the star, to meet the spe-cial king! _____

*For the storytelling today, you will need a doll to represent Baby Jesus lying in a manger or on white/gold cloth on your focal table.*

> **Tip**
>
> If the children in your group are more familiar with other names for the Magi, adapt the song and material accordingly, for instance to: 'the Three Kings', 'the Wise Men' or 'the Wise Ones'.

*If your group is using the What's in the Box? option (see Book 1, p. 221):*
*Invite a child to open the box.*
*Inside is a star.*

What's in the box?
*Accept the child's response.*

Today we're going to tell the story of 'the Magi' and the star.

To get ready for today's story,
we need to practise using our faces to show how we're feeling.
We're not going to use any sound at all!
Can you show me: sad . . . happy . . . important . . . shocked!
We're ready to tell our story.

In the time that Jesus was born
there were some people called 'Magi'.
Let's get ready to be Magi.

Some people call the Magi 'the Wise Men'
because they were very clever.
Can you show me very clever? *Lead the children in looking clever.*

Some people call the Magi 'the Three Kings'
because they were very important in their countries.
Can you show me very important?
And let's put on some important clothes . . .
a robe and a crown.
*Lead the children in putting on imaginary robes and crowns.*

So the Magi were very important and very clever.
They knew all about the stars in the sky.
One night, they were looking up to the sky . . .
Let's look up to the sky to see the stars like the Magi.
*Lead the children in looking up to the sky through an imaginary telescope or with hand over eyes.*
Look at all those stars!
Yes, we know all about them! *Look clever*

But look!
*Point upwards in surprise towards an imaginary star.*
Look! What's that!
That star wasn't there before!
The Magi were amazed!
Can you show me shocked and amazed?
*Lead the children in looking shocked and amazed.*

'That star means there's a new king!' they said.
'And he looks special . . . really special!
We need to meet this new king!'
So the Magi decided to follow the star on a very long journey.

Let's get up and get ready to go.
Don't forget your treasure chest – full of special gifts for the king!
*Lead the children in picking up an imaginary, very heavy treasure chest.*
Phew, that's heavy! Let's put it on our camel.
*Lead the children in putting the treasure chest onto an imaginary camel.*
Let's walk on the spot together and follow that star!

*Lead the children in walking on the spot throughout.*
**Let's follow, follow, follow the star,**
**follow the star, follow the star.**
**Let's follow, follow, follow the star,**
**to meet the special king!** *Crown on head*

Uh oh! *Point* Desert!
We can't walk through the sandy desert! *Shake head*
Let's climb on our camels.
*Lead the children in climbing onto the imaginary camel.*

Now when you ride a camel,
the camel doesn't go up and down like a donkey
*Mime trotting on a donkey.*
The camel goes from side to side:
*Lead the children in swaying jerkily from side to side as if on a camel.*
This way, that way, this way, that way . . .

*Continue the camel riding action as you sing.*
**Let's follow, follow, follow the star,**
**follow the star, follow the star.**
**Let's follow, follow, follow the star**
**to meet the special king!** *Crown on head*

Goodness! That was a long way through the desert.
Let's get off our camels.
*Lead the children in getting down off the camels.*

Uh oh! *Point* It's the sea! *Sound worried*
But look! *Point* There's a boat!
Let's get into our boat to cross the sea.
*Lead the children in sitting down on the floor as if in a boat.*
Don't forget your camel!
*Lead the children in helping a camel into the boat.*
Let's row!
*Row to the rhythm of the song.*
Row and row and row and row . . .

*Continue rowing in time as you sing.*
**Let's follow, follow, follow the star,**
**follow the star, follow the star.**
**Let's follow, follow, follow the star**
**to meet the special king!** *Crown on head*

Phew! We've reached the shore.
This is a long journey . . .
Let's get out of our boats . . .
*Lead the children in climbing out of the boat and standing up.*
Don't forget your camel!
*Lead the children in helping the camel out of the boat.*

Uh oh! Look! *Point upwards* Look at that mountain!
Time for some climbing!
Can camels climb? Let's find out . . .

*Lead the children in pretending to rock climb a very steep mountain.*
**Let's follow, follow, follow the star,**
**follow the star, follow the star.**
**Let's follow, follow, follow the star**
**to meet the special king!** *Crown on head*

Goodness me, this is a hard journey!
And now look! A dark valley!
It's bit scary! Ssssh!
*Whisper* We don't want to wake any scary animals up.
Let's tiptoe, tiptoe, tiptoe . . .
And whisper our song . . . Ssssssh!

**Let's follow, follow, follow the star,**
**follow the star, follow the star.**
**Let's follow, follow, follow the star,**
**to meet the special king!** *Crown on head*

Look! The star's stopped! *Point*
The new king must be there.
Shall we go and see?
*Accept the children's responses.*

First let's get ourselves ready!
That was a long journey and we look a bit scruffy.
Let's make sure our crown and robe are straight.
*Lead the children in straightening your crowns and robes.*

Remember! We're very clever!
Let's look very clever!
And we're very important!
We need to look important so the new king
knows how important we are!
*Lead the children in looking clever and important.*

Are we ready to meet the king?
Let's hold our heads high and march in on the spot.
March, march, march, march . . .
*Lead the children in marching on the spot.*

*Stop in surprise and confusion, looking around.*
But look! What's this?
This isn't a palace!
And look! What's this?
*Pick the Baby Jesus doll up in your arms.*
It's a baby! A tiny baby!
This can't be the new king . . . can it?

But the Magi looked and saw
that new king WAS a tiny, tiny baby.
And they looked even closer . . .
and they knelt down.
Let's kneel down together now.

*Lower your voice.*
And the Magi forgot about being clever.
They forgot about being important
because they saw that this wasn't just a new KING.
This baby was the KING OF KINGS.
This baby was GOD!
And the Magi bowed their heads.
Let's bow our heads . . . and worshipped.
*If there is silence, hold it for a moment.*

The Magi were amazed to see Baby Jesus.
We're going to pass Baby Jesus around the circle now.
Everyone's going to have a turn
so it will just be for a moment.

As we pass Baby Jesus around
let's imagine we're the Magi
meeting this tiny baby
and seeing that he's GOD!

Let's sing:
'Look! This is the King of Kings!
We've met the King of Kings!'

*Lead the children in singing quietly and with awe as you pass Baby Jesus around. You or another leader may need to be ready to help the children remember to pass him on and to skip over children who don't wish to hold Baby Jesus.*

**Look! This is the King of Kings,
the King of Kings, the King of Kings!**

**Look! This is the King of Kings!**
**We've met the King of Kings!**
*Repeat until all the children have had the opportunity to hold Baby Jesus.*

Next week, we'll find out what happened next.

# Week 2: The Magi's Gifts

→ Matthew 2.1–2, 9–11
→ Song: '1, 2, 3: three special gifts!' Words: © Sharon Moughtin-Mumby
→ Tune: 'The farmer's in his den' (traditional). For a taster see the Diddy Disciples website.

> ### Tip
>
> If the children in your group are more familiar with other names for the Magi, adapt the song and material accordingly, for instance to: 'the Three Kings', 'the Wise Men' or 'the Wise Ones'.

*For the storytelling today, you will need a doll to represent Baby Jesus, in a manger or on a gold/white cloth on your focal table.*

*Your group may also like to use items representing the three gifts as visual aids for this story for instance:*
*1 gold-coloured items such as jewellery (check these are safe for your group) or a picture of gold;*
*2 a cloth soaked in essential oil (frankincense or other) or a bowl filled with incense from your church, or a picture of frankincense;*
*3 a child-safe perfume bottle, essential oil bottle, myrrh resin (if your church has some) or a picture of myrrh.*
*If you're using the What's in the Box? option (Book 1, p. 221), these three gifts can be placed inside your usual box.*

Today we're going to tell the story of when the Magi gave 'gifts' – presents – to Baby Jesus.

> *If your group is using items to represent the gifts, show them at this point.*
> Let's count our 'gifts'.
> How many gifts are there?
> *Lead the children in counting on their fingers* **1, 2, 3!**
> *If appropriate, invite the children to name the three gifts: gold, frankincense and myrrh. Place the three gifts on the focal table.*
>
> *If you are going to imagine the gifts:*
> The Magi gave three 'gifts'.
> Let's count to 3 . . .
> *Lead the children in counting on their fingers* **1, 2, 3!**

*All groups:*
To tell our story about the Magi's gifts we need to learn a song.
It starts with counting . . .
*Lead the children in counting on their fingers again* **1, 2, 3!**

Now can you say: 'The Magi brought three special gifts'?
*Lead the children in saying these words to the rhythm that will be in the song.*

**The Magi brought three special gifts.**

That's quite a tongue twister, isn't it!

Shall we try it again?

**The Magi brought three special gifts.**

*Sing the Magi's gifts song to the children and encourage them to join in as you go.*

**1, 2, 3!** *Count on fingers*

**1, 2, 3!** *Count on fingers*

**The Magi brought three special gifts:** *Three fingers*

**1, 2, 3!** *Count on fingers*

*Repeat to give the group confidence in the song.*

We're ready to tell our story!

In the time that Jesus was born,
there were some people called Magi.
Now the Magi were very clever and VERY important.
Can you show me clever and important?
*Lead the children in looking clever and important.*

Let's put on some important clothes . . .
a robe and a crown.
*Lead the children in putting on imaginary robes and crowns.*

One night, the Magi were looking up to the sky . . .
Let's look up to the sky to see the stars like the Magi!
*Lead the children in looking up to the sky through an imaginary telescope
or with hand over eyes.*

Look! *Point with excitement*
The Magi saw a star that no one had seen before.
The star meant there was a brand new king!
The Magi decided to find the new king!
They followed the star on a long, long journey.
Let's walk together on a long journey.
*Lead the children in walking on the spot.*

Look! The star has stopped over that house!
Shall we go in?
The Magi tiptoed into the house.
Can you tiptoe on the spot with me?
*Lead the children in tiptoeing on the spot.*

They saw Baby Jesus with Mary.
*Place the Baby Jesus doll in the centre of the circle in a manger or on gold/white cloth.*

The Magi knelt before Jesus to worship him.
*Invite the children to kneel with you.*
Then the Magi gave the new king three special gifts.

> *If you think that some of the children might know the names of the gifts and you haven't done so already, ask:*
> Can anyone tell us what ONE of the gifts was?
> *Ask for the names of the three gifts one by one, from different children if possible.*

The three gifts were chosen very carefully by the clever Magi.
They show us what kind of king Jesus is going to be!
Shall we open them together?

Let's get our treasure chest with our gifts in.
*Lead the children in reaching to the side and each taking an imaginary, very heavy treasure chest with a lot of effort.*
Goodness! This is heavy! *Lift the chest and place it in front of you*

What's inside?
Shall we open our chests?
*Lead the children in opening your chests in front of you.*

Wow! This chest is bright inside!
*Lead the children in shielding your eyes from the brightness of this chest.*
It's shining, dazzling *jazz hands* and bright like the sun!

*Reach into the chest and take out an imaginary handful or two of gold.*
This is gold! The treasure of kings!
The gold shows that Jesus is born to be king!
Can you show me an action for 'king'?
*Choose one of the suggested actions for 'king' and use it for the song.*

Let's sing our song.
Let's sing 'Gold *jazz hands* is for a king'. *King action*

*Lead the children in singing to the same tune as you learned earlier:*
**Gold** *jazz hands* **is for a king!** *King action*
**Gold** *jazz hands* **is for a king!** *King action*
**The Magi brought three special gifts** *three fingers*
**and gold** *jazz hands* **is for a king!** *King action*

*If appropriate, encourage the children to respond with the word in bold.*
So, gold *jazz hands* is for a . . . **king**. *King action*
King Jesus!

What else are we going to take out of our treasure chest?
Let's reach in and take it out.
*Lead the children in taking an imaginary handful of something out of the chest.*
Mmmm! This smells nice . . .
*Invite the children to sniff with you.*

Goodness! *Rub bottom of nose* Atchoo!
After 3, let's all sneeze, 1, 2, 3 . . .
**Atchoo!**
This is frankincense! *Sniff again*
Atchoo!

> *Either:* It smells like the incense
> that people light in the Temple
> to show that their prayers are going up to God.
> *Sway hands upwards to show incense going up.*

> *Or:* It smells like the incense we use in our church
> to show we're in a holy place.

Let's stand up and show
the smoke of the incense
going up to God with our bodies.
*Lead the children in standing up and swaying your body and arms like smoke going upwards to God.*

Frankincense shows Jesus is born to be 'holy' and special.
Jesus is born to be God!
Let's sing 'Frankincense is holy'.

*Lead the children in swaying your body and arms like smoke as you sing.*
**Frankincense is holy!**
**Frankincense is holy!**
**The Magi brought three special gifts** *three fingers*
**and frankincense is holy!**

Let's sit down again.

*If appropriate, encourage the children to respond with the words in bold.*

So gold *jazz hands* is for a . . . **king** *king action*

Frankincense *sway arms* is . . . **holy** *sway arms*

I wonder what our third gift will be?

Let's reach into our treasure chest and see . . .

*Lead the children in taking a handful from the chest.*

That's strange! What's this? Let's taste it.

*Lead the children in imagining to eat something from the chest.*

*Screw your face up as you taste.*

Ugh! It tastes bitter: like lemons!

Can you show me what something bitter tastes like with your face?

*Lead the children in screwing your face up.*

This is myrrh! Myrrh means 'bitter' *(in Hebrew)*.

Normally we bring myrrh when someone dies!

Has someone died here?!

*Point to the baby. Invite the children to respond and accept their responses.*

No! Someone has been born!

But this gift of myrrh shows that Baby Jesus will die.

God's Son will die! *Sound confused*

What a strange thing.

What a bitter thing! *Lead the children in screwing your face up*

That could be our action for bitter – for myrrh.

*Invite the children to sing with you screwing your face up on 'very bitter' as you sing.*

**Myrrh is very bitter!** *Screw face up*

**Myrrh is very bitter!** *Screw face up*

**The Magi brought three special gifts:** *three fingers*

**and myrrh is very bitter!** *Screw face up*

*If appropriate, encourage the children to respond with the words in bold.*

So gold *jazz hands* is for a . . . **king** *king action*

Frankincense *sway arms* is . . . **holy** *sway arms*

and myrrh *screw face up* is . . . **very bitter** *screw face up*

The Magi brought three special gifts

that tell us all about King Jesus.

*If your group has chosen the Prayer Building Block for this unit, today you might like to use the following material in the place of your prayers.*

When we come to King Jesus,

sometimes WE want to give a 'gift', a present too!

Let's think – what could we give?

Let's stand up. *Lead the children in standing*

In this room, we have so many different gifts for Jesus:

all the things we're good at!

I wonder what our gifts are? Let's see . . .

Can you show me your best smile?

Maybe you have the gift of smiling!

Can you listen to this and clap/stamp the same back?

*Do a couple of simple clapping rhythms of three beats, or more advanced depending on your group. If they haven't done this before, you may need to remind them of the importance of listening well first!*

Wow! Some of you are really good!

Maybe you have the gift of music or listening!

33

Who's good at throwing and catching?
Let's throw . . . *lead the children in throwing an imaginary ball high in the air and catching it*
. . . and catch!
Maybe you have a gift for using your body!

We all have all sorts of gifts,
all sorts of things that we are good at.
But there's one gift we can all give to Jesus:
the gift of love. *Cross hands on chest*
Let's all wave at each other to show our love.
*Lead the children in waving to each other.*

So there's another treasure chest to open today: ours!
*Bend down and pick up an imaginary, very heavy treasure chest.*
*Encourage the children to do the same.*
Let's pick up our treasure chest.

This treasure chest is full of all of OUR gifts:
our smiling and moving and listening and loving,
all the things we're good at!

Let's imagine we're coming to Baby Jesus like the Magi.
Let's tiptoe on the spot into Baby Jesus' room.
*Lead the children in tiptoeing on the spot, carrying your imaginary treasure chest.*
Sssssh! Tiptoe, tiptoe, tiptoe . . .

*In a hushed tone* Let's kneel down.
Now let's open the treasure chest and show Jesus what's inside.
*Lead the children in opening the chest and showing the contents to Jesus.*

Look! Wow!
Look how beautiful your gifts are!
*Lead the children in reaching into the chest and taking big handfuls of the treasure out and holding it up high.*
Amazing!

Let's sing our song one more time.
This time let's give our gifts to Jesus.
Let's sing 'Jesus, take my gifts.'
Let's make our song into a prayer.

*Lead the children in holding out their hands full of their 'treasure' to Baby Jesus as they sing:*
**Jesus take my gifts!**
**Jesus take my gifts!**
**The Magi brought three special gifts:**
**and Jesus take my gifts!**

# Extra: Baby Jesus, the Refugee

→ **Matthew 2.13–18.**

*Today's material can involve an extended activity. To make time for it, you may like to omit some of your usual Building Blocks (for instance, the Prayer Building Block you've chosen).*

*For this week's story, you will need:*
- *figures or pictures of Mary, Joseph and Baby Jesus. At St Peter's, Walworth, we use the figures from our crib;*
- *either body templates (if you're using these for your Creative Responses, see p. 366 or website), small world people (see p. 95) or recent pictures of refugees from newspapers.*

   *If you are using the What's in the Box? option (Book 1, p. 221), show the children a suitcase or a form of travel bag. If you think the children would like to open it, you could put some clothes inside. If you have any baby clothes, include these.*

What's this?
*Invite the child to respond.*

We're going to need this suitcase for today's story.

Today's story starts with running!
After 3, we're going to stand up,
We're going to throw our things into a bag as quickly as we can.
*Mime throwing things into a bag.*
We're going to pick up our baby ever so carefully . . .
*Mime picking a baby up.*
and we're going to run on the spot!
Are you ready?

**1, 2, 3 . . .**
Stand up . . . *Lead the children in standing*
Pack, pack, pack, pack, pack . . .
*Lead the children in throwing clothes into an imaginary case*
Pick up our baby. *Lead the children in picking up an imaginary baby*
Gentle, careful . . .
And run! *Lead the children in running on the spot holding the baby*
Faster! Faster! Faster!
And freeze!

Let's sit down for a moment.

*When the group is ready:*
The king's found out about Baby Jesus!
The king knows that people are calling Jesus the new king!
And he's angry!
The king's coming to FIND Baby Jesus!
He wants to get rid of him!

*In a serious but calm voice:*
We're Joseph and we need to leave . . .
fast!
We need to go to another country,
where the king can't hurt us. *Shake head*
You know what we need to do.

After 3, we're going to stand up,
We're going to throw our things into a bag as quickly as we can.
*Briefly mime throwing things into a bag.*
We're going to pick up Baby Jesus ever so carefully.
*Briefly mime picking Baby Jesus up.*
And – with Mary – we're going to run on the spot!
Are you ready?

**1, 2, 3 . . .**
Stand up . . . *Lead the children in standing*
Pack, pack, pack, pack, pack . . .
*Lead the children in throwing clothes into an imaginary case.*
Pick up our baby. *Lead the children in picking up an imaginary baby*
Gentle, careful . . .
And run! *Lead the children in running on the spot holding the baby*
Faster! Faster! Faster!
And freeze!

Let's sit down again.

*When the group is ready:*
Phew! It's going to be all right. *Smile*
Joseph's found a safe place for Mary and Baby Jesus.
*Rock baby gently in arms.*
The king won't find him. *Shake head*
Jesus will grow up safe with his mummy and foster daddy.
*Rock baby gently in arms.*

But not every baby in our story stayed safe.
*Lead the children in crossing arms on chest.*
Let's bow our heads and cross our arms on our chest
and remember for a moment
the babies that were hurt by the king.
*Lead the children in bowing head and keeping arms crossed on chest. Keep a moment of silence – as long as is appropriate for your group.*

*Place figures or pictures of Mary, Joseph and Baby Jesus in the centre of the circle.*
Today we're remembering people
who've had to leave their country.
People who've had to pack *briefly mime packing*
and run very fast *briefly move arms as if running*
like Mary and Joseph and Baby Jesus. *Point to the figures/pictures*

People who've had to leave their home
because someone's going to hurt them.

People who've had to run from their homes
are often called 'refugees'.
Can you say 'refugees'?
**Refugees.**

There are 'refugees' who've come to OUR country,
looking for a safe place to live.
What do you think it feels like to have to pack and run away like that?
Can you show me with your face?

*If your group is creating person templates afterwards, place a representative number of these in the centre of the circle, or you may like to use 'small world' people (see p. 95) or recent pictures of refugees from newspapers.*
I'm going to place these people here now
with Baby Jesus, Mary and Joseph
in the middle of our circle
to remind us of the refugees in OUR country.

They've come a long way and they're still scared.
Let's open our hands out to them to show they're welcome.
*Lead the children in opening hands out to Mary, Joseph, Jesus and the other refugees.*
Let's help them to feel safe.

> *Either, if your group is familiar with Welcome Song: Option 1:*
> Let's sing 'Welcome friends to *St Peter's\**' to them!
>
> **Welcome friends to *St Peter's\**,** *wave to the centre of the circle*
> **Welcome friends to *St Peter's\**,** *wave to the centre of the circle*
> **Welcome friends to *St Peter's\**,** *wave to the centre of the circle*
> **you are welcome in the name of the Lord!**
>
> *\* Insert the name of your church or children's group, or sing 'our worship'.*
>
> *Or, if your group is familiar with Welcome Song: Option 2:*
> Let's sing our Welcome Song to them.

Let's wave with one hand. *Lead waving*
Then with our other hand. *Lead waving*
Then let's show God's 'glory' all over the refugees.
*Move arms up and down in front of you with fingers wiggling,*
*palms facing out, towards the centre of the circle.*
Then let's wave with both hands to give them a big welcome.
*Lead waving.*

**You are welcome in the name of the Lord!**
*Wave with right hand to the centre of the circle.*
**You are welcome in the name of the Lord!**
*Wave with left hand to the centre of the circle.*
**I can see all over you, the glory of the Lord!**
*Move arms up and down in front of you with fingers wiggling,*
*palms facing out, towards the centre of the circle.*
**You are welcome in the name of the Lord!**
*Wave with both hands to the centre of the circle.*

*Or, if your group is familiar with the Gathering Song for this unit:*
Let's sing 'You are welcome! You are welcome!' to them:

*Lead the group in singing the following words to the tune of 'We are marching in the light of God', waving throughout to the figures/pictures of the refugees:*
**You are welcome! You are we-elcome!**
**You are welcome! You are we-elcome!**
**You are welcome! You are we-elcome!**
**You are welcome! You are we-elcome!**
**You are welcome! You are welcome! Oh!** *Jazz hands*
**You are welcome! You are we-elcome!**
**You are welcome! You are welcome! Oh!** *Jazz hands*
**You are welcome! You are we-elcome!**

*Or sing another Welcome Song to the figures/pictures of refugees.*

*If possible, include one of the following activities as part of your worship, or another response to support refugees that's appropriate for your group and resources.*

We've been telling stories about Jesus, the Light of the World.
Jesus asks us to be little lights in the world, too.

*Either:*
Today we're going to be part of shining God's light in the dark.
We're going to make some pictures of refugees
and give them to our family and friends/people in our church.
We're going to ask them/our church to remember
people who've had to run and need a safe place to live.
We're going to ask them to pray that we will welcome them.

And if you're wondering what 'refugees' look like,
they might look just like you or just like me!
*See Weekly Starter Ideas on p. 47 for details.*

*Or:*
Today we're going to be part of shining God's light in the dark.
We're going to make _____ and sell them.
We're going to give the money to _____ *name of a local, national or international charity*
who are helping refugees
who've had to run and need a safe place to live.
*See Weekly Starter Ideas on p. 47 for ideas.*

**Tip**

If your group is meeting during a Sunday service, you might also like to invite the children, if they like, to present what they've made to the congregation at the end of the service. You could use this as an opportunity to challenge your congregation to wonder how we can be part of shining God's light in the darkness for all those who are looking for safety.

You may like to lead your congregation in a suitable prayer for refugees, for instance *Common Worship*'s Prayer for Refugees, below.[1] The children could then give their creations after the service to family, friends or members of the congregation.

Heavenly Father,

you are the source of all goodness, generosity and love.

We thank you for opening the hearts of many

to those who are fleeing for their lives.

Help us now to open our arms in welcome,

and reach out our hands in support.

That the desperate may find new hope,

and lives torn apart be restored.

We ask this in the name of Jesus Christ Your Son, Our Lord,

who fled persecution at His birth

and at His last triumphed over death. Amen.

# Week 3: Jesus, Light of the World!

→ **The presentation of Jesus/Candlemas**
→ **Luke 2.22–33**
→ **Song: 'Jesus, Light of the World (Epiphany)' Words: © Sharon Moughtin-Mumby**
→ **Tune: 'What shall we do with the drunken sailor?' (traditional). For a taster see the Diddy Disciples website.**

Some leaders/children might notice that this week's song shares its tune with Zechariah's song from Week 1 and the Gathering Song of Advent. In Luke's Gospel, the stories of Zechariah and Simeon are strongly connected with all sorts of similarities:

| | |
|---|---|
| Zechariah is an old man, | Simeon is an old man, |
| who encounters God (via an angel) | who encounters God (in the Spirit) |
| in the Temple, | and is sent to the Temple, |
| and sings a song | where he sings a song |
| about Jesus, the Light of the World. | about Jesus, the Light of the World. |
| Luke 1.5–23, 59–79 | Luke 2.25–32 |

In Luke, these stories are like 'bookends', showing the beginning and end of the stories about Jesus' birth. We've also used these stories as bookends in Diddy Disciples: Zechariah's song started off our stories about Baby Jesus in Advent and now Simeon's song (sung to the same tune) will bring them to an end. Both celebrate Jesus, Light of the World!

*If your group is using the What's in the Box? option (Book 1, p. 221):*
*Invite one of the children to open the box.*
*Inside are two pictures or figures: one is Baby Jesus and the other is an old man (Simeon). For Simeon, you could use a biblical painting, a picture from a children's Bible or a modern photo of an old man.*

What's in the box? *Invite the child to respond*

Today we're going to tell the story
about when this old man met Baby Jesus.

*Or, if your church calls this Sunday 'Candlemas', you may wish to use a candle:*
Today we're going to tell the story of 'Candlemas'.
Candlemas is the day when we celebrate
Jesus, the Light of the World, with candles.
*If appropriate:* Look out for the candles today in church.

## Introduction to the song: Option 1

*For groups that are familiar with the 'Jesus, Light of the World' song from the Getting Ready for Baby Jesus (Advent) unit:*

Today's our last story about Baby Jesus,
the Light of the World.
We sang a song when we were getting ready
for Baby Jesus before Christmas.
It's our 'busy, busy, busy' song about
*Say these words in way that invites the children to join in:*
Jesus, Light of the World . . . **DAWNING** in the darkness.
But this time Jesus isn't DAWNING in the darkness! *Action for the rising sun*
Jesus is SHINING in the darkness! *Jazz hands*
Can you show me your jazz hands for 'shining'? *Jazz hands*

Let's try singing our song with Jesus SHINING in the darkness at the end.
*Lead the children in singing:*
**Jesus, Light of the World,** *action for the rising sun then jazz hands*
**Jesus, Light of the World,** *action for the rising sun then jazz hands*
**Jesus, Light of the World . . .** *action for the rising sun then jazz hands*
*Interrupt the singing* Remember Jesus is SHINING!
**is SHINING in the darkness!** *Jazz hands*

*Continue with the material for all groups, below.*

## Introduction to the song: Option 2

*For groups that are not familiar with the 'Jesus, Light of the World' song from the Getting Ready for Baby Jesus (Advent) unit:*

We're going to learn a song today.
It's about Jesus being the Light of the World, like the sun.

Let's crouch down and show the sun hiding
before it comes up in the morning.
*Lead the children in crouching down.*
Now let's show the sun rising with our bodies . . .
Up, up, up and out!
*Raise hands upwards and outwards as you stand up.*

We're going to use that action for our song.
And then because Jesus is SHINING bright, *jazz hands*
we're going to finish with jazz hands! *Jazz hands*

Let's try that.
*Lead the children in singing with the actions of the rising sun:*
**Jesus, Light of the World,** *action for the rising sun*
**Jesus, Light of the World,** *action for the rising sun*
**Jesus, Light of the World . . .** *action for the rising sun*
**is SHINING in the darkness!** *Jazz hands*
*Repeat if necessary until the children are basically familiar with the tune.*

## All groups

We're ready to tell our story.
Our story today is about two people. *Show two fingers*
Number 1: *show one finger*
a tiny baby. He's only six weeks old! *Mime holding a baby*
It's Baby Jesus!

So number 1: *show one finger* a VERY young baby. *Mime holding a baby*
And number 2: *show two fingers* a VERY old man.
Let's look old and hunched over.
*Lead the children in bending over.*
Let's hold our stick to help us to walk.
*Lead the children in leaning on an imaginary walking stick.*

So 1: a VERY young baby. *Lead the children in holding the baby*
And 2: a VERY old man. *Lead the children in hunching over*

They're going to meet in the biggest house!
The Temple, God's House!
Can you show me big?
*Lead the children in stretching upwards and outwards as high as you can.*
Bigger and bigger! Reach up high!
That's God's House, the Temple,
where people go to meet with God, a bit like our church.

First, Baby Jesus is on the way to God's House.
*Lead the children in holding an imaginary baby in your arms.*
Mary and Joseph want to say thank you to God
for Baby Jesus, so they're taking him to the Temple.

Let's stand up and be Mary or Joseph.
*Lead the children in standing.*
Let's carry Baby Jesus in our arms.
Let's walk on the spot and sing: 'Walking, walking to the Temple'.

*Walk on the spot, cradling Jesus as you sing:*
**Walking, walking to the Temple,**
**walking, walking to the Temple,**
**walking, walking to the Temple!**
**The Light of the World is SHINING!** *Jazz hands*

*Sing louder and take the speed up a bit.*
**Jesus, Light of the World!** *Action for the rising sun then jazz hands*
**Jesus, Light of the World!** *Action for the rising sun then jazz hands*
**Jesus, Light of the World,** *action for the rising sun then jazz hands*
**is SHINING in the darkness!** *Jazz hands*

Someone else is on the way to the Temple, too:

> *If appropriate: hunch over an imaginary stick and ask the children:*
> Who else is in our story today?

The old man!
Let's hunch over and hold our stick and be the old man together.
*Lead the children in being the old man.*

We've been looking out for God's helper our whole life!
Let's hold our hand over our eyes and look . . .
*Lead the children in looking around.*

Let's sing together, 'Looking, looking, looking for God!'

*Lead the children in continuing to look around as you sing:*
**Looking, looking, looking for God!**
**Looking, looking, looking for God!**
*Interrupt the song.*

Sssssh! Can you hear that? *Hand behind ear*
Is that God? . . .
That's GOD whispering! *Look shocked*
What's God saying?

*Whisper loudly with hands around your mouth:*
'Go to the Temple!' *Point*

After 3, let's all be God and whisper, 'Go to the Temple'
*Lead the children in whispering loudly with hands around your mouth:*
**'1, 2, 3 . . . go to the Temple!'** *Point*

And what do you think the old man did?
*Invite responses from the children.*

He went to the Temple as fast as he could!
Let's be the old man again and sing our song quickly
to show how quickly we want to get to the Temple.

But, remember, we're very old so we can't run.
We can only hobble with our stick.

*At speed, hobbling on the spot, lead the children in singing:*
**Hurry, hurry, hurry, hurry to the Temple,**
**hurry, hurry, hurry, hurry to the Temple,**
**hurry, hurry, hurry, hurry to the Temple!**
**The Light of the World is SHINING!** *Jazz hands*

**Jesus, Light of the World,** *action for the rising sun*
**Jesus, Light of the World,** *action for the rising sun*
**Jesus, Light of the World** *action for the rising sun*
**is SHINING in the darkness!** *Jazz hands*

We're here! We're in God's House, the Temple.
Look around: it's huge!
Let's show with our bodies how big the Temple is!
*Lead the children in each making the biggest shape they can with their bodies.*

But wait a minute, *point* who's that?
Who do you think the old man saw?
*Accept the children's responses if there are any.*

The old man saw a tiny baby!
Baby Jesus!
Can you make the tiniest shape you can with your body?
*Lead the children in crouching down into a tiny shape.*

Baby Jesus was tiny.
But the old man saw that Jesus' light FILLED God's House!
Let's make the biggest shape we can with our body!
Let's show how big God's House is again.
*Lead the children in making a big shape with their body.*

Jesus' light FILLED God's House!
The tiny baby's light . . . *lead the children in making a tiny shape*
FILLED the massive Temple! *Lead the children in making their big shape*

Not only that! The baby's light filled the whole WORLD!
Let's make our shape even bigger! BIGGER!
*Lead the children in stretching out as far as they can.*
Freeze!

The old man saw the baby:
and he knew that's who he'd been looking for:
Jesus, the Light of the World!

How do you think he felt?
Can you show me?

The old man took the tiny baby in his arms. *Hold baby*
And he sang the song we've been singing, about
Jesus, the Light of the World.
That's the old man's song!

> *If appropriate:* Churches all through the world
> still sing the old man's song every day.

Let's be the old man singing to Baby Jesus.
Let's start by showing the tiny Baby Jesus with our bodies.
*Lead the children in making a tiny shape, e.g. crouching.*
Let's sing 'Shine, shine, shine' and show our tiny shape.

Then let's sing 'in all the world!' *big shape*
and show our biggest shape for the world.
'Shine, shine, shine' *tiny shape*
'in all the world.' *Biggest shape*

Let's sing!
*Lead the children in singing:*
**Shine, shine, shine in all the world!** *Tiny shape followed by big shape*
**Shine, shine, shine in all the world!** *Tiny shape followed by big shape*
**Shine, shine, shine in all the world!** *Tiny shape followed by big shape*
**The Light of the World is SHINING!** *Jazz hands*

**Jesus, Light of the World,** *action for the rising sun*
**Jesus, Light of the World,** *action for the rising sun*
**Jesus, Light of the World** *action for the rising sun*
**is SHINING in the darkness!** *Jazz hands*

Let's sit down for a moment.

*When the children are ready:*
Let me tell you something.
The Light of the World isn't just shining in Baby Jesus.

Jesus said that you *point to a child*
and you . . . and you . . . and you . . . *point to three more children*
All of us . . . *point in a circle to everyone in the room*
All of us are the light of the world!
Jesus' light shines inside all of us!
*Trace your finger in a circle around your heart.*

To finish our stories about Jesus, Light of the World,
let's make our song into a prayer.
Let's sing 'Shine, shine, shine in me, in me!'

Let's start off singing quietly
*Trace small circle on your heart.*
Then as we sing let's get louder and louder
and show our light shine brighter and brighter inside us.
*Show the circle that you are tracing on your heart getting bigger and bigger.*

Let's imagine Jesus' light filling us,
then filling our church/school/name of place,
then bursting out to fill the whole world! *Jazz hands*

Let's close our eyes and pray our song.
*Show the circle that you are tracing on your heart getting bigger and bigger as you lead the children in singing:*
**Shine, shine, shine, in me, in me-e!**
**Shine, shine, shine, in me, in me-e!**
**Shine, shine, shine, in me, in me-e!**
**The Light of the World is shining!** *Jazz hands*

*Lead the children in standing for the final verse.*
**Jesus, Light of the World,** *action for the rising sun*
**Jesus, Light of the World,** *action for the rising sun*
**Jesus, Light of the World** *action for the rising sun*
**is shining in the darkness!** *Jazz hands*

## Section 3

# Creative Response starter ideas: Jesus, Light of the World! unit

→ **Guide: Book 1, p. 228**

These starter ideas are designed to spark imaginations and open up opportunities for the children to respond creatively in their different ways to the worship and storytelling you've taken part in together.

### Tip

As outlined in the Guide of *Diddy Disciples* Book 1 from p. 228, we've found the following rules of thumb helpful for fostering an environment where children are encouraged to engage personally and openly.

1 Encourage the children to make their own choices.
2 Give the children space to develop their response as they wish.
3 Create space for 'bridge building'.
4 It's the act of responding that matters, not the final result.
5 These responses are 'holy ground'.

**Weekly Starter Ideas** relate directly to the Bible Storytelling of each session, including a print-and-go option.

**Sensory Starter Ideas** are designed for sensory explorers, including babies and toddlers. These can remain the same through the whole unit.

**Unit Starter Ideas** are designed to remain relevant throughout the whole unit. Keeping these resources available each week gives children the opportunity to deepen and develop their responses, while making preparation more manageable for leaders.

### Tip: Free response area

In addition to any other resources you provide, keeping a free response area available every week will give the children the opportunity to create anything they wish in response to the story they've told, building their sense of confidence and personal responsibility. In this area you could simply provide blank paper and crayons, pencils, paints or pastels. If you have them, other interesting media (see Book 1, p. 256) will provide even more scope for the children to nurture and strengthen their imaginative skills.

# Weekly Starter Ideas

## Week 1: The Magi's Journey

🏠 Invite the children to decorate their own star. What would they like to do with it: leave it as it is, add it to a picture or attach it to a hatband or lollipop stick or straw? Some children may even like to design their own star shape on blank paper. *Provide star template (p. 387 or website) and blank paper, scissors, pencils/pens/crayons. If you have glue, tinfoil, any collage materials (Book 1, p. 255), make these available too. You could even provide curling ribbon, ribbon, crepe/tissue paper strips to trail from the star.*

🏠 Give the children the opportunity to make their own telescope or pair of binoculars. Invite them to decorate a sheet of paper/card with patterns (and/or stars), then show them how to roll the paper up and secure it with tape to create a telescope (one roll) or binoculars (two rolls). *Provide A4 card/paper, masking/sticky tape. You could even provide readymade cardboard tubes (for example from kitchen roll, tinfoil or cling film rolls) for the children to decorate.*

🏠 Invite the children to make a star from salt dough and to make it shine with glitter or bright paints. *Provide salt dough (recipe in Book 1, p. 257), glitter or bright paints.*

🏠 Invite the children to create star shapes from spaghetti: these could be triangular stars or asterisk stars, or the children may like to explore other shapes. Your group may like to explore transient art (in which case simply provide dyed spaghetti). Alternatively, to create longer-lasting shapes (and for a messier option), provide cooked spaghetti and PVA glue (coloured by paint if you like) in small bowls. Encourage the children to dip the spaghetti into the glue, then to make shapes on waxed/baking paper. They could even add glitter for extra effect. Once the shapes have dried (overnight), they can be lifted off the waxed paper and hung up. *Provide cold cooked spaghetti, plus (optional) PVA glue in small bowls, glitter, waxed paper.*

🏠 It's an ancient Epiphany tradition for families to gather to ask for God's blessing on their home and all who visit or live there. Chalk is used to write **20 + C + M + B + 18** (or whichever year you are in) on the lintel, the doorstep or close to the door of the house, along with prayers asking Jesus to visit and be present in that home. Give the children the opportunity to lead their family in this Epiphany tradition by offering them a piece of chalk, instructions and the prayers to take home (see the Diddy Disciples website). At St Peter's, Walworth, we bless the chalk as a gathered church at the end of our Sunday service, before sending the congregation out to pray for God's blessing on their homes.

Note: C M B represents the traditional names of the Magi (Casper, Melchior and Balthazar) as well as the Latin words *Christus mansionem benedictat*, 'May Christ bless the house.'

## Week 2: The Magi's Gifts

Invite the children to design a Magi crown for themselves or a crown for Baby Jesus, the King of Kings. What will their unique crown look like? *Provide crown template (p. 371 or website), scissors, pencils/ crayons/pastels and masking or sticky tape. You could also provide collage materials (Book 1, p. 255) and glue if you have them.*

Give the children the opportunity to create their own treasure chest, filled with their gifts. They may like to write or draw what their gifts are inside, or they may prefer to use collage materials or pencils/crayons to fill the chest with 'treasure'. Remember to give them space to explore freely their own ideas. *Provide treasure chest template (p. 389 or website), pencils/crayons/pastels, scissors. If you have collage materials (Book 1, p. 255, especially gold/silver collage) and glue, make these available too.*

Invite the children to write or draw their gifts on a star or heart shape, or they may prefer to use their creative gifts to decorate one of these shapes with collage materials. You could even invite the children to wrap them up with Christmas wrapping paper as a present for Baby Jesus. *Provide star and/or large heart templates (p. 387 and p. 382, or website) and scissors plus pencils/crayons/paints/pastels. If you have collage materials (Book 1, p. 255), glue, wrapping paper and sticky/masking tape, make these available too.*

Give the children the opportunity to use their creative gifts as a gift for Jesus by creating new things from recycling. Encourage them to use their imagination and creativity freely. *Provide recycled items such as boxes, tubs, cartons, pots, paper, newspaper plus glue, string, sticky/masking tape.*

Invite the children to draw round their hands on paper or make handprints with paint or salt dough. As the children create and decorate their open hands, encourage them to wonder what gifts they have to give Baby Jesus. The most important gift that all of us are given is love. What ways do we like to show our love to God and other people? *Provide paper and pencils/crayons and scissors, or paper and paints, or salt dough (recipe in Book 1, p. 257) and dough cutters.*

Give the children the opportunity to explore their gifts and wonder what they could give to God by decorating a body template to look like themselves. In pictures, saints are often depicted holding something to symbolize who they are and the gifts they gave to God. What would the children like to show themselves holding as a gift they have to give to God? A pencil, a ball, a favourite toy, a heart? Give them lots of space to hold whatever they choose, or present themselves with empty, open hands. *Provide body template (p. 366 and website), pencils/crayons/pastels/paints. If you have collage materials (Book 1, p. 255), make these available too.*

## Tip

At St Peter's, Walworth, in Epiphany, we invite the children – if they would like – to present their Creative Responses – or another symbol of their gifts such as an undecorated heart or star or a battery tealight – to Baby Jesus at our Crib during the final hymn of our Sunday service. Some of these are wrapped up in Christmas wrapping paper. We've found it helpful to reassure the children that they can still take their responses home with them even if they choose to offer them up during the service like this. See Book 1, p. 230.

## Extra: Baby Jesus, the Refugee

*Starter ideas for Option 1:*

 Invite the children to make a body template into an image of a refugee, themselves, Joseph, Mary or someone else as a reminder of our shared humanity. If the children choose to make a refugee, they may also like to give them a name and age. *Provide body template (p. 366 or website), pencils/crayons/pastels, scissors. If you have glue and collage materials (Book 1, p. 255, including fabrics) make these available too.*

 Some children may like to explore Jesus, the baby refugee, and remember other baby refugees across the world. *Provide the baby template (p. 363 or website), pencils/crayons/paints and scissors.*

 Give the children the opportunity to make a refugee 'icon' from a body template, glued to thick card wrapped in tinfoil. *Provide body template (p. 366 or website), pencils/crayons/pastels, scissors, glue, card rectangles, tinfoil to wrap around the card.*

 Imagine having to pack your case quickly and run! What would the children take with them? Invite them to draw these things in their suitcase. *Provide suitcase template (p. 388 or website).*

## Tip

You could invite the children to give their creations to friends and family asking them to remember refugees who've had to flee their homes like Mary, Joseph and Jesus. You may like to provide the children with a note to attach to the back, for example:

Please pray with us for refugees. Thank you.

**Jesus, Light of the World,**
**as a baby, you were a refugee.**
**Help us to be part of shining your light**
**on refugees.**
**Help us to welcome them**
**and make a safe place for them. Amen.**

*Starter ideas for Option 2:*

 Invite the children to decorate bought or pre-made biscuits with coloured icing and sprinkles. Shapes of people (e.g. gingerbread people) or stars would be particularly appropriate. Sell the biscuits to raise money for an appropriate charity connected with refugees.

 Give the children the opportunity to make their own biscuits. Provide them with readymade biscuit mixture or scone dough and biscuit cutters and invite them to make their own shapes. Shapes of people (e.g. gingerbread people) or stars would be particularly appropriate. Bake the biscuits and then sell them to raise money for an appropriate charity connected with refugees.

 Choose another starter idea from the Jesus, Light of the World! unit or beyond to sell to raise money for a charity connected with refugees, or to give to people, asking them to remember refugees who've had to flee their homes like Mary, Joseph and Jesus.

## Week 3: Jesus, Light of the World!

📖 Invite the children to decorate a candle to celebrate Jesus, Light of the World. What would they like to do with their candle? Leave it as it is? Attach it to string to make a necklace or to a band of paper to make a hat? *Provide candle templates (p. 367 or website), scissors, crayons/pencils/pastels/paints. If you have collage materials (Book 1, p. 255), glue, string, hatbands (p. 360), masking tape, make these available too.*

📖 Invite older children to make paper lanterns to celebrate Jesus, Light of the World. Show the children how to fold the lantern template in half and cut down the lines. Then show them how to reopen the paper, make it into a circular lantern, and tape or glue it together and attach the handle. If your group has a longer time for Creative Response, you could invite the children to decorate their paper before cutting it. *Provide lantern template (p. 381 or website) on coloured paper if possible, scissors, glue or sticky/masking tape, pencils/crayons.*

📖 Invite the children to create an image of Jesus, Light of the World, shining in their hearts and filling them with light. The children may like to draw a picture of Jesus, or they may prefer to create something more impressionistic. Give them space to explore their own response. *Provide large heart templates (p. 382 or website), scissors, gold and silver collage materials (Book 1, p. 255) and glue.*

📖 Jesus is the Light of the World! Give the children the opportunity to create their own 2D globe by taking a paper plate and painting it with blue and green paints, sticking green and blue tissue/crepe paper to it or attaching green dried pasta with blue glue. Expect these 'globes' to be very impressionistic! *Provide paper plates, green and blue collage materials (Book 1, p. 255), paints, or green dried pasta (Book 1, p. 257) and PVA glue coloured with blue paint. Once the children have created their globe you could also provide yellow/gold collage materials and invite the children to add them on or around the paper plate to show Jesus, the Light of the World.*

📖 Invite the children to make a globe light-catcher by gluing green and blue tissue paper to a circle of wax paper. Expect these globes to be impressionistic! *Provide circles of wax/baking paper (some pound shops sell ready-cut circles), glue, green and blue tissue paper cut into small (if possible, irregular) shapes.*

📖 Make a Christingle and raise money for the Children's Society (see Children's Society website, <www.childrenssociety.org.uk>). At St Peter's we make mini versions from satsumas and birthday candles, using thin red sticky tape, which is easier for young children to manipulate than ribbon.

# Sensory Starter Ideas

Some of these Creative Responses can remain the same as those for the previous Getting Ready for Baby Jesus (Advent–Christmas) unit, giving young children the opportunity to strengthen and deepen their engagement with the stories around Baby Jesus.

Resources that you might provide for the children (including babies and toddlers) to explore for themselves include:

- a Baby Jesus doll along with a Moses basket, manger or cardboard box. You could even provide real hay for the children to explore;

- Christmas cards of famous paintings showing the Magi and star from the stories. You could also provide a box with a slot cut into it for the children to post the cards or make them into sewing cards by punching holes and providing shoelaces for threading;

- different terrain that the Magi may have travelled over for the children to explore (either on trays or in transparent plastic bottles): rocks, pebbles, sand, water;

- a durable nativity set that includes the Magi figures;

- building blocks to create an obstacle course for the Magi;

- torches, battery tealights or sensory light toys like flashing stars or light sticks;

- survival blankets and unwanted CDs (these make amazing sparkly sensory objects for young babies to explore light);

- a toddler-friendly globe, map jigsaw or laminated map for the children to explore;

- a light box. Put battery fairy lights (or similar) into a clear box and tape the lid firmly shut. Provide different coloured cellophane paper, tissue paper or other child-safe objects that light can shine through. Include some items that no light shines through to create a contrast;

- board books telling the story of the star and the Magi;

- dressing up: robes, crowns, gifts, telescopes, binoculars, stars, camel masks;

- playdough plus star, nativity, crown, camel cutters, etc.;

- Epiphany smells: add drops of essential oils of myrrh and frankincense to scraps of material and place in little pots for the children to explore;

- pictures of stars, star globes, telescopes, binoculars.

# Unit Starter Ideas

## Jesus, Light of the World!

📖 Invite the children to add stars to a night sky. *Provide dark paper, star stickers or star shapes and glue.*

📖 Give the children the opportunity to create a light painting. Invite them to draw a star, or any picture they like, using yellow/white wax crayons on white paper. Encourage the children to paint over this drawing with a thin blue/black watercolour or watered-down paint. Watch the light shining through the darkness! *Provide white paper, white/yellow wax crayons, blue/black watercolour or thinned paint, paintbrushes.*

📖 Invite the children to explore the contrast of light and dark with collage materials or chalks/pastels. *Provide black/dark paper and yellow/white/orange chalks or pastels, or gold/silver/white collage materials (Book 1, p. 255).*

📖 Give the children an opportunity to decorate a transparent candleholder with translucent paper and watch the different colours created by a candle shining within it. *Provide a transparent plastic cup or recycled plastic jar/ tub, different coloured tissue/crepe paper or cellophane cut into squares or small shapes, plus a battery tealight. Sweet wrappers work well! NB: these plastic containers are not suitable to hold real candles.*

📖 Give the children the opportunity to create a stained glass 'window' that they can watch the light shine through, just as Jesus, the Light of the World, can shine through our lives. Invite them to glue brightly coloured tissue/ cellophane/crepe paper to squares or circles of wax/baking paper. Older children may like to precede this by folding up a black or coloured piece of paper three to four times, cutting shapes out of it, opening it out again, then gluing this to the wax/baking paper to act as a backdrop or frame. *Provide baking/wax paper (the whiter the better, but brown paper still works), glue and brightly coloured tissue/crepe/cellophane paper (e.g. transparent sweet wrappers from Christmas). Optional: black/dark paper and scissors. If you do use black paper, the stained glass 'windows' may need to be trimmed after the paper has been added.*

📖 See also the options from Week 3, above.

## Magi

📖 Give the children the opportunity to create their own collages of the Magi from old Christmas cards that include pictures of the Magi, nativity and star. *Provide paper, old Christmas cards, glue, pencils/crayons/pastels. You may also like to provide glitter, if you have it.*

📖 Invite the children to make their own Magi from finger puppet templates. *Provide finger puppet template (p. 375 or website), pencils/crayons, scissors, glue. Optional extras: collage material (Book 1, p. 255, including fabric and coloured paper).*

📖 Invite the children to make their own Magi puppets from figures cut from Christmas cards then stood upright with plasticine, or attached to lollipop sticks/straws. You could even invite the children to make a backdrop for the Magi from Christmas cards or their own imagination (or a bit of both). *Provide Christmas cards featuring the Magi, scissors, plasticine or lollipop sticks/straws, plus glue/masking tape and plain paper.*

# UNIT 2
# JOHN THE BAPTIST (THE WEEKS BEFORE LENT)

The John the Baptist unit is designed to be used after the Jesus, Light of the World! unit in the weeks running up to the beginning of Lent. Together these units are designed to lead the children, week by week, from the joy of Christmas through to John the Baptist and Jesus the wilderness, in preparation for the quiet giving up of things in Lent and the journey to the cross.

'Extra' sessions are included, because the date for the beginning of Lent changes yearly. We suggest that you look at how many weeks your group will be meeting and construct your own timetable so that the final week of this unit is held in the week before Lent. Suggestions of how to fit the stories to the current year can be found on the Diddy Disciples website.

*In years with very few Sundays between Christmas and Lent, your group may need to combine Weeks 1 and 2 of John the Baptist into a single week. The storytelling material in that unit sets out how to combine the stories.

## Section 1

# The Building Blocks: John the Baptist unit

Pick and choose from these Building Blocks and their various options to build sessions for your group. Whatever choices you make, we suggest you keep to that pattern for the whole of the unit as this will open up opportunities for the children to participate fully and confidently during your time together.

> **Build your own Diddy Disciples session** (Book 1, p. 6.) provides an overview of the Building Blocks and a short introduction to fitting them together, along with examples.
>
> **Guide to the Building Blocks** (Book 1, p. 217) provides a step-by-step guide to each Building Block.

## Welcome

→ **Guide: Book 1, p. 218**

*Welcome your group.*

Let's start by going around the circle
and saying our name out loud.
My name's _____.

*Go around the circle so that every adult and child has the chance to say her or his name (and introduce any dolls, teddies or toys).*

*If any of the children don't want to say their name, or aren't able to, you (or a parent or carer) could say it for them and wave.*

It's time to sing our Welcome Song!

## Welcome Song: Option 1

→ **Song: 'The Diddy Disciples welcome song'. Words: © Sharon Moughtin-Mumby**
→ **Tune: 'Glory, glory, alleluia!' (traditional). For the music see p. 357, or for a taster see the Diddy Disciples website. For tips on teaching songs for the first time, see Book 1, p. 215.**

*Go around the circle the same way as above. See if you can remember each other's names and insert them into the song.*

**Welcome *Name 1* to *St Peter's*\***
**Welcome *Name 2* to *St Peter's*\***
**Welcome *Name 3* to *St Peter's*\***
**You are welcome in the name of the Lord!**

*\* Insert the name of your church or children's group, or sing 'our worship'.*

## Welcome Song: Option 2

→ **Song: 'You are welcome in the name of the Lord' (traditional)**
→ **Tune: traditional. For the music see p. 360, or for a taster see the Diddy Disciples website. For tips on teaching songs for the first time, see Book 1, p. 215.**

Let's wave with one hand. *Lead waving*
Then with our other hand. *Lead waving*
Then let's choose someone and show God's 'glory'!
*Move arms up and down in front of you with fingers wiggling, palms facing out, towards one person.*
And someone else! *Repeat*
Then let's wave with both hands all around the circle.
*Lead waving.*

We're ready to sing!

**You are welcome in the name of the Lord!**
*Wave with right hand to one person.*
**You are welcome in the name of the Lord!**
*Wave with left hand to another person.*
**I can see all over you, the glory of the Lord!**
*Move arms up and down in front of you with fingers wiggling,*
*palms facing out, towards one person and then another.*
**You are welcome in the name of the Lord!**
*Wave with both hands all around the circle.*

# Getting Ready to Worship

→ **Guide: Book 1, p. 218**

*Choose one of the following greetings according to which greeting is familiar in your church. (If your church uses a different greeting, you could use that here instead.)*

## Getting Ready to Worship: Option 1

→ **Action: the sign of the cross. Words: © Sharon Moughtin-Mumby**

*Invite the children to make the sign of the cross slowly with you. As the children become more confident, invite a child to lead the action as the whole group says the words and makes the sign of the cross.*

| In my head, | *touch head* |
| in my heart, | *touch chest* |
| and all around me, | *touch shoulders one by one* |
| Jesus is here. | *open hands in front, facing upwards* |

## Getting Ready to Worship: Option 2

→ **Action: 'The Lord be with you' (open hands)**

Let's start by clenching our hands together tightly.

*Lead children in clenching fists against your body to show a defensive posture.*

When we close ourselves up like this,
it's hard to let anyone into our heart.
It's hard even to let God into our heart!

When we get ready to worship,
we show that we're open to God and to each other.

*Open your hands out, facing up.*

Can you show me your open hands?
We're ready to let God and each other in!

The Lord be with you.
*Hold hands open to the children.*

**And also with you.**
*Invite the children to open their hands towards you.*

# Introducing the Unit

→ **Guide: Book 1, p. 218**

*If your group follows liturgical colours, try and keep in rhythm with the colour that your church is using each week. The rule of thumb is that the season changes on the Sunday between 28 January and 3 February and the colour changes then from white/gold to green.*

It's time to get ready [again]!
This time, it's time to get ready for Jesus the grown-up.

To help us get ready,

> *Week 1:* . . . we need to meet a man called John the Baptist.
> *Week 2:* . . . can anyone remember who we met last week?

*If necessary:* John the . . . **Baptist**

> *Week 1*
> *Hands on tummy:*
> Even when John was still in his mummy's tummy,
> God knew that John would have a special job:
> to get the world ready for Jesus!

Let's stand up and be John the Baptist together.
*Lead the children in standing.*

John wore clothes made from camel hair!
Let's put our camel-hair coat on!
*Lead the children in putting on a coat and scratching.*
It's very itchy!

John's job was to get the world ready for God!
John called out,
'Get ready for God!' *Cup hands around mouth*

After 3, let's shout, 'Get ready for God!'
**1, 2, 3 . . . Get ready for God!** *Cup hands around mouth*

*Look around* I'm not sure anyone heard that.
Let's try that again even louder.
**1, 2, 3 . . . Get ready for God!** *Cup hands around mouth*
*Move straight into your choice of Gathering Song.*

# Gathering Song

*Choose from one of the Gathering Song options below.*

## Gathering Song: Option 1

*For groups who aren't yet familiar with a Diddy Disciples' Sorry Song but would like to take part in the time of saying sorry at the end of the storytelling.*

→ Song: **'Wash me in the river'.** Words: © Sharon Moughtin-Mumby
→ Music: **'Alive, alive-o':** the chorus to the traditional Irish song 'Molly Malone'. For a taster see the Diddy Disciples website.

*This Gathering Song option is shorter so that all groups – even those with time limitations – can take part in the time for saying sorry at the end of the storytelling, if they wish. This song will be sung again by the group during this time of saying sorry.*

People heard John! And they came!
And do you know what John did?
> *If appropriate in Weeks 2+, accept responses.*
He washed the people in the river!

The people didn't feel ready to meet with God! *Shake head*
So they were sad.
Can you show me sad?
*Lead the children in looking sad.*

They asked John to wash them in the river. *Diddy Disciples 'I'm Sorry' sign (see p. 355)*
They wanted God to give them a new start.

> *In Week 1, you may find the following introduction helpful:*
> We're going to learn a new song!
> It's the people's song when they met John the Baptist.
> Let's say the words 'my turn', *point to self*, 'your turn' *leader's hands out to group.*

> Wash me in the river, *'I'm Sorry' sign*
> wash me in the river. *'I'm Sorry' sign*
> **Wash me in the river,** *'I'm Sorry' sign*
> **wash me in the river,** *'I'm Sorry' sign*

O wash me, O wash me, *'I'm Sorry' sign twice*
I need a new start! *Diddy Disciples 'New Start' sign (see p. 355)*
**O wash me, O wash me,** *'I'm Sorry' sign twice*
**I need a new start!** *'New Start' sign*

Now let's try and add the tune.
*Repeat the 'my turn, your turn' introduction above, this time with the tune. Then move straight into the following material.*

*All groups:*
Let's sing the people's song together.

*Lead the children in singing:*
**Wash me in the river,** *'I'm Sorry' sign*
**wash me in the river,** *'I'm Sorry' sign*
**O wash me, O wash me,** *'I'm Sorry' sign twice*
**I need a new start!** *'New Start' sign*
*Repeat as appropriate.*

We're ready to tell our story.

·················································································

: **Tip**

: If your group doesn't know one of the Diddy Disciples Sorry Songs, the extra week Jesus is Thrown into the
: Wilderness from this unit is a good opportunity for your group to learn Sorry Song: Option 2 in preparation
: for Lent. It shares the same tune and some of the words as 'Wash me in the river'. If you would like to learn
: this Sorry Song, we suggest introducing the new words immediately after singing 'Wash me in the river' as
: your Gathering Song during that session (before the storytelling). You may find the following introduction
: helpful.

·················································································

*Week 3 (for groups wanting to learn Sorry Song: Option 2)*
At the end of our story today,
we're going to sing our 'Wash me in the river' song again to say sorry.

But this week, we're going to use different words.
Let's learn them now:
'my turn' *point to self*, 'your turn' *leader's hands out to group*.

*Spoken in rhythm:*
For the things we have thought that we wish we'd not thought *both hands to self*
**For the things we have thought that we wish we'd not thought** *hands out to group*

Now let's try adding the tune and the rest of the words:
'my turn' *point to self*, 'your turn' *leader's hands out to group.*

*Singing:*
For the things we have tho-ught that we wish we'd not tho-ught *both hands to self*
**For the things we have tho-ught that we wish we'd not tho-ught** *both hands out to group*
We're sorry, we're sorry. We need a new start! *Both hands to self*
**We're sorry we're sorry. We need a new start!** *Both hands out to group*

Let's sing that altogether and add the actions.
Let's put our hands on our head.
**For the things we have tho-ught that we wish we'd not tho-ught,** *hands on head*
**we're sorry,** *'I'm Sorry' sign* **we're sorry.** *'I'm Sorry' sign*
**We need a new start!** *'New Start' sign*

The next verse is the same,
but this time the words are about what we've SAID.
Let's see if you can guess the words!
*Lead the group in singing:*

**For the things we have SA-ID that we wish we'd not SA-ID,**
**we're sorry,** *'I'm Sorry' sign* **we're sorry.** *'I'm Sorry' sign*
**We need a new start!** *'New Start' sign*

And then same again, but this time for the things we've DONE.
Let's try that together.
**For the things we have DO-NE that we wish we'd not DO-NE,**
**we're sorry,** *'I'm Sorry' sign* **we're sorry.** *'I'm Sorry' sign*
**We need a new start!** *'New Start' sign*

> ## Tip
>
> Remember, keep it simple! If your group is learning this Sorry Song for the first time today, this may not be the time to try and introduce lots of new resources for the storytelling and time of saying sorry, too (see Bible Storytelling on p. 81)!

## Gathering Song: Option 2

*For groups who are already familiar with a Diddy Disciples Sorry Song or have longer sessions.*

→ **Song: 'Get ready for our God!' Words: © Sharon Moughtin-Mumby**
→ **Music: 'She'll be coming round the mountain' (traditional). For a taster see the Diddy Disciples website.**

*In Week 1, you may find the following introduction helpful (before you distribute any imaginative aids that your group is using):*

We're going to learn a new song!
It's John the Baptist's song!
Let's say the words 'my turn' *point to self*, 'your turn' *leader's hands out to group.*

*Say the words in the rhythm in which you will sing them.*
Get ready, get ready for our God! *Both hands to self to show leader's turn*
**Get ready, get ready for our God!** *Hands out to group to show their turn*

It's time for a new start, time for a new start! *Diddy Disciples 'New Start' sign (see p. 355)*
**It's time for a new start, time for a new start!** *'New Start' sign*

Now let's try and add the tune:
*Singing:*
Get ready, get ready for our God! *Both hands to self to show leader's turn*
Get ready, get ready for our God! *Both hands to self to show leader's turn*
**Get ready, get ready for our God!** *Hands out to group to show their turn*
**Get ready, get ready for our God!** *Hands out to group to show their turn*

It's time for a new start, time for a new start! *'New Start' sign*
Get ready, get ready for our God! *Both hands to self to show leader's turn*

**It's time for a new start, time for a new start!** *'New Start' sign*
**Get ready, get ready for our God!** *Hands out to group to show their turn*

Let's try that all together . . .
*Lead the group in singing the song as a whole. When the group is ready, continue with the material below.*

*If you're using imaginative aids, ask two or three children to give them out at this point. Then invite the children to warm up their imaginations by exploring different shapes with their aids. See p. 220 of Book 1 for examples of actions for scarves or ribbons, but don't limit the children's imagination to these.*

Let's sing our song about getting ready for God.
We need some actions!
We already have an action for 'new start'.
*Lead the children in the Diddy Disciples 'New Start' sign (see p. 355)*
But we need an action for 'get ready'!
Who can show us a 'get ready' action?
*Choose one of the actions and ask the group to copy it.*

We're ready to sing!
*Lead the group in singing:*
**Get ready, get ready for our God!** *Get ready action*
**Get ready, get ready for our God!** *Get ready action*
**It's time for a new start, time for a new start!** *'New Start' sign*
**Get ready, get ready for our God!** *Get ready action*
*Repeat. If you like, you could choose a different action for 'get ready' each time.*

We're ready to tell our story about
*Week 1:* John the Baptist
*Weeks 2+:* John the Baptist and Jesus

# Getting Ready for Bible Storytelling

→ **Guide: Book 1, p. 220**

## Getting Ready for Bible Storytelling: Option 1

→ **Action: opening your group's box and naming this week's object**
→ **Guide: Book 1, p. 221**

*See the beginning of the weekly storytelling material for ideas of items to place in your box. Invite one of the children to open the box.*

What's in the box? *Ask the child to respond.*

## Getting Ready for Bible Storytelling: Option 2

→ **Song: 'Jesus, open up my eyes'. Words: © Sharon Moughtin-Mumby**
→ **Tune: 'Michael, row the boat ashore' (traditional). For the music see p. 359, or for a taster see the Diddy Disciples website. For tips on teaching songs for the first time, see Book 1, p. 215.**

It's time to open the Bible.
Let's get ready!
Let's take our thumb *lead children in showing thumb*
and draw our cross on our eyes, *draw cross*
and our lips, *draw cross*
and our heart. *Draw cross*
Let's ask Jesus to help us get ready to listen out for God!

**Jesus, open up my eyes. Alleluia!**
*Trace a cross between your eyes.*
**Jesus, open up my lips. Alleluia!**
*Trace a cross on your lips.*

**Jesus, open up my heart. Alleluia!**
*Trace a cross on your heart.*
**Jesus, help me hear your voice. Alleluia!**
*Cup your hands behind your ears.*

## Interactive Bible Storytelling

→ **Guide: Book 1, p. 221**

*See the Bible Storytelling material in Section 2 of this unit.*

## Saying Sorry to God/Prayers for Other People/ Thank You God

The Saying Sorry to God Building Block, with its strong echoes of repentance and baptism, works particularly well with the John the Baptist unit. For this reason, saying sorry is an optional part of the storytelling itself for this unit.
- If your group would prefer to continue with its usual Prayers for Other People or Thank You God Building Blocks, you can find these in other units, for instance p. 109 and p. 112.
- Prayer Actions with a spring theme can be found within the Journey to the Cross (Lent) unit on p. 110. Alternatively, Prayer Actions that can be used throughout the year can be found on pp. 47–8 of Book 1.

## Creative Response

→ **Guide: Book 1, p. 228**

*See the Creative Response starter ideas in Section 3 of this unit.*

## Sharing God's Peace

→ **Guide: Book 1, p. 231**

*This Building Block is particularly designed for children's groups that join the adult congregation to share communion but can also be used to end any session or Service of the Word.*

### Sharing God's Peace: Option 1

→ **Song: 'I've got peace like a river' (traditional), Isaiah 66.12, NIV**
→ **Tune: traditional. For a taster see the Diddy Disciples website. For tips on teaching songs for the first time, see Book 1, p. 215.**

> *Either: hold one end of the peace cloth (Book 1, p. 231) and ask one of the older children or an adult to hold the other end. Start singing the Peace Song. As the children begin to gather, invite them to join in holding a small section of the cloth, raising and lowering it so it 'flows' like a river as you sing together.*

> *Or: invite the children to sit in a circle in the worship space. Start singing the Peace Song. As the children begin to gather, invite them to join in raising and lowering their hands like the waters of a flowing river.*

**I've got peace like a river,**
**I've got peace like a river,**
**I've got peace like a river in my soul.**
**I've got peace like a river,**
**I've got peace like a river,**
**I've got peace like a river in my soul.**

*If your group is about to rejoin the adults for communion: when all the children are gathered, continue with the words of the Peace, below.*

## Sharing God's Peace: Option 2

→ Song: 'Peace is flowing like a river' (traditional), Isaiah 66.12, NIV
→ Tune: traditional. For a taster see the Diddy Disciples website. For tips on teaching songs for the first time, see Book 1, p. 215.

> *Either: hold one end of the peace cloth (Book 1, p. 231) and ask one of the older children or an adult to hold the other end. Start singing the Peace Song. As the children begin to gather, invite them to join in holding a small section of the cloth, raising and lowering it so it 'flows' like a river as you sing together.*
>
> *Or: invite the children to sit in a circle in the worship space. Start singing the Peace Song. As the children begin to gather, invite them to join in raising and lowering their hands like the waters of a flowing river.*

**Peace is flowing like a river,**
**flowing out through you and me.**
**Spreading out into the desert,**
**setting all the captives free.**

*If your group is about to rejoin the adults for communion: when all the children are gathered, continue with the words of the Peace, below.*

## Sharing God's Peace: Option 3

→ Song: 'I've got peace in my fingers'. Words: © 1995 Susan Salidor ASCAP
→ Tune: © 1995 Susan Salidor ASCAP
→ The words and music can be found on the album *Little Voices in My Head* by Susan Salidor © 2003 Peach Head. They can also be found on iTunes or YouTube, or at <www.susansalidor.com>. For tips on teaching songs for the first time, see Book 1, p. 215.

*If your group is about to rejoin the adults for communion: when all the children are gathered, continue with the words of the Peace, below.*

# The Peace

→ 2 Thessalonians 3.16; 1 Peter 5.14

*Once you have finished singing . . .*

The peace of the Lord be always with you.
*Hold hands open to the children.*
**And also with you.**

*Invite the children to open their hands towards you.*
Let's shake hands or hug each other
and say, 'Peace be with you' *or whatever is said on sharing the Peace in your church*
as a sign of God's peace.

*Lead the children in giving and receiving the Peace. Immediately following this, at St Peter's, Walworth, we lead the children back to join the rest of the congregation to continue our worship with the Eucharistic Prayer.*

# Taking God's Love into the World

→ Guide: Book 1, p. 232
→ Song: 'This little light of mine' (traditional)
→ Tune: traditional. For a taster see the Diddy Disciples website. For tips on teaching songs for the first time, see Book 1, p. 215.

*This Building Block is particularly designed for standalone groups or groups that are held during a Service of the Word. Alternatively, you could use one of the Peace Songs above to end your worship.*

Our time together is coming to an end.
*Invite the children to sit in a circle for a moment of quiet.*

God has lit a little light of love inside all of us.
*Trace a circle on your heart.*
Let's make our finger into a candle.
*Bring your finger from your heart and hold it out.*
Let's be God and light our little light of love together, after 3.
*Lead the children in lighting their finger candle by striking an imaginary match in the air on 3 and pretending to light your finger.*
**1, 2, 3 . . . Tssss!**
Let's imagine God's love shining and dancing like light in us.

*Wave your finger in front of you.*
**This little light of mine, I'm gonna let it shine!**
**This little light of mine, I'm gonna let it shine!**
**This little light of mine, I'm gonna let it shine!**
**Let it shine, let it shine, let it shine!**

*Blow on your finger as if blowing out a candle on 'puff'. Then hold it up high.*
**Won't let no one** *puff* **it out! I'm gonna let it shine!**
**Won't let no one** *puff* **it out! I'm gonna let it shine!**
**Won't let no one** *puff* **it out! I'm gonna let it shine!**
**Let it shine, let it shine, let it shine!**

*Hold your finger behind a cupped hand, then take your cupped hand away*
*to reveal the 'candle' and hold it high!*
**Hide it under a bushel? No! I'm gonna let it shine!**
**Hide it under a bushel? No! I'm gonna let it shine!**
**Hide it under a bushel? No! I'm gonna let it shine!**
**Let it shine, let it shine, let it shine!**

*Lead the children in placing your finger back on your heart.*
Now let's put our little light of love
back in our hearts, where it belongs.
Let's remember to let our little light shine
in all our playing and working today . . .

*If you're building a Service of the Word and this is your final Building Block, you may like to close with a familiar blessing, the Peace and/or one of the following. If you're using one of these call-and-responses with your group for the first time, see p. 25 for an introduction.*

| | | |
|---|---|---|
| *Either:* | Praise the Lord! *Both hands to self* | |
| | **Alleluia!** *Both arms upwards in 'V' shape* | |
| *Or:* | Let us bless the Lord. *Both hands to self* | |
| | **Thanks be to God.** *Both arms upwards in 'V' shape* | |
| *Or:* | And all the people said . . . *both hands to self* | |
| | **Amen!** *Both arms upwards in 'V' shape* | |

# Section 2

# The Bible Storytelling material: John the Baptist unit

## Week 1: Meet John

→ Matthew 3.1–6

> If your group is telling Weeks 1 and 2 as a single story to fit in the material before Lent begins, follow the instructions set out in boxes like this during the storytelling.

*If you are using the Saying Sorry material towards the end of the storytelling, you will need one or more bowls of water. You can simply use normal tap water, or, if your church is one that uses water liturgically, you could use water from your baptism font.*

*If you're using the What's in the Box? option (Book 1, p. 221) invite one of the children to open the box. Inside is a picture or statue of John the Baptist.*

What's in the box? *Invite the child to respond*

It's John the Baptist!
*If appropriate:*
Look what he's wearing! It's made of camel hair!

*Begin with this recap of the Gathering Song:*
Let's stand up and be John the Baptist together.
Let's make sure we've got our itchy camel-hair coat on.
*Lead the children in miming putting on a coat and feeling itchy.*

Let's call out after 3, 'Get ready for God!'
**1, 2, 3 . . . Get ready for God!**
And louder!
**1, 2, 3 . . . Get ready for God!**

Look! *Point* The people are coming!

*If you've just sung the 'Wash me in the river' song:*
Can anyone tell me what John the Baptist's going to do?
*Accept the children's responses.*

John's going to wash them in the river!
*Continue from the material for all groups, below.*

*If you have not sung the 'Wash me in the river' song:*
And do you know what John did?
He washed the people in the river!
Let's be the people coming to John.

The people wanted to get ready for God.
But they'd done wrong things that made them feel sad.
Can you show me sad?
*Lead the children in looking sad.*

They didn't really feel ready for God.
*Lead the children in shaking head.*
Let's shake our heads and look sad.
The people felt like they needed a new start!

*Confident groups that have sung 'Get ready for our God!' as their Gathering Song (Option 2) may also like to learn the 'Wash me in the river' song (Option 1) at this point using the material on p. 54. We've done this in our Diddy Disciples Sunday worship at St Peter's, Walworth, as the children are used to learning lots of new songs and enjoy singing 'Wash me in the river' as an alternative Sorry Song. It's too much for our nursery group at school, however. If you're already familiar with a Sorry Song then your group does not need to learn 'Wash me in the river' for the time of saying sorry.*

**Wash me in the river,** *Diddy Disciples 'I'm Sorry' sign (p. 355)*
**wash me in the river,** *'I'm Sorry' sign*
**O wash me, O wash me,** *'I'm Sorry' sign twice*
**I need a new start!** *Diddy Disciples 'New Start' sign (p. 355)*
*Repeat as appropriate.*

*When the group is ready, continue with the following material.*

*All groups:*
It's time to get into the river with John!
Let's dip our toe in.
*Lead the children in dipping a toe in imaginary water.*

Is the water warm or cold today?
*Let one of the children decide. According to their response:*
> *Either:* Oh no! It's freezing!
> *Or:* Oooh! It's lovely and warm!

Let's walk on the spot into the river . . .
*Lead the children in walking in slowly on the spot into warm/cold water.*
Deeper . . . *show the water level on your ankle*
and deeper . . . *show the water level at your knee*
and deeper . . . *show the water level at your thighs*
and deeper . . . *show the water level at your waist*
until the river's up to our waist!

We're in the river!
Now we're going to let John baptize us.
After 3, we're going to take a deep breath,
then we're going to go down *point down* right under the water . . .
and up again. *Point up*
Down . . . *point down*
then up . . . *Point up*

Are you ready to take a deep breath?
Don't forget to hold your nose!

1, 2, 3, breathe! *Lead the children in taking a deep breath then hold nose*
and down . . . *lead the children in crouching down to go under the water*
and up! *Lead the children in standing up again*

This was called BAPTISM.
Can you say 'baptism'?
**Baptism.**

Let's go down again and this time we're going to stay underwater.
1, 2, 3 . . . *deep breath, hold nose*
Down into the water . . . and FREEZE!
*Stay crouched down with the children.*

In the water, God made the people clean.
Not just clean OUTside *rub arms*
but clean INside too. *Trace a circle on your heart*
God gave them a new start!

After 3, let's go up out of the water and shout,
'God gives me a new start!'
**1, 2, 3 . . .** *lead the children in jumping up*
**God gives me a new start!**

So John called to the people.
Let's stand up and after 3,
let's be John calling, 'Get ready for God' again.
**1, 2, 3 . . . Get ready for God!** *Hands around mouth*

And more and more and more people came!
Let's show John's baptism one more time.
After 3, let's go down and stay down. *Point down*
**1, 2, 3 . . .** *deep breath, hold nose*
*Lead the children in crouching down.*
and FREEZE!

Now we're going to jump back up *point up*
and shout *hands cupped around mouth*
'God gives me a new start!'
**1, 2, 3 . . .** *jump up* **God gives me a new start!**

■ If you're telling Weeks 1 and 2 as a single story, move straight to Week 2 at this point.
■ If you'd like to continue with a time of saying sorry, use the following material. Your group will need to be using the 'Wash me in the river' Gathering Song or be familiar with one of the Diddy Disciples Sorry Songs (p. 356).

Let's sit down for a moment.
*When the group is ready:*
I wonder how the people felt when God gave them a new start?
Can you show me with your face?
*Accept the children's responses.*

Sometimes we do things we wish we hadn't done.
Sometimes it can feel like we've done it all wrong.
We wish we could have a new start!

Let's put our hands on our head.
I wonder if there's anything we've thought this week
that we wish we hadn't thought?

*If you haven't learned the 'Wash me in the river' Gathering Song, use the words from your usual Sorry Song at this point and below.*
**Wash me in the river,** *Diddy Disciples 'I'm Sorry' sign (p. 355)*
**wash me in the river,** *'I'm Sorry' sign*
**O wash me, O wash me,** *'I'm Sorry' sign twice*
**I need a new start!** *Diddy Disciples 'New Start' sign (p. 355)*

Let's put our hands by our mouths.
I wonder if there's anything we've said this week
that we wish we hadn't said?

**Wash me in the river,** *'I'm Sorry' sign*
**Wash me in the river,** *'I'm Sorry' sign*
**O wash me, O wash me,** *'I'm Sorry' sign twice*
**I need a new start!** *'New Start' sign*

Let's cross our hands on our chest.
I wonder if there's anything we've done this week
that we wish we hadn't done?

**Wash me in the river,** *'I'm Sorry' sign*
**Wash me in the river,** *'I'm Sorry' sign*
**O wash me, O wash me,** *'I'm Sorry' sign twice*
**I need a new start!** *'New Start' sign*

Let's open our eyes again.
The Good News is that God LOVES giving new starts!
God can wash us, not just OUTside, *rub arms*
but INside too! *Trace a circle on your heart*

One very special way God does this is through baptism,
like John's baptisms.
Put your hand up if you've seen a baptism or been baptized?
We'll be talking more about baptism next week.

But God loves giving new starts all the time!
Not just in baptism.
We don't have to go to a river!
We don't even have to use water, but we're going to today!

*If there is an older child present who is unlikely to spill the water you could invite her or him to take the water around the circle. You may wish to ask more than one child to take bowls around the circle, going opposite ways or starting at different points in the circle. Alternatively take a bowl around yourself and/or ask adults to help.*

Here I have a bowl of water
        *If appropriate* taken from our baptism font at church.
*Name* is going to bring this bowl of water around.

If you'd like a new start from God,
You could dip your finger in the water in the bowl and
        *Either:* draw a cross on your forehead.
        *Or:* draw a smile on your forehead to show that God is happy with you.

Let's ask God to wash us INside as well as OUTside!
Let's ask God to give us a brand new start!
Let's sing as we wait for the water.

*Lead the children in singing the following, or the 'I'm sorry' refrain from your usual Sorry Song.*
**Wash me in the river,** *'I'm Sorry' sign*
**Wash me in the river,** *'I'm Sorry' sign*
**O wash me, O wash me,** *'I'm Sorry' sign*
**I need a new start!** *'New Start' sign*

*When all the children and adults who wish to take water have done so:*
Look at all those beautiful new starts! *Point around the room*
After 3, let's shout, 'God gives me a new start!'
**1, 2, 3 . . . God gives me a new start!**

I wonder how you'll use your new start today?

## Tip

In St Peter's School, following this session, we send each class back with the water in a little dish to place on their RE table in the classroom:

> I'm going to give *Name* this water
> to take back to your classroom.
> When you do something
> you wish you hadn't done,
> if you like, you can come and ask God
> to give you a new start.
> You can dip your finger in here
> *mime dipping finger into the bowl*
> and draw a cross/smile on your forehead!
> *Mime drawing a cross/smile on your own forehead*
> God always loves to give new starts!

# Week 2: John Baptizes Jesus

→ **Matthew 3.13–17**

This storytelling starts with a recap of Week 1. If your group is telling Weeks 1 and 2 as a single story, start with the material immediately following the box like this below.

*If you're using the What's in the Box? option (Book 1, p. 221):*
*invite one of the children to open the box. Inside is a picture or statue of John the Baptist.*

What's in the box? *Invite the child to respond*

This is John the Baptist!
*If appropriate:*
Look what he's wearing! It's made of camel hair!

Let's stand up and be John the Baptist together.
Let's call out after 3, 'Get ready for God!'
**1, 2, 3 . . . Get ready for God!**

Look! *Point* The people are coming!
Can anyone tell me what John the Baptist's going to do?
*Accept the children's responses.*

John's going to wash them in the river!
It's time to get into the river with John!
Let's dip our toe in.
*Lead the children in dipping a toe in imaginary water.*

Is the water warm or cold today?
*Let one of the children decide. According to their response:*
> *Either:* Oh no! It's freezing!
> *Or:* Oooh! It's lovely and warm!

Let's walk on the spot into the river . . .
*Lead the children in walking in slowly on the spot into warm/cold water.*
Deeper . . . *show the water level on your ankle*
and deeper . . . *show the water level at your knee*
and deeper . . . *show the water level at your thighs*

and deeper . . . *show the water level at your waist*
until the river's up to our waist!

Now we're going to let John baptize us.
After 3, we're going to take a deep breath,
then we're going to go down *point down*
and up again. *Point up*
Don't forget to hold your nose!

1, 2, 3, breathe! *Lead the children in taking a deep breath. Hold nose*
and down . . . *lead the children in crouching down to go under the water*
and up! *Lead the children in standing up again*

This was called baptism.
Can you say 'baptism'?
**Baptism.**

Let's go down again.
1, 2, 3 . . . *deep breath, hold nose*
Down into the water . . .
and FREEZE!
*This time stay crouched down with the children.*

In the water, God made the people clean.
Not just clean OUTside *rub arms*
but clean INside too. *Trace a circle on your heart*
God cleaned their hearts! *Trace a circle on your heart*
God gave them a new start!

After 3, let's go up out of the water and shout
'God gives me a new start!'
**1, 2, 3 . . .** *up out of the water*
**God gives me a new start!**

> If your group is holding Weeks 1 and 2 as a single session, move straight from the place indicated in Week 1 to pick up the story again from here.

So John was at the river baptizing people.
Then, one day, JESUS came to the river!
Let's stand up tall and be the grown-up Jesus.
*Lead the children in standing up tall.*

Jesus said, 'Baptize me!'
After 3 let's say, 'Baptize me!' *Point to self* like Jesus.
1, 2, 3 . . . **Baptize me!** *Point to self*
John was shocked!
Can you show me your shocked face?
*Lead the children in looking shocked.*

John shook his head.
Let's shake our head. *Lead the children in shaking head*

I can't baptize YOU!' said John. *Point in front of you*
You don't need a new start!
You're clean ALREADY!
You should baptize ME!' *Point to self*

Let's all shake our heads like John again and say, 'No!'
**'No!'** *Shaking head*

But Jesus said, 'Yes!' *Nod head*
After 3 let's say, 'Baptize me!' *point to self* like Jesus.
1, 2, 3 . . . **Baptize me!** *Point to self*

Jesus stepped into the river.
Let's be Jesus and get into the river together.
*Lead the children in miming walking on the spot and showing the water level rising with your hands up to your waist.*
Deeper and deeper until the water is up to our waist.

So John baptized Jesus.
Jesus went down into the river and then back up again.
After 3, let's be Jesus.
Let's go down into the river . . .
1, 2, 3 . . . *deep breath, hold nose*
. . . and up again!

Then when Jesus came up out of the water, *point back up*
Something amazing happened!
Look! *Point heavenwards*

The sky is opening up!
*Move arms from both pointing upwards, down to your sides.*
The Holy Spirit is flying down like a dove!
*Show a dove flying down with your hands.*

Let's make a dove shape with our hands.
*Show the children how to make a dove shape by linking your thumbs.*
Let's make the dove fly down from heaven.
*Lead the children in making a dove fly down from the sky.*

Let's sit down for a moment.

*When the group is ready:*
God flew down like a dove and landed on Jesus
and a voice said . . .
Can you say these very special words after me,
'my turn' *point to self*, 'your turn' *leader's hands out to group*?

'This is my child.' *Mime rocking a baby*
**'This is my child.'** *Mime rocking a baby*
'I love him!' *Hands crossed over chest*
**'I love him!'** *Hands crossed over chest*
'I am very happy with him!' *Trace smile on face*
**'I am very happy with him!'** *Trace smile on face*

Jesus' baptism made baptism special.
Now, if we want to follow Jesus, we get baptized too!
Can you put your hand up if you've been baptized?
*Acknowledge those who've put their hands up.*

*When the group is ready:*
God has said those special words to you!
God wants to say those special words to ALL of us!

Let's all close our eyes for a moment . . .
Let's imagine getting baptized like Jesus:
going down . . . then up . . .
Let's imagine the Holy Spirit
flying down on us like a dove.

Let's say God's special words again
but this time let's say them quietly.
Let's imagine God saying them to us too!

'You are my child.'
**'You are my child.'**
'I love you!'
**'I love you!'**
'I am very happy with you!'
**'I am very happy with you!'**

Let's open our eyes.
I wonder how those words make you feel?
Can you show me?
*Accept all responses.*

---

■ If you would like to continue with a time of saying sorry, use the following material. Groups that have told the stories from Week 1 and 2 in a single session may need to think about time considerations.

■ Your group will need to be using the 'Wash me in the river' Gathering Song (p. 54) or be familiar with one of the Diddy Disciples Sorry Songs (p. 356).

---

God is VERY happy with us! *Trace a smile on face*
There's nothing we can do to make God love us less. *Shake head and smile*
And there's nothing we can do to make God love us more.[2] *Shake head and smile*
But sometimes we don't feel READY to be with God.
Like the people who came to John didn't feel ready. *Shake head*

The people asked John to wash them in the river first. *Diddy Disciples 'I'm Sorry' sign (p. 355)*
Sometimes WE can feel not ready for God. *Shake head*
Sometimes we feel like we need a new start.

The Good News is:
God LOVES to give us a new start.
Let's have a time of saying sorry to God now.

Sometimes we do things we wish we hadn't done.
Sometimes it can feel like we've done it all wrong.
We wish we could have a new start!

Let's put our hands on our head.
I wonder if there's anything we've thought this week
that we wish we hadn't thought?

*If you haven't learned the 'Wash me in the river' Gathering Song, use the words from your usual Sorry Song at this point and below.*

**Wash me in the river,** *'I'm Sorry' sign*
**wash me in the river,** *'I'm Sorry' sign*
**O wash me, O wash me,** *'I'm Sorry' sign twice*
**I need a new start!** *Diddy Disciples 'New Start' sign (p. 355)*

Let's put our hands by our mouths.
I wonder if there's anything we've said this week
that we wish we hadn't said?

**Wash me in the river,** *'I'm Sorry' sign*
**Wash me in the river,** *'I'm Sorry' sign*
**O wash me, O wash me,** *'I'm Sorry' sign twice*
**I need a new start!** *'New Start' sign*

Let's cross our hands on our chest.
I wonder if there's anything we've done this week
that we wish we hadn't done?

**Wash me in the river,** *'I'm Sorry' sign*
**Wash me in the river,** *'I'm Sorry' sign*
**O wash me, O wash me,** *'I'm Sorry' sign twice*
**I need a new start!** *'New Start' sign*

Let's open our eyes again.
The Good News is that God LOVES giving new starts!
God can wash us, not just OUTside, *rub arms*
but INside too! *Trace a circle on your heart*

One very special way God does this is through baptism,
But God loves giving new starts all the time!
We don't have to go to a river!
We don't even have to use water, but we're going to today!

*If there is an older child present who is unlikely to spill the water you could invite him or her to take the water around the circle. You may wish to ask more than one child to take bowls around the circle, going opposite ways or starting at different points in the circle. Alternatively take a bowl around yourself and/or ask adults to help.*

Here I have a bowl of water
    *If appropriate:* taken from our baptism font at church.
*Name* is going to bring this bowl of water around.

If you'd like a new start from God,
You could dip your finger in the water in the bowl and
    *Either:* draw a cross on your forehead.
    *Or:* draw a smile on your forehead to show that God is happy with you.

Let's ask God to wash us INside as well as OUTside!
Let's ask God to give us a brand new start!
Let's sing as we wait for the water.

*Lead the children in singing the following, or the 'I'm sorry' refrain from your usual Sorry Song.*
**Wash me in the river,** *'I'm Sorry' sign*
**Wash me in the river,** *'I'm Sorry' sign*
**O wash me, O wash me,** *'I'm Sorry' sign*
**I need a new start!** *'New Start' sign*

*When all the children and adults who wish to take water have done so:*
Look at all those beautiful new starts! *Point around the room*
After 3, let's shout, 'God gives me a new start!'
**1, 2, 3 . . . God gives me a new start!**

I wonder how you'll use your new start today?

## Tip

In St Peter's School, following this session, we send each class back with the water in a little dish to place on their RE table in the classroom:

> I'm going to give *Name* this water
> to take back to your classroom.
> When you do something
> you wish you hadn't done,
> if you like you can come and ask God
> to give you a new start.
> You can dip your finger in here
> *mime dipping finger in the bowl*
> and draw a cross/smile on your forehead!
> *Mime drawing a cross/smile on your forehead*
> God always loves to give new starts!

# Extra: Our Baptism

*Optional: a baptism roleplaying workshop*

## Introductory notes

Baptism roleplaying workshops that involve simulating baptism with a doll are becoming increasingly common in primary schools and churches. Witnessing or taking part in roleplay has been shown to both accelerate and deepen learning experiences among children (and adults!). The following material is offered as an optional week for churches, groups or schools who would like to offer a baptism roleplaying workshop to give the children opportunities to make connections between the Bible stories about baptism that you've been telling together and the Christian baptisms they see in their place.

Baptism looks different in every church and setting. The following material is based on infant baptism material in *Common Worship* (both *Christian Initiation* 2006 and *Additional Baptism Texts in Accessible Language* 2015) and BCP 2004 (Church of Ireland). However, please adapt the Diddy Disciples resources freely so your workshop reflects baptism in your church as closely as possible. It may also be appropriate for your group to omit some sections because of time limitations.

The words and symbols of baptism are full of meaning! This workshop concentrates solely on the meanings brought to baptism by the stories about John the Baptist and the baptism of Jesus, building on the songs and actions that the children have learned over the weeks. For an opportunity to explore more meanings of these rich symbols, see the similar baptism roleplaying workshop in the God's Best Friend, Moses, unit (p. 307). Other Diddy Disciples workshops for baptism (for instance, exploring baptism in the context of the Easter stories and the death and resurrection of Jesus) will become available on the website over time.

## Tip

The titles used for the different sections in this workshop match the ones used in *Common Worship* and BCP 2004 so, if you like, you can compare the material easily. Some of the order of the service has been changed for practical reasons (e.g. the Signing with the Cross is before the Prayer over the Water): to bring together the parts of the workshop that will take place at the tables. If you prefer, you can adapt the material to follow *Common Worship*'s order of service.

## Practical notes

At St Peter's, Walworth, we find that we're all shattered at the end of our baptism roleplaying workshops (so be prepared and perhaps find extra helpers!) but everyone who's taken part thinks they're hugely worthwhile for the way in which they make links between the stories and baptism material for churches.

For today's session, you will need:

- a range of baby dolls or figures set out in a line in front of the group: one for each child. For 'babies' we provide a baby doll. For 'adults' we provide a 'small world' figure (see p. 95). We enjoy seeing the range of farmers, police officers, shopkeepers, soldiers, elderly people, etc., who are brought to 'baptism'. If your church does not have infant baptism, you could use adult figures only.

> ## Tip
>
> - We don't give the children access to the dolls/figures until later in the session, as we've found that they can prove really distracting to the children if given out early on. If children have brought toys with them, you could ask them to place them at the end of the line so you can make sure they're reunited for the workshop.
> - As our group is large, we don't give children the choice of exactly which doll/figure they'll baptize (unless they've brought their own) – this would prove too disruptive – but smaller groups may like to do this.

For the baptism demonstration (leader) in the first part of the session:

- a baby doll (or adult figure if your church does not have infant baptism);
- a large, transparent bowl of water;
- a white robe or dress, or a piece of white cloth to act as a robe (if your church dresses baptism candidates in white after baptism);
- a pot of oil (if your church uses oil for the Signing with the Cross).

For the baptism workshop (whole group) in the second part of the session, you will need to set up tables beforehand with:

- a bowl of water for each child. At St Peter's we use a range of bowls including recyclable cartons. We fill them with water beforehand, just deep enough for the children to be able to scoop water out easily;
- a piece of white cloth to act as a robe for each child (if your church dresses baptism candidates in white after baptism);
- access to towels to dry hands and for inevitable spillages;
- two or more pots of oil on each table that the children can easily access (if your church uses oil for the Signing with the Cross and/or anointing).

> ## Tip
>
> You may like (or need) to invite children to bring their own dolls or figures to the baptism workshop. If you do invite children to bring a favourite toy, it's important to then honour this invitation (even if the favourite toy turns out to be a teddy or a rabbit, for instance). Psychology suggests that favourite toys can represent much more than the toy itself for many children. The danger of rejecting such a toy as 'not quite right' is that children may then feel rejected themselves. If your group might find this challenging, then it may be best not to make an invitation like this.

# Introduction

*As the baptism workshop this week is longer, you can go straight into this material after your usual Welcome and Getting Ready to Worship Building Blocks.*

*If appropriate, encourage the children to join in at the dots.*
We've been telling stories about John the . . . **Baptist**.
Let's stand up, put our itchy camel-hair coat on . . .
*Lead the children in standing up, putting coat on and scratching*
and be John the Baptist together.

John's job was to get the world ready for God!
*Cup hands around mouth*
After 3, let's shout, 'Get ready for God!'

**1, 2, 3 . . . Get ready for God!** *Cup hands around mouth*
*Look around* I'm not sure anyone heard that.
Let's try that again even louder.
**1, 2, 3 . . . Get ready for God!** *Cup hands around mouth*

People heard John! And they came!
*If appropriate:* Can anyone tell us what John did?
*Accept responses.*

John washed the people in the river!
Let's show John's baptisms.
After 3, we're going to take a deep breath,
then we're going to go down under the water and stay down.
*Point down.*

Don't forget to hold your nose!
1, 2, 3, breathe! *Lead the children in taking a deep breath. Hold nose*
and FREEZE!
*Go down and stay crouched down with the children.*
In the water, God made the people clean.
Not just clean OUTside *rub arms*
but clean INside too. *Trace a circle on your heart*
God gave them a new start!
After 3, let's go up out of the water and shout
'God gives me a new start!'
**1, 2, 3 . . .** *up out of the water*
**God gives me a new start!**

We get baptized in our church.

> *If appropriate:*
> Put your hand up if you've been baptized.

*All groups:*
Put your hand up if you've seen a baptism in our church.
Baptism in our church LOOKS different
from John's baptisms but it's doing the same thing.

Today we're going to 'baptize' one of these friends.
*Indicate dolls/teddies/figures to be 'baptized'.*

## Presentation of the Candidates

→ **Song: 'I am going to follow Jesus'. Words: © Sharon Moughtin-Mumby**
→ **Tune: 'Bobby Shaftoe' (traditional). For a taster see the Diddy Disciples website.**

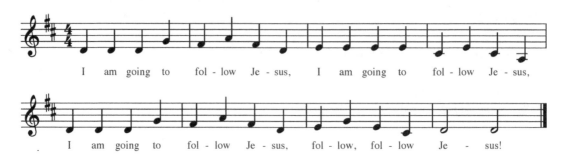

I am going to fol-low Je-sus, I am going to fol-low Je-sus,

I am going to fol-low Je-sus, fol-low, fol-low Je - sus!

*'I am going to follow Jesus' will become the Gathering Song for Lent so will become a very familiar song over time. As the words are so repetitive, don't worry about teaching the song, just start singing and the children will naturally begin to join in.*

When our friends are baptized,
they promise to 'follow Jesus'.
Let's show our friends how to follow Jesus.
Let's stand up and march on the spot.
*Lead the children in marching on the spot, counting in beat with the song you'll sing.*
**1, 2, 3, 4! 1, 2, 3, 4!**

*Continue marching as you sing.*
**I am going to follow Jesus,**
**I am going to follow Jesus,**
**I am going to follow Jesus,**
**follow, follow Jesus!**

Let's practise following Jesus!
*Invite one of the children to stand in the centre of the circle or at the front.*
*Name* is going to be Jesus!
*To the child:* 'Jesus!' Can you show us an action?
Let's all copy what 'Jesus' does.
Let's 'follow Jesus'.

*Continue 'following' the child's action as you sing:*
**I am going to follow Jesus,**
**I am going to follow Jesus,**
**I am going to follow Jesus,**
**follow, follow Jesus!**
*Invite another child to be 'Jesus' and repeat.*

*When the group is ready to finish:*
Let's sit down for a moment.

*When the group is ready:*
We've shown our friends how to follow Jesus. *Indicate dolls/figures*
Now I'm going to ask three questions. *Hold three fingers up*

If our friends are going to be baptized,
we need to answer, 'We will!' for our friends. *Thumbs up*
Let's practise saying, 'We will!' *Thumbs up*
**We will!** *Thumbs up*

Question number 1: *show one finger*
Will you welcome these friends into God's family?
**We will!** *Thumbs up*

Question number 2: *show two fingers*
We've been practising how to do this in our song!
Will you show these friends how to follow Jesus?
**We will!** *Thumbs up*

Question number 3: *show three fingers*
Will you help these friends be part of the Church?
**We will!** *Thumbs up*

# The Decision

*Either:*

→ Song: 'Wash me in the river' (the Gathering Song for the John the Baptist unit). Words: © Sharon Moughtin-Mumby

→ Tune: 'Alive, alive-o' from 'Molly Malone' (traditional). For the music see p. 54, or for a taster see the Diddy Disciples website.

*Or:*

→ Song: 'The Diddy Disciples sorry song'. Words: © Sharon Moughtin-Mumby

→ Tune: © Sharon Moughtin-Mumby. For the music see p. 356, or for a taster see the Diddy Disciples website.

*Or:*

*You may prefer to use the words from The Decision* (Common Worship *or BCP 2004) that you use for baptism in your church.*

*If your church lights the Easter Candle visibly during baptisms, you could light a real candle in a safe place or light a battery candle at this point. At St Peter's, Walworth, we use our church's Pascal Candle from the previous year.*

Now we light a candle to remind us
of God's bright light, shining in the darkness.

When we're baptized, Jesus gives us a new start.
Before we get baptized,
we say a really big sorry to God.

> *If you've lit a candle:*
> We promise to walk in God's light! *Point to the lit candle*

Let's teach our friends *point to dolls/figures* how we say sorry.
Let's put our hands on our head
I wonder if there's anything we've thought this week
That we wish we hadn't thought?

*Lead the children in singing the following. Or change the words to your usual Sorry Song here and below.*

**Wash me in the river,** *Diddy Disciples 'I'm Sorry' sign (p. 355)*
**Wash me in the river,** *'I'm Sorry' sign*
**O wash me, O wash me,** *'I'm Sorry' sign twice*
**I need a new start!** *Diddy Disciples 'New Start' sign (p. 355)*

Let's put our hands by our mouths.
I wonder if there is anything we've said this week
That we wish we hadn't said?

*Lead the children in singing*
**Wash me in the river,** *'I'm Sorry' sign*
**Wash me in the river,** *'I'm Sorry' sign*
**O wash me, O wash me,** *'I'm Sorry' sign*
**I need a new start!** *'New Start' sign*

Let's cross our hands on our chest
I wonder if there is anything we've done this week
That we wish we hadn't done?

*Lead the children in singing*
**Wash me in the river,** *'I'm Sorry' sign*
**Wash me in the river,** *'I'm Sorry' sign*
**O wash me, O wash me,** *'I'm Sorry' sign*
**I need a new start!** *'New Start' sign*

The Good News is that God
always wants to give us a new start!
Let's tell our friends about our amazing new start.

After 3, let's shout, 'God gives us a new start!'
**1, 2, 3: God gives us a new start!**

> ## Tip
>
> At St Peter's, Walworth, we move to the font at this point when we're holding the sessions with the school, but on Sundays this isn't possible and so we stay in our places. With the school group, we show the children the font, then put the lid back on and place a transparent bowl filled with water on top of the font. This is partly because the font has baptism water in it and partly so the children can then see the water inside the bowl and the 'baptism' itself more easily.
>
> If you're moving to the font, you could take this opportunity to ask a helper to move the dolls/figures to the baptism tables ready for their 'baptism'. We place the dolls/teddies/figures on the floor around the tables: one for each bowl. You can place figures on top of the tables: one next to each bowl. If any children have brought their own toys, keep these to one side and make sure the children are reunited with them for the workshop.

*If you're going to show the children the font:*
It's time to go to the 'font'.
Let's sing 'I am going to follow Jesus'
while we go there.
Let's tiptoe! *We've found that this helps the children not to run from excitement!*
*Lead the children in singing as you move to the font.*

*Invite the children to sit around the font.*
This is a 'font'. It's like a big bowl filled with water.

*All groups:*
Now we need some water.
*Show the children water in a transparent bowl so they can see it.*
This is just ordinary water.
But we say a prayer over the water to make it special.

> *If appropriate:* Let's hold our hands up
> over the water to show our prayer.
> *Lead the children in holding hands up over the water.*

* The prayer remembers
how important water is in our Bible stories.
One of the prayers remembers
John baptizing Jesus in the river.

Let's tell the story together.
Let's stand up and be Jesus.

*When the group is ready:*
After 3, let's go down into the river . . .
**1, 2, 3 . . .** *deep breath, hold nose*
. . . and up again!

Jesus made baptism special!
When we follow Jesus we get baptized too!
But we don't have a river in our church!

> *If appropriate:* and WE don't go right under the water, *point down*
> though some churches do!

Let's show how we baptize in our church.

# Signing with the Cross

*If your church does not make the sign of the cross here, skip this section and continue at Baptism, below.*

*Pick up the doll that you will demonstrate baptism with.*
First, when we baptize someone,
we draw a cross on their forehead.

> *If your church uses oil for the Signing with the Cross.*
> I'm going to dip my finger/thumb in this oil.
> *Dip finger in oil and show the oily finger/thumb.*
>
> *If it's the oil of catechumens:*
> This oil is the oil of getting ready and learning.
> It shows that we're getting ready to be baptized.

*All groups:*
I'm going to draw a cross on this baby's forehead.
Can you say the words after me,
'my turn' *point to self,* 'your turn' *leader's hands out to group*?

You belong to Jesus. *Look baby in the eyes*
**You belong to Jesus.**
I sign you with the cross. *Sign cross on forehead*
**I sign you with the cross.**

# Baptism

*Continue from here if your church doesn't make the sign of the cross before the baptism.*

[Now] I'm going to 'baptize' this baby.
Let's see if you can count on your fingers
how many times I pour water.

*Hold the doll like a baby in one arm and look into its eyes.*
Alex, *or another unisex name*
I baptize you in the name of . . . *pause*
the Father, *pour*
and of the Son, *pour*
and of the Holy Spirit. *Pour* Amen.
Can you show me on your fingers
how many times I poured water?
*Accept the children's responses.*

Three times! *Show three fingers*
The three are:
Father, *bend first finger up and down*
Son *bend second finger up and down*
and Holy Spirit. *Bend third finger up and down*

When we're baptized, we show that's what we believe.
Can you show me one finger?
*Lead the children in holding up index finger.*

*When the group is ready:*
Watch this!
*Demonstrate to the children:*

I believe in the Father. Nod, nod, nod. *Nod first finger three times*
Let's try that together.
**I believe in the Father. Nod, nod, nod.** *Nod first finger three times*

Now two fingers: *lead the children in holding up two fingers*
I believe in the Son. **Nod, nod, nod.** *Nod second finger*

Three fingers: *lead the children in holding up three fingers.*
I believe in the Holy Spirit. **Nod, nod, nod.** *Nod third finger*

So we pour water THREE times.
Father, Son and Holy Spirit!

> *If your church places a white robe on the newly baptized, you could do this at this point.*
> Then we put a white robe on our friend
> to show they've been 'baptized'.

> *If your church makes the sign of the cross at this point,*
> Now I'm going to make the sign of the cross
> on the baby's forehead
> *Demonstrate to the group.*

> *If your church anoints with oil of Chrism:*
> Now we're going to 'anoint' the baby's head with oil.
> This oil is the same oil
> used to sign the Queen with the cross
> when she was made Queen!
> We could say it's 'Royal Oil'.
> Can you say 'Royal Oil'?
> **Royal Oil!**

> The oil reminds us that our baby or adult
> is going to be part of a ROYAL family: God's family!

> I'm going to dip my finger/thumb in this oil.
> *Dip finger in oil and show the oily finger/thumb.*

> *Either:* Now I'm going to rub oil on the baby's head.
> *Or:* Now I'm going to draw a cross on the baby's head with oil.
> *Demonstrate to the group.*

## Baptism workshop

So you've watched how we baptize in our church.
I think you're ready for our baptism roleplay.
At the tables, there's a bowl of water

> *If you've moved the toys to the tables:*
> and a friend who's asked to be 'baptized'.

> *If the toys are still lined up at the front of the group:*
> On the way, we'll give you a friend to 'baptize'.
> *Get ready to distribute the toys to the children. If any of the children have brought toys, make sure they're reunited with the right toy!*

Let's go to our table(s) and find a place.
But wait!
Don't touch the water until we're all ready!
Let's sing as we go . . .

Let's tiptoe!

*Lead the children in singing 'I am going to follow Jesus' as they find a place next to a bowl of water.*

## Roleplay: Signing with the Cross

*As in the demonstration above, if your church does not make the sign of the cross here, skip this section and continue from Roleplay: Baptism, below.*

*When the group is ready:*
Can anyone remember what we did just before we poured water on our friend?
*Encourage the children to join in after the dots:*
We signed our friend with the . . . **cross**!

Let's make the sign of the cross on our friend's forehead.

> *If you're using oil:*
> Let's dip our finger/thumb in the oil
> and hold it up in the air to show we're ready.
> *Show the children your oily finger/thumb and wait as all the children dip their finger/thumb in oil and hold it up.*

*When the group is ready:*
Let's say the words 'my turn' *point to self*, 'your turn' *leader's hands out to group*.
You belong to Jesus.
**You belong to Jesus.**
I sign you with the cross. *Draw a cross on the doll's forehead*
**I sign you with the cross.** *Draw a cross on the doll's forehead*

## Roleplay: Baptism

Now let me tell you something important!
You can't be baptized without a name!
So let's call our babies and adults 'Alex', *or another unisex name*.

Now say these words after me,
and copy my actions,
'my turn' *point to self*, 'your turn' *leader's hands out to group*.

Alex! *Look into the doll/figure's eyes*
**Alex!**
I baptize you
**I baptize you**
in the name of . . .
**in the name of . . .**

*Aside to the children quietly:* Now let's put our hand in the water ready . . .
*Scoop one:* the Father,
*Scoop one:* **the Father,**
*Scoop two:* and of the Son,
*Scoop two:* **and of the Son,**
*Scoop three:* and of the Holy Spirit.
*Scoop three:* **and of the Holy Spirit.**
Amen!
**Amen!**

> *If your church places a white robe on the newly baptized,*
> Then we put a white robe on our friends
> to show they've been 'baptized'.

> *Lead the children in placing white robes on their friends.*

*If your church makes the sign of the cross at this point:*
Now we're going to make the sign of the cross
on the baby's forehead.
*Demonstrate to the group.*

*If your church anoints with oil of Chrism:*
Now we're going to 'anoint' the baby's head with oil.

Let's dip our finger/thumb in the oil
and hold it up in the air to show we're ready.
*Lead the group in rubbing oil on the toy's head or drawing the sign of the cross.*

## The Welcome

Then we welcome our friends into the church family.
Welcoming our new brothers and sisters
into God's family is really important!

> *Either:*
> Let's sing our Welcome Song to them!
> *If your group uses one of the Welcome Songs, sing your Welcome Song here. If you're using Welcome Song: Option 1, you could sing 'Welcome frie-ends to God's family!' throughout.*
>
> *Or:*
> Let's give them all a big clap!
> *Lead the children in clapping.*

## Opportunity for 'overlearning'

Now, we only ever need to get baptized once
in our whole lives.
But as this is role play, shall we do that again?
*Use the same pattern as you used earlier.*

> *If appropriate:*
> Can anyone remember what we did first?
> *Encourage the children to join in after the dots:*
> We signed our friends with the . . . **cross**!
>
> *If you're using oil:*
> Let's dip our finger/thumb in the oil
> and hold it up in the air to show we're ready.
>
> *When the group is ready:*
> Let's say the words 'my turn' *point to self*, 'your turn' *leader's hands out to group.*
>
> *Lead the children in signing cross and saying words.*
> You belong to Jesus.
> **You belong to Jesus.**
> I sign you with the cross.
> **I sign you with the cross.**

Let's pretend to baptize our friends!
Alex! *Look into the doll/figure's eyes*
**Alex!**
I baptize you
**I baptize you**
in the name of . . .
**in the name of . . .**

*Aside quietly:* Now let's put our hand in the water ready . . .
*Scoop one:* the Father,
*Scoop one:* **the Father,**
*Scoop two:* and of the Son,
*Scoop two:* **and of the Son,**
*Scoop three:* and of the Holy Spirit.
*Scoop three:* **and of the Holy Spirit.**
Amen!
**Amen!**

> *If appropriate:*
> Then what do we do?
> *Accept children's responses.*
>
> *If your church places white robes on the newly baptized,*
> Then we put white robes on our friends
> to show they've been 'baptized'.
> *Lead the children in placing a white robe on their friends.*
>
> *If your church makes the sign of the cross at this point:*
> Now I'm going to make the sign of the cross on the baby's forehead.
> *Demonstrate to the group.*
>
> *If your church anoints with oil of Chrism:*
> We 'anoint' our friend's head with oil.
>
> Let's dip our finger/thumb in the oil
> And hold it up in the air to show we're ready.
> *Lead the group in rubbing oil on the head or drawing the sign of the cross.*

And let's welcome our friends into the church family.
*Use the same welcome as you did earlier.*

**Tip**

At St Peter's, Walworth, by the third time, we don't use 'my turn, your turn' but have a go at saying the words together all at the same time: 'You're baptism experts now! You don't need to copy me any more! You can do this yourself!'

## Roleplay: Giving of a Lighted Candle

*If your group includes children who are likely to want to continue exploring the water, you may find it helpful to say something like:*
*'Now let's take our friend and take one step back from our tables.'*

*When the group is ready:*
> *if your church gives a candle at the end of the service, show one of the candles you use to the children.*
> The last thing we do in a baptism is give a candle
> to remind our friends to shine like little lights
> in the world for Jesus.
>
> Let's hold our friends in one hand
> and make our other finger into a candle now.
> *Lead the children in holding your finger up in front of you.*
>
> After 3, I'm going to light your friends' candles.
> Are you ready?
> **1, 2, 3 . . . Tsssssss!**
> *Mime striking a match in the air and hold it out towards the children's finger candles to 'light' them.*

*End with a suitable song. For example:*

*Either:*

Let's sing to our friends and help them remember to be little lights in the world for Jesus.

*Lead the children in waving their candle finger in front of their friend.*

**This little light of mine, I'm gonna let it shine!**
**This little light of mine, I'm gonna let it shine!**
**This little light of mine, I'm gonna let it shine!**
**Let it shine, let it shine, let it shine!**
*Continue with the rest of the song, if appropriate.*

*Or:*

We give this candle to remind our friends
that everything they do is in the light of God.
Let's celebrate that they've been 'baptized'!
Let's dance and sing:
'We are living in the light of God'!
*Lead the children in waving their candle finger as they sing.*

**We are living in the light of God,**
**we are living in the light of God!**
**We are living in the light of God,**
**we are living in the light of God!**
**We are living, we are living, oh!**
**We are living in the light of God!**
**We are living, we are living, oh!**
**We are living in the light of God!**

*Or: close by singing another song with which the group is familiar, either about living in God's light or being welcomed into God's family.*

## Tip

If you're planning to have a time of Creative Response (bearing in mind that this session will already have been longer than normal), remember that the tables (and possibly the floor) will be wet from the baptisms so you may need to rethink your space.

# Extra: Jesus Is Thrown into the Wilderness

→ Mark 1.9–12
→ Poem: 'Look at that rubbish! Throw it away!' © Sharon Moughtin-Mumby

*For today's session and the following weeks (moving into Lent), you may like to use the following:*

*For the storytelling (optional)*
- *a wilderness tray to support the children in imagining the wilderness. At St Peter's, Walworth, we use a tray filled with sand (or brown sugar) with a few rocks and stones placed around so that it looks desolate;*
- *a Jesus figure: at St Peter's, Walworth, we use the Joseph figure from my daughters' nativity set. If you have no appropriate figures, you could print a picture of Jesus to lay on the sand.*

*If your group is using the time of saying sorry (these resources can remain the same throughout the following unit during Lent):*
- *a 'bare tree':*
  *either: a large tree branch tree held in a Christmas tree holder or in a bucket filled with stones plus sticky tack;*
  *or: the bare tree template (see p. 364 or website). At St Peter's, Walworth, we print three copies of this onto three A4 sheets of bright blue paper and glue them next to each other on a landscape piece of cardboard from an old box that looks like 'rubbish' from the back. We continue to use this throughout the next unit (Lent);*
- *a wastepaper basket/battered cardboard box or old container with white and/or pink crumpled tissue/crepe/coloured paper torn into pieces that will look like blossom when crumpled up into a ball (not too big). If you've printed your tree outline on white paper, pink tissue paper will help to create a contrast.*

```
Tip
Remember, keep it simple! If your group is learning a Sorry Song for the first time today (see p. 356), this
probably isn't the time to introduce lots of new resources as well!
```

To tell our story today, we need to learn a chant.
Let's see if you can say this after me:
'my turn' *point to self*, 'your turn' *leader's hands out to group*.

Look at that rubbish! *Point to self to show your turn*
Throw it away! *Continue pointing to self to show your turn continues*
**Look at that rubbish!** *Hands out to group*
**Throw it away!**

*Within the leader's material, different words are emphasized each time to help bring variety. Don't worry about the children*
*following you precisely: the group can emphasize different words.*

Let's try that again this time with the actions:
**LOOK at that rubbish!** *Point and make a disgusted face*
**Throw it away!** *Mime picking up rubbish and throwing it*
**Look at that RUBBISH!** *Point elsewhere and make a disgusted face*
**Throw it away!** *Mime picking up rubbish and throwing it*
**Look at THAT rubbish!** *Point elsewhere and make a disgusted face*
**Throw it away!** *Mime picking up rubbish and throwing it*

We're ready to tell our story.
Jesus was baptized by John the Baptist.
Jesus stepped into the river.
What's the water like today? Hot or cold? *Let one of the children decide.*
Let's be Jesus and get into the *cold/warm* river together.
*Lead the children in walking on the spot into the river, as if it's cold/warm according to the child's choice. With your hands, show the*
*water rising higher and higher, starting with your ankles until it reaches your waist.*
Deeper and deeper until the water is up to our waist.

After 3, let's be Jesus.
Let's go down into the river . . .
1, 2, 3 . . . *deep breath, hold nose*
. . . and up again!

When Jesus came up out of the water,
he was ready!
Ready to give the world a BIG new start! *Diddy Disciples 'New Start' sign (p. 355)*

Then something VERY surprising happened.
The Holy Spirit **THREW\* JESUS OUT** into the wilderness!
*\*This is actually the word that Mark's Gospel uses:* ekballo, *to throw out.*

Can you show me how you throw something.
*Lead the children in pretending to throw.*
The Spirit THREW Jesus out into the wilderness!
Let's be the Spirit
and throw Jesus out into the wilderness.
*Encourage the children to 'throw' Jesus out into the wilderness.*

> *If you're using a wilderness tray:*
> This is like the 'wilderness'.
> *Place your wilderness tray in front of the children. If you're using the What's in the Box? option (Book 1, p. 221), this can*
> *become this week's object. You may like to have a cloth over it, in which case invite a child to remove the cloth at this point.*

What do you see? *Invite a child to respond*

Sand, rocks and sky and nothing else. *Shake head*
*Place the Jesus figure in the wilderness.*
The Spirit threw Jesus into the wilderness!

Let's stand up and be Jesus.
Jesus looked one way.

Let's look this way . . . *point one way*
*Lead the children in looking the way you've pointed.*
And there was sand and rocks and sky.

And Jesus looked the other way . . .
*Lead the children in looking the other way.*
And there was sand and rocks and sky.

Jesus looked behind him . . .
*Lead the children in looking behind.*
What do you think he saw?
*Encourage the children to join you:*
**Sand and rocks and sky!**

When Jesus was alive,
the 'wilderness' was where people went
when no one wanted them any more. *Shake head*
When people were thrown out like rubbish.
Let's see if we can remember our chant
about throwing rubbish out.

**LOOK at that rubbish!** *Point and make a disgusted face*
**Throw it away!** *Mime picking up rubbish and throwing it*
**Look at that RUBBISH!** *Point elsewhere and make a disgusted face*
**Throw it away!** *Mime picking up rubbish and throwing it*
**Look at THAT rubbish!** *Point elsewhere and make a disgusted face*
**Throw it away!** *Mime picking up rubbish and throwing it*

The wilderness was where the world threw people out
that they didn't want any more. *Shake head*
Let's pretend to pick people up and throw them out.

**LOOK at that rubbish!** *Point and make a disgusted face*
**Throw it away!** *Mime picking up rubbish and throwing it*
**Look at that RUBBISH!** *Point elsewhere and make a disgusted face*
**Throw it away!** *Mime picking up rubbish and throwing it*

*Look sad* The world can be mean to people sometimes.
But let me tell you a secret! *Whisper behind hand*
God loves rubbish!

Let's sit down for a moment.
After 3, can you whisper our secret together:
*Lead the children in whispering behind hand*
**1, 2, 3 . . . God loves rubbish!**

*Talk normally again.*
God loves things that have been thrown out.
God knows AMAZING things can be made from things
and people that have been thrown out.

God doesn't see rubbish like we do. *Shake head*
When we see rubbish *both hands to self*, we say:
**LOOK at that rubbish!** *Point and make a disgusted face*
**Throw it away!** *Mime picking up rubbish and throwing it*

God doesn't see rubbish like that. *Shake head*
God says . . . listen! . . .

**Look at that RUBBISH!** *Point and make an excited face*
**What can I make?!** *Pick it up and look excited*

Let's be God together. Let's say:
**LOOK at that rubbish!** *Point and make an excited face*
**What can I make?!** *Pick it up and look excited*
**Look at THAT rubbish!** *Point elsewhere and make an excited face*
**What can I make?!** *Pick it up and look excited*
**Look at that RUBBISH!** *Point elsewhere and make an excited face*
**What can I make?!** *Pick it up and look excited*

God loves rubbish!
So when Jesus began the big new start,
he began in the wilderness,
with all the things and all the people no one wants:
ready to make something exciting!

Let's be God together again.
Let's say:
**Look at that RUBBISH!** *Point and make an excited face*
**What can I make?!** *Pick it up and look excited*

---

At this point, your group can:
■ sing one of the Diddy Disciples Sorry Songs (p. 356) as indicated below;
■ move straight to the Saying Sorry Action below;
■ end the storytelling with the words: 'We'll find out what happens to Jesus in the wilderness next week . . .'

---

*Invite the children to sit down for a moment of quiet.*
Let's close our eyes.
Sometimes we can feel like rubbish.
Sometimes it can feel like we've done everything wrong.
It's time to say sorry.

## Saying Sorry to God: Option 2

*For groups who are using Sorry Song: Option 2 for the first time, the song is as follows. Sorry Song: Option 1 can be found on p. 356.*

→ Song: 'We need a new start'. Words: © Sharon Moughtin-Mumby
→ Tune: 'Molly Malone' (traditional). For the music see p. 356, or for a taster see the Diddy Disciples website. For tips on teaching songs for the first time, see Book 1, p. 215. For a description of the 'I'm Sorry' and 'New Start' signs, see p. 355 or the website

### Tip

This song can be sung using 'we're sorry' as indicated, or as 'I'm sorry', adapting the material accordingly.

Let's put our hands on our head.
I wonder if there's anything we've thought this week
that we wish we hadn't thought?

*Lead the children in placing your hands on head, singing:*
**For the things we have thou-ght**
**that we wish we'd not thou-ght,**
**we're sor-ry, we're sor-ry.** *Diddy Disciples 'I'm Sorry' sign twice (see p. 355)*
**We need a new start.** *Diddy Disciples 'New Start' sign (see p. 355)*

Let's put our hands by our mouths.
I wonder if there's anything we've said this week
that we wish we hadn't said?

*With hands by mouth, singing:*
**For the things we have sa-id**
**that we wish we'd not sa-id,**
**we're sor-ry, we're sor-ry.** *'I'm Sorry' sign twice*
**We need a new start.** *'New Start' sign*

Let's cross our hands on our chest.
I wonder if there's anything we've done this week
that we wish we hadn't done?

*With hands crossed on chest, singing:*
**For the things we have do-ne**
**that we wish we'd not do-ne,**
**we're sor-ry, we're sor-ry.** *'I'm Sorry' sign twice*
**We need a new start.** *'New Start' sign*

*Continue with the Saying Sorry Action below or, if you've only learned this Sorry Song today, this may have been enough for your group. There will be other opportunities to use the following Saying Sorry Action throughout Lent. You may like to simply end with the following words.*

The Good News is:
God always loves to give us a new start!
After 3, let's shout, 'God gives us a new start!'
**1, 2, 3: God gives us a new start!**

## Saying Sorry Action

This paper has been thrown out as rubbish.
In a moment, *Name* and *Name*
are going to come around with this rubbish.
If you like you can take a piece and hold it in the air.
Let's remember what it feels like to feel rubbish!

*While all the children and adults who wish to take a piece of rubbish do so, lead the group in humming your Sorry Song or another song, such as your Gathering Song.*

*When the group is ready:*
When we do things that make God or other people sad,
it can make us feel like rubbish!
Let's crumple our paper up to show how we can feel
when we feel like rubbish.

*When the group is ready:*
Let's open our eyes again.
The Good News is, that when we feel like rubbish
God LOVES rubbish!
Let's be God again.
Let's imagine we're God,
looking at us
when we're feeling rubbish.

**Look at that RUBBISH!** *Point and make an excited face*
**What can I make?!** *Pick it up and look excited*
**Look at THAT rubbish!** *Point elsewhere and make an excited face*
**What can I make?!** *Pick it up and look excited*

It's time to give our rubbish to God the Maker.

*Show the group the bare tree (see p. 364) you have chosen and a container/wastepaper basket filled with crumpled paper.*

> *If your group is using a tree branch (small groups only):*
> Let's take our rubbish paper and some sticky tack
> and stick our paper on our tree.

> *If your group is using a printed tree (large groups):*
> *Either:* Let's take our rubbish paper
> and place it on our trees.

> *Or: Name* and *Name* are going to come around now
> with these 'bare trees' *on trays.*
> If you like, you can place your rubbish paper on the trees.

*While all the children and adults who wish to give their rubbish to God do so, lead the group in humming or singing again. Expect some of the blossom to end up looking as if it's blown from the tree or fallen to the floor. This is what blossom does!*

*When the group is ready:*
What looked like rubbish becomes beautiful blossom,
a sign of new life!
God can make amazing things with rubbish!
After 3, let's say, 'God gives us a new start!'
**1, 2, 3 . . . God gives us a new start!**

# The Week before Lent: Jesus Gives Up Everything For Us

→ Luke 4.1–2; Matthew 4.1–2
→ Song: 'I am going to follow Jesus'. Words: © Sharon Moughtin-Mumby
→ Tune: 'Bobby Shaftoe' (traditional). For the music see p. 72, or for a taster see the Diddy Disciples website. For tips on teaching songs for the first time, see Book 1, p. 215.

*This session is designed for groups who would like to explore the giving up of chocolate, food, alleluias or other things for Lent. As this session is a pivotal week between the John the Baptist unit and Lent, you may wish to omit the John the Baptist Gathering Song. Following your usual Welcome Song, continue with the following material.*

*For today's session, you may like to use the following:*
*For the storytelling (optional)*
- *a wilderness tray to support the children in imagining the wilderness. This is a tray filled with sand (or brown sugar) with a few rocks and stones placed around so that it looks desolate;*
- *a Jesus figure: at St Peter's, Walworth, we use the Joseph figure from my daughters' nativity set. If you have no appropriate figures, you could print a picture of Jesus to lay on the sand.*

*Especially with young children (optional):*
- *a pancake or a picture of a pancake;*
- *an egg or a picture of an egg and a bowl to break the egg into.*

*If your group would like to experience giving something up for Lent (optional):*
*This material opens up lots of opportunities for children to make connections between the things they see taking place in the world around them (pancake parties/Easter eggs/mini eggs in the shops/people talking about 'giving things up for Lent') and your time together with God.*
- *One hollow chocolate Easter egg (taken out of its box) that can be shared by the group at Easter. It needs to be hollow as it will represent the empty tomb during the Easter unit.*
- *A box to put the egg in and tape/ribbon to fasten it shut.*
- *A mini egg for each child and adult. Check if any children have allergies (e.g. dairy/nuts).*

*You could adapt the material to share pancakes with the children (or hold a pancake party!) but in our experience some young children don't like pancakes, which takes away some of the significance of the experience.*

*If your church gives up alleluias during Lent:*
This week is the last time we're going to say 'Alleluia!'
for a very long time!
We'll find out why later.
That's why this week we're going to be
saying 'Alleluia!' as much as we can!

---

## Tip

If your group will be using this call-and-response for the first time, you may find it helpful to say, for example:

> Now it's 'my turn' *point to self*, 'your turn' *leader's hands out to group*.
> When I say, 'Praise the Lord', *both hands to self*
> you say, 'Alleluia!' *Both arms upwards in 'V' shape*
>
> Praise the Lord!
> **Alleluia!** *Both arms upwards in 'V' shape*

---

It's time to get ready!
Lent starts *this Wednesday*!
Can you say 'Lent'?
**Lent**
In 'Lent' we go to the 'wilderness' with Jesus!

> *If you're using a wilderness tray place this in the centre of the circle. If your group is using the What's in the Box? option (Book 1, p. 221), this can act as the object for the week. You may like to cover it with fabric and change the question to 'What's under the cloth?'*
> *Invite a child to uncover the wilderness.*

> What can you see?
> *Accept the child's response.*

> This is the 'wilderness':
> sand, rocks and sky and nothing else.
> Jesus went to the wilderness!
> *Place Jesus figure in the wilderness.*

Let's imagine we're going to the 'wilderness' with Jesus.
Let's get up and march on the spot:
**1, 2, 3, 4! 1, 2, 3, 4!**
Let's sing 'I am going to follow Jesus'.

*This song will become the Gathering Song for Lent. The words are so repetitive that it won't need teaching. Start singing and the children will gradually join in.*
**I am going to follow Jesus,**
**I am going to follow Jesus,**
**I am going to follow Jesus,**
**follow, follow Jesus!**

We're in the 'wilderness' with Jesus.

> *If your church is giving up alleluias:*
> Praise the Lord!
> **Alleluia!** *Both arms upwards in 'V' shape*

Jesus looked one way . . .
Let's look this way . . .
*Lead the children in looking to one side.*
And there was sand and rocks and sky.

And Jesus looked the other way . . .
*Lead the children in looking to the other side.*
And there was sand and rocks and sky.

Jesus looked behind him . . .
*Lead the children in looking behind.*
And there was . . . *encourage the children to join in*
**sand and rocks and sky.**

> *If your church is giving up alleluias:*
> Praise the Lord!
> **Alleluia!** *Both arms upwards in 'V' shape*

In the wilderness there's no food! *Shake head*
Jesus was very, very hungry! *Rub tummy*
Can you show me hungry? *Rub tummy*
Can you show me thirsty? *Pant with thirst*

Jesus was hungry and thirsty in the wilderness:
not just for one minute, *shake head and wag finger from side to side*
not just for one day, *shake head and wag finger*
but for *show ten fingers four times as you say* FORTY whole days!

In Lent some people give up food and drink for forty days
so they can feel how Jesus felt,
hungry and thirsty in the wilderness.

Let's imagine we're giving up food for Lent.
Let's sing again and rub our tummy
to show we're feeling hungry the way Jesus felt hungry.

*Rubbing tummy throughout:*
**I am going to follow Jesus,**
**I am going to follow Jesus,**
**I am going to follow Jesus,**
**follow, follow Jesus!**

Let's sit down for a moment.
*When the group is ready:*

> *If you're using an egg or picture of an egg, show it to the children.*
> Can anyone tell me what this is?
> Eggs are amazing!
> We can make lots of treats with eggs like cakes! Mmmm!

A long time ago, people started giving up EGGS for Lent.
They wanted to be like Jesus, hungry, in the wilderness.
Let's go back in time 200 years ago . . .
Let's put our hands over our eyes and count to 3 . . .
**1, 2, 3!** *If appropriate, you could count backwards.*
We've done it! We've gone back in time!
Let's open our eyes!

> *If your church is giving up alleluias:*
> Praise the Lord!
> **Alleluia!** *Both arms upwards in 'V' shape*

We're going to give up eggs for Lent!
Quick! Lent starts tomorrow!
We need to use up all our eggs!
We're going to make pancakes! Mmmmm!

*If you're using a pancake or picture of a pancake, show it to the children.*

*If your group has a real egg, you could ask a child or one of the helpers to demonstrate breaking the egg into a bowl. Make sure you have washing facilities handy. It's best not to do this yourself.*

Let's all break our eggs.
*Lead the children in imagining picking up an egg.*
1, 2, 3 . . . Crack! *Mime tapping your egg on the bowl*
Put your thumbs inside and open it up!
We've got two more eggs! Let's break them.

**1, 2, 3 . . . Crack!**
Put your thumbs inside and open it up!
*Repeat.*

> *If your church is giving up alleluias:*
> Praise the Lord!
> **Alleluia!** *Both arms upwards in 'V' shape*

Now let's add some flour . . . *mime tipping in flour*
and milk. *Tip in milk*
Let's stir and stir and stir.
We're ready to cook our pancake.

Let's pour our mixture into the pan *pour action*
And cook it . . . *mime holding pan over stove*
Now let's toss our pancake. *Demonstrate*
After 3, let's toss our pancake . . .
**1, 2, 3 . . .** *Lead the children in tossing their pancake high*
Make sure you catch it again!
*Lead the children in catching their pancake in the pan.*
Did you catch it?
I hope there's none on the ceiling!

> *If your church is giving up alleluias:*
> Praise the Lord!
> **Alleluia!** *Both arms upwards in 'V' shape*

People used to eat pancakes to use up all their eggs.
Then they wouldn't eat eggs for the whole of Lent
so they could feel hungry like Jesus.
Let's toss our pancakes and imagine we're giving up eggs for Lent.

*Lead the children in tossing and catching pancakes as you sing:*
**I am going to follow Jesus,**
**I am going to follow Jesus,**
**I am going to follow Jesus,**
**follow, follow Jesus!**

It's time to come back in time to nowadays.
Let's put our hands over our eyes and count to 3 . . .
**1, 2, 3 . . .** We're back! Phew!

> *If your church is giving up alleluias:*
> Praise the Lord!
> **Alleluia!** *Both arms upwards in 'V' shape*

Let's open our eyes.
We still eat pancakes on the day before Lent
on 'Shrove Tuesday'.

> If your group is not giving up a chocolate egg or sharing mini eggs, skip the next section and continue from the box like this below.

*Show the hollow chocolate egg to the children.*
But can anyone tell me what this is?
*Accept responses.*

Chocolate is a wonderful treat!
Lots of people give up chocolate for Lent too.
They want to be like Jesus, hungry in the wilderness.
We're going to give up this chocolate egg for Lent
so we can be like Jesus.

Shall we have a last taste of chocolate before Lent starts?
*Show chocolate mini eggs.*
I have some mini chocolate eggs here,
enough for everyone.

> *If your church is giving up alleluias:*
> Praise the Lord!
> **Alleluia!** *Both arms upwards in 'V' shape*

*Name* and *Name* are going to bring the eggs around.
If you'd like one, hold your hands out like this.
*Model putting both your hands out in a cupped shape.*
Don't eat it straight away!
Keep it on your hand and wait till everyone has an egg.
Make sure you keep your hand open so the egg doesn't melt!
*Ask a responsible child to show everyone how to hold their egg on their hand. Don't worry too much if the very young children eat theirs straight away.*

**I am going to follow Jesus,**
**I am going to follow Jesus,**
**I am going to follow Jesus,**
**follow, follow Jesus!**

Let's smell our chocolate egg . . . Mmmmm!
Now let's taste our chocolate egg!
Let's really enjoy it!

*As the children eat . . .*
Now we're going to give up our big chocolate egg!
We're going to wrap it up and put it in this box.
*Wrap up the egg.*
We're going to keep it _____ *name the place it will be kept*
until Lent is finished and it's Easter.
Then we can eat our Easter egg!

> *If your church gives up alleluias in Lent:*
> So we've given up our chocolate egg.
> We're also going to give up singing our special alleluia!
> Let's get ready to give our alleluias up now
> by making our alleluia action. *Hands up in a 'V' shape*
> for the last time as we sing.
>
> *Lead them in repeatedly making the alleluia action as you sing.*
> **I am going to follow Jesus,**
> **I am going to follow Jesus,**

**I am going to follow Jesus,
follow, follow Jesus!**

*As appropriate:*
So we've been very busy getting ready for Lent!

- We've used up all our eggs and made pancakes!
  *Toss pancake.*
- We've eaten our chocolate eggs. Mmm!
  *Rub tummy.*
- We've given up our big egg.
  *Show Easter egg.*
- And we've given up our, ssshhh! *whisper* alleluia.

But we need to remember to get ready INside for Lent, too.
*Trace a circle around your heart.*

> If your group is not giving up a chocolate egg, continue from here (unless you would like to
> give up alleluias, in which case add the relevant 'Alleluia!' material from above). You may like
> to add:
>
> Giving up eggs and eating pancakes
> [and giving up alleluias]
> help people get ready for Lent.
> But we need to remember to get ready INside for Lent, too.

Let's put our hands on our heart
*model placing hands like a cross on your heart*
and close our eyes for a moment.
Let's ask Jesus to help us get ready for Lent INside.

Let's sing our song one last time very gently.
Let's make it into a prayer to Jesus.
Let's ask Jesus to help us get ready INside.

**I am going to follow Jesus,
I am going to follow Jesus,
I am going to follow Jesus,
follow, follow Jesus!**

## Section 3

# Creative Response starter ideas: John the Baptist unit

→ **Guide: Book 1, p. 228**

These starter ideas are designed to spark imaginations and open up opportunities for the children to respond creatively in their different ways to the worship and storytelling you've taken part in together.

### Tip

As outlined in the Guide of *Diddy Disciples* Book 1 from p. 228, we've found the following rules of thumb helpful for fostering an environment where children are encouraged to engage personally and openly.

1  Encourage the children to make their own choices.
2  Give the children space to develop their response as they wish.
3  Create space for 'bridge building'.
4  It's the act of responding that matters, not the final result.
5  These responses are 'holy ground'.

**Weekly Starter Ideas** relate directly to the Bible Storytelling of each session, including a print-and-go option.

**Sensory Starter Ideas** are designed for sensory explorers, including babies and toddlers. These can remain the same through the whole unit.

**Unit Starter Ideas** are designed to remain relevant throughout the whole unit. Keeping these resources available each week gives children the opportunity to deepen and develop their responses, while making preparation more manageable for leaders.

### Tip: Free response area

In addition to any other resources you provide, keeping a free response area available every week will give the children the opportunity to create anything they wish in response to the story they've told, building their sense of confidence and personal responsibility. In this area you could simply provide blank paper and crayons, pencils, paints or pastels. If you have them, other interesting media (see Book 1, p. 256) will provide even more scope for the children to nurture and strengthen their imaginative skills.

## Weekly Starter Ideas

*The stories told in this unit share a number of strong themes, for instance the River Jordan and baptism. For this reason, there are more Unit Starter Ideas than Weekly Starter Ideas for this unit.*

## Week 1: Meet John

〰 Invite the children to make their own figure of John the Baptist wearing sackcloth. Give them the chance to explore what they think the prophet may have looked like. Would they like to model John on a strong person they know themselves? They might like to attach a straw/lollipop stick to their figure with masking tape. *Provide body template (p. 366 or website), pencils/pastels/crayons/paints. Optional: glue and camel/sand/brown coloured collage materials (Book 1, p. 255).*

〰 Invite the children to make a moving picture of someone being baptized in the River Jordan. First, give them the opportunity to create their own man, woman or child (freehand or by decorating a body template). This could be someone they know, someone from the story or themselves. Older children may then like to have a go at making their own 'river', by folding the long edge of a piece of A4 blue paper approximately in half, cutting a wavy slit into the fold, then opening the paper up again. You may like to add the wavy slits before the session for very young children. Show the children how to slide the figure into the slit and move them up and down. They may even like to attach a straw/lollipop stick to their baptism candidate. *Provide body templates (p. 366 or website), plain paper, pencils/pastels/crayons/paints and blue paper. Sticky tape will come in handy for when the slits inevitably break or are cut close to the edges of the paper!*

〰 Give the children the opportunity to make their own John the Baptist figure from a dolly peg. *Provide dolly pegs, sackcloth/brown fabric/felt, felt tips, glue.*

〰 See also the various River Jordan and baptism starter ideas below.

## Week 2: John Baptizes Jesus

〰 Invite the children to make their own dove. What would they like to do with it? Keep it as it is? Or add it to a bigger picture or collage, attach string to make a necklace or tape it to a hatband (p. 360). Would they like to add wings? If you have curling ribbon/crepe streamers, would they like to add these to the dove's tail or elsewhere? Or do they have their own ideas? *Provide bird template (p. 365), scissors and glue. Optional extras: straws/lollipop sticks, masking tape, string, white collage materials/feathers (Book 1, p. 255), curling ribbon/crepe streamers (give the children the choice between blue/green for water or red/gold/orange/yellow for fire; they may even like to choose a bit of both!).*

〰 Invite the children to make giant medals to show how God is very happy with them! What will they draw on their medal? A smiley face, their name, a picture of Jesus or the water? Or do they have other ideas? *Provide circle templates (p. 369 or website), string/ribbon/wool and masking tape.*

〰 Give the children the opportunity to use interesting media to draw Jesus' face as they imagine it. I wonder what Jesus looked like? You could use different paintings or people you know as inspiration. *Provide interesting media (Book 1, p. 256).*

〰 Give the children the opportunity to create their own icons of the baptism of Jesus. *Provide pencils/crayons/ pastels, scissors, glue, a card rectangle, tinfoil to wrap around the card (to create a silver icon background), paper for the children's picture (which can then be glued to the icon background).*

〰 Invite the children to make a moving picture of Jesus being baptized. See Week 1 above, but add Jesus to the suggestions of the people they might choose to make.

〰 See also the various River Jordan and Our Baptism starter ideas below.

## Extra: Our Baptism

≋ Give the children the opportunity to make a baptism card for their friends. If you like, you could provide a choice of templates (see below) for the children to use as they wish. Or you could leave it entirely up to their imaginations! *Provide card plus pencils/paints/pastels/crayons. Optional: bird template (p. 365 or website), candle templates (p. 367 or website), body template (p. 366 or website), blue collage materials for water (Book 1, p. 255) and glue.*

≋ See also the various Our Baptism starter ideas below.

## Extra: Jesus is Thrown into the Wilderness

≋ Give the children a (lightly) screwed up piece of paper and ask them to open it out. God can make amazing things from rubbish! What can they make from this piece of rubbish? There's nothing on this paper, just as there's nothing in the wilderness! What can they do with it? *Provide lightly screwed up paper and pencils/crayons/pastels/paints.*

≋ Invite the children to make their own wilderness scene. All we can see in the wilderness is sand and rocks and sky! The children may like to draw Jesus in the wilderness, or to leave it empty. *Provide paper, glue, sand (or brown sugar) and small pebbles.*

≋ Invite the children to make something amazing from rubbish! God loves rubbish! Give them space to use their imaginations freely. *Provide a range of recycling materials plus craft materials and masking tape.*

≋ Give the children the opportunity to witness new life growing from 'rubbish'. Invite the children to decorate a recyclable container that can act as a plant pot with collage materials. When they're ready, invite them to place a few pieces of folded paper towel and a discarded carrot top (top upwards) in the container. When they get home, they can put a little water on the paper towel and keep it damp (not soaked). Green leaves will grow up from the carrot top! *Provide recyclable containers, collage materials (Book 1, p. 255), glue, paper towel (or cotton wool), discarded carrot tops.*

≋ Invite the children to make their own wilderness tray (see p. 86). *Provide sand, pebbles and a box or tub from recycling. Tubs with lids (e.g. margarine tubs, takeaway containers) are ideal for transportation home.*

## The Week before Lent: Jesus Gives Up Everything for Us

≋ Invite the children to decorate a 'pancake' with their favourite toppings. What would it be like to give those things up for Lent? Jesus gave up everything for us! *Provide circle template (p. 369 or website), pencils/crayons/pastels/paints.*

≋ Invite the children to draw around their open hand and to write/draw on the shape what they plan to give up for Lent. Encourage them to put it up somewhere at home to remind themselves. *Provide paper, pencils/crayons.*

≋ If you haven't done this in the previous week: give the children the opportunity to make their own wilderness tray (see p. 86). *Provide sand, pebbles and a box or tub from recycling. Tubs with lids (e.g. margarine tubs, takeaway containers) are ideal.*

≋ If you haven't done this in the previous week: invite the children to make their own wilderness scene. All we can see in the wilderness is sand and rocks and sky! The children may like to draw Jesus in the wilderness, or to leave it empty. *Provide paper, glue, sand (or brown sugar) and small pebbles.*

≋ If your church gives up alleluias for Lent, you could give the group the opportunity to create a joint 'Alleluia! Alleluia!' poster, with as many alleluias (or half alleluias) as the children create. Invite the children to design one of the letters from 'alleluia' in bubble writing, or to decorate one of the 'alleluia' letters from the website. When the children are ready, attach the letters with string or glue them onto a large roll of paper. Your group may prefer to draw and decorate individual alleluias to take home. *Provide paper, pencils/crayons/paints/pastels, glue, scissors, string and tape, or a large roll of paper and glue. Optional: 'Alleluia!' template (website only).*

## Tip

Think about whether your group would like to take part in the traditional custom of 'burying the alleluia' in preparation for Lent. Having made a group 'Alleluia!' banner (see above), you could sing or say 'Alleluia!' a number of times (with or without the wider congregation), then invite the children to wrap the group's 'Alleluia!' banner and place it in a box. 'Bury' the box either outside (make sure it's waterproof), under the altar or somewhere dark for Lent. The 'Alleluia!' banner can then be brought out/dug up for Easter Day. At St Peter's, Walworth, we invite the children to carry out the 'Alleluia!' banner in its 'coffin' during the final hymn of the Sunday before Lent.

- Your group may like to hold a pancake party, with mini pancakes or traditional pancakes and toppings.
- You may like to hold an egg hunt to make sure you're taking all the eggs out of the room for Lent!
  *Provide eggs to find: paper eggs, plastic eggs or even mini foil-wrapped eggs.*

# Sensory Starter Ideas (including for babies and toddlers)

You could provide:

≋ sand (or brown sugar) in clear bottles filled to different levels. Tape the lids tight shut!

≋ water in clear bottles filled to different levels. You could even add glitter/food colouring or both. Tape the lids tight shut!

≋ a river cloth and sackcloth;

≋ different sizes of stones and rocks in a box/feely bag/socks. Where Jesus went into the wilderness there were only rocks and sand. Make sure these are a suitable size for under threes. If they present a choking hazard place these also in a clear bottle and tape the lid tight shut;

≋ a long roll of paper taped to the floor for children and parents to add wavy blue or green lines with chunky crayons;

≋ a sand and/or water tray if appropriate for your setting;

≋ pictures of rivers or water made into sewing cards by punching holes, with blue or white wool/shoelaces to thread through the picture to look like waves;

≋ a wilderness tray (see p. 86);

≋ shallow tubs of water/blue fabric and 'small world' figures (such as Happyland or Fisher Price plastic figures, or wooden or knitted figures) for the children to roleplay baptizing the people in the water, just as John baptized people in the River Jordan.

## Tip

At St Peter's, Walworth, we use the Happyland set my children used to play with at home. You could borrow 'small world' figures for the week from a family or your local school, or you may like to buy some for your group, as they're useful to provide during the Creative Response sessions across the different units.

# Unit Starter Ideas

## The River Jordan

≋ Invite the children to make a wavy River Jordan from spaghetti dyed in different shades of blue and green. *Provide cooked, dyed spaghetti (Book 1, p. 257).*

≋ Invite the children to create a wavy River Jordan from string or wool. *Provide string/wool of lots of different lengths, glue, paper. Choose between blue/green wool and white PVA glue, or white string/wool and PVA glue dyed with blue/green paint.*

≋ Give the children the opportunity to finger paint the River Jordan. *Provide lots of different pots of cornflour paint (Book 1, p. 258) in different shades of green and blue (created by adding varying amounts of green/blue paint).*

≋ Invite the children to make a River Jordan necklace by threading blue/green dried pasta onto wool or string. *Provide green/blue dried pasta (Book 1, p. 257), wool/string. At St Peter's, we've found it can help to tape both ends of the wool/string and to knot one piece of threaded pasta with the string beforehand.*

≋ Invite the children to collage the River Jordan. *Provide blue paper and green/blue/silver/white/grey collage resources (Book 1, p. 255).*

≋ Give the children the opportunity to explore the different colours in water by looking at a photograph or painting, for instance Monet's *Water-Lily Pond*, then creating their own River Jordan. Remember to give the children space to develop their own responses, even if these differ from the example given. *Provide a photograph or famous picture of water, plus paper and watercolours/pastels.*

≋ Invite the children to create the scene of John the Baptist by the River Jordan. *Provide rocks, blue fabric and 'small world' people (see p. 95). If your facilities allow for it, you could even provide a water tray instead of blue fabric.*

≋ Invite the children to create the River Jordan on a paper plate. Will they show the banks of the river, or just the water? *Provide paper plates and either blue/green and yellow/brown paints, or glue and blue/green yellow/brown collage materials (Book 1, p. 255). You may also like to provide sand/soil.*

## Our Baptism

≋ Invite the children to design a baptism candle with pictures of Jesus' baptism. *Provide candle template (p. 367 or website), pencils/crayons/pastels/paints. Optional: glue and water-coloured collage materials (Book 1, p. 255).*

≋ Give the children the opportunity to design their own baptism font. They may like to use the template as a starter, or to create their own shape. Remind them to show the water inside! They might like to decorate the font with patterns, with pictures of John the Baptist or Jesus, or with pictures from the same stories as your church's font. Younger children may like to use collage materials. Remember to give them the space to develop their own ideas. *Font template (p. 378 or website), pencils/crayons/pastels/paints. Optional: glue, scissors, collage materials (Book 1, p. 255).*

≋ Give the children the opportunity to design their own font, using interesting media. *Provide interesting media (see ideas in Book 1, p. 256).*

≋ Invite the children to draw an observational picture of your church's font, either in situ or from a photograph. *Provide paper, pencils/pastels/paints/crayons or interesting media (see ideas in Book 1, p. 256).*

≋ Your group may like to create a giant picture of your church's font surrounded by the people of your church. *Provide a large piece of paper/card, body templates (p. 366 or website), pencils/crayons/pastels/ paints, a simple outline of your church's font, scissors and glue. Optional: collage materials (Book 1, p. 255) to dress the people and/or to collage the font.*

≋ Give the children the opportunity to roleplay 'baptizing' dolls or figures as in your church (particularly if you're not going to do the optional Our Baptism session. Show them how to 'baptize' the dolls with three scoops of water ('In the name of the Father, and of the Son and of the Holy Spirit') or by full immersion and invite them to 'baptize' a range of 'baptism candidates'. *Provide shallow tubs of water and dolls or 'small world' figures (see p. 95).*

≋ Invite the children to make a baptism candle from a cardboard roll wrapped in white/coloured paper or from white card, rolled and taped. Invite them to decorate the candle in their own way. They may like to collage it with blue/green collage to show the waters of baptism, to draw pictures of John the Baptist or Jesus' baptism, or they may have their own ideas. If they're using pencils, they may find it easier to decorate the candle before rolling it up. *Provide cardboard rolls (e.g. kitchen/tinfoil/cling film rolls) or white card and sticky tape, blue/green collage materials (Book 1, p. 255), glue and pencils/crayons/pastels/paints.*

≋ If your church uses a shell to scoop baptismal water, give the children the opportunity to design their own baptism shell. *Provide the children with light coloured shells from the seaside and invite them to decorate them with felt tips/pastels/paints.*

# UNIT 3
# THE JOURNEY TO THE CROSS (LENT)

For Lent, the Bible stories have been chosen from the Last Week of Jesus' life (apart from the Temptations, which are at the beginning of Jesus' ministry). While many churches normally tell these stories in the last week of Lent, they are central to our Christian faith and relationship with Jesus, so it's worth devoting time to explore them with small children. The Gospels themselves give these stories – and Jesus' Last Week as a whole – considerable weight.

At St Peter's, Walworth, we've found that familiarizing the children with these stories through Lent – as well as introducing them to acts of worship like waving palm branches and foot washing in meaningful ways – gives our young children confidence to join in with our whole-church acts of worship during Holy Week itself and a deeper understanding of the story unfolding around them.

## Section 1

# The Building Blocks: The Journey to the Cross unit

Pick and choose from these Building Blocks and their various options to build sessions for your group. Whatever choices you make, we suggest you keep to that pattern for the whole of the unit as this will open up opportunities for the children to participate fully and confidently during your time together.

> **Build your own Diddy Disciples session** (Book 1, p. 6) provides an overview of the Building Blocks and a short introduction to fitting them together, along with examples.
>
> **Guide to the Building Blocks** (Book 1, p. 217) provides a step-by-step guide to each Building Block.

> **Tip**
>
> The Saying Sorry to God Building Block, with its strong echoes of repentance and baptism works particularly well with the Lent unit.

# Welcome

→ **Guide: Book 1, p. 218**

*Welcome your group.*

Let's start by going around the circle
And saying our name out loud.
My name's _____.

*Go around the circle so that every adult and child has the chance to say her or his name (and introduce any dolls, teddies or toys). If any of the children don't want to say their name or aren't able to, you (or a parent or carer) could say it for them and wave.*

It's time to sing our Welcome Song!

## Welcome Song: Option 1

→ **Song: 'The Diddy Disciples welcome song'. Words: © Sharon Moughtin-Mumby**
→ **Tune: 'Glory, glory, alleluia!' (traditional). For the music see p. 357, or for a taster see the Diddy Disciples website. For tips on teaching songs for the first time, see Book 1, p. 215.**

*Go around the circle the same way as above. See if you can remember each other's names and insert them into the song.*

**Welcome *Name 1* to *St Peter's\****
**Welcome *Name 2* to *St Peter's\****
**Welcome *Name 3* to *St Peter's\****
**You are welcome in the name of the Lord!**

*\*Insert the name of your church or children's group, or sing 'our worship'.*

## Welcome Song: Option 2

→ **Song: 'You are welcome in the name of the Lord' (traditional)**
→ **Tune: traditional. For the music see p. 360, or for a taster see the Diddy Disciples website. For tips on teaching songs for the first time, see Book 1, p. 215.**

Let's wave with one hand. *Lead waving*
Then with our other hand. *Lead waving*
Then let's choose someone and show God's 'glory'!
*Move arms up and down in front of you with fingers wiggling, palms facing out, towards one person.*
And someone else! *Repeat*
Then let's wave with both hands all around the circle.
*Lead waving.*

We're ready to sing!

**You are welcome in the name of the Lord!**
*Wave with right hand to one person.*
**You are welcome in the name of the Lord!**
*Wave with left hand to another person.*
**I can see all over you, the glory of the Lord!**
*Move arms up and down in front of you with fingers wiggling,*
*palms facing out, towards one person and then another.*
**You are welcome in the name of the Lord!**
*Wave with both hands all around the circle.*

# Getting Ready to Worship

→ **Guide: Book 1, p. 218**

*Choose one of the following greetings according to which greeting is familiar in your church. (If your church uses a different greeting, you could use that here instead.)*

## Getting Ready to Worship: Option 1

→ **Action: the sign of the cross. Words: © Sharon Moughtin-Mumby**

*Invite the children to make the sign of the cross slowly with you. As the children become more confident, invite a child to lead the action as the whole group says the words and makes the sign of the cross.*

| | |
|---|---|
| **In my head,** | *touch head* |
| **in my heart,** | *touch chest* |
| **and all around me,** | *touch shoulders one by one* |
| **Jesus is here.** | *open hands in front, facing upwards* |

## Getting Ready to Worship: Option 2

→ **Action: 'The Lord be with you' (open hands)**

Let's start by clenching our hands together tightly.

*Lead children in clenching fists against your body to show a defensive posture.*

When we close ourselves up like this,
it's hard to let anyone into our heart.
It's hard even to let God into our heart!

When we get ready to worship,
we show that we're open to God and to each other.

*Open your hands out, facing up.*

Can you show me your open hands?
We're ready to let God and each other in!

The Lord be with you.
*Hold hands open to the children.*

**And also with you.**
*Invite the children to open their hands towards you.*

# Introducing the Unit

→ **Guide: Book 1, p. 218**

## Introducing the Unit: Option 1

→ **Optional focus: a cross**

> *Week 1:* This week we're starting on a journey with Jesus:
> *All other weeks:* We're on a journey with Jesus:
>
> *If you're using a cross, show the children the cross.*
> the journey to the cross.

The way of the cross is the way of love.
Let's cross our arms on our chest to show love.
*Lead the children in crossing arms on chest.*

*Look down at your own arms.*

Look! Our sign for love is a cross.
The way of love is the way of the cross.
*For the first couple of weeks, you may like to trace your finger on the crossed arms of a child sitting next to you to show the cross shape she or he is making.*

In our stories,
we're following Jesus on the way of love to the cross.

## Introducing the Unit: Option 2

→ **Focus: the liturgical colour purple**
→ **Optional focus: a cross**

*If your church uses visible liturgical colours:*
Can anyone tell me what colour season we're in now?
*If appropriate:* You may have seen it in church.

> *Week 1:*
> Today is the *first Sunday* of an important time for the Church.
> It's the start of the season of Lent!

The special colour of Lent is purple.
It's the colour that reminds us to get ready!
We're getting ready to follow Jesus on a journey:
> *If you're using a cross, show the children the cross.*
the journey to the cross.

The way of the cross is the way of love.
Let's cross our arms on our chest to show love.
*Lead the children in crossing arms on chest.*

*Look down at your own arms.*
Look! Our sign for love is a cross.
The way of love is the way of the cross.
> *For the first couple of weeks, you may like to trace your finger on the crossed arms of a child sitting next to you to show the cross shape he or she is making.*
In Lent we follow Jesus to the cross.
*If you're using a cross, or there's one in the building, show the group the cross.*

## Introducing the Unit: Option 3

→ **Focus: the use of sackcloth during Lent**
→ **Optional focus: a cross**

*If your church uses visible sackcloth as a sign of repentance for Lent, you may also like to choose Saying Sorry to God for your Prayer Building Block (p. 103) to support children as they make the connections between what they see in the church building and their own acts of worship.*

> *Week 1:*
> Today is the *first Sunday* of an important time for the Church.
> It's the start of the season of Lent!

In Lent our church wears sackcloth.
It's the colour that reminds us to say sorry.
In Lent we do lots of saying sorry to get ready.

We're getting ready to follow Jesus on a journey:
> *If you're using a cross, show the children the cross.*
the journey to the cross.

The way of the cross is the way of love.
Let's cross our arms on our chest to show love.
*Lead the children in crossing arms on chest.*

*Look down at your own arms.*

Look! Our sign for love is a cross.

The way of love is the way of the cross.

> *For the first couple of weeks, you may like to trace your finger on the crossed arms of a child sitting next to you to show the cross shape she or he is making.*

In Lent we follow Jesus to the cross.

*If you're using a cross, or there's one in the building, show the group the cross.*

# Gathering Song

→ **Guide: Book 1, p. 219**
→ **Song: 'I am going to follow Jesus'. Words: © Sharon Moughtin-Mumby**
→ **Tune: 'Bobby Shaftoe' (traditional). For the music see p. 72, or for a taster see the Diddy Disciples website. For tips on teaching songs for the first time, see Book 1, p. 215.**

Our song [for Lent] is all about following Jesus.

Let's get ready to follow Jesus.

Let's get up and march on the spot:

*Lead the children in march in time to the beat:*

1, 2, 3, 4! 1, 2, 3, 4!

> ## Tip
>
> The words to this song are so repetitive that you won't need to teach them to the children, they will naturally begin to join in as you sing.

*Continue marching as you sing:*

**I am going to follow Jesus,**
**I am going to follow Jesus,**
**I am going to follow Jesus,**
**follow, follow Jesus!**

> *Distribute imaginative aids if you have them.*

Let's practise following Jesus!

*Invite one of the children to stand in the centre of the circle or at the front.*

*Name* is going to be Jesus!

*To the child:* 'Jesus!' Can you show us an action?

Let's all copy what 'Jesus' does.

Let's 'follow Jesus'.

*Continue 'following' the child's action as you sing:*

**I am going to follow Jesus,**
**I am going to follow Jesus,**
**I am going to follow Jesus,**
**follow, follow Jesus!**

*Invite another child to be 'Jesus' and repeat as appropriate.*

*When the group is ready to finish:*

In Lent, we follow Jesus!

*Week 1:*

The place we start is the 'wilderness'

> *If you're using a wilderness tray (see p. 86) place this in the centre of the circle.*
> This is the 'wilderness': sand, rocks and sky and nothing else.
> Jesus went to the wilderness!
> *Place Jesus figure in the wilderness.*

It's time to follow Jesus into the wilderness!
*Lead the children in marching on the spot.*
**1, 2, 3, 4 . . . 1, 2, 3, 4 . . .**

**I am going to follow Jesus,**
**I am going to follow Jesus,**
**I am going to follow Jesus,**
**follow, follow Jesus!**

*Weeks 2+:*
We follow Jesus all the way to the cross. *If you're using a cross, show the cross to the group.*
*Lead the children in crossing arms on your chest.*
Let's show the way of love –
the cross – on our chest as we follow Jesus.

*Cross and uncross your arms across your chest as you sing:*
**I am going to follow Jesus,**
**I am going to follow Jesus,**
**I am going to follow Jesus,**
**follow, follow Jesus!**

# Getting Ready for Bible Storytelling

→ **Guide: Book 1, p. 220**

*Some people give up the word 'alleluia' for Lent and so Option 2 is not included in this unit.*

## Getting Ready for Bible Storytelling: Option 1

→ **Action: opening your group's box and naming this week's object**
→ **Guide: Book 1, p. 221**

*See the beginning of the weekly storytelling material for ideas of items to place in your box. Invite one of the children to open the box.*

What's in the box? *Ask the child to respond*

# Interactive Bible Storytelling

→ **Guide: Book 1, p. 221**

*See the Bible Storytelling material in Section 2 of this unit.*

# Saying Sorry to God

→ **Guide: Book 1, p. 223**

*Cross arms on chest.*
[In Lent/In life] we follow Jesus on the way of love,
the way of the cross. *Look down at your crossed arms*
Let's say sorry for the times
we haven't followed Jesus well.
When we haven't loved as Jesus loves.
Let's sing/say sorry to God with our Sorry Song.

## Saying Sorry to God: Option 1

→ Song: 'The Diddy Disciples sorry song'. Words: © Sharon Moughtin-Mumby
→ Tune: © Sharon Moughtin-Mumby. For the music see p. 356, or for a taster see the Diddy Disciples website. For tips on teaching songs for the first time, see Book 1, p. 215. For a description of the 'I'm Sorry' and 'New Start' signs, see p. 355 or the website.

Let's put our hands on our head.
I wonder if there's anything we've thought this week
that we wish we hadn't thought?

*Lead the children in placing your hands on head, singing:*
**With my hands on my head,**
**I remember the things I've thought today,**
**I remember the things I wish I'd thought a different way.**

**I'm sorry, I'm sorry,** *Diddy Disciples 'I'm Sorry' sign twice (see p. 355)*
**I wish I could start again.** *Diddy Disciples 'New Start' sign (see p. 355)*
**I'm sorry, I'm sorry,** *'I'm Sorry' sign twice*
**I wish I could start again.** *'New Start' sign*

Let's put our hands by our mouths.
I wonder if there's anything we've said this week
that we wish we hadn't said?

*With hands by mouth, singing:*
**With my hands on my mouth,**
**I remember the things I've said today,**
**I remember the things I wish I'd said a different way.**

**I'm sorry, I'm sorry,** *'I'm Sorry' sign twice*
**I wish I could start again.** *'New Start' sign*
**I'm sorry, I'm sorry,** *'I'm Sorry' sign twice*
**I wish I could start again.** *'New Start' sign*

Let's cross our hands on our chest.
I wonder if there's anything we've done this week
that we wish we hadn't done?

*With hands crossed on chest, singing:*
**With my hands on my chest,**
**I remember the things I've done today,**
**I remember the things I wish I'd done a different way.**

**I'm sorry, I'm sorry,** *'I'm Sorry' sign twice*
**I wish I could start again.** *'New Start' sign*
**I'm sorry, I'm sorry,** *'I'm Sorry' sign twice*
**I wish I could start again.** *'New Start' sign*

*Continue with a Saying Sorry Action or move straight to God Gives Us a New Start, below.*

## Saying Sorry to God: Option 2

→ Song: 'We need a new start'. Words: © Sharon Moughtin-Mumby
→ Tune: 'Molly Malone' (traditional). For the music see p. 356, or for a taster see the Diddy Disciples website. For tips on teaching songs for the first time, see Book 1, p. 215. For a description of the 'I'm Sorry' and 'New Start' signs, see p. 355 or the website.

> **Tip**
>
> This song can be sung using 'we're sorry' as indicated, or as 'I'm sorry', adapting the material accordingly.

Let's put our hands on our head.
I wonder if there's anything we've thought this week
that we wish we hadn't thought?

*Lead the children in placing your hands on head, singing:*
**For the things we have thou-ght**
**that we wish we'd not thou-ght,**
**we're sor-ry, we're sor-ry.** *Diddy Disciples 'I'm Sorry' sign twice (see p. 355)*
**We need a new start.** *Diddy Disciples 'New Start' sign (see p. 355)*

Let's put our hands by our mouths.
I wonder if there's anything we've said this week
that we wish we hadn't said?

*With hands by mouth, singing:*
**For the things we have sa-id**
**that we wish we'd not sa-id,**
**we're sor-ry, we're sor-ry.** *'I'm Sorry' sign twice*
**We need a new start.** *'New Start' sign*

Let's cross our hands on our chest.
I wonder if there's anything we've done this week
that we wish we hadn't done?

*With hands crossed on chest, singing:*
**For the things we have do-ne**
**that we wish we'd not do-ne,**
**we're sor-ry, we're sor-ry.** *'I'm Sorry' sign twice*
**We need a new start.** *'New Start' sign*

*Continue with a Saying Sorry Action or move straight to God Gives Us a New Start, below.*

# Saying Sorry Action

→ **Guide: Book 1, p. 223**

*For alternative actions that can be used during any unit at any time of year, see Saying Sorry Actions: Options 2, 3 and 4 on pp. 40–2 of Book 1.*

## Saying Sorry Action: Option 1

*For small groups*
Action: taking some 'rubbish' and giving it to God the Maker to be transformed into blossom.

*You will need:*
- a 'sorry tree'
  either: a large tree branch held in a Christmas tree holder or in a bucket filled with stones and sticky tack;
  or: bare tree template (see Option 2), p. 106;
- white and/or pink crumpled tissue/crepe/coloured paper in a box or wastepaper basket. If you're using a printed tree on white paper, pink tissue paper will help to create a contrast.

*Tip white and/or pink crumpled tissue paper on the floor in the centre of the circle, to look like rubbish.*

Here's some rubbish.
When we do things that make God or other people sad,
it can make US feel like rubbish:
If you like, you could tear a little piece of paper off this rubbish
and crumple it up.
Let's show how we feel when we're feeling rubbish!

*While this is taking place, lead the group in either:*

> *Option 1: singing the 'I'm sorry' refrain, or:*
>
> *Option 2: humming the first two lines of the 'We need a new start' song, followed by singing the refrain 'We're sorry, we're sorry. We need a new start'.*

*When everyone who wishes to take some paper has done so:*

The Good News is:

when we feel like rubbish . . . God LOVES rubbish!

It's time to give our rubbish to God the Maker.

*Place your tree in the centre of the circle.*

> *Either (real tree):* Let's take our rubbish paper
>
> and stick it on our sorry tree.
>
> *Or (printed tree):* Let's place our rubbish paper on our sorry tree.

*While this takes place, lead the group in humming/singing again.*

*When the group is ready:*

What looked like rubbish becomes beautiful blossom,

a sign of new life!

God can make amazing things with rubbish!

After 3, let's say, 'God gives us a new start!'

**1, 2, 3 . . . God gives us a new start!**

*Expect some of the blossom to end up looking as if it's blown from the tree or fallen to the floor. This is what blossom does!*

## Saying Sorry Action: Option 2

*For large groups*

Action: crumpling a piece of tissue/crepe paper to show how you feel when you're feeling 'rubbish' and giving it to God the Maker to be transformed into blossom.

*You will need:*

- 'sorry trees': at St Peter's, Walworth, we print three copies of the bare tree template (see p. 364 or website) onto three A4 sheets of bright blue paper and glue these next to each other on a landscape piece of cardboard from an old box that looks like 'rubbish' from the back;
- white and/or pink tissue/crepe/coloured paper cut into squares that will look like blossom when crumpled up into a ball (not too big). If you've printed your tree outline on white paper, pink tissue paper will help to create a contrast.

When we do things that make God or other people sad,

it can make us feel 'rubbish':

Like we're ruined everything!

*Name* and *Name* are going to bring some paper around now.

If you like, take a piece and crumple it up.

Let's make our paper into rubbish!

Let's show how we feel when we're feeling rubbish!

*While this takes place, lead the group in either:*

> *Option 1: singing the 'I'm sorry' refrain, or*
>
> *Option 2: humming the first two lines of the 'We need a new start' song, followed by singing the refrain 'We're sorry, we're sorry. We need a new start'.*

*When the group is ready:*

The Good News is:

when we feel like rubbish . . . God LOVES rubbish!

It's time to give our rubbish to God the Maker.

*Place your trees in the centre of the circle upside down to show the 'rubbish' back.*

Here's another piece of rubbish!

*Turn it over to show the trees.*

But look, this rubbish has been made into saying sorry trees!

*Either:*
As we sing, let's give our rubbish to God.
Let's put our crumpled up paper on our sorry trees.
*Or:*
*Name* and *Name* are going to come around now
and collect our rubbish to give to God.

*While this takes place, lead the group in humming/singing again. If the paper has been collected by children, ask them to gently tip it out over the pictures of the bare trees so they look like blossom.*

*When the group is ready:*
What looked like rubbish becomes beautiful blossom,
a sign of new life!
God can make amazing things with rubbish!
After 3, let's say, 'God gives us a new start!'
**1, 2, 3 . . . God gives us a new start!**

*Expect some of the blossom to end up looking as if it's blown from the tree or fallen to the floor. This is what blossom does!*

## Saying Sorry Action 3

→ **Action: dipping finger in water and drawing a cross on forehead.**

*This option is particularly appropriate for churches that use sprinkling with water ('asperges') during Lent.*

*If relevant, it's particularly appropriate to use the same water that will be used in your main church service.*

*If there is an older child present who is unlikely to spill the water you could invite him or her to take the water around the circle. You may wish to ask more than one child to take a bowl around the circle, going opposite ways or starting at different points in the circle. Alternatively take a bowl around yourself and/or ask adults to help.*

One of the ways we get ready in Lent
is by making sure our hearts are clean and ready.
In Lent, we're sprinkled with water *action like rain falling*
and we ask God to make us clean
Not just on the OUTside *rub arm*
but on the Inside. *Trace circle around heart*

> *If appropriate (adapt accordingly):*
> Did you see the water being sprinkled in church?
> *Or:* Right now the adults are being sprinkled with water!

*Name* is going to bring this bowl of water around.
If you like, you can dip your finger into it *show finger*
and draw a cross on your forehead. *Demonstrate*
Let's ask God to wash our hearts clean.

*While this takes place, lead the group in either:*
> *Option 1: singing the 'I'm sorry' refrain, or*
> *Option 2: humming the first two lines of the 'We need a new start' song, followed by singing the refrain 'We're sorry, we're sorry. We need a new start'.*

*When the group is ready:*
The Good News is:
God always wants to give us a new start!
After 3, let's shout, 'God gives us a new start!'
1, 2, 3: **God gives us a new start!**

# God Gives Us a New Start

→ **Guide: Book 1, p. 225**

*Every time of Saying Sorry should end by assuring the children that God gives them a new start. Most Diddy Disciples Saying Sorry Actions already include this promise of a new start. If they don't – or if you've created your own Saying Sorry Action – you should choose from one of the following New Start options, or create your own assurance of forgiveness. You could also choose to move straight from the Sorry Song to God's promise of a new start, without any Saying Sorry Action.*

## New Start Action: Option 1

→ **Action: tracing a cross/smile on each other's forehead**

The Good News is:
God always wants to give us a new start!

Let's turn to the person next to us
and show that God gives us a new start.
Let's take our thumb/finger *show thumb/finger*
And draw a cross/smile on that person's forehead *draw a cross/smile in the air*

> *If your group is drawing a smile, add:*
> to show that God is very happy with us!

Let's say, 'God gives you a new start!'
Then let the other person give you a new start, too!

*When the group has finished showing each other God's new starts:*
Let's use our new start to share God's love this week!

## New Start Action: Option 2

→ **Action: standing up and hugging each other**

The Good News is:
God always wants to give us a new start!

Let's help someone next to us stand up from the floor.
Then let that person help you stand up too!
*Lead the children in helping each other stand up.*

Then let's give each other a hug and say:
'God gives you a new start!'

*When the group has finished showing each other God's new starts:*
Let's use our new start to share God's love this week!

## New Start Action: Option 3

→ **Song: 'God loves to give me a new start!' Words: © Sharon Moughtin-Mumby**
→ **Tune: 'Give me oil in my lamp' (traditional). For the music see p. 357, or for a taster see the Diddy Disciples website. For tips on teaching songs for the first time, see Book 1, p. 215.**

The Good News is:
God always wants to give us a new start!
Let's sing our New Start song together.

**[Yes, my] God loves to give me a new start!** *Trace a smile/cross on own forehead*
**How amazing God's love for me!** *Cross hands on chest*
**[Yes, my] God loves to give me a new start!** *Trace a smile/cross on own forehead*
**How amazing is God's love for me!**

**Sing hosanna! Sing hosanna!** *Wave hands in the air*
**Sing hosanna to the King of Kings!**

*Wave hands in the air followed by crown on head.*

**Sing hosanna! Sing hosanna!** *Wave hands in the air*
**Sing hosanna to the King!**
*Wave hands in the air followed by crown on head.*

# Introduction to Prayers

It's time for us to take ourselves to a quiet place
to pray like Jesus.
Let's sit in a circle and have a moment of quiet.

# Prayers for Other People

→ **Guide: Book 1, p. 223 and p. 225**

*Invite the children to sit in a circle in a moment of quiet.*
Let's imagine holding our prayer gently,
*hands together gently in traditional prayer gesture, but cupped so you can imagine a prayer inside*
and then let it go up in prayer to God.
*Hands opened upwards to God*

> *If you're using Option 1:*
> Jesus *hands together, cupped*
> hear our prayer. *Hands opened upwards to God*
> Let's pray . . .

## Prayers for Other People: Option 1

→ **Song: 'Jesus, hear our prayer!'** Words: © Sharon Moughtin-Mumby
→ **Tune: 'Brown girl in the ring'** (traditional). For the music see p. 358, or for a taster see the Diddy Disciples website. For similar words designed to fit with the alternative tune, 'He's got the whole world in his hands', see p. 359. For tips on teaching songs for the first time, see Book 1, p. 215.

| | |
|---|---|
| **For the world:** | **Jesus, hear our prayer!** |
| *Make a circle shape* | *Open hands upwards to God* |
| **For the Church:** | **Jesus, hear our prayer!** |
| *Praying hands* | *Open hands upwards to God* |
| **For our place,** *Walworth\** | **Jesus, hear our prayer!** |
| *Hands down moving out in* | *Open hands upwards to God* |
| *a semi-circle to show the land* | |
| *around us* | |
| **Lord Jesus, hear our prayer. Amen.** | |
| *Open hands upwards to God* | |

*\* Insert local area/school/church/community/parish.*

| | |
|---|---|
| **For the sick and lonely:** | **Jesus, hear our prayer!** |
| *Fingers showing tears falling* | *Open hands upwards to God* |
| *down cheeks* | |
| **For our friends and family:** | **Jesus, hear our prayer!** |
| *Arms around yourself* | *Open hands upwards to God* |
| **For ourselves:** | **Jesus, hear our prayer!** |
| *Both hands on heart* | *Open hands upwards to God* |
| **Lord Jesus, hear our prayer. Amen.** | |
| *Open hands upwards to God* | |

Let's close our eyes for a moment.
I wonder if there's someone special
you'd like to pray for?
Let's imagine that person now.

Now, let's imagine Jesus coming to them.

Does Jesus say anything?

Does Jesus do anything?

Let's open our eyes.

*Continue with one of the Prayer Action options outlined below. Once the Prayer Action has been completed, you may like to use the following verse to close this time of prayer.*

| | |
|---|---|
| **Take our prayers:** | **Jesus, hear our prayer!** |
| *Hands together gently* | *Open hands upwards to God* |
| **Make them holy:** | **Jesus, hear our prayer!** |
| *Hands together gently* | *Open hands upwards to God* |
| **Make them beautiful:** | **Jesus, hear our prayer!** |
| *Hands together gently* | *Open hands upwards to God* |
| **Lord Jesus, hear our prayer! Amen.** | |
| *Hands together gently, then open hands upwards to God* | |

## Prayers for Other People: Option 2

→ **Song: 'The Diddy Disciples little prayers song'. Words: © Sharon Moughtin-Mumby**
→ **Tune: 'Frère Jacques' (traditional). For the music see p. 356, or for a taster see the Diddy Disciples website. For tips on teaching songs for the first time, see Book 1, p. 215.**

*These prayers are especially suited to churches that prefer less traditional prayer forms.*

> *Either: choose what you'd like the group to pray for before the session.*

> *Or: ask the children at this point if there is anything or anyone that they'd like to pray for. Ask them or others to suggest actions.*

*You will need two different 'thank you' suggestions and two different 'hear our prayer' suggestions. Try to encourage at least one prayer for other people outside the group.*

*Invite the children to sing after you, repeating your words and their actions. Sometimes it might be almost impossible to fit the child's own words in! It's really valuable to do this where possible, resisting the urge to try and 'neaten' their suggestions. For examples, see p. 17.*

*Having sung your prayers, you could insert a Prayer Action, repeat the process or move straight on to close with the following (or other words that remain the same each week).*

| | |
|---|---|
| For today, | *Point hands down for 'now'* |
| **For today,** | *Point hands down for 'now'* |
| Thank you, God! | *Open hands upwards to God or hands together in prayer* |
| **Thank you, God!** | *Open hands upwards to God or hands together in prayer* |
| | |
| Fo-r your love, | *Cross hands on chest* |
| **Fo-r your love,** | *Cross hands on chest* |
| Thank you, God! | *Open hands upwards to God or hands together in prayer* |
| **Thank you, God!** | *Open hands upwards to God or hands together in prayer* |

# Prayer Actions

→ **Guide: Book 1, p. 225**

## Prayer Action: Option 1

*For small groups*

→ **Action: placing leaves on a prayer tree**

*You will need:*

- *a 'prayer tree': a large tree branch held in a Christmas tree holder or in a bucket filled with stones and sticky tack;*
- *little green leaves cut from green paper.*

*Place your tree in the centre of the circle.*

Lent means 'springtime'.

In the spring we see new life
and new beginnings starting all around us.
We see tiny leaves growing on the trees.
We can be part of bringing
God's new life to the world when we pray.

*Place your baskets of leaves and sticky tack at the base of the tree.*
If you like, you can take a leaf.
You can stick it on our prayer tree
and ask God to hear it as a prayer.

*While this takes place, hum the tune together, singing the words 'Jesus, hear our prayer'*
*or 'Hear our prayer' as a refrain. When the group is ready:*
This Lent, let's watch new life grow
on our prayer tree and in our lives as we pray.

> **Tip**
>
> You could leave the leaves on the tree each week so that the tree gains more and more leaves through Lent.

## Prayer Action: Option 2

*For small or large groups*

→ **Action: placing blossom on prayer trees**

*You will need:*
- *'prayer trees': at St Peter's, Walworth, we print three copies of the bare tree template (see p. 364 or website) onto three*
  *A4 sheets of bright blue paper and glue these next to each other on a landscape piece of cardboard from an old box*
  *that looks like 'rubbish' from the back;*
- *'blossom': either real blossom, or white/pink tissue/crepe/coloured paper crumpled up into small balls. If you've printed your tree*
  *outline on white paper, pink tissue paper will help to create a contrast.*

*Place your trees in the centre of the circle.*
Lent means 'springtime'.
In the spring we see new life
and new beginnings starting all around us.
We see blossom growing on the trees.
We can be part of bringing
God's new life to the world when we pray.

*Show baskets of 'blossom'.*
In a moment, *Name* and *Name*
are going to bring around these baskets of 'blossom'.
If you like, you could take some and hold it up.
Let's ask God to hear our blossom as a prayer.

*While this takes place, hum the tune together, singing the words 'Jesus, hear our prayer'*
*or 'Hear our prayer' as a refrain. When the group is ready:*

> *Either:*
> As we sing, let's give our blossom prayers to God.
> Let's sprinkle our blossom on our prayer trees!
>
> *Or:*
> *Name* and *Name* are going to come around
> with our trees.
> As we sing, let's give our blossom prayers to God.

*While this takes place, lead the group in humming/singing again. When your group is ready, end this time of prayer with the final*
*verse of the Prayer Song you've chosen.*

This Lent, let's watch new life grow
on our prayer trees and in our lives as we pray.

*Expect some of the blossom to end up looking as if it's blown from the tree or fallen to the floor. This is what blossom does!*

## Prayer Action: Option 3

→ **Action: placing a small cross as a prayer on a large cross (Jesus' cross) placed on a cloth (purple, if your church uses liturgical colours)**

*If you're going to ask a child to carry the cross around the group, place the cloth and cross on a tray.*

In Lent we follow Jesus on the way to the cross.

*Invite two children to take around two baskets of small crosses.*
*Name* and *Name* are going to bring around these baskets of crosses now.
If you like, you can take one of these crosses
and hold it high.
Let's ask God to hear our crosses as a prayer
for ourselves and a special person.

*While the crosses are taken around, hum the tune together, singing the words 'Jesus, hear our prayer' or 'Hear our prayer' as a refrain. When your group is ready:*

The way of the cross isn't always easy
but we know Jesus is there with us.

> *Either: place your large cross in the centre.*
> You can place your cross prayer with Jesus' cross here.
> Let's ask Jesus to be with us and our special person.

> *Or: ask a child to take a large cross around on a tray.*
> *Name* is going to bring Jesus' cross around.
> If you like you can give your cross prayer to Jesus.
> Let's ask Jesus to be with us and our special person.

*While this takes place, hum the tune together, singing the words 'Jesus, hear our prayer' or 'Hear our prayer' as a refrain. When the group is ready, end this time of prayer with the final verse of the Prayer Song you've chosen.*

# Thank You, God

→ **Guide: Book 1, p. 227**

## Thank You, God: Option 1

→ **Song: 'My hands were made for love'. Words: © Sharon Moughtin-Mumby**
→ **Tune: 'Hickory, dickory, dock' (traditional). For the music see p. 360, or for a taster see the Diddy Disciples website. For tips on teaching songs for the first time, see Book 1, p. 215.**

*Invite the children to sit in a circle for a moment of quiet.*
It's time to remember all the things we've done this week.
It's time to say 'thank you' to God
for when we've been part of showing God's love.

Let's wiggle our fingers!
I wonder when you've shown love
with your hands this week?

*Wiggle fingers as you sing.*
**My hands were made for love!**
**My hands were made for love!**
**Thank you for the love they've shown.**
**My hands were made for love!**

Let's wiggle our feet!
I wonder when you've shown love
with your feet this week?

*Wiggle feet as you sing.*
**My feet were made for love!**
**My feet were made for love!**
**Thank you for the love they've shown.**
**My feet were made for love!**

Let's put our hands gently on our neck.
Let's sing 'Ahhh!'
**Ahhhhh!**
Can you feel your throat vibrating and dancing with your voice?
I wonder when you've shown love
with your voice this week?

*Hold neck and feel your voice 'dancing' as you sing.*
**My voice was made for love!**
**My voice was made for love!**
**Thank you for the love it's shown.**
**My voice was made for love!**

## Thank You, God: Option 2

→ Song: 'For the love we've shown'. Words: © Sharon Moughtin-Mumby
→ Tune: 'All through the night' (traditional). For the music see p. 357, or for a taster see the Diddy Disciples website. For tips on teaching songs for the first time, see Book 1, p. 215.

*Most suitable for use with children over the age of four.*

*Invite the children to sit in a circle for a moment of quiet.*
It's time to remember all the things we've done this week.
It's time to say 'thank you'
for when we've been part of showing God's love.

> *Either:* Let's wiggle our fingers.
> *Or:* Let's hold up our hands.

I wonder when you've shown love
with your hands this week?

> *Either:* Let's wiggle our feet.
> *Or:* Let's show our feet.

I wonder when you've shown love
with your feet this week?

Let's put our hands gently on our neck.
Let's sing 'Ahhh!'
**Ahhhhh!**
Can you feel your neck vibrating and dancing with your voice?
I wonder when you've shown love
with your voice this week?

Let's sing our 'thank you' song to God
For the times we've been part of sharing God's love.

**For the love we've shown with our hands,**
*Hold hands up or wiggle fingers.*
**Thank you, God!**
**For the love we've shown with our feet,**
*Point to feet or wiggle feet.*

**Thank you, God!**
**When we love all those around us,**
*Cross hands on chest.*
**It's the same as loving Jesus!**
**For the love we've shown with our voice,**
*Hands on neck or point to singing mouth*
**Thank you, God!**

# Creative Response

→ **Guide: Book 1, p. 228**

*See the Creative Responses in Section 3 of this unit.*

# Sharing God's Peace

→ **Guide: Book 1, p. 231**

*This Building Block is particularly designed for children's groups that join the adult congregation to share communion but can also be used to end any session or Service of the Word.*

## Sharing God's Peace: Option 1

→ **Song: 'I've got peace like a river' (traditional), Isaiah 66.12, NIV**
→ **Tune: traditional. For a taster see the Diddy Disciples website. For tips on teaching songs for the first time, see Book 1, p. 215.**

*Either: hold one end of the peace cloth (Book 1, p. 231) and ask one of the older children or an adult to hold the other end. Start singing the Peace Song. As the children begin to gather, invite them to join in holding a small section of the cloth, raising and lowering it so it 'flows' like a river as you sing together.*

*Or: invite the children to sit in a circle in the worship space. Start singing the Peace Song. As the children begin to gather, invite them to join in raising and lowering their hands like the waters of a flowing river.*

**I've got peace like a river,**
**I've got peace like a river,**
**I've got peace like a river in my soul.**
**I've got peace like a river,**
**I've got peace like a river,**
**I've got peace like a river in my soul.**

*If your group is about to rejoin the adults for communion: when all the children are gathered, continue with the words of the Peace, below.*

## Sharing God's Peace: Option 2

→ **Song: 'Peace is flowing like a river' (traditional), Isaiah 66.12, NIV**
→ **Tune: traditional. For a taster see the Diddy Disciples website. For tips on teaching songs for the first time, see Book 1, p. 215.**

*Either: hold one end of the peace cloth (Book 1, p. 231) and ask one of the older children or an adult to hold the other end. Start singing the Peace Song. As the children begin to gather, invite them to join in holding a small section of the cloth, raising and lowering it so it 'flows' like a river as you sing together.*

*Or: invite the children to sit in a circle in the worship space. Start singing the Peace Song. As the children begin to gather, invite them to join in raising and lowering their hands like the waters of a flowing river.*

**Peace is flowing like a river,**
**flowing out through you and me.**
**Spreading out into the desert,**
**setting all the captives free.**

*If your group is about to rejoin the adults for communion: when all the children are gathered, continue with the words of the Peace, below.*

## Sharing God's Peace: Option 3

→ Song: 'I've got peace in my fingers'. Words: © 1995 Susan Salidor ASCAP
→ Tune: © 1995 Susan Salidor ASCAP
→ The words and music can be found on the album *Little Voices in My Head* by Susan Salidor © 2003 Peach Head. They can also be found on iTunes or YouTube, or at <www.susansalidor.com>. For tips on teaching songs for the first time, see Book 1, p. 215.

*If your group is about to rejoin the adults for communion: when all the children are gathered, continue with the words of the Peace, below.*

# The Peace

→ 2 Thessalonians 3.16; 1 Peter 5.14

*Once you've finished singing . . .*

The peace of the Lord be always with you.
*Hold hands open to the children.*
**And also with you.**

*Invite the children to open their hands towards you.*
Let's shake hands or hug each other
and say, 'Peace be with you' *or whatever is said on sharing the Peace in your church*
as a sign of God's peace.

*Lead the children in giving and receiving the Peace. Immediately following this, at St Peter's, Walworth, we lead the children back to join the rest of the congregation to continue our worship with the Eucharistic Prayer.*

# Taking God's Love into the World

→ Guide: Book 1, p. 232
→ Song: 'This little light of mine' (traditional)
→ Tune: traditional. For a taster see the Diddy Disciples website. For tips on teaching songs for the first time, see Book 1, p. 215.

*This Building Block is particularly designed for standalone groups or groups that are held during a Service of the Word. Alternatively, you could use one of the Peace Songs above to end your worship.*

Our time together is coming to an end.
*Invite the children to sit in a circle for a moment of quiet.*
God has lit a little light of love inside all of us.
*Trace a circle on your heart.*

Let's make our finger into a candle.
*Bring your finger from your heart and hold it out.*
Let's be God and light our little light of love together, after 3.
*Lead the children in lighting their finger candle by striking an imaginary match in the air on 3 and pretending to light your finger.*
**1, 2, 3 . . . Tssss!**

Let's imagine God's love shining and dancing like light in us.

*Wave your finger in front of you.*
**This little light of mine, I'm gonna let it shine!**
**This little light of mine, I'm gonna let it shine!**
**This little light of mine, I'm gonna let it shine!**
**Let it shine, let it shine, let it shine!**

*Blow on your finger as if blowing out a candle on 'puff'. Then hold it up high.*
**Won't let no one** *puff* **it out! I'm gonna let it shine!**
**Won't let no one** *puff* **it out! I'm gonna let it shine!**
**Won't let no one** *puff* **it out! I'm gonna let it shine!**
**Let it shine, let it shine, let it shine!**

*Hold your finger behind a cupped hand, then take your cupped hand away to reveal the 'candle' and hold it high!*

**Hide it under a bushel? No! I'm gonna let it shine!**
**Hide it under a bushel? No! I'm gonna let it shine!**
**Hide it under a bushel? No! I'm gonna let it shine!**
**Let it shine, let it shine, let it shine!**

*Lead the children in placing your finger back on your heart.*
Now let's put our little light of love
back in our hearts, where it belongs.
Let's remember to let our little light shine
in all our playing and working today . . .

*If you're building a Service of the Word and this is your final Building Block, you may like to close with a familiar blessing, the Peace and/or one of the following. If you're using one of these call-and-responses with your group for the first time, see p. 25 for an introduction.*

*Either:*

Let us bless the Lord. *Both hands to self*
**Thanks be to God.** *Both arms upwards in 'V' shape*

*Or:* And all the people said . . . *Both hands to self*
**Amen!** *Both arms upwards in 'V' shape*

# Section 2

# The Bible Storytelling material: The Journey to the Cross unit

## Week 1: Jesus Is Tested in the Wilderness

→ **Matthew 4.1–11; Luke 4.1–13**
→ Song/poem: 'God's way of love I'll go'. Words: © Sharon Moughtin-Mumby
→ Tune: either say this as a poem or use the tune from 'Zoom, zoom, zoom! We're going to the moon! (traditional). For a taster see the Diddy Disciples website.

No! No! No! God's way of love I'll go!     No! No! No! God's way of love I'll go!

*For today's session, you may like to use:*

• *a wilderness tray to support the children in imagining the wilderness. This is a tray filled with sand (or brown sugar) with a few rocks and stones placed around so that it looks desolate. See the website for images;*

• *a Jesus figure: at St Peter's, Walworth, we use the Joseph figure from my daughters' nativity set. If you have no appropriate figures, you could print a picture of Jesus to lay on the sand.*

*If your group is not using the 'I am going to follow Jesus' Gathering Song, begin by imagining going to the wilderness together, for example:*

It's time to go the 'wilderness'!
*If you're using a wilderness tray place this in the centre of the circle.*

This is the 'wilderness':
sand, rocks and sky and nothing else.
Jesus went to the wilderness!

*Place Jesus figure in the wilderness.*
In Lent we go to the wilderness with Jesus.
Let's get up and march on the spot:
**1, 2, 3, 4 . . . 1, 2, 3, 4 . . .**

*All groups:*
We're here! We're in the wilderness with Jesus.
Look over here! *Point one way*
All we can see is sand and rocks and sky!

Look over there! *Point opposite way*
*Encourage the children to join in after the dots.*
All we can see is sand and rocks . . . **and sky!**

And look behind us! *Point behind*
*Encourage the children to join in after the dots.*
All we can see is . . . **sand and rocks and sky!**

We're going to tell the story of Jesus in the wilderness.
But, first, we need to learn a song.
*Start off by saying the words without any tune.*
Let's say the words 'my turn' *point to self*, 'your turn' *leader's hands out to group*.

No! No! No! *Wag finger from side to side*
God's way of love I'll go! *Cross arms before chest*
**No! No! No!** *Wag finger from side to side*
**God's way of love I'll go!** *Cross arms before chest*

> *You can keep this as a poem, or add the tune at this point.*
> Now let's add the tune:
> 'my turn' *point to self*, 'your turn' *leader's hands out to group*.
> No! No! No! *Wag finger from side to side*
> God's way of love I'll go! *Cross arms before chest*
> **No! No! No!** *Wag finger from side to side*
> **God's way of love I'll go!** *Cross arms before chest*
> *Repeat until the children are confident.*
>
> *If your group is using the What's in the Box? option (Book 1, p. 221):*
> *Invite a child to open the box.*
> *Inside are: stones, a globe (or picture of the world) and an angel (or a picture of an angel).*
>
> What's in the box?
> *Accept the child's response.*

In the wilderness, Jesus is given three tricky choices about:
stones, the world and an angel!
We need three actions!

> *If you're using the What's in the Box? option, show each items as you ask for the action.*

Number 1: *show one finger*
Who can show us an action for stones?
*Choose one of the children's actions.*

Number 2: *show two fingers*
Who can show us an action for EVERYTHING in the world?
*Choose one of the children's actions.*

And number 3: *show three fingers*
Who can show us an action for an angel?

We're ready to tell our story!
Jesus was in the wilderness, all by himself.
All he could see anywhere was . . .
*Encourage the children to join in:*
**. . . sand and rocks and sky!**

Jesus was very hungry and very thirsty.
Can you show me hungry?
Can you show me thirsty?
*Lead the children in looking very hungry and thirsty.*

Then at the point that Jesus was MOST hungry
And MOST thirsty, a tester came!
The tester wanted to see if Jesus was ready
to follow God's way of love. *Cross arms on chest*

The tester asked THREE tricky questions.
*Show three fingers.*
And Jesus had to make THREE tricky choices:
**1, 2, 3.** *Count on fingers*
Will Jesus follow God's way of love?! *Rhetorical question*
Let's find out!

Choice number 1: let's hold up one finger.
*Lead the children in holding up one finger.*

The tester showed Jesus some stones.

> *If you're using the What's in the Box? option, show the stones.*

What's our action for stones?
*Encourage the children to show their 'stone action'.*

The tester said, 'Jesus, you're very hungry!
You don't have to follow God! *Shake head*
Why don't you just make these stones *stone action* into bread?'

Mmmmm! Imagine how much Jesus wanted to eat bread!
Can you show me again how hungry Jesus was?
*Lead the group in rubbing tummy and looking hungry.*

But Jesus knew the tester was trying to trick him!
THAT's not God's way of love! *Shake head and cross arms on chest*
So Jesus said . . .
*aside:* Let's see if you can join in . . .

**No! No! No!** *Wag finger side to side*
**God's way of love I'll go!** *Cross arms*
*If the children don't join in naturally, encourage them to join in now.*
**No! No! No!** *Wag finger side to side*
**God's way of love I'll go!** *Cross arms*

Choice number 2: let's hold up two fingers.
*Lead the children in showing two fingers.*

> *If you're using the What's in the Box? option, show the globe.*

Can you show me our action for EVERYTHING in the world!?
*Ask a child to lead the group in the 'everything' action.*

The tester showed Jesus the whole world! *Everything action*
The tester said, 'Why don't you follow me and not God?!
I'll give you the whole world and EVERYTHING in it!'
Can you imagine being given EVERYTHING as a present?!

But Jesus knew the tester was trying to trick him!
THAT's not God's way of love! *Shake head and cross arms on chest*
So Jesus said:

*Lead the children in singing/saying:*
**No! No! No!** *Wag finger side to side*
**God's way of love I'll go!** *Cross arms*
**No! No! No!** *Wag finger*
**God's way of love I'll go!** *Cross arms*

Choice number 3: let's hold up three fingers.
*Lead the children in showing three fingers.*

> *If you're using the What's in the Box? option, show the angel.*
> *If appropriate:* Can anyone remember our third action?
> *Accept responses.*

Let's show our angel action.

The tester took Jesus up to the top of a tall, tall tower.
*Reach up high.*

The tester said: 'Why don't you throw yourself off?!
Angels will catch you!
Then everyone will see how special you are!'

It's nice to feel special, isn't it!
But Jesus knew the tester was trying to trick him!
THAT's not God's way of love! *Shake head and cross arms on chest*
So Jesus said:

**No! No! No!** *Wag finger side to side*
**God's way of love I'll go!** *Cross arms*
**No! No! No!** *Wag finger*
**God's way of love I'll go!** *Cross arms*
**No! No! No!** *Wag finger*
**God's way of love I'll go!** *Cross arms*

Jesus chose God's way of love!
Let's all cross our arms to show love.
*Lead the children in crossing arms on your chest.*

The way of love is also called the way of the cross.
Look at our arms! We've made the sign of the cross.
*Show the children how their arms look like a cross.*

Let's close our eyes for a moment.

*When the group is ready:*
Sometimes we have to make tricky choices.
There are things we really, really want to do,
but we know they're wrong.
We know they don't show love. *Shake head and cross arms on chest*
*Hold silence for a few seconds.*

Let's open our eyes again.
When we follow Jesus, we choose to say, 'No!' *wag finger side to side*
to things we know are wrong.
We choose to follow God's way of love. *Cross arms*

If we like, we can make Jesus' words into OUR words. *Point to self*
Let's sing/say them as a prayer and a promise to Jesus [this Lent].

*Lead the children in singing/saying:*
**No! No! No!** *Wag finger side to side*
**God's way of love I'll go!** *Cross arms*
**No! No! No!** *Wag finger*
**God's way of love I'll go!** *Cross arms*

# Week 2: Jesus Enters Jerusalem

→ **The story behind Palm Sunday**
→ Matthew 21.1–11; Mark 11.1–10; Luke 19.28–38
→ Song: 'Jesus came riding on a donkey' Words: © Sharon Moughtin-Mumby
→ Tune: 'Sing hosanna' (traditional). For a taster see the Diddy Disciples website.

*If your group is using the What's in the Box? option (Book 1, p. 221):*
*Invite a child to open the box.*
*Inside is a palm leaf (real or a picture).*

What's in the box?
*Accept the child's response.*

This is a 'palm leaf'
Today we're going to tell the story of
when all the people waved palm leaves for Jesus.

To tell our story today, we're going to learn a song.
Let's sing the words 'my turn' *point to self*, 'your turn' *leader's hands out to group*.
Jesus came riding on a donkey. *Hold reins and jig up and down*
**Jesus came riding on a donkey.** *Hold reins and jig up and down*

And the people all danced and sang! *Wave hands above head*
**And the people all danced and sang!** *Wave hands above head*

They threw down their cloaks before him.
*Lift two hands above head and then bring them down to show throwing cloaks on the floor. If your group is familiar with 'You are welcome in the name of the Lord!' (Welcome Song: Option 2), use the action from 'I can see all over you the glory of the Lord!'*
**They threw down their cloaks before him**
and waved gree-een palm leaves in their hands! *Wave hands above head*
**and waved gree-een palm leaves in their hands!** *Wave hands above head*

That song has lots of words!
Let's try and sing it all together.
If you can't remember all the words,
can you help with the actions?

**Jesus came riding on a donkey** *hold reins and jig up and down*
**and the people all danced and sang!** *Wave hands above head*
**They threw down their cloaks before him** *'Glory of the Lord' sign (see p. 99)*
**and waved gree-een palm leaves in their hands!** *Wave hands above head*

Then we're going to sing the song that the people sang!

*If appropriate:* You might recognize it.

I'm going to sing it: see if you can join in!

*Lead the children in singing while waving hands above head:*

**Sing hosanna! Sing hosanna!** *Wave hands*

**Sing hosanna** *wave hands* **to the King of Kings!** *Crown action twice*

**Sing hosanna! Sing hosanna!**

**Sing hosanna** *wave hands* **to the King!** *Crown action*

Let's try that all together:

**Jesus came riding on a donkey** *hold reins and jig up and down*

**and the people all danced and sang!** *Wave hands above head*

**They threw down their cloaks before him** *'Glory of the Lord' sign (see p. 99)*

**and waved gree-een palm leaves in their hands!** *Wave hands above head*

**Sing hosanna! Sing hosanna!** *Wave hands above head*

**Sing hosanna** *wave hands* **to the King of Kings!** *Crown action twice*

**Sing hosanna! Sing hosanna!**

**Sing hosanna** *wave hands above head* **to the King!** *Crown action*

We're ready to tell our story.

Jesus and his friends, the disciples, were going to the big city.

Let's stand up and show a big shape with our body.

*Lead the children in stretching out your body into the biggest shape.*

Bigger! Even bigger!

Jerusalem was the biggest city in the whole land!

The disciples were feeling excited.

Can you show me excited?

*Lead the children in looking excited.*

And the disciples were feeling scared.

Can you show me scared?

*Lead the children in looking scared.*

The big city was busy and full of people.

What if no one liked them there?

Let's be the disciples and look:

excited . . . *excited*

and scared . . . *scared*

Then Jesus said:

'Look! *Point* There's a donkey over there.

Go and get the donkey for me!' *Point*

Can you hear the donkey? *Hand behind ear*

*If the children don't naturally make the sound:*

What sound does a donkey make?

**Eeyore! Eeyore!**

*Lead the children in showing the donkey's ears flapping with your hands.*

Let's take the donkey for Jesus.

*Lead the children in holding an imaginary rope.*

Let's stroke our donkey's nose

so it knows we'll be gentle. *Stroke imaginary donkey's nose.*

Now let's take our donkey to Jesus.

Listen to this and see if you can do the same!

*Tongue click to make a 'clip clop' sound and walk in time with the rhythm.*

*'Clip clop' Holding reins* **Ee – yore!** *Ears flapping*
*'Clip clop' Holding reins* **Ee – yore!** *Ears flapping*
*'Clip clop' Holding reins* **Ee – yore!** *Ears flapping*
*'Clip clop' Holding reins* **Ee – yore!** *Ears flapping*

The disciples gave the donkey to Jesus.
*Lead the children in miming passing the donkey's rope over.*
Then Jesus got on the donkey.
Let's be Jesus and get on our donkey.
*Lead the children in being Jesus getting on the donkey.*
*Bob up and down on the spot holding reins as if you're riding a donkey.*
Let's ride our donkey to the big city.

*Lead children in trotting on the spot:*
*'Clip clop' Holding reins* **Ee – yore!** *Ears flapping*
*'Clip clop' Holding reins* **Ee – yore!** *Ears flapping*
*'Clip clop' Holding reins* **Ee – yore!** *Ears flapping*
*'Clip clop' Holding reins* **Ee – yore!** *Ears flapping*

And freeze!
In Jerusalem, the people heard Jesus coming!
Let's be the people together.
Sssssh! Listen! *Hand behind ear* Can you hear?
What can we hear?

*Lead the children in very quietly saying:*
*'Clip clop' Holding reins* **Ee – yore!** *Ears flapping*
*'Clip clop' Holding reins* **Ee – yore!** *Ears flapping*
*Interrupt* Who's that?
Let's stand on our tiptoes and try to see . . .
*Lead the children in tiptoeing up with hand shading eyes.*
Look! Can you see Jesus? *Point*

The people saw Jesus coming on the donkey.!
They thought Jesus was going to be the new king!
They whispered to each other.
After 3, let's whisper, 'Jesus is the new king!' *Sound excited and amazed*
*Lead the children in whispering louder and louder, turning to each other.*
**1, 2, 3 . . . Jesus is the new king!**
**Jesus is the new king!**
**Jesus is the new king!**

Everyone was so excited!
They pulled their cloaks off.
*Lead the children in miming ripping a cloak off.*
They threw them in front of Jesus.
*Lift two hands above head and then bring them down to show throwing cloaks on the floor.*

> *If your group is familiar with 'You are welcome in the name of the Lord!' (Welcome Song: Option 2):*
> Look, the people can see the 'glory of the Lord' all over Jesus!

*Lead the children in shouting 'Hosanna', getting louder and louder. They will almost certainly instinctively copy you. If not, encourage them to.*
Hosanna! *Raise hands above head*
**Hosanna!** *Raise hands above head*
Hosanna! *Raise hands above head*
**Hosanna!** *Raise hands above head*
Hosanna! *Raise hands above head*
**Hosanna!** *Raise hands above head*

Then they began to pull branches off the palm trees!

Let's climb up the tree . . .

*Lead the children in miming shimmying up a tree.*

Let's pull branches off to wave for Jesus.

*Lead the children in reaching up and pulling down branches.*

Not little leaves. *Show little with your fingers*

But huge green branches with long green leaves.

*Lead the children in reaching up tall to show a tall long branch.*

Branches taller than me.

They waved their palm branches in the air!

*Mime being the branch, swaying with your whole body with your hands raised above your head.*

Let's wave our whole body, like a branch, in the air.

*Lead the children in shouting 'hosanna', getting louder and louder.*

*If they don't instinctively copy you, encourage them to:*

Hosanna! *Raise hands above head*

**Hosanna!** *Raise hands above head*

Hosanna! *Raise hands above head*

**Hosanna!** *Raise hands above head*

Hosanna! *Raise hands above head*

**Hosanna!** *Raise hands above head*

Jesus is HERE!

That was exciting, wasn't it?

That's the story of Palm Sunday!

Let's tell our story again with our song.

> *If appropriate, you could distribute branches, leaves, green imaginative aids (or a mixture).*

> *You might like to try singing the song while moving around the room or even leaving the room if appropriate. At St Peter's Church, we use the chairs we've set out for the adults as an 'island' to walk around in a circle as we sing. With the school, we take the procession around the church or even out into the churchyard if it's not raining.*

*When the group is ready:*

What do we need to get on to start our song?

*If the children need a clue:* What did Jesus ride into Jerusalem on?

*Accept the children's responses.*

Let's get on our donkey!

*'Clip clop' Holding reins* **Ee – yore!** *Ears flapping*

*'Clip clop' Holding reins* **Ee – yore!** *Ears flapping*

**Jesus came riding on a donkey** *hold reins and jig up and down*

**and the people all danced and sang!** *Wave hands above head*

**They threw down their cloaks before him** *'Glory of the Lord' sign (see p. 99)*

**and waved gre-en palm leaves in their hands!** *Wave hands above head*

   [and they sang]

**Sing hosanna! Sing hosanna!** *Wave hands above head*

**Sing hosanna** *wave hands* **to the King of Kings!** *Crown action twice*

**Sing hosanna! Sing hosanna!**

**Sing hosanna** *wave hands above head* **to the King!** *Crown action*

*Repeat.*

*Continue singing as you collect any imaginative aids, leaves or branches. When the group is ready:*

Hosanna! *Raise hands above head*

**Hosanna!** *Raise hands above head*

Hosanna! *Raise hands above head*

**Hosanna!** *Raise hands above head*

Hosanna! *Raise hands above head*
**Hosanna!** *Raise hands above head*

We'll find out what happens to Jesus
in the big city next week.

# Week 3: Jesus Cleans the Temple

*Aka: 'Jesus makes a mess!' This is what the Diddy Disciples at St Peter's, Walworth, call it!*

→ Matthew 21.8–13; Luke 19.45–46
→ Song: 'The people in the Temple'. Words: © Sharon Moughtin-Mumby
→ Tune: 'The wheels on the bus' (traditional). For a taster see the Diddy Disciples website.

*If your group is using the What's in the Box? option (Book 1, p. 221):*
*Invite a child to open the box.*
*Inside are cows and/or sheep (toys or a picture).*

What's in the box?
*Accept the child's response.*

We're going to tell the story of when Jesus
CHASED the cows and sheep out of God's House.

Today's story starts with a BIG house.
Let's stand up and make a big shape with our bodies.
*Lead the children in reaching out big with their arms.*
Bigger! Bigger!
This house is God's House, the Temple.
It's huge!
It's the biggest house in the biggest city in the whole land.
Can you show me big again?
And freeze!
That's big!

People went to the Temple to pray,
a bit like our church.

Let's sit down quietly and PRAYERfully.
*When the children are seated say slowly and clearly:*
'The people in the Temple, they pray, pray, pray.'
Let's sing that – ssssshhhh! – ever so peacefully.
*Either hold your hands upwards or put them together in prayer.*

*Lead the children in singing. The words are so repetitive they won't need teaching: the children will naturally begin to join in as you sing.*

**The people in the Temple**
**they pray, pray, pray,** *prayer action*
**pray, pray, pray,** *prayer action*
**pray, pray, pray . . .** *prayer action*
**The people in the Temple**
**they pray, pray, pray,** *prayer action*
**all day long!**

Very peaceful . . .
But the problem was
there were other people in the Temple!
There were people trying to sell things!

First of all they were selling cows!
What noise do cows make?
*Accept the children's responses.*
And what action could we use for cows?
*Choose one or more of the actions suggested by one of the children and invite the others to follow their lead.*

**The cows in the Temple**
**go 'Moo, moo, moo,** *cow action*
**moo, moo, moo,** *cow action*
**moo, moo, moo!'** *Cow action*
**The cows in the Temple**
**go 'Moo, moo, moo,'** *cow action*
**all day long!**

Hmm. It's getting a bit noisy.
This feels more like a cow shop than God's House.

And that wasn't the only animal in the Temple.
The sellers were also selling sheep!
What noise do sheep make?
*Accept the children's responses.*
And what action could we use for sheep?
*Choose one or more of the actions suggested by one of the children and invite the others to follow their lead.*

**The sheep in the Temple**
**go 'Baa, baa, baa,** *sheep action*
**baa, baa, baa,** *sheep action*
**baa, baa, baa!'** *Sheep action*
**The sheep in the Temple**
**go 'Baa, baa, baa,'** *sheep action*
**all day long!**

The sellers in the Temple were making lots of money
selling cows and sheep. .
The sellers were taking money from poor people!

Let's be the poor people and hold our empty hands out.
*Lead the children in holding empty hands out.*
No more money! *Shake head and look sad*

Let's be the sellers and hold our bags of money in our hands.
*Lead the children in holding imaginary money bags.*
Let's jingle our money bags to show ALL the money!
Jingle, jingle, jingle! *Shake money bags*
Listen to all that money:
all the money we're taking from the poor people.

**The sellers in the Temple**
**go jingle, jingle, jingle,** *shake money bags*
**jingle, jingle, jingle,** *shake money bags*
**jingle, jingle, jingle!** *Shake money bags*
**The sellers in the Temple**
**go jingle, jingle, jingle** *shake money bags*
**all day long!**

What a lot of noise! *Hold hands on ears*
*Encourage the children to fill in the gaps.*
We have cows going . . .
Sheep going . . .
Sellers and their money going . . .
What a lot of noise! *Hold hands on ears*
I can't pray!
I can't even hear myself think!

Then one day Jesus came riding on a donkey.
*Hold reins and move hands up and down as if on a donkey.*

> *If appropriate, you could recap the story from last week here with the words:*
>
> *'Clip clop' Holding reins* **Ee – yore!** *Ears flapping*
> *'Clip clop' Holding reins* **Ee – yore!** *Ears flapping*
>
> *and/or the Palm Sunday song:*
>
> **Jesus came riding on a donkey** *hold reins and jig up and down*
> **and the people all danced and sang!** *Wave hands above head*
> **They threw down their cloaks before him** *'Glory of the Lord' sign (see p. 99)*
> **and waved green palm leaves in their hands!** *Wave hands above head*
> > [And they sang]
> **Sing hosanna! Sing hosanna!** *Wave hands above head*
> **Sing hosanna** *wave hands* **to the King of Kings!** *Crown action twice*
> **Sing hosanna! Sing hosanna!**
> **Sing hosanna** *wave hands above head* **to the King!** *Crown action*

Jesus came riding on a donkey!
And Jesus went straight to the Temple.
He wanted to pray in God's House.

Let's be Jesus and walk on the spot into the Temple.
*Lead the children in walking on the spot.*
And freeze!

We're here! We're in the Temple!
Let's pray.
Hang on a minute!
What can Jesus hear? *Hand behind ear*

*Encourage the children to fill in the gaps.*
We have cows going . . .
Sheep going . . .
Sellers and their money going . . .
And the poor people with no more money.
*Shake head and hold hands out and look sad.*

Jesus was CROSS!
Can you show me angry like Jesus?
*Lead the children in looking angry.*

Jesus was ANGRY!
Can you show me angry?
*Lead the children in looking furious.*
Even MORE angry!

And Jesus shouted . . .
Can you shout after me:
'my turn' *point to self*, 'your turn' *leader's hands out to group*?

*Loudly and authoritatively in outrage:*
This is GOD's House! *Two hands pointing down*
**This is GOD's House!**
You've turned it into a SHOP! *Arms folded*
**You've turned it into a SHOP!**
*Raise voice and sound even more angry.*
And now you're taking money from POOR people! *Hands on hips*
**And now you're taking money from POOR people!**

Then Jesus THREW OVER all the shop tables! *Pushing action*
He turned the tables upside down! Topsy turvy! *Diddy Disciples 'New Start' sign (p. 355)*
And all the money fell on the floor! *Throw arms outwards*

Let's show Jesus turning the tables topsy turvy!
*Lead the children in the 'New Start' sign.*

> *If appropriate:* Look! Jesus is giving the Temple a new start!

Jesus in the Temple said, 'This is God's House.'
Let's sing and show Jesus turning over the tables
with our arms. *'New Start' sign*

> *If appropriate:*
> But for the rest of our song we won't sing 'all day long' at the end
> we'll sing 'on that day!'
> Let's practise that:
> *Lead the children in singing* 'on that day!'
> *Don't worry too much if this last change of words is too much for your group when you come to singing the rest of the song.*

And remember, Jesus is CROSS! *Show cross face*
Let's sound cross as we sing!

**Jesus in the Temple said, 'This is God's House!'** *'New Start' sign*
**'This is God's House!'** *'New Start' sign*
**'This is God's House!'** *'New Start' sign*
**'This is God's House!'** *'New Start' sign*
**Jesus in the Temple said, 'This is God's House!'** *'New Start' sign*
**on that day!**

Then Jesus chased all the cows and sheep out!
Let's be the cows for the first half of the song.
Then let's be the sheep!

*Lead the children in sounding unsettled as you 'moo' and 'baa'.*
**The cows in the Temple**
**went 'Moo, moo, moo,** *cow action*
**moo, moo, moo,** *cow action*
**moo, moo, moo!'** *Cow action*
*Interrupt:* And now the sheep!
**The sheep in the Temple**
**went 'Baa, baa, baa,'** *sheep action*
**on that day!**

Now the leaders in the Temple saw this.
Let's be the leaders in the Temple and look important.
*Lead the children in looking important.*

How do you think the leaders felt
when Jesus turned the tables topsy turvy? *'New Start' sign*
Can you show me with your face?
*Accept all suggestions.*

In our story, some of the leaders were cross!
Can you show me cross?
*Lead the children in looking cross.*
Now angry! Really angry!
*Lead the children in looking angry.*

The leaders wanted Jesus OUT of the Temple! *Point outwards in anger*
OUT of the big city! *Point outwards in anger*
The leaders wanted NO MORE JESUS! *Shake head and point finger*
Let's be the angry leaders and sing
*Speak in the rhythm of the last line of the song:*
'NO MORE JESUS!' on . . . that . . . day. *Point finger in anger in time*

**The leaders in the Temple**
**said, 'No more Jesus!'** *Point finger in anger three times*
**'No more Jesus!'** *Point finger in anger three times*
**'No more Jesus!'** *Point finger in anger three times*
**The leaders in the Temple**
**said, 'No more Jesus!'** *Point finger in anger three times*
**on that day.**

That was when the leaders decided to put Jesus on the cross.
*Hold arms out in a cross shape.*
We'll find out what happens next *in two weeks.*
*(Next week is Mothering Sunday.)*

# Week 4: Jesus Is like a Mother Hen (Mothering Sunday)

→ Luke 13: 34–35 and Matthew 23.37–39
→ Song: 'I am so important! Look, look, look at me!' Words: © Sharon Moughtin-Mumby
→ Tune: 'Chick, chick, chick, chick, chicken! (Lay a little egg for me!)' (traditional)

*The fourth Sunday of Lent is traditionally held as Mothering Sunday. The following material is designed to enable groups to celebrate the themes of this day while continuing the unit's exploration of Jesus' journey to Jerusalem and the cross.*

If your group is using the *What's in the Box?* option (Book 1, p. 221):
*Invite a child to open the box.*
*Inside is a chick (either a toy or a picture).*

What's in the box?
*Accept the child's response.*

Today's story is all about little chicks!
Can you show me what a little chick looks like?
What does a little chick sound like?
*Lead the children in pretending to be a chick.*

Freeze!
We're going to sing a chicken song!
Let's learn it 'my turn' *point to self*, 'your turn' *leader's hands out to group*.

*Sing it with the tune straight away.*
Chick, chick, chick, chick, chicken!
Cheep, cheep, cheep, cheep, cheep!
**Chick, chick, chick, chick, chicken!**
**Cheep, cheep, cheep, cheep, cheep!**

Chicks don't know what they're doing
or where they're going.
They wander this way and that and get lost.
Then they cheep for their mummy hen.
Let's turn around on the spot and look lost while we sing our song.
*Lead the children in pretending to be a lost chick.*

**Chick, chick, chick, chick, chicken!** *Flap wings*
**Cheep, cheep, cheep, cheep, cheep!**
**Chick, chick, chick, chick, chicken!** *Flap wings*
**Cheep, cheep, cheep, cheep, cheep!**

Freeze!
Chicks also spend a lot of time hiding and resting
under their mummy's wing.
Let's sit down and pretend we're hiding under our mummy's wing,
while she keeps us safe and warm.
*Lead the children in sitting down. Make your arm into a wing and pretend it's your mummy hen's wing to hide behind.*
Sssssh! Let's sing our song ever so quietly.
**Chick, chick, chick, chick, chicken!**
**Cheep, cheep, cheep, cheep, cheep!**
**Chick, chick, chick, chick, chicken!**
**Cheep, cheep, cheep, cheep, cheep!**

I wonder how the little chicks feel
when they're with their mummy hen?
*Accept responses.*

We're ready to tell our story.

Jesus went to the big city Jerusalem.
Let's make a big shape with our body
to show the big city!
*Lead the children in making a big shape.*
Bigger! Even bigger!

Lots of people in the big city
saw themselves as ever so important.
Can you show me how you look
when you're being important?
*Lead the children in looking important and a little snooty.*

We're going to sing a song for the important people.
It goes like this:
'my turn' *point to self*, 'your turn' *leader's hands out to group*.

*To the same tune as 'Chick, chick, chick, chick, chicken'.*
I am so important! *Puff chest up and stand tall*
Look, look, look at me! *Point at yourself with both hands*
**I am so important!** *Puff chest up and stand tall*
**Look, look, look at me!** *Point at yourself with both hands*

The people in the big city
saw themselves as always right.
Can you show me what you look like
when you think you're completely right?
Let's sing our song again.

**I am so important!** *Puff chest up and stand tall*
**Look, look, look at me!** *Point at yourself with both hands*
**I am so important!** *Puff chest up and stand tall*
**Look, look, look at me!** *Point at yourself with both hands*

But when JESUS looked at the people of the big city.
They didn't look important or right at all! *Shake head*
They looked like little lost chicks,
running around getting lost
and cheeping for their mummy.

Can you show me little chicks again?
*Lead the children in being little chicks.*
**Chick, chick, chick, chick, chicken!**
**Cheep, cheep, cheep, cheep, cheep!**

So the people in the big city
thought they looked important and always right.
*Lead the children in singing:*
**I am so important!** *Puff chest up and stand tall*
**Look, look, look at me!** *Point at yourself with both hands*

But when Jesus saw them they looked like little chicks.
*Lead the children in singing:*
**Chick, chick, chick, chick, chicken!** *Flap wings*
**Cheep, cheep, cheep, cheep, cheep!**

Let's sit down for a moment.

*When the group is ready:*
Jesus wanted to keep the people of the big city safe,
to love them, to cuddle them under his wing
like a mummy hen.

And so Jesus did a very surprising thing.
Jesus cried. *Run fingers down cheeks to show tears*

Can you make your fingers run down your cheeks
to show Jesus crying?
*Lead the children in the crying action.*

And Jesus said a beautiful thing to Jerusalem.
Let's say Jesus' words together,
'my turn' *point to self*, 'your turn' *leader's hands out to group*.

Jesus said . . .
Like a mummy hen *flap wings gently*
**Like a mummy hen** *flap wings gently*
Keeps her chicks safe and warm *cross arms on chest*

**Keeps her chicks safe and warm** *cross arms on chest*
I want to take care of you! *Hands outwards, palms up*
**I want to take care of you!** *Hands outwards, palms up*

Let's close our eyes for a moment.
*When the group is ready:*
Sometimes we feel very small.
Sometimes we feel lost.
And everyone else around us can look so big and important
and always right.

When we feel like that, let's imagine Jesus saying those words to us.
Let's say them after Jesus
and take them deep in our heart.
Jesus said . . .

Like a mummy hen *flap wings gently*
**Like a mummy hen** *flap wings gently*
Keeps her chicks safe and warm *cross arms on chest*
**Keeps her chicks safe and warm** *cross arms on chest*
I want to take care of you! *Hands outwards, palms up*
**I want to take care of you!** *Hands outwards, palms up*

Let's imagine we're with Jesus, our mummy hen, right now.
Let's imagine hiding safe under our mummy's wing.
*After a moment.*
Let's open our eyes.
How did that feel to be safe with Jesus?
Can you show me with your face?

Today is Mothering Sunday when we celebrate mummies.
We celebrate mummies in three ways.

> *If your church also celebrates Mary as Jesus' mother, adapt the material to read four.*

Let's count to 3.
*Lead the children in counting to three on fingers.*
**1, 2, 3.**
1: *lead the children in showing one finger*
We remember how Jesus wants to be like a mummy hen to us
2: *lead the children in showing two fingers*
We remember how the Church can be like a mummy to us.

> *If your church also celebrates Mary as Jesus' mother, add:*
> 3: *lead the children in showing three fingers*
> We remember Mary, Jesus' mummy.

And, what's next?
**3 or 4**: *lead the children in showing three (or four) fingers*
We remember all the people who have been like mummies to us:
men like Jesus, and women too.

I wonder who's been like a mummy to you?
*At this point, you can:*
- *either end this time of storytelling;*
- *or lead into the Prayers for Other People, using the material below as the Prayer Action;*
- *or move straight into the following material that gives thanks for and prays for everyone who has been like a mother to us.*

## Mothering Sunday thank you prayers

*Either: placing flowers as prayers on a 'garden' (a tray with brown cloth/paper folded on it). The flowers could be real flowers, silk flowers, paper flowers, 'flowers' made from tissue/crepe paper, or pictures of flowers, etc. At St Peter's, Walworth, we pick daisies on the way to church and use these;*
*or: placing little chicks onto a mother hen template (p. 379 or website);*
*or: placing paper hearts on a cross (continuing the theme of Lent).*

Let's close our eyes for a moment.
Let's remember someone who's been like a mummy to us.
Let's say thank you to God for all our mummies!

Let's open our eyes again.
*Show the children the symbols you have chosen in one or more baskets or trays.*
*Name* and *Name* are going to bring around these flowers/hearts/chicks.
If you like, you can take a flower/heart/chick and hold it up.
Let's ask God to see these flowers/hearts/chicks as a thank you prayer
for someone who's been like a mummy to us.

*As the symbols are taken around, lead the group in:*

> *Either: humming the refrain of your prayer song together, with the words 'Jesus, hear our prayer' as a refrain as usual.*

> *Or: singing new words to the tune of 'Chick, chick, chick, chick, chicken'.*
> Let's sing our song again. This time let's sing:
> 'Thank you for our mummies!
> Thank you, thank you God!'
> **Thank you for our mummies!**
> **Thank you, thank you God!**
> *Repeat as appropriate.*

*When the group is ready, place your 'garden'/cross/mother hen in the centre of the circle.*

> *Either:*
> If you like, you can place your flower in our 'garden' as a prayer.
> Let's say thank you for everyone who's like a mummy
> and makes the world beautiful.

> *Or:*
> If you like, you can place your heart on this cross as a prayer.
> Let's say thank you for everyone who's like a mummy
> and shows us how to love as Jesus loves.

> *Or:*
> If you like, you can place your chick on this mummy hen as a prayer.
> Let's say thank you for everyone who's like a mummy
> and shows us how to love as Jesus loves.

*Hum or sing together again while the children place their symbols. Some groups may like to invite two children to carry the 'garden'/ cross/hen around the group to collect the symbols. These can then be placed in the centre.*

*End by singing the final verse of your prayer song, or by singing the 'Thank you for our mummies' song one last time.*

# Week 5: Jesus Washes the Disciples' Feet

→ **John 13.1–17**
→ **Song: 'I am going to follow Jesus'. Words: © Sharon Moughtin-Mumby**
→ **Tune: 'Bobby Shaftoe'. For the music see p. 72, or for a taster see the Diddy Disciples website. For tips on teaching songs for the first time, see Book 1, p. 215.**

Today's session includes the option of an act of footwashing. If your group takes part in this, it's important to think through the logistics beforehand and it may make sense to have extra helpers available. You may find it helpful to think through:

- Where will the footwashing take place? At St Peter's, Walworth, we don't set up tables for the Creative Response time this week. Instead, we place a ring of chairs (with a space left for entry!) where the tables normally stand. Ideally, there should be one chair for every pair of children.
- Where will you place the towels? We place one towel under each chair so they don't get sat on!
- Where will the water come from? Footwashing really requires warm water to be poured out by an extra helper during the Bible Storytelling. We recommend giving out the bowls of water when the children are in place, to prevent spillages. This is where your extra helpers will come in handy. We place the bowls of water in the centre of the circle of chairs while the children who will sit on the chairs find their places. We then move a bowl next to each child's feet and send their partners over one by one to kneel by the bowl.
- How will you manage taking shoes and socks off? At St Peter's, Walworth, we ask the children to take their shoes and socks off at the beginning of the session as they enter the room to keep the flow of our worship time together.
  - We make sure they place their socks inside their shoes!
  - Be aware that there will be children who do not wish to take their socks/tights/shoes off. They can take the role of 'footwasher' in the footwashing or they can simply watch.
  - If there are children wearing tights who need help to remove them, make sure that the child does want to take her/his tights off, then **make sure that this is done by their parent/carer or that you check the safeguarding procedures for your church/group for helping children change clothes**. At St Peter's we make an announcement in the weeks prior to the session asking children and parents to make sure that tights aren't worn to that session. However, it inevitably happens!
  - For children wearing tights and shorts, who want to join in, we provide spare skirts in different sizes that they can slip on in order to take their shorts and tights off appropriately.

---

### Tip

For the storytelling this week, it's preferable to use the language of 'king' for both girls and boys as it will be the 'Servant KING', Jesus, that we're talking about later.

---

*If your group is using the What's in the Box? option (Book 1, p. 221):*
*Invite a child to open the box.*
*Inside is a crown.*

What's in the box?
*Accept the child's response.*

Today we're going to tell a story about a king.
King Jesus, the Servant King.

To get ready for today's story,
we're going to practise being servants and kings!

*Invite a child to be 'king'.*
*Name* is going to be our king!
Here's your crown! *Place an imaginary crown on the king's head*
Can you show us your crown on your head?
*If necessary help the king in making a crown action with her/his hands.*
The rest of us are going to be servants! *Point around the group*

*Name*, we're your servants.
What would you like us to do?
> *If necessary, aside to the king*: Say, 'Mop the floor!' or 'Cook some food!'
> *King:* 'Mop the floor!'
We're King *Name*'s servants, we have to do as the king says!
Let's *mop the floor*! *Lead the children in miming mopping the floor*

*Choose another child to be king.*
Now *Name* is going to be our king!
Here's your crown! *Place an imaginary crown on king's head*

Can you show us your crown on your head?
*If necessary help the king in making a crown action with her/his hands.*

*Name*, we're your servants.
What would you like us to do?

> *If necessary, aside to the king*: Say, 'Wash my clothes!' or 'Run on the spot!'
> *King:* 'Run over there!'

We're King *Name*'s servants, so let's run on the spot.
*Lead the children in running on the spot.*
*Repeat as appropriate.*

Let's sit down.

*When the group is ready:*
We're ready to tell our story about Jesus the King.
Jesus' friends, the disciples, were excited!
Can you show me excited?
*Lead the children in looking excited.*
Really excited!
Jesus had invited them to a special party!
*If appropriate:* the Passover!

And . . . ssssh! *Look around*
Listen! *Hand behind ear*
*Whispering:* 'Jesus is going to tell us he's the King!'
Let's turn to each other and whisper, 'Jesus is the King!'
*Lead the group in whispering to each other:*
**Jesus is the King!**
**Jesus is the King!**
**Jesus is the King!**

So the disciples were sitting down ready to eat.
Let's look ready for our special meal.
Let's sit up!
*Lead the children in sitting up and looking expectant.*
Then Jesus the King did something very surprising!

Let's all be Jesus.
Jesus stood up.
Let's stand up! *Lead the children in standing.*
He tied a towel around his waist like an apron.
Let's put our apron on . . . *Lead the children in tying apron on*
Then Jesus poured water into a bowl.
*Lead the children in miming pouring water*
Jesus knelt on the floor. *Lead the children in kneeling*
and washed the feet of one of his disciples. *Diddy Disciples 'New Start' sign (p. 355)*

*The words to this song are so straightforward, if you start singing the children will gradually join in.*
**Washing, washing, washing feet,** *'New Start' sign*
**washing, washing, washing feet,** *'New Start' sign*
**washing, washing, washing feet,** *'New Start' sign*
**washing, washing feet.** *'New Start' sign*

The room went silent!
This is the hard bit of the story!
Let's try one second of complete silence after 3!
Let's put our hands over our mouth to show silent!

> **1, 2, 3 . . .**

*Lead the children in clamping hands on mouth.*

*Leave a second or as long as you think the group can, then:*
Silence!
The room went silent!

The disciples looked at each other shocked.
Let's be the disciples again.
Can you show me your shocked face?
*Lead the group in look at each other shocked.*
Nobody spoke.

Kings don't wash feet! *Crown action and shake head*
Kings don't kneel on the floor! *Crown on head and shake head*
Servants wash feet! *'New Start' sign*
Not kings!
The disciples were shocked!
Can you show me shocked? *Lead the group in shocked action*

Then it was Peter's turn.
Let's be Peter.
Let's put our feet in front of us and wiggle them.
*Lead the children in wiggling feet.*
Wiggle, wiggle, wiggle!

Jesus came to wash Peter's feet. *Keep wiggling feet*
But Peter said, 'NO! *Wag finger*
Not MY feet! No!' *Wag finger*
Let's be Peter and say, 'No! *Wag finger*
**No!'** *Wag finger*
Peter wanted Jesus to act like a REAL king. *Crown on head*
Not like a servant. *'New Start' sign and shake head*

But Jesus said, 'Yes!'
Jesus washed Peter's feet!
Let's be Peter. *Wiggle feet*
Let's close our eyes and imagine Jesus
Kneeling down before us and washing our feet.

*Singing gently and making the 'New Start' sign throughout:*
**Washing, washing, washing feet,**
**washing, washing, washing feet,**
**washing, washing, washing feet,**
**washing, washing feet.**

I wonder how Peter felt when Jesus washed his feet?
Can you show me with your face?

That was when the disciples knew:
Jesus wasn't just the king! *Crown action*
Jesus was the SERVANT *'New Start' sign* KING! *Crown action*

Let's say that 'my turn' *point to self*, 'your turn' *leader's hands out to group*.

*Slowly:* Jesus is the SERVANT *'New Start' sign* KING! *Crown action*
**Jesus is the SERVANT** *'New Start' sign* **KING!** *Crown action*
And again:
**Jesus is the SERVANT** *'New Start' sign* **KING!** *Crown action*

*Optional footwashing:*
Then Jesus said something surprising.

Let's be Jesus.
Let's say these words 'my turn' *point to self*, 'your turn' *leader's hands out to group*.

YOU must wash each other's feet! *Point to children then feet*

**YOU must wash each other's feet!** *Point to children then feet*

YOU must be like a servant! *Point to children then 'New Start' sign*

**YOU must be like a servant!** *Point to children then 'New Start' sign*

When we wash each other's feet.
We're showing we're ready to be a servant like Jesus.
We're following Jesus!

> *If your group is taking part in the act of footwashing:*
> We're going to wash each other's feet this morning.
> We're going to follow Jesus.

## Tip

If there are a range of ages in your group, pair up younger children with older children for the footwashing where possible. Where there are parents/carers with babies and toddlers, the baby/toddler can sit on their knee on the chairs.

- We've found it's easier to assume that the children will join in with the footwashing unless they make it clear that they don't want to. It's hard for young children to imagine what's involved until it happens, so it doesn't seem to work to ask them. Instead, we follow their reactions when they have seen what will take place.
- If there are children who have not wanted to take their shoes and socks off, ask them to join the second half of the group (who will become the 'footwashers').
- If it emerges at any point that any of the children do not want to have their feet washed, simply swap them over to become the 'footwasher'. If they also don't want to do this, then simply let them watch and help the group sing. They may like to take part in the drying of feet later.

*Be very clear about what you would like the children to do, according to your resources and space. This is especially important if you have a large group.*

*For example:*

> *Either (in groups of the same age):* Can this half of the room go and sit on the chairs?
> *Or (in mixed age groups):* Can everyone who doesn't go to school sit on the chairs? *These children may need some help to identify themselves and go to the chairs.*
> Now everyone in nursery. Now everyone in reception. *Until half the group is sitting*

As they find their places, let's sing:
**I am going to follow Jesus,**
**I am going to follow Jesus,**
**I am going to follow Jesus,**
**follow, follow Jesus!**

*When the children are sitting ready, ask helpers to move the bowls of water in front of each seated child. Continue singing as this takes place.*

*When the bowls are in place, to the remaining children (which should be half the group):*
Can you go and kneel next to one of the children sitting on a chair?
*In large groups, you may find it helpful to send the children over one by one, telling them the name of the child they should kneel in front of.*

As they find their places, let's sing:
**I am going to follow Jesus,**
**I am going to follow Jesus,**
**I am going to follow Jesus,**
**follow, follow Jesus!**

*When the group is ready:*
It's time for our foot washing.

If you're sitting on a chair,
you're going to have your feet washed!
If you're kneeling on the floor,
you're going to be washing feet!
Let's sing as we wash.

*Lead the children in singing as they wash feet.*
**Washing, washing, washing feet,**
**washing, washing, washing feet,**
**washing, washing, washing feet,**
**washing, washing feet.**

**I am going to serve like Jesus,**
**I am going to serve like Jesus,**
**I am going to serve like Jesus,**
**serve like, serve like Jesus.**

**I am going to follow Jesus,**
**I am going to follow Jesus,**
**I am going to follow Jesus,**
**follow, follow Jesus!**
*Repeat as appropriate.*

*When the group is ready:*
Now if you're kneeling,
it's time to dry your friend's feet.
Let's take our towel . . .
                *If appropriate:* it's under the chair!

Let's dry our friend's feet.
*Lead the children in singing as they wash feet.*
**Drying, drying, drying feet,**
**drying, drying, drying feet,**
**drying, drying, drying feet,**
**drying, drying feet.**

**I am going to serve like Jesus,**
**I am going to serve like Jesus,**
**I am going to serve like Jesus,**
**serve like, serve like Jesus.**

**I am going to follow Jesus,**
**I am going to follow Jesus,**
**I am going to follow Jesus,**
**follow, follow Jesus!**
*Repeat as appropriate.*

*If there's time, you could invite the children to swap and repeat the material. If there are pairs where this doesn't work, the helpers could join that pair to have their feet washed by both children at this point, now the children know what they're doing. Or groups of two to three children could wash one child's feet.*

*When the footwashing is over:*
When we wash each other's feet
We're showing we're ready to serve people like Jesus.
We're following Jesus, the SERVANT *'New Start' sign* KING! *Crown action*

Let's say that 'my turn' *point to self*, 'your turn' *leader's hands out to group*.

We follow the SERVANT *'New Start' sign* KING! *Crown action*
**We follow the SERVANT** *'New Start' sign* **KING!** *Crown action*
Let's say that three times!

Lead the children in saying:

**We follow the SERVANT** *'New Start' sign* **KING!** *Crown action*

Louder!

**We follow the SERVANT** *'New Start' sign* **KING!** *Crown action*

Even louder!

**We follow the SERVANT** *'New Start' sign* **KING!** *Crown action*

*Encourage the children to find their shoes and put them on again before any time of Creative Response.*

# Week 6: Jesus' Last Meal

→ **The Last Supper**
→ **Luke 22.14–23**
→ **Poem: 'Do this to remember me'** © Sharon Moughtin-Mumby

*To tell the story of Jesus' Last Supper, you'll need to have ready two or more trays: one set holding a piece of bread for each child and adult; the other set holding a cup with a small amount of grape juice at the bottom for each child and adult.*

## Tip

You could use matzo (unleavened) bread, pitta bread or everyday bread for this action. We cut the bread into small squares beforehand with scissors.

There are benefits in making connections both with the kind of bread that you use in your church's communion service and with the kind that your children will be familiar with from home, school or nursery. As this story is told at Easter time as well, you could move between the different kinds of bread to support the children in making these connections.

> *If you're using the What's in the Box? option (Book 1, p. 221):*
> *Invite one of the children to open the box. Inside will be bread and a cup or chalice.*
>
> What's in the box? *Ask the child to respond.*
>
> We're going to tell the story of when Jesus shared bread and wine.
> *Show cup and bread.*

Jesus' friends, the disciples, were excited!

Can you show me excited?

*Lead the children in looking excited.*

Really excited!

They were in the big city, Jerusalem!

> *If you're telling this story on Palm Sunday before or after a procession:*
> Jesus had ridden into the city on a donkey!
> Everyone had waved palm leaves and shouted:
> *Lead the children in shouting Hosanna, getting louder and louder.*
> *If necessary:* Let's shout 'my turn' *point to self*, 'your turn' *leader's hands out to group*.

Hosanna! *Raise hands above head*

**Hosanna!** *Raise hands above head*

Hosanna! *Raise hands above head*

**Hosanna!** *Raise hands above head*

Hosanna! *Raise hands above head*

**Hosanna!** *Raise hands above head*

Now Jesus had invited them to a special party!

> *If appropriate:* The Passover!

and . . . ssssh! *Look around*

Listen! *Hand behind ear*

*Whispering with finger near lips:* 'Jesus is going to tell us he's the King!'

Let's turn to each other and whisper, 'Jesus is the King!'
*Lead the group in whispering to each other:*
**Jesus is the King!**
**Jesus is the King!**
**Jesus is the King!**

The sun had gone down . . .
Let's show the sun going down with our arms.
*Lead the children in raising your arms then lowering them to your sides to show the sun setting.*
It was dark!
It was time!

Then after dinner, Jesus did something new.

> *If appropriate:*
> We tell this story every week in church.
> It's one of our most important stories!

*Invite two children to take around small pieces of bread in two baskets for everyone who wants to receive them.*

*Name* and *Name* are going to
bring around some bread now.
If you'd like some bread,
can you hold your hands out like this?
*Model to the children holding out cupped hands.*
*Name* and *Name* will give you a piece.
Keep the bread in your hands till everyone has some.
Don't eat it yet!

*If your group is using 'I am going to follow Jesus' as a Gathering Song, you may like to sing this as you wait for your bread. Or you could sing another appropriate song that the group is familiar with.*

*When the group is ready:*
After dinner, Jesus did something new.

Can you say these words after me and copy my actions,
'my turn' *point to self*, 'your turn' *leader's hands out to group*?

| | |
|---|---|
| Jesus took the bread. | *Take bread in one hand* |
| **Jesus took the bread.** | *Take bread in one hand* |
| He said, 'Thank you, God!' | *Hold bread up if this is in your tradition* |
| **He said, 'Thank you, God!'** | *Hold bread up if this is in your tradition* |
| Jesus broke the bread. | *Break bread* |
| **Jesus broke the bread.** | *Break bread* |
| Then he shared it. | *Mime handing bread out in a circle* |
| **Then he shared it.** | *Mime handing bread out in a circle* |

| | |
|---|---|
| This is my body, | *Hold bread or point to it* |
| **This is my body,** | *Hold bread or point to it* |
| broken for you. | *Hold bread back together then separate it again* |
| **broken for you.** | *Hold bread back together then separate it again* |
| Do this to remember me! | *Hold bread up if this is in your tradition* |
| **Do this to remember me!** | *Hold bread up if this is in your tradition* |

*Invite the children to eat their bread slowly, really tasting and enjoying it. Once the children's hands are empty, distribute cups with just 1–2 cm of grape juice at the bottom. These cups are best distributed by adults or responsible older children.*

While you finish eating,
we're going to bring around cups.
If you'd like a cup,
can you hold your hands out like this? *Model to the children*

Keep the cup in your hands till everyone has one.
Don't drink from it yet!

*If your group is using 'I am going to follow Jesus' as a Gathering Song, you may like to sing this as you wait for your cup. Or you could sing another appropriate song that the group is familiar with. Once all the children and adults who wish to receive a cup have done so:*

When they'd finished eating,
Jesus took the cup.

Can you say these words after me and copy my actions,
'my turn' *point to self*, 'your turn' *leader's hands out to group*?

| | |
|---|---|
| Jesus took the cup. | *Take cup in both hands* |
| **Jesus took the cup.** | *Take cup in both hands* |
| He said, 'Thank you, God!' | *Hold cup up if this is in your tradition* |
| **He said, 'Thank you, God!'** | *Hold cup up if this is in your tradition* |
| Jesus poured the wine. | *Mime pouring wine* |
| **Jesus poured the wine.** | *Mime pouring wine* |
| Then he shared it. | *Mime handing cup out in a circle* |
| **Then he shared it.** | *Mime handing cup out in a circle* |
| | |
| This is my blood, | *Lift cup or point to it* |
| **This is my blood,** | *Lift cup or point to it* |
| poured out for you. | *Mime pouring wine* |
| **poured out for you.** | *Mime pouring wine* |
| Do this to remember me! | *Hold cup up if this is in your tradition* |
| **Do this to remember me!** | *Hold cup up if this is in your tradition* |

*Invite the children to drink the grape juice slowly and to really taste and enjoy it. When they've finished, ask for a moment of quiet.*

I wonder how you feel when you eat the bread
and drink from your cup?
Can you show me?

*The children may respond silently, inside themselves, or they may offer a facial expression, or a single word or more. Accept all of their responses.*

Then Jesus said to his friends:
'Tonight, all of you will run away!
You'll leave me all alone!'
I wonder how the disciples felt now?
Can you show me with your face?

Peter said, 'No!' *Shake head, looking cross*
Can you shake your head and say, 'No!'
**'No!** *Shake head*
'I will never leave you!' Peter said.
'I *point to self* will stay with you!'

And all the other disciples said the same thing.
Let's all shake our heads and say,
'We will never leave you!' *Shake head*
**'We will never leave you!** *Shake head*
**We will never leave you!'** *Shake head*

Then Jesus went with his friends to a quiet garden to pray.
We'll hear the rest of this story next time we meet as a church [*or, if there will be a children's session for Good Friday* next time we meet together].

# Section 3

# Creative Response starter ideas: The Journey to the Cross unit

→ **Guide: Book 1, p. 228**

These starter ideas are designed to spark imaginations and open up opportunities for the children to respond creatively in their different ways to the worship and storytelling you've taken part in together.

---

**Tip**

As outlined in the Guide of *Diddy Disciples* Book 1 from p. 228, we've found the following rules of thumb helpful for fostering an environment where children are encouraged to engage personally and openly.

1  Encourage the children to make their own choices.
2  Give the children space to develop their response as they wish.
3  Create space for 'bridge building'.
4  It's the act of responding that matters, not the final result.
5  These responses are 'holy ground'.

---

**Weekly Starter Ideas** relate directly to the Bible Storytelling of each session, including a print-and-go option.

**Sensory Starter Ideas** are designed for sensory explorers, including babies and toddlers. These can remain the same through the whole unit.

**Unit Starter Ideas** are designed to remain relevant throughout the whole unit. Keeping these resources available each week gives children the opportunity to deepen and develop their responses, while making preparation more manageable for leaders.

---

**Tip: Free response area**

In addition to any other resources you provide, keeping a free response area available every week will give the children the opportunity to create anything they wish in response to the story they've told, building their sense of confidence and personal responsibility. In this area you could simply provide blank paper and crayons, pencils, paints or pastels. If you have them, other interesting media (see Book 1, p. 256) will provide even more scope for the children to nurture and strengthen their imaginative skills.

# Weekly Starter Ideas

## Week 1: Jesus is Tested in the Wilderness

✝ Invite the children to decorate a cross made from wood or card to remind them to walk the way of love like Jesus. You may like to show the children a photograph of one or more of the crosses that are used in your own church or local area or around the world as inspiration. However, encourage them to explore their own unique ideas and designs. *Provide wooden crosses or the cross template (p. 370 or website), pencils/crayons/ paints and scissors. If you have collage materials (Book 1, p. 255) and glue, make these available too. If you have string or wool, you could see if any children would like to make necklaces or bookmarks with their cross.*

✝ Invite the children to decorate a heart to remind them to walk the way of love like Jesus. *Provide large heart template (p. 382 or website), pencils/crayons/paints and scissors. If you have collage materials (Book 1, p. 255) and glue, make these available too. If you have string or wool, you could see if any children would like to make necklaces or bookmarks with their hearts.*

✝ Give older children the opportunity to make their own cross from simple materials. *Provide twigs/lollipop sticks/ straws and short pieces of pipe cleaner, or larger sticks and string/jumbo pipe cleaners.*

✝ Invite the children to paint or draw a cross or a heart on a stone or safe piece of wood to carry in their pocket. *Provide smooth pebbles (check they aren't a choking hazard) or a piece of wood (check for splinters) and felt tips/pastels/paints.*

✝ Give the children the opportunity to make their own wilderness tray (see p. 117). *Provide sand, pebbles and a box or tub from recycling. Tubs with lids (e.g. margarine tubs, takeaway containers) are ideal for transporting home.*

## Week 2: Jesus Enters Jerusalem

✝ Invite the children to colour or collage palm leaves. *Provide the palm leaf template (p. 383 or website), scissors pencils/crayons, etc. If you have green collage materials (Book 1, p. 255) and glue, make these available too. If you have lollipop sticks/straws/twigs and masking tape, you could see if any children would like to add a branch to their palm leaf.*

✝ Give the children the opportunity to make palm leaf hats. *Provide palm leaf templates (p. 383 or website) printed on green paper, plus scissors, glue and paper hatbands (see p. 360).*

✝ Give the children the opportunity to contribute to a group giant palm branch with their handshapes. Show the children how to draw around their hand on green paper then cut it out. Invite them to write their name on their handshape(s) then stick them to a branch with sticky tack. Make it clear that the tack means they can take their hand home afterwards if they like! *Provide green paper, scissors, sticky tack and a stick or branch (suitably sized for your group).*

✝ Invite the children to make palm leaves by rolling and taping green paper into a roll they can hold in their hand, then cutting lengthways halfway down the roll all the way around, to create strip leaves. *Provide green paper, scissors, masking tape.*

✝ Give the children the opportunity to enter into the part of the story when the crowd are crying out for King Jesus! Invite them to make and decorate a crown for Jesus. *Provide hatbands for crowns (see p. 360 or website) or crown templates (p. 371), scissors, masking tape, collage materials (Book 1, p. 255).*

✝ Invite the children to imagine what they would wave for Jesus if Jesus came to their place. You could take them outside into the churchyard to find branches/leaves/grasses to wave. Or you could provide materials to make placards/flags/banners/balloons, etc. *Provide an appropriate range of materials with lots of choice.*

## Week 3: Jesus Cleans the Temple

✝ You could give the children the opportunity to draw or paint a picture in a frame of a place where they feel close to God. *Provide picture frame template (p. 384 or website), paints/pastels/pencils/crayons.*

*This week's story also opens up an important opportunity for children to explore anger as a positive force for justice:*

✝ Invite the children to explore the expressions on Jesus' face when he was cleaning out the Temple. *Provide the face template (p. 374 or website), scissors pencils/crayons/pastels, etc.*

✝ Invite the children to create a picture of Jesus cleaning out the Temple. *Provide blank paper, or the body template (p. 366 or website), scissors, pencils/crayons, etc.*

✝ Invite the children to help you clean out and tidy your group's resources or meeting space. *Provide (for example): damp cloths or wipes, brushes and dustpans, grimy resources (you could always add grime!), resources that need tidying and organizing, crayons/pens/pencils that need sorting, appropriate silver and a soft cloth, used fabric/ paper/card that could be cut into squares and sorted into collage materials for the group to create with (Book 1, p. 255), or ask those who clean your meeting space or church for more ideas. If appropriate in your space, you could even provide a water tray with soapy water.*

## Week 4: Jesus is like a Mother Hen

✝ Give the children the opportunity to make a thank you card for someone who's been like a mummy to them. They might like to make their card for Jesus, Mum, Dad, a carer, Grandma, Granddad, the church, a leader or someone else who has looked after them like a mummy. *Provide A4 card folded in half, pencils/ crayons/pastels. You may also like to provide the mother hen and chick templates (p. 379 or website) for children who'd like to use these pictures in their own design. Encourage the children to explore their own ideas. Some children may prefer to use a postcard template (p. 385 or website).*

✝ Some places share Simnel cakes on Mothering Sunday (others at Easter). You could give the children the opportunity to decorate either a mini Simnel-like cake for someone who's looked after them like a mummy, or a large cake for your church to share with your congregation after the service. To decorate the cakes: spread apricot jam on the top, roll out the marzipan, cut out a circle shape from it and place it onto the jam layer. Next, roll the marzipan into small balls (traditionally 11) and 'glue' them to the top of the cake using the jam. Give the children space to develop the Simnel cake tradition in their own ways. *Provide a large sponge cake or one cupcake per child, marzipan, rolling pins, circle cutters (plate/cup/cutter with a similar circumference to the cake), apricot jam.*

## Week 5: Jesus Washes the Disciples' Feet

If you've held an actual footwashing in your group, there may be little time for a Creative Response this week. Bear in mind that you may not have space to put your usual tables out and that the floor may be wet!

✝ Invite the children to draw around their foot and then to cut it out. If you have blue/green collage materials available, you could also invite the children to create a water collage around their footprint(s). *Provide coloured paper, pencils/crayons, scissors. Optional: blue/green collage materials (Book 1, p. 255) and glue.*

✝ Give the children the opportunity to make a miniature clay bowl or jug for footwashing. *Provide playdough, salt dough (Book 1, p. 257) or clay (airdrying clay would mean that children could take their bowls home), facilities for the children to wash and dry their hands afterwards. Optional: clay modelling tools.*

✝ See John the Baptist Unit Starter Ideas (River Jordan) for more water-themed creative starter ideas.

## Week 6: Jesus' Last Meal

✝ Give the children the opportunity to decorate their own cup or chalice from Jesus' Last Supper. If you have examples in your own church that are available, you could show these to the children but encourage the children to create their own unique designs. *Provide chalice template (p. 368), pencils/crayons, scissors. Optional: different coloured collage materials (Book 1, p. 255) and glue.*

✝ Invite the children to make an image of Jesus, Peter, themselves or someone they know at Jesus' Last Supper. *Provide body template (p. 366), pencils/crayons/pastels, scissors. Optional: collage materials (Book 1, p. 255) and glue.*

✝ Give the children the opportunity to spend time kneading and shaping bread dough into a roll to take home, bake and share. *Provide a simple bread dough for the children (use a readymade mix, see Book 1, p. 258 for a recipe, or use your own recipe), a floured container or cling film to take the roll home in, and appropriate instructions for baking the bread. Optional: if you have the facilities, you may even like to bake the bread on site.*

✝ Give the children the opportunity to decorate a paper cup with the story of Jesus' Last Supper. If you have examples of decorated communion cups or chalices in your own church that are available, you could show these to the children. *Provide paper cups that can be drawn on, pencils/crayons, scissors. Optional: different coloured collage materials (Book 1, p. 255) and glue.*

✝ Invite the children to decorate mini wooden chalices and patens. *Provide felt tip pens or good quality pencils, wooden mini cups and plates. At St Peter's, Walworth, we use wooden egg cups and coasters, available from Baker Ross; check other online stockists and craft shops.*

✝ Give the children the opportunity to create their own artwork of Jesus' Last Supper. Show them examples of famous or local paintings then encourage them to use these as a starting point to paint or draw their own picture. *Provide paper, paints/pastels, famous paintings for inspiration (e.g. The Last Supper by Leonardo da Vinci, Joos van Cleve, Hans Holbein the Younger, Fra Angelico). Optional: picture frame template (p. 384 or website) or an 'icon background' (a piece of card wrapped in tinfoil that's slightly larger than the paper provided).*

### Tip

At St Peter's, Walworth, we use compostable paper cups for our tea and coffee after the Sunday service. These can easily be drawn on with pencils, crayons or pens and come in useful for all sorts of things, including as compostable plant pots!

# Sensory Starter Ideas (including for babies and toddlers)

You could provide:

✝ a plastic or soft donkey;

✝ a Jesus figure (we use Joseph from our nativity set);

✝ child-safe crosses (holding crosses are particularly appropriate);

✝ wooden/metal or other child-safe cup and plate or chalice and paten for children to explore and tell the story of Jesus' Last Meal. Alternatively you could provide wooden egg cups and coasters (at St Peter's, Walworth, we source them from Baker Ross, but check other online suppliers and craft shops);

✝ purple imaginative aids;

✝ if your church ashes people on Ash Wednesday, you could provide a bowl of ash in a little oil for the children to explore, plus dolls or 'small world' people (see p. 95) that can receive an ash cross on their forehead;

✝ building blocks to build Jerusalem, the Temple or the tallest tower from the Jesus is Tested in the Wilderness, or other creations;

✝ resources for exploring real footwashing (a bowl of water and towel) or roleplaying footwashing (a bowl filled with blue fabric, a doll/teddy and towel);

✝ if you've used a wilderness tray and Jesus figure in the last unit, you could make it available for the children to explore for themselves towards the beginning of Lent (make sure the rocks/pebbles don't present a choking hazard);

✝ if your group is using a 'sorry tree' (p. 105) or 'prayer tree' (p. 110) during the session in Lent, you could leave this and tissue paper available for the children to continue adding their prayers or 'sorries' during the Creative Response time;

✝ board books that tell the story of Jesus' Last Week;

✝ dressing up: robes (to look like important people and to throw down before Jesus), palm leaves, cow and sheep masks, a till with money (for Jesus cleaning the Temple);

✝ playdough plus shape cutters of the animals that feature in the unit's stories (donkeys, cows, sheep, hens, chicks), people shape cutters and modelling tools if you have them;

✝ animal jigsaws or plastic models of the animals that feature in the unit's stories (donkeys, cows, sheep, hens, chicks);

✝ palm leaves and/or palm crosses for the children to explore;

✝ books with pictures of ancient Jerusalem;

✝ small tree branches that are growing spring leaves and/or blossom. You could take these out of water for the session itself for the children to explore, but replace them in water between sessions. Different branches for the children to compare and contrast would be wonderful.

# Unit Starter Ideas

✝ An important theme of Lent in Diddy Disciples is that God can create beautiful things from what looks like rubbish. Invite the children to use recyclable materials to create amazing sculptures. *Provide recycling materials such as boxes, tubes, cartons, egg boxes, paper, etc., along with masking tape, string, glue sticks.*

✝ Another important Lenten theme is saying sorry to God and letting God make us clean again. Invite the children to help you clean out and tidy your group's resources or meeting space. *Provide (for example): damp cloths or wipes, brushes and dustpans, grimy resources (you could always add grime!), resources that need tidying and organizing, crayons/pens/pencils that need sorting, appropriate silver and a soft cloth, or ask those who clean your meeting space or church for more ideas. If appropriate in your space, you could even provide a water tray with soapy water.*

✝ Invite some of the children to help sharpen pencils/crayons then to use the sharpenings to create pictures. *Provide pencils (good quality pencils/crayons make this easier as the wood or wax doesn't disintegrate on sharpening), sharpeners, paper, PVA glue and glue sticks.*

✝ If your church ashes people on Ash Wednesday, you could invite the children to decorate then ash a person template. Who will their person look like? *Provide body templates (p. 366 or website), crayons/ pencils/paints/pastels, scissors plus a bowl of ash and a drop of water/oil.*

✝ Give the children the opportunity to contribute to the group's resources by transforming used patterned paper, sweet wrappers, etc., into collage materials for the group to create. Invite the children to cut the paper into squares and other shapes, then to sort them into different containers. *Provide a range of recyclable materials that can become collage materials (Book 1, p. 255). You could even encourage them to bring recyclable material to contribute themselves the next time they come.*

✝ Invite the children to make a picture of themselves in one of the stories you've told together. *Provide body templates (p. 366 or website) and pencils/crayons/paints. If it's Palm Sunday, you may also like to provide real or paper leaves and glue so the children can add leaves to their creations.*

✝ Lent means 'springtime'. Give the children the opportunity to plant seeds and watch them grow. *Provide plant pots, recyclable containers, appropriate compost/soil, seeds/bulbs.*

✝ Give the children the opportunity to witness new life growing from 'rubbish'. Invite the children to decorate a recyclable container that can act as a plant pot with collage materials. When they're ready, invite them to place a few pieces of folded paper towel and a discarded carrot top (top upwards) in the container. When they get home, they can put a little water on the paper towel and keep it damp (not soaked). Green leaves will grow up from the carrot top! *Provide recyclable containers, collage materials (Book 1, p. 255), glue, paper towel (or cotton wool), discarded carrot tops.*

✝ Invite the children to explore different tree branches that are growing spring leaves or blossom. *Provide a range of tree branches (take these out of water for the session), notepads and pencils to take notes or make observational drawings, rulers, scales, magnifying glasses, torches, even a child microscope if you have one.*

✝ Invite the children to make a spring scene picture or their own mini spring garden in a box using real materials. *Provide either paper and glue or small boxes (e.g. recyclable tubs) plus natural materials such as grass, leaves, twigs, fallen blossom, etc. If you have a churchyard, you could even go and find some spring materials together there.*

✝ Give the children the opportunity to make a Lent or Holy Week wheel to tell six stories from Holy Week, with an arrow to move around the stories. At St Peter's, Walworth, we depict the following six stories: Jesus Enters Jerusalem (Palm Sunday), Jesus Cleans the Temple, Jesus Washes the Disciples' Feet, the Last Supper, the Crucifixion and Easter Day. Your group of children may like to choose differently. *Provide wheel with arrow template (p. 390 or website), paper fasteners, pencils/crayons]/pens.*

Section 3: Creative Response starter ideas

## Prayer

✝ Invite the children to make their own 2D version of your group's sorry/prayer tree. *Provide bare tree template (p. 364 or website) plus glue and squares of white/pink tissue paper (prayer tree) or crumpled and torn white/pink tissue paper (sorry tree).*

✝ Give the children the opportunity to make their own 3D version of your group's sorry/prayer tree. *Provide appropriate twigs plus glue and squares of white/pink tissue paper (prayer tree) or crumpled and torn white/pink tissue paper (sorry tree).*

✝ Invite one or more children to create a prayer space for Lent (or beyond) in the room in which you hold your session. Encourage them to find or make symbols or pictures to place in the prayer space that help them feel close to God. This 'prayer space' could be packed into a box at the end of each session and re-created (the same or different) during the Creative Response each week. *Provide a wide range of materials and objects for the children to choose from: Bible, books, crosses, candles, pictures, icons, flowers, paper, crayons/pencils/pastels, recyclable materials, etc.*

✝ Give the children the opportunity to draw or paint a picture of a place where they feel close to God in a picture frame. *Provide picture frame template (p. 384 or website), paints/pastels/pencils/crayons.*

## The Way of the Cross

See Week 1 for simple ideas, or try one of the following:

✝ Give the children the opportunity to make a stained glass cross. Invite them to glue brightly coloured tissue/cellophane/crepe paper to cross-shaped wax/baking paper. *Provide scissors, glue and brightly coloured tissue/crepe/cellophane paper (e.g. transparent sweet wrappers) plus baking/wax paper (the whiter the better, but brown paper still works) in the shape of a cross. You (or older children) can make a cross shape by folding square or rectangular wax/baking paper into quarters then cutting an L-shape into it (making sure you don't cut into any side that's a fold).*

✝ Invite the children to make a cross with playdough, salt dough or airdrying clay. They may also like to etch patterns into it. *Provide playdough, salt dough (Book 1, p. 257) or airdrying clay, clay modelling tools or plastic (safe) knives and forks.*

# UNIT 4

# JESUS IS ALIVE! ALLELUIA! (EASTER)

The Jesus is Alive! unit gathers together some of the most famous Bible stories about the Risen Jesus. It invites the children to stand alongside the loyal women at the tomb, the confused friends on the road to Emmaus, the conflicted Peter who has betrayed his friend and teacher, and the amazed disciples as they encounter Jesus, risen from the dead. Many of these stories are from John's Gospel and include some of the most beautiful storytelling in the New Testament.

The unit ends (after Jesus Goes Up! in Week 7) with the extraordinary arrival of the Holy Spirit on the Day of Pentecost (Week 8). It also includes extra material for Trinity Sunday, giving the children the opportunity to explore the creative relationships between God the Father, Jesus Christ and the Holy Spirit.

## Tip

Throughout this unit, we have an Easter Garden at St Peter's visible on our focal table. This Easter Garden can be as simple as a large hollowed rock to show the tomb (or cave) with a stone to the side. At times we've added grass (either real turf or greengrocer's 'grass') or used a flowerpot (on its side and covered with grass) for the tomb. In some years, we've used one of the simple Easter Gardens made and donated by the children (see p. 205). In others, we've planted a larger garden together on Good Friday with mini rosemary bushes for the Garden of Gethsemane, three crosses on a hill for Golgotha and a rock and stone for the Easter tomb surrounded by mini daffodils. Choose what's right for your group.

## Section 1

# The Building Blocks: Jesus Is Alive! Alleluia! unit

Pick and choose from these Building Blocks and their various options to build sessions for your group. Whatever choices you make, we suggest you keep to that pattern for the whole of the unit as this will open up opportunities for the children to participate fully and confidently during your time together.

> **Build your own Diddy Disciples session** (Book 1, p. 6) provides an overview of the Building Blocks and a short introduction to fitting them together, along with examples.
>
> **Guide to the Building Blocks** (Book 1, p. 217) provides a step-by-step guide to each Building Block.

## Welcome

→ **Guide: Book 1, p. 218**

*Welcome your group.*

Let's start by going around the circle
And saying our name out loud.
My name's _____.

*Go around the circle so that every adult and child has the chance to say his or her name (and introduce any dolls, teddies, or toys). If any of the children don't want to say their name or aren't able to, you (or a parent or carer) could say it for them and wave.*

It's time to sing our Welcome Song!

## Welcome Song: Option 1

→ Song: 'The Diddy Disciples welcome song'. Words: © Sharon Moughtin-Mumby
→ Tune: 'Glory, glory, alleluia!' (traditional). For the music see p. 357, or for a taster see the Diddy Disciples website. For tips on teaching songs for the first time, see Book 1, p. 215.

*Go around the circle the same way as above. See if you can remember each other's names and insert them into the song.*

Welcome *Name 1* to *St Peter's\**
Welcome *Name 2* to *St Peter's\**
Welcome *Name 3* to *St Peter's\**
**You are welcome in the name of the Lord!**

*\* Insert the name of your church or children's group, or sing 'our worship'.*

## Welcome Song: Option 2

→ Song: 'You are welcome in the name of the Lord' (traditional)
→ Tune: traditional. For the music see p. 360, or for a taster see the Diddy Disciples website. For tips on teaching songs for the first time, see Book 1, p. 215.

Let's wave with one hand. *Lead waving*
Then with our other hand. *Lead waving*
Then let's choose someone and show God's 'glory'!
*Move arms up and down in front of you with fingers wiggling, palms facing out, towards one person.*
And someone else! *Repeat*
Then let's wave with both hands all around the circle.
*Lead waving.*

150

We're ready to sing!

**You are welcome in the name of the Lord!**
*Wave with right hand to one person.*
**You are welcome in the name of the Lord!**
*Wave with left hand to another person.*
**I can see all over you, the glory of the Lord!**
*Move arms up and down in front of you with fingers wiggling,*
*palms facing out, towards one person and then another.*
**You are welcome in the name of the Lord!**
*Wave with both hands all around the circle.*

# Getting Ready to Worship

→ **Guide: Book 1, p. 218**

*Choose one of the following greetings according to which greeting is familiar in your church. (If your church uses a different greeting, you could use that here instead.)*

## Getting Ready to Worship: Option 1

→ **Action: the sign of the cross. Words: © Sharon Moughtin-Mumby**

*Invite the children to make the sign of the cross slowly with you. As the children become more confident, invite a child to lead the action as the whole group says the words and makes the sign of the cross.*

| | |
|---|---|
| **In my head,** | *touch head* |
| **in my heart,** | *touch chest* |
| **and all around me,** | *touch shoulders one by one* |
| **Jesus is here.** | *open hands in front, facing upwards* |

## Getting Ready to Worship: Option 2

→ **Action: 'The Lord be with you' (open hands)**

Let's start by clenching our hands together tightly.

*Lead children in clenching fists against your body to show a defensive posture.*

When we close ourselves up like this,
it's hard to let anyone into our heart.
It's hard even to let God into our heart!

When we get ready to worship,
we show that we're open to God and to each other.

*Open your hands out, facing up.*

Can you show me your open hands?
We're ready to let God and each other in!

The Lord be with you.
*Hold hands open to the children.*

**And also with you.**
*Invite the children to open their hands towards you.*

# Introducing the Unit

→ **Guide: Book 1, p. 218**

## Introducing the Unit: Option 1

*If your group is using an Easter Garden (see p. 149), place it in the middle of the circle.*
Can anyone tell me what this is?
*Accept children's responses and ways of naming the garden.*
This is our Easter Garden
with the dark cave in the middle.

We're telling the stories of what happened
when Jesus burst from the 'tomb', the dark cave.
and won a new start for us.

*If your church shouts a special 'Alleluia!' at Easter, you could introduce it here. Examples follow, but adapt these to introduce the children to the words that they will hear around them in your church services. Encourage them to join in in church, too!*
We celebrate Easter with the Church's special shout of joy:
Alleluia!

*Either:*
When I say, 'The Lord is risen!',
can you shout: **'He is risen indeed, Alleluia!'**

The Lord is risen!
**He is risen indeed, Alleluia!**
*Repeat until the children are confident.*

*Or:* When I say, 'Praise the Lord!'
can you shout: **'Alleluia!'**

Praise the Lord!
**Alleluia!**
*Repeat until the children are confident.*

## Introducing the Unit: Option 2

→ **Focus: the liturgical colour, white and gold and 'Alleluia!'**

Can anyone tell me what colour season we're in now?

*If appropriate:* You may have seen it in church.

*Accept responses.*

At the moment, the Church is in Easter!
The special colours of Easter are white and gold!
The colours of joy and celebration!

*If your group is using an Easter Garden (see p. 149), place it in the middle of the circle.*
Can anyone tell me what this is?
*Accept children's responses and ways of naming the garden.*
This is our Easter Garden
with the dark cave in the middle.

At Easter, we celebrate Jesus
bursting from the 'tomb', the dark cave,
and winning a new start for us.

We celebrate Easter with the Church's special shout of joy:
Alleluia!

*Either:*
When I say, 'The Lord is risen!',
can you shout: **'He is risen indeed, Alleluia!'**

The Lord is risen!
**He is risen indeed, Alleluia!**
*Repeat until the children are confident.*

*Or:* When I say, 'Praise the Lord!'
can you shout: **'Alleluia!'**

Praise the Lord!
**Alleluia!**
*Repeat until the children are confident.*

At Easter, we celebrate Jesus bursting out of the dark cave
and winning new life for all of us!

# Gathering Song

→ **Guide: Book 1, p. 219**

*Choose from one of the Gathering Song options below.*

## Gathering Song: Option 1

→ **Tune: 'Wide awake' © Mollie Russell-Smith and Geoffrey Russell-Smith, also known as 'The dingle, dangle scarecrow'. It is now published by EMI Harmonies Ltd. For a taster see the Diddy Disciples website.**

*Skip this Gathering Song in Week 1 as it features as part of the Interactive Bible Storytelling. Even if you're not using Week 1, see the material on p. 171 for learning this song for the first time. For the music see p. 170.*

Let's tell the story of Easter Day with our song.

On Good Friday, Jesus died on the cross.
Let's hold our hands out in love like Jesus on the cross.
*Lead the children in stretching arms out to the side.*

His friends took Jesus' body down from the cross.
Let's be Jesus' friends.
*Lead the children in miming holding Jesus' body gently.*

They put it gently into the dark cave
*Lead the children in miming placing Jesus' body in the tomb,*
and rolled the stone across.
*Lead the children in rolling a large stone across.*

They went home feeling very, very, very sad.
Nothing happened for one whole night and day after that.
But then the night after, something very, very special . . .
something amazing happened!

*Lead the children in curling up on the floor or crouching to sing:*
**When all the world was sleeping**
**and the sun had gone to bed . . .**
**up jumped Lord Jesus** *jump up with hands in the air*
**and this is what he said:** *hands out, palms up*
**'I am risen, risen, risen,** *wave hands high in the air*
**I have won us a new start!** *'New Start' sign (see p. 355) over head*
**I am risen, risen, risen,** *wave hands high in the air*
**I have won us a new start!'** *'New Start' sign over head*
*Repeat.*

## Gathering Song: Option 2

We're going to sing a song
that is full of the Church's 'Alleluia!' shout of joy now.

*If your group is singing this song for the first time, you may find the following introduction helpful.*
Let's learn the words to a new song,
'my turn' *point to self*, 'your turn' *leader's hands out to group.*

*Singing:* 'Allelu, allelu, allelu, alleluia!
Let's praise the Lord!
**Allelu, allelu, allelu, alleluia!**
**Let's praise the Lord!**
*And again:* 'Allelu, allelu, allelu, alleluia!
Let's praise the Lord!
**Allelu, allelu, allelu, alleluia!**
**Let's praise the Lord!**

Then our words go the other way around!
*Singing:* Let's praise the Lord! Alleluia!
Let's praise the Lord! Alleluia!
**Let's praise the Lord! Alleluia!**
**Let's praise the Lord! Alleluia!**

*Singing:* Let's praise the Lord! Alleluia!
Let's praise the Lord!
**Let's praise the Lord! Alleluia!**
**Let's praise the Lord!**

Let's try that all together.
**Allelu, allelu, allelu, alleluia!**
**Let's praise the Lord!**
**Allelu, allelu, allelu, alleluia!**
**Let's praise the Lord!**
**Let's praise the Lord! Alleluia!**
**Let's praise the Lord! Alleluia!**
**Let's praise the Lord! Alleluia!**
**Let's praise the Lord!**
*Repeat until the children are confident. If you feel the group is ready, you could split the group as indicated below, or you may like to leave this for another week.*

We're going to split into two groups.
*Split the group in half, making sure there are confident singers in both groups.*
Over here *indicate clearly* is the 'Alleluia!' team.
Over here *indicate clearly* is the 'Let's praise!' team.

You're going to sing the 'Alleluias!' *Point to the 'Alleluia!' team*
You're going to sing the 'Let's praise the Lords!' *Point*

When you're singing, you can stand up!
When you're not singing, sit down again!

And remember. We're going to show 'Alleluia!' with our whole body.
Let's raise our hands to sing 'Alleluia!' and 'Praise the Lord!' *Arms in 'V' shape*

Let's go:
**Allelu, allelu, allelu, alleluia!** *'Alleluia!' team stand to sing with arms raised*
**Let's praise the Lord!** *'Let's praise' team stand to sing with arms raised*
**Allelu, allelu, allelu, alleluia!** *'Alleluia!' team stand to sing with arms raised*
**Let's praise the Lord!** *'Let's praise' team stand to sing with arms raised*

154

**Let's praise the Lord!** *'Let's praise' team continue standing to sing with arms raised*

**Alleluia!** *'Alleluia!' team stand to sing with arms raised*

**Let's praise the Lord!** *'Let's praise' team stand to sing with arms raised*

**Alleluia!** *'Alleluia!' team stand to sing with arms raised*

**Let's praise the Lord!** *'Let's praise' team stand to sing with arms raised*

*Repeat.*

# Getting Ready for Bible Storytelling

→ Guide: Book 1, p. 220

## Getting Ready for Bible Storytelling: Option 1

→ Action: opening your group's box and naming this week's object
→ Guide: Book 1, p. 221

*See the beginning of the weekly storytelling material for ideas of items to place in your box. Invite one of the children to open the box.*

What's in the box? *Ask the child to respond.*

## Getting Ready for Bible Storytelling: Option 2

→ Song: 'Jesus, open up my eyes'. Words: © Sharon Moughtin-Mumby
→ Tune: 'Michael, row the boat ashore' (traditional). For the music see p. 359, or for a taster see the Diddy Disciples website. For tips on teaching songs for the first time, see Book 1, p. 215.

It's time to open the Bible.
Let's get ready!
Let's take our thumb *Lead children in showing thumb*
and draw our cross on our eyes, *Draw cross*
and our lips, *Draw cross*
and our heart. *Draw cross*
Let's ask Jesus to help us get ready to listen out for God!

**Jesus, open up my eyes. Alleluia!**
*Trace a cross between your eyes.*
**Jesus, open up my lips. Alleluia!**
*Trace a cross on your lips.*
**Jesus, open up my heart. Alleluia!**
*Trace a cross on your heart.*
**Jesus, help me hear your voice. Alleluia!**
*Cup your hands behind your ears.*

# Interactive Bible Storytelling

→ Guide: Book 1, p. 221

*See the Bible Storytelling material in Section 2 of this unit.*

# Saying Sorry to God

→ Guide: Book 1, p. 223

*Invite the children to sit in a circle for a moment of quiet.*
Jesus burst from the dark cave.
Jesus showed us how strong love is!

But we don't always love like God loves. *Shake head*
Sometimes we get it wrong and make God or other people sad.
It's time to sing our Sorry Song.

## Saying Sorry to God: Option 1

→ Song: 'The Diddy Disciples sorry song'. Words: © Sharon Moughtin-Mumby
→ Tune: © Sharon Moughtin-Mumby. For the music see p. 356, or for a taster see the Diddy Disciples website. For a description of the 'I'm Sorry' and 'New Start' signs, see p. 355 or the website. For tips on teaching songs for the first time, see Book 1, p. 215.

Let's put our hands on our head.
I wonder if there's anything we've thought this week
that we wish we hadn't thought?

*Lead the children in placing your hands on head, singing:*
**With my hands on my head,**
**I remember the things I've thought today,**
**I remember the things I wish I'd thought a different way.**

**I'm sorry, I'm sorry,** *Diddy Disciples 'I'm Sorry' sign twice (see p. 355)*
**I wish I could start again.** *Diddy Disciples 'New Start' sign (see p. 355)*
**I'm sorry, I'm sorry,** *'I'm Sorry' sign twice*
**I wish I could start again.** *'New Start' sign*

Let's put our hands by our mouths.
I wonder if there's anything we've said this week
that we wish we hadn't said?

*With hands by mouth, singing:*
**With my hands on my mouth,**
**I remember the things I've said today,**
**I remember the things I wish I'd said a different way.**

**I'm sorry, I'm sorry,** *'I'm Sorry' sign twice*
**I wish I could start again.** *'New Start' sign*
**I'm sorry, I'm sorry,** *'I'm Sorry' sign twice*
**I wish I could start again.** *'New Start' sign*

Let's cross our hands on our chest.
I wonder if there's anything we've done this week
that we wish we hadn't done?

*With hands crossed on chest, singing:*
**With my hands on my chest,**
**I remember the things I've done today,**
**I remember the things I wish I'd done a different way.**

**I'm sorry, I'm sorry,** *'I'm Sorry' sign twice*
**I wish I could start again.** *'New Start' sign*
**I'm sorry, I'm sorry,** *'I'm Sorry' sign twice*
**I wish I could start again.** *'New Start' sign*

*Continue with a Saying Sorry Action or move straight to God Gives Us a New Start, below.*

## Saying Sorry to God: Option 2

→ Song: 'We need a new start'. Words: © Sharon Moughtin-Mumby
→ Tune: 'Molly Malone' (traditional). For the music see p. 356, or for a taster see the Diddy Disciples website. For tips on teaching songs for the first time, see Book 1, p. 215. For a description of the 'I'm Sorry' and 'New Start' signs, see p. 355 or the website.

### Tip

This song can be sung using 'we're sorry' as indicated, or as 'I'm sorry', adapting the material accordingly.

Let's put our hands on our head.
I wonder if there's anything we've thought this week
that we wish we hadn't thought?

*Lead the children in placing your hands on head, singing:*
**For the things we have thou-ght**
**that we wish we'd not thou-ght,**
**we're sor-ry, we're sor-ry.** *Diddy Disciples 'I'm Sorry' sign twice (see p. 355)*
**We need a new start.** *Diddy Disciples 'New Start' sign (see p. 355)*

Let's put our hands by our mouths.
I wonder if there's anything we've said this week
that we wish we hadn't said?

*With hands by mouth, singing:*
**For the things we have sa-id**
**that we wish we'd not sa-id,**
**we're sor-ry, we're sor-ry.** *'I'm Sorry' sign twice*
**We need a new start.** *'New Start' sign*

Let's cross our hands on our chest.
I wonder if there's anything we've done this week
that we wish we hadn't done?

*With hands crossed on chest, singing:*
**For the things we have do-ne**
**that we wish we'd not do-ne,**
**we're sor-ry, we're sor-ry.** *'I'm Sorry' sign twice*
**We need a new start.** *'New Start' sign*

*Continue with a Saying Sorry Action or move straight to God Gives Us a New Start, below.*

# Saying Sorry Action

→ **Guide: Book 1, p. 223**

*For alternative actions that can be used during any unit at any time of year, see Saying Sorry Actions: Options 2, 3 and 4 on pp. 40–2 of Book 1.*

## Saying Sorry Action: Option 1

→ **Action: bursting out of a 'dark cave'**

When we do things that make God or other people sad,
it can make us feel like we're in a dark cave.
Let's curl up in a ball as if we're inside a dark cave
feeling sad and lost.
*Lead the children in curling up on the floor, or crouching.*

Jesus' love is stronger than the dark!
Jesus burst out from the dark cave!
We can burst from OUR dark caves with Jesus.

After 3, let's get ready to burst out of our cave with Jesus.
Let's jump and shout, 'Alleluia! God gives me a new start!'
**1, 2, 3 . . .** *Lead the children in jumping up with hands in the air*
**Alleluia! God gives me a new start!**

## Saying Sorry Action: Option 2

→ **Action: dipping finger in water and drawing a cross on forehead**

*This option is particularly appropriate for churches that use sprinkling with water ('asperges') during Easter.*

*If relevant, it's particularly appropriate to use the same water that will be used in your main church service.*

*If there's an older child present who is unlikely to spill the water you could invite her or him to take the water around the circle. You may wish to ask more than one child to take bowls around the circle, going opposite ways or starting at different points in the circle. Alternatively take a bowl around yourself and/or ask adults to help.*

At Easter, we remember our baptism!
The special moment when we promised to follow Jesus
and to love everyone as Jesus loves.

We sprinkle everyone with water
to help us remember when water was sprinkled on our head.
*Mime sprinkling water.*

> *If appropriate (adapt accordingly):*
> Did you see the water being sprinkled in church?
> *Or:* Right now the adults are being sprinkled with water!

*Name* is going to bring this bowl of water around.
If you like, you can dip your finger into it *show finger*
and draw a cross on your forehead. *Demonstrate*

Let's remember our baptism
and our promise to follow Jesus.
If you haven't been baptized,
you could ask God
to help you get ready for baptism.

*While this takes place, lead the group in either:*
> *Option 1: singing the 'I'm sorry' refrain, or*
> *Option 2: humming the first two lines of the 'We need a new start' song, followed by singing the refrain 'We're sorry, we're sorry. We need a new start'.*

*When the group is ready:*
The Good News is:
God always wants to give us a new start!
After 3, let's shout, 'God gives us a new start!'
1, 2, 3: **God gives us a new start!**

Let's use our new start to follow Jesus.

## Saying Sorry Action: Option 3

→ **Action: placing coloured tissue paper on a cross (on a tray if it will be carried around the group) or an Easter Garden (see p. 149)**

*Invite two children to give out pieces of coloured tissue paper.*
*Name* and *Name* are going to bring around some paper.
If you like, you can take a piece and hold it in the air
to show that there are things that you wish you hadn't done.

*As the paper is given out, lead the group in either*
> *Option 1: singing the 'I'm sorry' refrain, or*
> *Option 2: humming the first two lines of the 'We need a new start' song, followed by singing the refrain 'We're sorry, we're sorry. We need a new start'.*

*When the group is ready:*
When we do things that make God or other people sad,

it can make us feel sad and cross inside.

Let's crumple our paper up to show how we can feel

when we know we've made someone feel sad.

Let's put our feelings into the paper.

Jesus' love was stronger than *either* the dark cave *or* the cross,

and stronger than every wrong thing.

Jesus' love is so strong that it can change

even dark things into beautiful things.

As we sing, let's give our paper and feelings to God.

Let's put it on *either* our empty cave *or* our cross.

*As leader, place your paper on the garden/cross as an example.*

Look! The paper looks like little flowers

springing up to new life.

Let's watch God's love changing *either* the dark cave *or* the cross

into something beautiful with our sorries.

*Lead the group in singing again as the paper is placed. Some groups may like to ask two children to take the cross or garden around the group as you sing so the other children can stay in their places. Once the paper has been collected, the cross or garden can then be placed in the centre of the circle.*

*When the group is ready:*

Look at our beautiful garden/cross!

After 3, let's shout, 'Alleluia! *Hands raised* God gives me a new start!

**1, 2, 3 . . . Alleluia!** *Hands raised* **God gives me a new start!**

## Saying Sorry Action: Option 4

→ **Action: sunbathing in God's love**

*Optional:*

→ **Song: 'Alleluia! Jesus Christ, the Son, is ris'n!'** Words: © Sharon Moughtin-Mumby

→ **Tune: 'If you're happy and you know it, clap your hands'** (traditional).

> There is a uniquely English traditional wordplay on the 'Son rising' and the 'sun rising' on Easter Day that's worth celebrating!

When we do things that make God or other people sad,

it can make us feel dark inside,

like the sun's stopped shining.

Let's close our eyes and feel the dark.

*Lead the children in closing eyes for a moment.*

On Easter Day, Jesus 'rose',
like the sun 'rises' in the morning!

Let's open our eyes and show the light of God's love
rising like the sun.
Let's crouch down low . . .
*Lead the children in crouching down.*
Let's show the sun coming up and up and out . . .
in the morning:
*lead the children in showing the sun rising with your hands as you stand up: holding hands together in front of your chest then reaching up and out*
up, and up, and out!

Now let's hold our faces up to the sun
and imagine the God's love,
warm and bright,
shining on our face and body,
and all over us like the warm sun!
Let's hold our arms out.
*Lead the children in holding arms forwards with hands up.*
Imagine sunbathing in the warm light of God!

> *Optional:*
> *Lead the children in singing:*
> **Alleluia! Jesus Christ, the Son, is ris'n!**
> **Alleluia! Jesus Christ, the Son, is ris'n!**
> **And God's love will shine on us!**
> **God's love will shine on us!**
> **Alleluia! Jesus Christ, the Son, is ris'n!**
>
> *When learning this song for the first time, you could teach it 'my turn', 'your turn' first.*
>
> Let's learn a song about sunbathing in God's love!

> " There's something about sunbathing that tells us more about what prayer is like than any amount of religious jargon. When you're lying on the beach or under the lamp, something is happening, something that has nothing to do with how you feel or how hard you're trying. You're not going to get a better tan by screwing up your eyes and concentrating. You give the time, and that's it. All you have to do is turn up. And then things change, at their own pace. You simply have to be there where the light can get at you . . .
>
> [To pray] all you need to do is to be where the light can get at you – in this case, the light of God's love. Give the time and let go of trying hard (actually this is the difficult bit). God is there always. You don't need to fight for his attention or make yourself acceptable. He's glad to see you. And he'll make a difference while you're not watching, just by radiating who and what he is in your direction. All he asks is that you stay there with him for a while, in the light. For the rest, you just trust him to get on with it.
>
> ARCHBISHOP ROWAN WILLIAMS[3] "

## Saying Sorry Action: Option 5

→ **Action: placing small 'x' shapes on a cross or Easter Garden (see p. 149)**

*For groups with school-aged children, who might be familiar with the idea of an 'x' and 'getting it wrong'.*

## Tip

At St Peter's, Walworth, we use pipe cleaners twisted into the shape of the cross or small twigs in an 'x shape' fastened with pipe cleaners. We tried making these during the Sorry Action with the children, but it was too fiddly to do in this prayerful context for this age group. If you like, however, you could make the crosses together in place of a Creative Response early in the unit.

Sometimes it can feel like we've got it wrong.
*Name* and *Name* are going to bring around a basket of 'x's as we sing.
If you like, you can take an 'x' shape
and hold it up to show
you know you've got some things wrong.
*Model holding up the 'x' show it looks like an 'x' (and not Jesus' cross).*

*As the crosses are given out, lead the group holding up their 'x' and either*

>  Option 1: singing the 'I'm sorry' refrain, or
>  Option 2: humming the first two lines of the 'We need a new start' song, followed by singing the refrain 'We're sorry, we're sorry. We need a new start'.

*When the group is ready:*
We all do things that are wrong.
When Jesus died,
he took all our wrong things onto HIS cross.
Jesus' cross is our cross as well.

Let's turn our 'x' shapes around . . .
*Lead the children in turning the 'x' shape around to look like a † shape.*
Look! They look like Jesus' cross!
Let's give our 'x's to Jesus
and make his cross into our cross too.

*Lead the group in singing again as the crosses are placed on either your Easter Garden next to Jesus' cross, or onto a larger cross. Some groups may like to ask two children to carry the garden or cross around the circle on a tray to collect the little crosses. The garden/cross can then be placed in the centre of the circle.*

*When the group is ready:*

If we give our cross to Jesus,
the dark cave becomes our dark cave too!

Let's curl up in the dark cave with Jesus.
*Lead the children in curling up on the floor.*

After 3, let's burst out of the cave with Jesus.
Let's shout, 'Alleluia! *Hands raised* God gives me a new start!'
**1, 2, 3: Alleluia! God gives me a new start!**

# God Gives Us a New Start

→ **Guide: Book 1, p. 225**

*Every time of Saying Sorry should end by assuring the children that God gives them a new start. Most Diddy Disciples Saying Sorry Actions already include this promise of a new start. If they don't – or if you've created your own Saying Sorry Action – you should choose from one of the following New Start options, or create your own assurance of forgiveness. You could also choose to move straight from the Sorry Song to God's promise of a new start, without any Saying Sorry Action.*

## New Start Action: Option 1

→ **Action: tracing a cross/smile on each other's forehead**

The Good News is:
God always wants to give us a new start!

Let's turn to the person next to us
and show that God gives us a new start.
Let's take our thumb/finger *show thumb/finger*
and draw a cross/smile on that person's forehead *Draw a cross/smile in the air*

> *If your group is drawing a smile, add:*
> to show that God is very happy with us!

Let's say, 'God gives you a new start!'
Then let the other person give you a new start, too!

*When the group is ready:*
Let's use our new start to share God's love this week!

## New Start Action: Option 2

→ **Action: standing up and hugging each other**

The Good News is:
God always wants to give us a new start!

Let's help someone next to us stand up from the floor.
Then let that person help you stand up too!
*Lead the children in helping each other stand up.*

Then let's give each other a hug and say:
'God gives you a new start!'

*When the group is ready:*
Let's use our new start to share God's love this week!

## New Start Action: Option 3

→ **Song: 'God loves to give me a new start!' Words: © Sharon Moughtin-Mumby**
→ **Tune: 'Give me oil in my lamp' (traditional). For the music see p. 357, or for a taster see the Diddy Disciples website. For tips on teaching songs for the first time, see Book 1, p. 215.**

The Good News is:
God always wants to give us a new start!
Let's sing our New Start song together.

**[Yes, my] God loves to give me a new start!** *Trace a smile/cross on own forehead*
**How amazing is God's love for me!** *Cross hands on chest*
**[Yes, my] God loves to give me a new start!** *Trace a smile/cross on own forehead*
**How amazing is God's love for me!**

**Sing hosanna! Sing hosanna!** *Wave hands in the air*
**Sing hosanna to the King of Kings!**
*Wave hands in the air followed by crown on head.*
**Sing hosanna! Sing hosanna!** *Wave hands in the air*
**Sing hosanna to the King!**
*Wave hands in the air followed by crown on head.*

# Introduction to Prayers

It's time for us to bring our prayers to the Risen Jesus,
who loves to meet with us.

# Prayers for Other People

→ Guide: Book 1, p. 223 and p. 225

*Invite the children to sit in a circle in a moment of quiet.*

Let's imagine holding our prayer gently,

*hands together gently in traditional prayer gesture, but cupped so you can imagine a prayer inside*

and then let it go up in prayer to God.

*Hands opened upwards to God*

> *If you're using Option 1:*
> Jesus *hands together, cupped*
> hear our prayer *hands opened upwards to God*
> Let's pray . . .

## Prayers for Other People: Option 1

→ Song: 'Jesus, hear our prayer!' Words: © Sharon Moughtin-Mumby
→ Tune: 'Brown girl in the ring' (traditional). For the music see p. 358, or for a taster see the Diddy Disciples website. For similar words designed to fit with the alternative tune 'He's got the whole world in his hands', see p. 359. For tips on teaching songs for the first time, see Book 1, p. 215.

| | |
|---|---|
| **For the world:** | **Jesus, hear our prayer!** |
| *Make a circle shape* | *Open hands upwards to God* |
| **For the Church:** | **Jesus, hear our prayer!** |
| *Praying hands* | *Open hands upwards to God* |
| **For our place,** *Walworth*\* | **Jesus, hear our prayer!** |
| *Hands down moving out in* | *Open hands upwards to God* |
| *a semi-circle to show the land around us* | |
| **Lord Jesus, hear our prayer. Amen.** | *Open hands upwards to God* |

\* *Insert local area/school/church/community/parish.*

| | |
|---|---|
| **For the sick and lonely:** | **Jesus, hear our prayer!** |
| *Fingers showing tears falling* | *Open hands upwards to God* |
| *down cheeks* | |
| **For our friends and family:** | |
| **Jesus, hear our prayer!** | |
| *Arms around yourself* | *Open hands upwards to God* |
| **For ourselves:** | **Jesus, hear our prayer!** |
| *Both hands on heart* | *Open hands upwards to God* |
| **Lord Jesus, hear our prayer. Amen.** | |
| *Open hands upwards to God* | |

Let's close our eyes for a moment.
I wonder if there's someone special
you'd like to pray for?
Let's imagine that person now.

Now, let's imagine Jesus coming to them.
Does Jesus say anything?
Does Jesus do anything?
Let's open our eyes.

*Continue with one of the Prayer Action options outlined below. Once the Prayer Action has been completed, you may like to use the following verse, to close this time of prayer.*

| | |
|---|---|
| **Take our prayers:** | **Jesus, hear our prayer!** |
| *Hands together gently* | *Open hands upwards to God* |
| **Make them holy:** | **Jesus, hear our prayer!** |
| *Hands together gently* | *Open hands upwards to God* |

| | |
|---|---|
| **Make them beautiful:** | **Jesus, hear our prayer!** |
| *Hands together gently* | *Open hands upwards to God* |
| **Lord Jesus, hear our prayer! Amen.** | |

*Hands together gently, then open hands upwards to God*

## Prayers for Other People: Option 2

→ **Song: 'The Diddy Disciples little prayers song'. Words: © Sharon Moughtin-Mumby**
→ **Tune: 'Frère Jacques' (traditional). For the music see p. 356, or for a taster see the Diddy Disciples website. For tips on teaching songs for the first time, see Book 1, p. 215.**

*These prayers are especially suited to churches that prefer less traditional prayer forms.*
> *Either: choose what you'd like the group to pray for before the session.*
> *Or: ask the children at this point if there is anything or anyone that they'd like to pray for. Ask them or others to suggest actions.*

*You will need two different 'thank you' suggestions and two different 'hear our prayer' suggestions. Try to encourage at least one prayer for other people outside the group.*

*Invite the children to sing after you, repeating your words and their actions. Sometimes it might be almost impossible to fit the child's own words in! It's really valuable to do this where possible, resisting the urge to try and 'neaten' their suggestions. For examples, see p. 17.*

*Having sung your prayers, you could insert a Prayer Action, repeat the process, or move straight on to close with the following (or other words that remain the same each week).*

| | |
|---|---|
| For today, | *Point hands down for 'now'* |
| **For today,** | *Point hands down for 'now'* |
| Thank you, God! | *Open hands upwards to God or hands together in prayer* |
| **Thank you, God!** | *Open hands upwards to God or hands together in prayer* |
| | |
| Fo-r your love, | *Cross hands on chest* |
| **Fo-r your love,** | *Cross hands on chest* |
| Thank you, God! | *Open hands upwards to God or hands together in prayer* |
| **Thank you, God!** | *Open hands upwards to God or hands together in prayer* |

# Prayer Actions

→ **Guide: Book 1, p. 225**

*Continue with one of the Prayer Action options outlined below, or you can use the Prayer Actions: Options 2 and 3 on pp. 47–8 of Book 1 at any time of year.*

## Prayer Action: Option 1

→ **Action: placing flowers as prayers on an Easter Garden (p. 149). These could be real flowers, silk flowers, paper flowers, 'flowers' made from tissue/crepe paper, or pictures of flowers, etc. At St Peter's, Walworth, we pick daisies on the way to church and use these.**

*Show the children the flowers you have chosen in one or more baskets or trays.*
Name *and* Name *are going to bring around these baskets of flowers.*
*If you like, you can take a flower.*
*Let's ask God to see these flowers as a prayer for a special person.*

*Hum the tune together, with the words 'Jesus, hear our prayer!' as a refrain, until all the children and adults who wish to take a flower have done so.*

*Place your Easter Garden in the centre of the circle.*

> *If you have not already asked this question:*
> Can anyone tell me what this is?
> *Accept the child's response.*

The Easter Garden and empty cave
remind us that Jesus burst from the dark cave at Easter.
We all have new life!

If you like, you can place your flower in our garden as a prayer.
This Easter, let's watch new life and beautiful things
growing in our garden and our lives as we pray.

*Hum the tune together again while everyone places their flowers. Some groups may like to invite two children to carry the 'garden'*
*around the group to collect the flowers. The garden can then be placed in the centre.*
*End this time of prayer with the final verse of the Prayer Song you've chosen.*

## Prayer Action: Option 2

→ **Action: placing flowers as prayers on a cross (if it will be taken around the group, on a tray). These could be real flowers, silk flowers, paper flowers, 'flowers' made from tissue/crepe paper, or pictures of flowers, etc. At St Peter's, Walworth, we pick daisies on the way to church and use these.**

*Show the children the flowers you have chosen in one or more baskets or trays.*
*Name* and *Name* are going to bring around these baskets of flowers.
If you like, you can take a flower.
Let's ask God to see these flowers as a prayer for a special person.

*Hum the tune together, with the words 'Jesus, hear our prayer!' as a refrain, until all the children and adults who wish to take a*
*flower have done so.*

*When the group is ready, place the cross in the centre of the circle.*
Jesus' love is stronger than every sad thing.
Stronger even than the cross!
If you like, you can place your flower on Jesus' cross as a prayer.
Jesus' love changes the cross into a beautiful thing.
When we pray, we can be part of sharing that love!

*Hum the tune together again while everyone places their flowers. Some groups may like to invite two children to carry the cross (on*
*a tray) around the group to collect the flowers. The cross can then be placed in the centre.*

*End this time of prayer with the final verse of the Prayer Song you've chosen.*

## Prayer Action: Option 3

→ **Action: placing flowers as prayers on a 'garden': a tray filled with soil or with brown cloth/paper folded on it. The flowers could be real flowers, silk flowers, paper flowers, 'flowers' made from crumpled tissue/crepe paper, or pictures of flowers, etc. At St Peter's, Walworth, we pick daisies on the way to church and use these.**

At Easter, we see new life starting all around us.
We see trees becoming green with leaves
and flowers beginning to 'blossom'.
We can be part of bringing GOD's new life and love
to the world when we pray!

*Show the children the flowers you have chosen in one or more baskets or trays.*
*Name* and *Name* are going to bring around these baskets of flowers.
If you like, you can take a flower.
Let's ask God to see these flowers as a prayer for a special person.

*Hum the tune together, with the words 'Jesus, hear our prayer!' as a refrain, until all the children and adults who wish to take a*
*flower have done so.*

*Place your 'garden' in the centre of the circle.*
If you like, you can place your flower in our garden as a prayer.
This Easter, let's watch new life and beautiful things
'blossoming' in our garden and our lives as we pray.

*Hum the tune together again while everyone places their flowers. Some groups may like to invite two children to carry the 'garden' around the group to collect the flowers. The garden can then be placed in the centre.*

*End this time of prayer with the final verse of the Prayer Song you've chosen.*

# Thank You, God

→ **Guide: Book 1, p. 227**

## Thank You, God: Option 1

→ **Song:** 'My hands were made for love'. Words: © Sharon Moughtin-Mumby
→ **Tune:** 'Hickory, dickory, dock' (traditional). For the music see p. 360, or for a taster see the Diddy Disciples website. For tips on teaching songs for the first time, see Book 1, p. 215.

*Invite the children to sit in a circle for a moment of quiet.*
It's time to remember all the things we've done this week.
It's time to say 'thank you' to God
for when we've been part of showing God's love.

Let's wiggle our fingers!
I wonder when you've shown love
with your hands this week?

*Wiggle fingers as you sing.*
**My hands were made for love!**
**My hands were made for love!**
**Thank you for the love they've shown.**
**My hands were made for love!**

Let's wiggle our feet!
I wonder when you've shown love
with your feet this week?

*Wiggle feet as you sing.*
**My feet were made for love!**
**My feet were made for love!**
**Thank you for the love they've shown.**
**My feet were made for love!**

Let's put our hands gently on our neck.
Let's sing 'Ahhh!'
**Ahhhhh!**
Can you feel your throat vibrating and dancing with your voice?
I wonder when you've shown love
with your voice this week?

*Hold neck and feel your voice 'dancing' as you sing.*
**My voice was made for love!**
**My voice was made for love!**
**Thank you for the love it's shown.**
**My voice was made for love!**

## Thank you, God: Option 2

→ **Song:** 'For the love we've shown'. Words: © Sharon Moughtin-Mumby
→ **Tune:** 'All through the night' (traditional). For the music see p. 357, or for a taster see the Diddy Disciples website. For tips on teaching songs for the first time, see Book 1, p. 215.

*Most suitable for use with children over the age of four.*

*Invite the children to sit in a circle for a moment of quiet.*

It's time to remember all the things we've done this week.
It's time to say 'thank you'
for when we've been part of showing God's love.

> *Either:* Let's wiggle our fingers.
> *Or:* Let's hold up our hands.

I wonder when you've shown love
with your hands this week?

> *Either:* Let's wiggle our feet.
> *Or:* Let's show our feet.

I wonder when you've shown love
with your feet this week?

Let's put our hands gently on our neck.
Let's sing 'Ahhh!'
**Ahhhhh!**
Can you feel your neck vibrating and dancing with your voice?
I wonder when you've shown love
with your voice this week?

Let's sing our 'thank you' song to God
For the times we've been part of sharing God's love.

**For the love we've shown with our hands,**
*Hold hands up or wiggle fingers.*
**Thank you, God!**
**For the love we've shown with our feet,**
*Point to feet or wiggle feet.*
**Thank you, God!**
**When we love all those around us,**
*Cross hands on chest.*
**It's the same as loving Jesus!**
**For the love we've shown with our voice,**
*Hands on neck or point to singing mouth*
**Thank you, God!**

# Creative Response

→ **Guide: Book 1, p. 228**

*See the Creative Responses in Section 3 of this unit.*

# Sharing God's Peace

→ **Guide: Book 1, p. 231**

*This Building Block is particularly designed for children's groups that join the adult congregation to share communion but can also be used to end any session or Service of the Word. During Advent and Christmas, you might like to keep to your normal option for Sharing God's Peace.*

## Sharing God's Peace: Option 1

→ **Song: 'I've got peace like a river' (traditional), Isaiah 66.12, NIV**
→ **Tune: traditional. For a taster see the Diddy Disciples website. For tips on teaching songs for the first time, see Book 1, p. 215.**

> *Either: hold one end of the peace cloth (Book 1, p. 231) and ask one of the older children or an adult to hold the other end. Start singing the Peace Song. As the children begin to gather, invite them to join in holding a small section of the cloth, raising and lowering it so it 'flows' like a river as you sing together.*

*Or: invite the children to sit in a circle in the worship space. Start singing the Peace Song. As the children begin to gather, invite them to join in raising and lowering their hands like the waters of a flowing river.*

**I've got peace like a river,**
**I've got peace like a river,**
**I've got peace like a river in my soul.**
**I've got peace like a river,**
**I've got peace like a river,**
**I've got peace like a river in my soul.**

*If your group is about to rejoin the adults for communion: when all the children are gathered, continue with the words of the Peace, below.*

## Sharing God's Peace: Option 2

→ Song: 'Peace is flowing like a river' (traditional), Isaiah 66.12, NIV
→ Tune: traditional. For a taster see the Diddy Disciples website. For tips on teaching songs for the first time, see Book 1, p. 215.

*Either: hold one end of the peace cloth (Book 1, p. 231) and ask one of the older children or an adult to hold the other end. Start singing the Peace Song. As the children begin to gather, invite them to join in holding a small section of the cloth, raising and lowering it so it 'flows' like a river as you sing together.*

*Or: invite the children to sit in a circle in the worship space. Start singing the Peace Song. As the children begin to gather, invite them to join in raising and lowering their hands like the waters of a flowing river.*

**Peace is flowing like a river,**
**flowing out through you and me.**
**Spreading out into the desert,**
**setting all the captives free.**

*If your group is about to rejoin the adults for communion: when all the children are gathered, continue with the words of the Peace, below.*

## Sharing God's Peace: Option 3

→ Song: 'I've got peace in my fingers'. Words: © 1995 Susan Salidor ASCAP
→ Tune: © 1995 Susan Salidor ASCAP
→ The words and music can be found on the album *Little Voices in My Head* by Susan Salidor © 2003 Peach Head. They can also be found on iTunes or YouTube, or at <www.susansalidor.com>. For tips on teaching songs for the first time, see Book 1, p. 215.

*If your group is about to rejoin the adults for communion: when all the children are gathered, continue with the words of the Peace, below.*

# The Peace

→ 2 Thessalonians 3.16; 1 Peter 5.14
*Once you have finished singing . . .*

The peace of the Lord be always with you.
*Hold hands open to the children.*
**And also with you.**

*Invite the children to open their hands towards you.*
Let's shake hands or hug each other
and say, 'Peace be with you' *or whatever is said on sharing the Peace in your church*
as a sign of God's peace.

*Lead the children in giving and receiving the Peace. Immediately following this, at St Peter's, Walworth, we lead the children back to join the rest of the congregation to continue our worship with the Eucharistic Prayer.*

# Taking God's Love into the World

→ Guide: Book 1, p. 232
→ Song: 'This little light of mine' (traditional)
→ Tune: traditional. For a taster see the Diddy Disciples website. For tips on teaching songs for the first time, see Book 1, p. 215.

*This Building Block is particularly designed for standalone groups or groups that are held during a Service of the Word. Alternatively, you could use one of the Peace Songs above to end your worship.*

Our time together is coming to an end.
*Invite the children to sit in a circle for a moment of quiet.*

God has lit a little light of love inside all of us.
*Trace a circle on your heart.*
Let's make our finger into a candle.
*Bring your finger from your heart and hold it out.*
Let's be God and light our little light of love together, after 3.
*Lead the children in lighting their finger candle by striking an imaginary match in the air on 3 and pretending to light your finger.*
**1, 2, 3 . . . Tssss!**
Let's imagine God's love shining and dancing like light in us.

*Wave your finger in front of you as you sing.*
**This little light of mine, I'm gonna let it shine!**
**This little light of mine, I'm gonna let it shine!**
**This little light of mine, I'm gonna let it shine!**
**Let it shine, let it shine, let it shine!**

*Blow on your finger as if blowing out a candle on 'puff'. Then hold it up high.*
**Won't let no one** *puff* **it out! I'm gonna let it shine!**
**Won't let no one** *puff* **it out! I'm gonna let it shine!**
**Won't let no one** *puff* **it out! I'm gonna let it shine!**
**Let it shine, let it shine, let it shine!**

*Hold your finger behind a cupped hand, then take your cupped hand away*
*to reveal the 'candle' and hold it high!*
**Hide it under a bushel? No! I'm gonna let it shine!**
**Hide it under a bushel? No! I'm gonna let it shine!**
**Hide it under a bushel? No! I'm gonna let it shine!**
**Let it shine, let it shine, let it shine!**

*Lead the children in placing your finger back on your heart.*
Now let's put our little light of love
back in our hearts, where it belongs.
Let's remember to let our little light shine
in all our playing and working today . . .

*If you're building a Service of the Word and this is your final Building Block, you may like to close with a familiar blessing, the Peace and/or one of the following. If you're using one of these call-and-responses with your group for the first time, see p. 25 for an introduction.*

*Either:* Praise the Lord! *Both hands to self*
   **Alleluia!** *Both arms upwards in 'V' shape*

*Or:* Let us bless the Lord. *Both hands to self*
   **Thanks be to God.** *Both arms upwards in 'V' shape*

*Or:* And all the people said . . . *both hands to self*
   **Amen!** *Both arms upwards in 'V' shape*

# Section 2

# The Bible Storytelling material: Jesus Is Alive! Alleluia! unit

## Week 1: Jesus Is Risen! Alleluia!

→ **John 19.40—20.1a**
→ Song/poem: **'When all the world was sleeping'.** Words: © Sharon Moughtin-Mumby
→ Tune: **'Wide awake'** © Mollie Russell-Smith and Geoffrey Russell-Smith, also known as **'The dingle, dangle scarecrow'.** It is now published by EMI Harmonies Ltd. For a taster see the Diddy Disciples website.

*If your group is using an Easter Garden (see p. 149), place it in the middle of the circle. If your group is using the What's in the Box? option (Book 1, p. 221), this can be the object of the week. You may like to place a cloth over it and invite one of the children to remove the cloth.*

Can anyone tell me what this is?
*Accept children's responses and ways of naming the garden.*

This is our Easter Garden with the tomb, the dark cave, in the middle.

170

On Good Friday, Jesus died on the cross.
Let's hold our hands out in love like Jesus on the cross.
*Lead the children in stretching arms out to the side.*

His friends took Jesus' body down from the cross.
Let's be Jesus' friends.
*Lead the children in miming holding Jesus' body gently.*

They put it gently into the dark cave
*Lead the children in miming placing Jesus' body in the tomb.*
and rolled the stone across.
*Lead the children in miming rolling a large stone across.*
They went home feeling very, very, very sad.

Nothing happened for one whole night and day after that.
But then the night after, something very, very special,
Something amazing happened.
Let's tell the story together with a song.

To tell our story, we need to imagine we're in a dark cave.
Let's curl up in a ball on the floor and shut our eyes.
Let's feel the dark.

Now we're ready to learn the words of our song.
Let's say them 'my turn' *point to self*, 'your turn' *leader's hands out to group*.

*For the first time, say the words rather than sing them so the children can understand that they are different from the usual words to this very recognizable (and excitable) tune.*

*Still curled up on the floor or crouching down*
When all the world was sleeping
**When all the world was sleeping**
and the sun had gone to bed.
**and the sun had gone to bed.**

*Jump up with hands in the air.*
Up jumped Lord Jesus!
**Up jumped Lord Jesus!**

And this is what he said . . . *Hands out, palms up*
**And this is what he said . . .**

'I am risen, risen, risen!'
*Wave hands victoriously high in the air*
**'I am risen, risen, risen!'**

'I have won us a new start!'
*Diddy Disciples 'New Start' sign (p. 355)*
**'I have won us a new start!'**

'I am risen, risen, risen!' *Wave hands high in the air*
'I have won us a new start!' *'New Start' sign over head*
**'I am risen, risen, risen!'** *Wave hands high in the air*
**'I have won us a new start!'** *'New Start' sign over head*

Now we're ready to sing our song together.
Let's see if you recognize the tune.
Listen carefully for our new words!
Let's start off by curling up on the floor . . .

*Lead the children in curling up on the floor or crouching.*
**When all the world was sleeping**
**and the sun had gone to bed . . .**

**up jumped Lord Jesus** *jump up with hands in the air*
**and this is what he said:** *hands out, palms up*

**'I am risen, risen, risen,** *wave hands high in the air*
**I have won us a new start!** *'New Start' sign over head*
**I am risen, risen, risen,** *wave hands high in the air*
**I have won us a new start!'** *'New Start' sign over head*
*Repeat until the children are confident.*

Let's sit down!

> *If you're using the What's in the Box? option (Book 1, p. 221), invite one of the children to open the box. Inside will be an Easter egg.*
>
> What's in the box? *Ask the child to respond*
>
> Today is Easter Day! [*Or:* It's Easter!]
> Who's been given an Easter egg?
>
> Today we're going to tell the story
> of why we give Easter eggs at Easter.

*Show the children a hollow chocolate Easter egg.*
At Easter, we celebrate Jesus bursting from the dark cave.
Can anyone tell me what this is?
*Accept the children's responses.*

Easter eggs help to show us what Jesus did.
They remind us of the dark cave,
the tomb, that Jesus was put in.
They're round and dark inside.
*Show the group how the egg is round.*

In our country, we use CHOCOLATE eggs,
because Easter is a time of joy and happiness.
Chocolate is a very happy, joyful thing!
Put your hand up if you like chocolate!

But what's inside real eggs when they are left to grow?
*Accept responses from the children.*
A tiny chick: new life!
Chicks burst out of their egg
when they're ready to be born.
Jesus burst from the dark cave
like a little chick
bursting out of an egg into new life!

Let's all imagine that we're a tiny chick
curled inside an egg in the dark.
*Lead the children in curling up into a ball as if you're inside an egg.*

Ssssh! Now let's tap on the egg three times.
After three taps,
we're going to burst out of the egg and shout, 'New life'!
*Lead the children in tapping the imaginary egg that you are inside.*
**Tap one! Tap two! Tap three**!
*Lead the children in jumping up.*
**New life!**

So at Easter we break open eggs.
We remember Jesus bursting from the dark cave
and giving us new life and a new start.

*If your group wrapped an egg up at the beginning of Lent (p. 86):*
Some of us wrapped up a chocolate egg at the beginning of Lent.
Now Lent's finished! The time for giving things up is gone!
It's time to celebrate because Jesus has burst from the dark cave!
*Use the egg that you left wrapped up through Lent.*

*All groups: show the children a hollow chocolate Easter egg.*
We're going to use this chocolate egg to celebrate Easter together.
In a moment, we're going to count to 3 and break open this egg.

> *Either:* Then I'm going to say, 'Alleluia! Christ is risen!'
> You can shout, **'He is risen indeed! Alleluia!'**

> **1, 2, 3 . . .** *Break open the egg*
> Alleluia! Christ is risen!
> **He is risen indeed! Alleluia!**

> *Or:* I'm going say, 'Praise the Lord!' and you can shout, '**Alleluia!'**
> **1, 2, 3 . . .** *Break open the egg*
> Praise the Lord!
> **Alleluia!**

You could say that with every Easter egg you break open this Easter!

*Break the chocolate egg up into little pieces and place in one or two bowls or baskets.*

*Name* and *Name* are going to bring around this egg now.
If you'd like a piece, hold your hands out like this.
*Model putting both your hands out in a cupped shape.*

Don't eat it straight away!
Keep it on your hand and wait till everyone has a piece.
Make sure you keep your hand open so the chocolate doesn't melt!

*Ask a responsible child to show everyone how to hold their egg on their hand. Don't worry too much if the very young children eat theirs straight away.*

*Sing the 'He is risen, risen, risen!' chorus from the Gathering Song, an 'Alleluia!' song or another Easter song that the children are very familiar with as the chocolate egg is taken around.*

*When the group is ready:*
There's a Bible verse that says
'Taste and see that the Lord is good!'
Let's say that 'my turn' *point to self*, 'your turn' *leader's hands out to group*.
Taste and see that the Lord is good!
**Taste and see that the Lord is good!**

Let's taste our chocolate egg together now.
Lead the children in eating the egg.
Mmmm! That tastes really, really good!
'Taste and see that the Lord is good!'

> *Either:*
> Alleluia! Christ is risen!
> **He is risen indeed! Alleluia!**

> *Or:*
> Praise the Lord!
> **Alleluia!**

# Week 2: On Easter Day in the Morning

→ **John 20.1–10**
→ **Song: 'On Easter Day in the morning'. Words: © Sharon Moughtin-Mumby**
→ **Tune: 'I saw three ships come sailing in' (traditional). For a taster see the Diddy Disciples website.**

Let's sit down!
At Easter, Jesus burst from the tomb, the dark cave!

> *If you're using the What's in the Box? option (Book 1, p. 221), invite one of the children to open the box. Inside will be*
> *NOTHING!*
>
> What's in the box? *Ask the child to respond.*
>
> There's nothing in the box! It's empty!

Today we're going to tell the story
of when Jesus' friends found the dark cave empty!

To tell our story, we need to learn a song.
Let's say the words 'my turn' *point to self,* 'your turn' *leader's hands out to group.*
*Lead the children in saying the words to the rhythm that will be used in the song.*

Tiptoe, tiptoe to the tomb.
**Tiptoe, tiptoe to the tomb.**
On Easter Day, on Easter Day.
**On Easter Day, on Easter Day.**
On Easter Day in the morn-ing.
**On Easter Day in the morn-ing.**

We're ready to add the tune.
Let's sing 'my turn' *point to self,* 'your turn' *leader's hands out to group.*

Tiptoe, tiptoe to the tomb
on Easter Day, on Easter Day.
**Tiptoe, tiptoe to the tomb**
**on Easter Day, on Easter Day.**

Tiptoe, tiptoe to the tomb
on Easter Day in the morn-ing.
**Tiptoe, tiptoe to the tomb**
**on Easter Day in the morn-ing.**

Let's try that all together.
*Lead the children in singing:*
**Tiptoe, tiptoe to the tomb**
**on Easter Day, on Easter Day.**
**Tiptoe, tiptoe to the tomb**
**on Easter Day in the morn-ing.**

We're ready to tell our story.
Jesus' friends don't know that
Jesus has burst from the dark cave!
They still think Jesus has gone!

174

Let's be the women, Jesus' friends.
We're feeling very, very sad.
Can you show me sad?
*Lead the children in showing a sad face and body.*
We're fast asleep in bed.
Can you show me fast asleep?
*Lead the children in being asleep.*

It's time to get up,
but we're still feeling sad.
Let's get up really slowly.
Let's yawn and stretch and stand up.
*Lead the children in getting up sadly and slowly.*
Jesus has died. He's gone!
How are we feeling?
*Lead the children in looking very sad.*

We're going to the dark cave.
We want to say goodbye to Jesus properly.
Let's tiptoe on the spot.
Ssssh! We don't want anyone to see us. Ssssh!

*Lead the children in singing quietly and sadly.*
**Tiptoe, tiptoe to the tomb**
**on Easter Day, on Easter Day.**
**Tiptoe, tiptoe to the tomb**
**on Easter Day in the morning.**

We're here.
But look! *Point and gasp*
What's happened?! *Look confused and shocked*
Look! The stone is rolled away!

Let's show the stone that was rolled away with our arms. *Diddy Disciples 'New Start' sign (p. 355)*
Has someone taken Jesus away? *Sound worried*
How are we feeling?
Can you show me with your face?
*Accept the children's responses, which may range from sad/shocked/worried to happy/excited or confused.*

We're feeling all sorts of things!
How confusing!
Let's sing 'Look! The stone is rolled away!'
and show the stone rolling with our arms.

*Lead the children in singing in a confused voice with the 'New Start' sign.*
**Look! The stone is rolled away**
**on Easter Day, on Easter Day.**
**Look! The stone is rolled away**
**on Easter Day, on Easter Day.**

What's happening? *Hands out in question*
Let's tiptoe on the spot a bit closer.
*Lead the children in tiptoeing.*
**Tiptoe, tiptoe, tiptoe . . .**

Let's bend down and look inside the cave . . .
*Lead the children in bending down and peering low.*
Look! *Gasp and point*
There are two angels there!
Angels!

How do you think the women are feeling now?
Can you show me with your face?
Let's keep our faces looking like that,
And sing 'Look! *Point* Two angels in the cave!'

*Lead the children singing in amazement.*
**Look! Two angels in the cave!**
**On Easter Day, on Easter Day!**
**Look! Two angels in the cave!**
**On Easter Day in the morning.**

We've got to tell someone!
After 3, let's run on the spot
and sing 'Run and run to tell our friends . . .'

1, 2, 3 . . . Run!

*Lead the children in singing faster and running on the spot.*
**Run and run to tell our friends**
**on Easter Day, on Easter Day!**
**Run and run to tell our friends**
**on Easter Day in the morning!**

*Excitedly:*
Look! *Point* There's Peter and John!
After 3, let's shout: 'Look! Two angels in the cave!'
1, 2, 3: **Look! Two angels in the cave!**
And do you know what Peter and John did? *Rhetorical question*
They ran!

After 3, let's be Peter and John and run on the spot.
Let's sing: 'Run and run and run and run!'
1, 2, 3: Run!

*Lead the children in singing even faster and running on the spot.*
**Run and run and run and run**
**on Easter Day, on Easter Day!**
**Run and run and run and run**
**on Easter Day in the morning!**

Freeze!
John got to the cave first!
He bent down and looked inside.
Let's kneel down and look into the cave together.
*Lead the group in kneeling and peering into an imaginary cave.*

Then Peter came running up.
And he RAN inside the cave
Who's feeling brave?
Let's get up and imagine
we've just stepped into the dark cave together.
*Lead the children in standing up.*

Let's look around . . .
*Lead the children in looking as described with hands shielding eyes.*
Let's look left . . .
and right . . .
Behind us . . . *twirl around*
Let's look up . . . and down . . .

Nothing!

176

The dark cave is empty!
Jesus is gone! *Look confused*

*Gasp* Jesus is RISEN!
Jesus is ALIVE!
How do you think Peter is feeling?
Can you show me with your face?

Let's keep our faces looking like that
and sing 'Look! The cave is empty!'

*Lead the children in singing in amazement as you look around the cave on the spot.*
**Look! The cave is e-empty,**
**on Easter Day, on Easter Day!**
**Look! The cave is e-empty,**
**on Easter Day in the morning!**

Peter and John were amazed!
Can you show me your amazed faces?
Freeze!

Let's shout our special Easter shout of joy.

> *Either:* Alleluia! Jesus is risen!
> **He is risen indeed! Alleluia**!
> *Or:* Praise the Lord!
> **Alleluia!**

Our story for today ends here.
Next week we'll tell the story of
two friends MEETING the Risen Jesus.

# Week 3: The Walk to Emmaus

→ **Luke 24: 13–35**
→ **Poem: 'Do this to remember me' © Sharon Moughtin-Mumby**

*In Luke's story of the road to Emmaus, it's only when the 'stranger' breaks the bread that the disciples' eyes are opened to recognize him as Jesus. This week's story therefore begins with a recap of Jesus' Last Supper. At St Peter's, Walworth, we ask one of the children who is familiar with the storytelling from Lent (p. 139) to take the role of Jesus, leading the group.*

*For this week's session, you'll need to have ready two or more trays: one set holding a piece of bread for each child and adult; the other set holding a cup with a small amount of grape juice at the bottom for each child and adult.*

*For the storytelling while the children are finishing their bread, you may like to use three 'small world' people (see p. 95) to represent the two friends and Jesus, the stranger. There is a tradition that the two friends are a man (Cleopas) and a woman (unnamed).*

> ## Tip
>
> You could use matzo (unleavened) bread, pitta bread or everyday bread for this action. We cut the bread into small squares beforehand with scissors.
>
> There are benefits in making connections both with the kind of bread that you use in your church's communion service and with the kind that your children will be familiar with from home, school or nursery. As this story is told during Lent as well, you could move between the different kinds of bread to support the children in making these connections.

*If you've sung the 'Jesus, open up my eyes' song as part of the Getting Ready to Open the Bible Building Block (Option 1),*
*you may like to begin with the following material:*
Today's story is all about our 'Open up my eyes' song.
It's the story of when Jesus opened up his FRIENDS' eyes *Trace cross on eyes*
and helped them hear his voice in their Bible stories. *Hands behind ears*
Let's watch out for the moment the stranger breaks the bread! *Breaking bread action*
That's when the friends' eyes are opened! *Trace cross on eyes*

*All other groups:*
Today we're going to tell one of the stories
about Jesus after he burst from the dark cave.

But first, let's remember the story
of what Jesus did just BEFORE he died.
At Jesus' last dinner with his friends,
Jesus said, 'Do this to remember me.'

*If appropriate:*
Can anyone tell me what Jesus asked his friends to remember him with?
*Accept the children's responses.*

*If you're using the What's in the Box? option (Book 1, p. 221):*
*Invite one of the children to open the box. Inside will be bread and a cup or chalice.*

What's in the box? *Ask the child to respond*
*Show cup and bread.*

Jesus told his friends to remember them with bread and wine.
This morning we're going to tell that story together.

*If appropriate:*
We tell this story every week in church.
It's one of our most important stories!

Jesus and his friends were at
a very special party called 'the Passover'.
They sat down to eat together,
like we're sitting here.
Then Jesus did something new.

*Invite two children to take around small pieces of bread in two baskets for everyone who wants to receive them.*
*Name* and *Name* are going to
bring around some bread now.
If you'd like some bread,
can you hold your hands out like this?
*Model to the children holding out cupped hands.*

*Name* and *Name* will give you a piece.
Keep the bread in your hands till everyone has some.
Don't eat it yet!

*If your group is familiar with the 'I am going to follow Jesus' song from Lent, you may like to sing this as you wait for your bread. Or*
*you could sing another appropriate song that the group is familiar with. Once all the children and adults who wish to receive bread*
*have done so:*

After dinner, Jesus did something new.
Can you say these words after me and copy my actions,
'my turn' *point to self,* 'your turn' *leader's hands out to group*?

| | |
|---|---|
| Jesus took the bread. | *Take bread* |
| **Jesus took the bread.** | *Take bread* |
| He said, 'Thank you, God!' | *Hold bread up if this is in your tradition* |
| **He said, 'Thank you, God!'** | *Hold bread up if this is in your tradition* |
| Jesus broke the bread. | *Break bread* |
| **Jesus broke the bread.** | *Break bread* |
| Then he shared it. | *Mime handing bread out in a circle* |
| **Then he shared it.** | *Mime handing bread out in a circle* |
| This is my body, | *Hold bread or point to it* |
| **This is my body,** | *Hold bread or point to it* |
| Broken for you. | *Hold bread back together then separate it again* |
| **Broken for you.** | *Hold bread back together then separate it again* |
| Do this to remember me! | *Hold bread up if this is in your tradition* |
| **Do this to remember me!** | *Hold bread up if this is in your tradition* |

*Invite the children to eat their bread slowly, really tasting and enjoying it. Once the children's hands are empty, distribute cups with just 1–2 cm of grape juice at the bottom. These cups are best distributed by adults or responsible older children.*

While you finish eating,
we're going to bring around cups.
If you'd like a cup,
can you hold your hands out like this? *Model to the children*
Keep the cup in your hands till everyone has one.
Don't drink from it yet!

*If your group is familiar with the 'I am going to follow Jesus' song from Lent, you may like to sing this as you wait for your cup. Or you could sing another appropriate song that the group is familiar with. Once all the children and adults who wish to receive a cup have done so:*

When they'd finished eating,
Jesus took the cup.
Can you say these words after me and copy my actions,
'my turn' *point to self*, 'your turn' *leader's hands out to group*?

| | |
|---|---|
| Jesus took the cup. | *Take cup in both hands* |
| **Jesus took the cup.** | *Take cup in both hands* |
| He said, 'Thank you, God!' | *Hold cup up if this is in your tradition* |
| **He said, 'Thank you, God!'** | *Hold cup up if this is in your tradition* |
| Jesus poured the wine. | *Mime pouring wine* |
| **Jesus poured the wine.** | *Mime pouring wine* |
| Then he shared it. | *Mime handing cup out in a circle* |
| **Then he shared it.** | *Mime handing cup out in a circle* |
| This is my blood, | *Lift cup or point to it* |
| **This is my blood,** | *Lift cup or point to it* |
| Poured out for you. | *Mime pouring wine* |
| **Poured out for you.** | *Mime pouring wine* |
| Do this to remember me! | *Hold cup up if this is in your tradition* |
| **Do this to remember me!** | *Hold cup up if this is in your tradition* |

*Invite the children to drink the grape juice slowly and to really taste and enjoy it.*
Now as you finish your grape juice and bread,
let's tell our Easter story of Jesus after he had risen.

> *If you're using 'small world' people (see p. 95), place the two friends in front of you.*

Two of Jesus' friends were walking on the road to Emmaus.

> *Place the Jesus figure next to the two friends.*

A stranger came and walked with them.
The friends looked sad.
*To the group*: Can you show me sad?
*Lead the children in looking sad.*

'What's wrong?' the stranger asked.
*To the group:* Can anyone tell us why the friends are looking sad?
*Accept responses.*

Jesus had died on the cross. *Hold out arms in a cross shape*
The friends told the stranger about Jesus dying. *Cross shape*
The stranger said, 'Don't you understand?' *Shake head*
He started to tell them the stories of Moses [*or:* of the Bible]
but it was getting late and dark.

'Come and eat with us,' said the friends.
The stranger said, 'Yes'.

> *If you're using 'small world' people (see p. 95), place them on your focal table or to the side as the group will now become these people.*

and then . . .

Let's tell the story with OUR bodies now.
Can you repeat after me and help me with the actions.
*This time mime the actions, without bread.*

| | |
|---|---|
| The STRANGER took the bread. | *Mime taking bread* |
| **The STRANGER took the bread.** | *Mime taking bread* |
| He said, 'Thank you, God!' | *Hold bread up if this is in your tradition* |
| **He said, 'Thank you, God!'** | *Hold bread up if this is in your tradition* |
| The STRANGER broke the bread. | *Mime breaking bread* |
| **The STRANGER broke the bread.** | *Mime breaking bread* |
| Then he shared it. | *Mime handing bread out in a circle* |
| **Then he shared it.** | *Mime handing bread out in a circle* |

Then the eyes of the friends were opened.

> *If your group is familiar with the 'Jesus, open up my eyes' song:*
> Just like we ask Jesus to open up OUR eyes in our song.
> *Singing:* Jesus open up my eyes, Alleluia! *Trace cross on forehead*

I wonder who it was breaking bread?
*Accept responses.*

It was Jesus!
Jesus is RISEN!
Jesus is ALIVE!
I wonder how the friends felt when they realized it was Jesus?!
Can you show me with your face?
*Follow the children's suggested expressions.*

Let's shout our special Easter shout of joy!
> *Either:* Alleluia! Jesus is risen!
> **He is risen indeed! Alleluia!**

> *Or:* Praise the Lord!
> **Alleluia!**

But Jesus had already gone!
I wonder how the friends felt when they saw that Jesus had gone?
Then the friends got up and ran to tell the other disciples.

# Week 4: The Good Shepherd

→ **John 10.11–15**

*The Good Shepherd is traditionally told on the fourth week of Easter in the lectionary. We like to join in with this tradition. If your group has already told the story together in the Jesus' Wonderful Love unit, don't be concerned: repetition and 'overlearning' is an important part of learning for young children.*

→ **Song: 'The good shepherd song'. Words:** © Sharon Moughtin-Mumby
→ **Tune: 'Mary had a little lamb'** (traditional). For a taster see the Diddy Disciples website. Alternatively, use the tune for 'Have you seen the muffin man?'

*If you're using the What's in the Box? option (Book 1, p. 221), invite one of the children to open the box. Inside will be a picture of a sheep, or a toy sheep.*

What's in the box? *Ask the child to respond*

Today churches all over the world tell a story that Jesus told
about sheep and a shepherd.
We're going to tell the story together.

To tell Jesus' story we need to be sheep!
What do sheep say?
*Accept responses.*
Freeze!
Can you say 'Baa, baa! Bleat! Baa, baa!'
**Baa, baa! Bleat! Baa, baa!**

Let's wiggle our tail to show we're sheep.
*Lead the children in wiggling hand behind back and saying:*
**Baa, baa! Bleat! Baa, baa!**

Now can you say our sheep words and sound scared?
Don't forget to wiggle your tail to show how you're feeling!
*Lead the children in sounding and looking scared as you repeat the words together, and likewise with the following emotions:*
**Baa, baa! Bleat! Baa, baa!** *Scared*
And happy?
**Baa, baa! Bleat! Baa, baa!** *Happy*
And cross?
**Baa, baa! Bleat! Baa, baa!** *Cross*

We're ready to tell our story about a little flock of sheep.
This flock didn't have their own shepherd. *Shake head*
A different person came every day to look after them.

Let's sing 'We are all little sheep'.
Let's wiggle our tails like sheep as we sing.
*Wiggle tails or other sheep action as you sing:*
**We are a-ll little sheep,**
**little sheep, little sheep.**
**We are a-ll little sheep.**
**Baa, baa! Bleat! Baa, baa!**

But look! What's that over there?! *Point and look scared*
It's a wolf!
A big, bad wolf!
*Hold your hands out like claws, ready to pounce.*

How are you feeling?!
Can you show me?
How do you think the sheep will sound when they bleat now?
Shall we practise that together?
**Baa, baa! Bleat! Baa, baa!** *Sounding scared*

Let's sing and be the big bad wolf together. *Make as if ready to pounce*
Then we'll turn into the sheep for our scared baas at the end.
Let's sing 'Look! Here comes a big bad wolf!'
*Hold your hands out like claws, ready to pounce on the word 'wolf'.*

*Lead the children in pouncing on the word 'wolf' as you sing.*
**Look! Here comes a big, bad wolf,** *Pounce*
**a big, bad wolf,** *Pounce* **a big, bad wolf!** *Pounce*
**Look! Here comes a big, bad wolf!** *Pounce*
**Baa, baa! Bleat! Baa, baa!** *Sounding scared*

It's all right. Our shepherd will help us . . .
But look! *Point*
Our shepherd's running away! *Shocked*

How are we feeling now with no shepherd? *Shake head*
The wolf can catch us!
We need to get away!!
After 3, let's sing: 'The sheep they ran and ran and ran!'
And run on the spot like the sheep!
**1, 2, 3 . . . Run!**

*Lead the children in running on the spot and singing:*
**The sheep, they ran and ran and ran,**
**ran and ran, ran and ran!**
**The sheep, they ran and ran and ran!**
**Baa, baa! Bleat! Baa, baa!**

Let's sit down for a moment.
Oh dear! Poor sheep! That shepherd wasn't very good!

Jesus said, 'Then there was another flock of sheep.'
Let's be the other flock of sheep,
happily chewing our grass.

Now this flock has a GOOD shepherd.
Our shepherd loves us!
Let's pretend that our hand is our shepherd's hand. *Hold up hand*
Let's stroke our arm like the shepherd stroking us.
*Lead the children in stroking your arm with your hand.*

How are you feeling?
Let's practise our baas now . . .
**Baa, baa! Bleat! Baa, baa!**
Let's sing 'We are little sheep' and sound like that.

*Waggle tails or other sheep action as you sing.*
**We are a-ll little sheep,**
**little sheep, little sheep.**
**We are a-ll little sheep.**
**Baa, baa! Bleat! Baa, baa!**

But look! What do you think I can see?!
*Give the children opportunity to respond, then go straight into . . .*

*Hold your hands out like claws, ready to pounce on the word 'wolf'.*
**Look! Here comes a big, bad wolf,** *Pounce*
**A big, bad wolf,** *Pounce* **a big, bad wolf!** *Pounce*
**Look! Here comes a big, bad wolf!** *Pounce*
**Baa, baa! Bleat! Baa, baa!** *Sounding scared*

Oh no! What's the shepherd going to do?
*Give the children opportunity to respond.*

This shepherd is the good shepherd.
He won't run! *Shake head*
He won't leave us!
He'll keep us safe!

Let's stand up and be the good shepherd together.
Let's put our feet firmly on the ground: 1, 2 . . .
*Lead the children in placing feet.*
And fold our arms.
*Lead the children in folding arms.*

We're NEVER going to leave the sheep.
Let's sing 'I will never, never leave . . .' *shake head gently*
**I will never, never leave,** *shake head gently*
**never leave, never leave.**
**I will never, never leave.** *Shake head gently*
**Baa, baa! Bleat! Baa, baa!**

This time it was the wolf who ran off!
The sheep were safe!
After 3, let's sing 'The wolf, it ran and ran and ran'.
Let's be the wolf, running on the spot as fast as we can.
1, 2, 3 . . . Run!

*Lead the children in running on the spot as you sing:*
**The wolf, it ran and ran and ran,**
**ran and ran, ran and ran!**
**The wolf, it ran and ran and ran!**
Freeze! *Interrupt the singing*

Wait!
How do you think the sheep will sound now?
The wolf has gone!
The sheep are safe!
**Baa, baa! Bleat! Baa, baa!**
*Lead the children in repeating the joyful, calm, etc., singing of the sheep two or three times.*

We're safe! The good shepherd will never leave us!
Let's sit down for a moment.

Jesus said, 'I am the good shepherd!'
You're my little sheep, my little lambs. *Point to the children*
I love you and I will never leave you. *Shake head*

Let's close our eyes for a moment.
Let's imagine Jesus coming to us.
Let's sing the good shepherd's song quietly:
'I will never, never leave!'
Let's imagine Jesus singing it to us.
Instead of singing our 'baas' at the end,
Let's sing 'thank you, thank you, Je-sus'.

**I will never, never leave,**
**never leave, never leave.**
**I will never, never leave.**
**Thank you, thank you, Je-sus!**
*Repeat if appropriate.*

# Week 5: The Catch of Fishes

→ **John 21.1–14**
→ **Song: 'Back in Galilee'. Words: © Sharon Moughtin-Mumby**
→ **Tune: 'Row, row, row your boat' (traditional). For a taster see the Diddy Disciples website.**

Row, row, row the boat, back in Gal-i-lee. Throw the net then pull it in . . . What _can we see?

To tell our story this week, we need to learn a song.
Let's sit on the floor and pretend to row a boat.
Lead the children in sitting down and rowing in time:
Row and row and row and row . . .
And freeze!

Let's learn the words to our song:
'my turn' *point to self*, 'your turn' *leader's hands out to group*.

*Sing the words with the tune.*
Row, row, row the boat, *Rowing action*
**Row, row, row the boat,** *Rowing action*

back in Galilee. *Rowing action*
**back in Galilee.** *Rowing action*

Throw the net then pull it in . . . *Mime throwing a net out of the boat then pulling it in*
**Throw the net then pull it in . . .** *Net out, then in*

What can we see? *Mime looking in the nets*
**What can we see?** *Mime looking in the nets*

Let's try singing that all together.
*Lead the children in singing:*
**Row, row, row the boat,** *rowing action*
**back in Galilee.** *Rowing action*
**Throw the net then pull it in . . .** *net out, then in*
**What can we see?** *Mime looking in the nets*

184

We're ready to tell our story.

Jesus has burst from the dark cave!

Jesus is alive!

Some of Jesus' friends, the disciples, have seen Jesus.

But they don't understand. *Shake head*

What does it mean that Jesus is alive?

Jesus isn't with his friends every day any more. *Shake head*

They have nothing to do.

Can you show me how you look when you have nothing to do?

The disciples had nothing to do! *Look fed up and bored*

> *If appropriate (e.g. we are St Peter's Church and school!):*
> Can anyone tell me what Peter did before he met Jesus?
> *Accept all responses.*

Before Peter met Jesus he was a fisherman.

So what do you think Peter decided to do?

*Accept responses.*

> *If you're using the What's in the Box? option (Book 1, p. 221), invite one of the children to open the box. Inside will be fish: either plastic or paper fish or a picture of a shoal of fish.*

> What's in the box? *Ask the child to respond*

Peter said, 'Come on, let's go fishing!' *Beckon action*

So Jesus' friends went back home to Galilee.

They got in their boat . . .

*Lead the children in miming getting in the boat*

and fished all night.

Let's row our boat out and sing our song.

**Row, row, row the boat,** *rowing action*

**back in Galilee.** *Rowing action*

**Throw the net then pull it in . . .** *net out, then in*

**What can we see?** *Mime looking in the nets*

Let's have a look!

*Lead the children in looking in the imaginary nets.*

What have we caught?

Nothing! *Shake head*

I wonder how Peter and the disciples are feeling now?

Can you show me?

Let's sing our song feeling like Peter.

*Lead the children in singing the song in the mood one of the children has chosen. For instance, fed up, cross, sad, bored, unsure, etc.*

**Row, row, row the boat,** *rowing action*

**back in Galilee.** *Rowing action*

**Throw the net then pull it in . . .** *net out, then in*

**What can we see?** *Mime looking in the nets*

Let's have a look!

*Lead the children in looking in the imaginary nets.*

What have we caught?

Nothing! *Shake head*

*Upset:* Nothing! Oh no!

Have we forgotten how to fish?

I wonder how Peter and the disciples are feeling now?

Can you show me?

*Lead the children in singing the song in the mood one of the children has chosen.*

**Row, row, row the boat,** *rowing action*

**back in Galilee.** *Rowing action*

**Throw the net then pull it in . . .** *net out, then in*

**What can we see?** *Mime looking in the nets*

Let's have a look!

*Lead the children in looking in the imaginary nets.*

What have we caught?

Nothing! *Shake head*

*Sadly:* We really HAVE forgotten how to fish!

We can't do ANYTHING right without Jesus!

I wonder how Peter and the disciples are feeling now?

Can you show me?

This time, let's sing our song and row

really quietly and slowly and sadly

like we're really missing Jesus.

**Row, row, row the boat,** *rowing action*

**back in Galilee.** *Rowing action*

*Interrupt the singing and point.*

Wait! Look! Who's that?

A stranger was standing far away on the beach.

The stranger said: *hands cupped around mouth*

'Have you caught anything?'

The disciples said . . .

Well, what do you think they said?

*Accept responses.*

The disciples said, 'No!' *Hands cupped around mouth*

The stranger said: *hands cupped around mouth*

'Throw your net on the OTHER SIDE of the boat! *Point*

There are fish there!'

Now the stranger didn't really look like a fisherman. *Shake head*

*Look suspicious:* He didn't look like he'd know anything about fishing!

But the disciples were so sad and fed up

that they shrugged their shoulders.

Let's shrug our shoulders.

*Lead the children in shrugging shoulders.*

'We may as well try,' they said.

So they tried again.

Let's sing our song together, but still a bit fed up.

**Row, row, row the boat,** *rowing action*

**back in Galilee.** *Rowing action*

**Throw the net then pull it in . . .** *net out, then in*

**What can we see?** *Mime looking in the nets*

Let's have a look!

*Lead the children in looking in the imaginary nets.*

What have we caught?

Still nothing? . . .

No! Not nothing!
Oh my goodness!
This net is too heavy to pull in!
*Lead the children in imagining pulling a net that's too heavy.*
It's full to bursting with fish!
How is this net not breaking!

Then one of the disciples said:
'I know who the stranger is!'
Who do you think it is?
*Accept responses.*
It's Jesus!
And do you know what Peter did?

He jumped straight into the water
and swam as fast as he could to Jesus!
Let's swim on the spot as fast as we can!
*Lead the children in swimming.*
Faster! Faster!

And the other friends rowed their boat
as fast as they could to the shore.
Let's sit down and row as fast as we can to the shore,
pulling our heavy nets . . .
*Lead the children in rowing fast.*

And do you know what Jesus said to them? *Rhetorical question*
*Say in a calm, matter-of-fact voice*
Jesus said, 'Come and have breakfast!'
So they did!

Let's kneel down. *Lead the children in kneeling*
Let's make a fire.
*Lead the children in miming building a fire from wood.*
Let's light our fire.
*Lead the children in miming striking a match and lighting the wood.*
**1, 2, 3 . . . Tssss!**

They cooked the fish together.
*Lead the children in cooking the fish on the fire.*
And they ate it! *Lead the children in taking a bite of fish*
Mmmm! Delicious!

Then let's say this 'my turn' *point to self*, 'your turn' *leader's hands out to group.*

| | |
|---|---|
| Jesus took the bread. | *Take bread* |
| **Jesus took the bread.** | *Take bread* |
| He said, 'Thank you, God!' | *Hold bread up if this is in your tradition* |
| **He said, 'Thank you, God!'** | *Hold bread up if this is in your tradition* |
| Jesus broke the bread. | *Break bread* |
| **Jesus broke the bread.** | *Break bread* |
| Then he shared it. | *Mime handing bread out in a circle* |
| **Then he shared it.** | *Mime handing bread out in a circle* |

And then the disciples knew absolutely
that this was the Risen Jesus!

# Week 6: Peter's Story

→ **John 18.15–27, 21.15–19**
→ **Song: 'I am going to follow Jesus'. Words: © Sharon Moughtin-Mumby**
→ **Tune: 'Bobby Shaftoe' (traditional). For the music see p. 72, or for a taster see the Diddy Disciples website. For tips on teaching songs for the first time, see Book 1, p. 215.**

*If you're using the What's in the Box? option (Book 1, p. 221), invite one of the children to open the box. Inside will be screwed up paper, looking like rubbish.*

What's in the box? *Ask the child to respond*

Today we're going to tell the story of someone
who'd made a bad choice.
Such a bad choice he felt he should be thrown away
like rubbish.

This week we're going to tell Peter's story.

Before Jesus died on the cross,
Jesus' friends, the disciples, followed Jesus everywhere.
Let's march on the spot:
**1, 2, 3, 4! 1, 2, 3, 4!**

*Continue marching on the spot as you sing:*
**I am going to follow Jesus,**
**I am going to follow Jesus,**
**I am going to follow Jesus,**
**follow, follow Jesus!**

The disciples followed Jesus everywhere!
But one dark night, Jesus said,
'I'm going somewhere and you can't follow me.' *Shake head*
Jesus meant the cross. *Hold arms out in cross shape*

Peter said, *Point to self*
'I will follow you EVERYWHERE!'
Let's be Peter.
Can you show me really brave and proud and confident?
*Lead the children in looking brave, proud and confident.*
Let's go!

*Lead the children in singing the song looking brave and marching confidently on the spot.*
**I am going to follow Jesus,**
**I am going to follow Jesus,**
**I am going to follow Jesus,**
**follow, follow Jesus!**

But Jesus shook his head. *Shake head*
Let's shake our heads together.
*Lead the children in shaking heads.*
'No, Peter!
A cockerel will crow three times.'

Who can show me what a cockerel crowing sounds like?
*Give the children a few moments to crow like a cockerel.*
Freeze!

Let's crow three times like a cockerel together.
Ready . . .
*Count crows on fingers as you lead the children in crowing.*

Jesus said, 'Before the cockerel crows three times,
You will choose NOT to follow me.'

That night Jesus was taken away!
Everyone was very scared.
Can you show me scared?
*Lead the children in looking scared.*

Peter tried to follow Jesus.
Let's tiptoe like Peter in the dark.
Let's sing like we're really quite scared!

*Tiptoe and sing quietly and hesitatingly:*
**I am going to follow Jesus,**
**I am going to follow Jesus,**
**I am going to follow Jesus,**
**follow, follow Jesus . . .**

Then a woman saw Peter.
She said, 'Do you follow Jesus?'
And do you know what Peter said?

Peter said, 'No! *Shake head*
I do not follow Jesus!'
Let's sing that in a very quiet, scared voice.

*Lead the children in singing timidly:*
**No, I do not follow Jesus,**
**No, I do not follow Jesus,**
**No, I do not follow Jesus,**
**follow, follow Jesus!**

Peter crept away and sat by a fire.
Let's sit down and warm our hands by the fire.
*Lead the children in sitting and miming warming hands.*
But some men asked him: 'Do you follow Jesus?'

What do you think Peter said?
*Accept responses.*
Peter said, 'No, *shake head*
I do not follow Jesus.'
Let's sing in an even quieter and more scared voice.

*Lead the children in singing as if very scared:*
**No, I do not follow Jesus,**
**No, I do not follow Jesus,**
**No, I do not follow Jesus,**
**follow, follow Jesus!**

But another man said, 'Yes you do! I saw you! *Point*
This time Peter jumped up.
Let's jump up together.
*Lead children in jumping up.*
Let's sing: *loudly and angrily*
'No! *Stamp* I do not follow Jesus!'

*Lead the children in singing loudly and angrily:*
**No! *Stamp* I do not follow Jesus!**
**No! *Stamp* I do not follow Jesus!**
**No! *Stamp* I do not follow Jesus,**
**follow, follow Jesus!**

And at that very moment Peter heard a terrible sound.
What do you think it was?
*Crow like a cockerel:* Cock-a-doodle doo!

Let's crow like a cockerel three times.
*Count crows on fingers as you lead the children in crowing three times.*

I wonder how Peter felt.
Can you show me with your face?
*Accept the children's responses.*

Let's sit down for a moment.
That was before Jesus died.
Now Jesus has risen! *Sound excited*
Jesus is alive!

*Sound more concerned:*
And Jesus is standing in front of Peter.
I wonder how Peter is feeling?
He said that he didn't follow Jesus! *Shake head*
Can you show me with your face?

Then Jesus asked Peter three questions.
They were questions that would give Peter a whole new start.

Question number 1. Let's hold one finger up.
*Lead the children in holding up one finger.*
Jesus asked, 'Peter, do you love me?
In a very quiet, sad voice, Peter said . . . 'Yes.' *Thumbs up*

Question number 2. Let's hold two fingers up.
*Lead the children in holding up two fingers.*
Jesus asked, 'Peter, do you love me?'
What do you think Peter said?
*Accept responses.*
In a little bit louder voice, Peter said . . .
*Encourage the children to join in:* **'Yes.'** *Thumbs up*

Question number 3. Let's hold three fingers up.
*Lead the children in holding up three fingers.*
Jesus asked, 'Peter, do you love me?'

This time Peter got a bit fed up.
Jesus wasn't listening properly!
Let's stand up.
After 3, let's shout, 'Yes!' and stamp our feet!
**1, 2, 3: Yes!** *Stamp*

Then Jesus said to Peter:
*In a matter-of-fact, gentle voice, smiling:*
'Follow me!'
And that was how Jesus gave Peter a new start.
Peter was Jesus' follower again!

Let's sing our song.
And this time, let's sing it really joyfully!
Like we really mean it!
Let's stand up and follow!
**1, 2, 3, 4! 1, 2, 3, 4!**
*Continue marching happily as you sing:*
**I am going to follow Jesus,**
**I am going to follow Jesus,**

**I am going to follow Jesus,**
**follow, follow Jesus!**

Let's sit down for a moment.
In our story today, Peter got it really wrong.
But Jesus gave him a brand new start.

Peter became the leader of all the disciples!
Then the leader of the whole Church!

> *If you're going to make keys later:*
> Jesus put Peter in charge and gave him some special keys:
> the keys to heaven!

When we make mistakes and feel good for nothing,
let's remember Peter's story.
God can always, always, always give us a new start.
God can do amazing things when we show we're sorry.

*This week, you may wish to use the Sorry Song at this point instead of the Prayers for Other People, even if you haven't chosen it as a Building Block for the rest of the unit.*

# Week 7: Jesus Goes Up!

→ **The Ascension (Luke 24.42–53; Acts 1.8–14)**
→ **Song: 'Go! And wait for the Holy Spirit!' Words: © Sharon Moughtin-Mumby**
→ **Tune: 'London Bridge is falling down' (traditional). For a taster see the Diddy Disciples website.**

*If you're using the What's in the Box? option (Book 1, p. 221), invite one of the children to open the box. Inside will be an 'Alleluia!' (written or printed).*

What's in the box? *Ask the child to respond. Don't worry if the child can't read it: he or she might say 'a word' or 'writing' or 'a piece of paper' or 'a drawing', etc.*

The writing/word on this piece of paper says 'Alleluia!'

Today's the last week of Easter.
So our song today ends every time with the joyful shout of Easter.

> *If appropriate:*
> Can anyone tell me what our joyful Easter word is?
> *Accept children's responses.*
> Alleluia! *Hands raised*

Let's practise: 'my turn' *point to self*, 'your turn' *leader's hands out to group.*

*Sing to the tune of the last line of 'London Bridge is falling down':*
'Alleluia!' *Hands raised*
**'Alleluia!'** *Hands raised*
And again: 'Alleluia!' *Hands raised*
**'Alleluia!'** *Hands raised*

We're ready to tell our story.
Jesus was sitting with his disciples, eating fish.

Let's kneel down. *Lead the children in kneeling*
Let's make a fire.
*Lead the children in miming building a fire from wood.*
Let's light our fire.
*Lead the children in miming striking a match and lighting the wood.*
**1, 2, 3 . . . Tssss!**
Let's cook our fish.
*Lead the children in cooking the fish on the fire.*
Now let's eat it!
*Lead the children in taking a bite of fish.*
Mmmm! Delicious!

Let's sing: 'We are eating fish! Yum! Yum!' *Eating action*
And remember our special 'Alleluia!' *hands raised* at the end!

*Don't worry about teaching this song. Its tune and shape are so recognizable that the children will naturally join in when you start singing.*
**We are eating fish! Yum! Yum!** *Eating action*
**Fish! Yum! Yum! Fish! Yum! Yum!** *Eating action*
**We are eating fish! Yum! Yum!** *Eating action*
**Alleluia!** *Raise arms to form a 'V' shape in the air*

So the disciples were eating fish. Yum! Yum!
Then Jesus said, 'Time to go! Get up!'
Let's get up! *Lead the children in standing*

Jesus led the disciples up a hill.
Put your hand up if you've ever climbed a very high hill.
It's hard work!
Can you show me walking up a hill on the spot?
**Climb, climb, climb, climb! Climb, climb, climb, climb!**
Let's keep on climbing and sing:
'Climb the hi-ill, 1, 2, 3!'

**Climb the hi-ill, 1, 2, 3!**
**1, 2, 3! 1, 2, 3!** *Climb the hill together*
**Climb the hi-ill, 1, 2, 3!**
**Alleluia!** *'V' shape in the air*

Phew! We're at the top.
Wow! Look at the amazing view! *Hand sheltering eyes*
*Lead the children in looking around!*
Let's look left! And right!
And in front of us! And behind us!
We can see everything!

Then Jesus said, 'Listen!' *Hand behind ear*
Let's say Jesus' words together:
'my turn' *point to self*, 'your turn' *leader's hands out to group*.

Go! And wait for the Holy Spirit! *Point*
**Go! And wait for the Holy Spirit!** *Point*

Let's sing Jesus' words together.
**Go and wait for the Holy Spirit,** *Point*
**the Holy Spirit, the Holy Spirit!** *Point*
**Go and wait for the Holy Spirit** *Point*
**Alleluia!** *'V' shape in the air*

*Hold hands out in a questioning shape.*

But who or what is the Holy Spirit? *Look confused*
The disciples haven't met the Holy Spirit yet! *Shake head*
Jesus said, 'The Holy Spirit will make you strong!' *Strong action*
Can you show me an action for strong?
*Accept the children's actions.*

When the Holy Spirit comes, it will be in fire!
Can you make your bodies into flames of fire
by waving and swaying them?
*Lead the children in swaying with hands stretched upwards like flames of fire.*
Let's sing:
The Holy Spirit *fire action* will make you strong!' *Strong action*

**The Holy Spirit** *fire action* **will make you strong,** *Strong action*
**make you strong, make you strong!** *Strong action*
**The Holy Spirit** *fire action* **will make you strong!** *Strong action*
**Alleluia!** *Hands upwards*

Look! *Point upwards*
Look! *Point again* Jesus is going up!
Up and up and up! *Point higher and higher*
The disciples were amazed!
Can you show me your amazed face?

Look! Jesus is going up!
*Lead the children in singing with amazement:*
**Look! Jesus is going up,** *point upwards*
**going up, going up!** *point upwards*
**Look! Jesus is going up!** *point upwards*
**Alleluia!** *'V' shape in the air*

*Lead the children in looking upwards with your hand sheltering your eyes.*
The disciples watched Jesus go up and up and up . . .
Till they could only see his feet disappearing into a cloud!

*Gasp* Jesus is going!
Let's wave goodbye to Jesus.
Who likes waving goodbye?
Let's wave and sing goodbye as loudly as we can!

**Wave goodbye to Je-e-sus!** *Waving with both arms*
**Je-e-sus, Je-e-sus!** *Waving with both arms*
**Wave goodbye to Je-e-sus!** *Waving with both arms*
**Alleluia!** *'V' shape in the air*

Jesus has gone!
How do you feel when someone special comes visit, then goes again?
It can be fun waving goodbye.
Then how does it feel when they've gone?
Can you show me your face?
Jesus has gone! What shall we do now?
*Look confused and leave a moment's pause.*

Can anyone remember what Jesus told us to do?
*If necessary:* 'Go and wait for . . .'
*Accept responses.*

So what shall we do?
*Lead the children straight into singing:*
**Go and wait for the Holy Spirit,** *point*
**the Holy Spirit,** *point* **the Holy Spirit!** *Point*

**Go and wait for the Holy Spirit!** *Point*
**Alleluia!** *'V' shape in the air*

Can anyone remember what the Holy Spirit will do?
*If necessary:* The Holy Spirit will make us . . . ?
*Accept the children's responses.*

*Lead the children in singing:*
**The Holy Spirit** *fire action* **will make us strong,** *strong action*
**make us strong, make us strong!** *Strong action*
**The Holy Spirit** *fire action* **will make us strong!** *Strong action*
**Alleluia!** *Hands upwards*

That's where our story ends for today:
with waiting . . .

> *If appropriate:* Can anyone remember who the disciples are waiting for?
> *Help the children out if necessary:* The . . . Holy . . . Spirit!

Next week we'll find out what happens
when the Holy Spirit comes . . .

# Week 8: Come, Holy Spirit!

→ **The Day of Pentecost, Acts 2.1–4**
→ Song: 'Holy Spirit, come!' Words: © Sharon Moughtin-Mumby
→ Tune: 'Wind the bobbin up' (traditional). For a taster see the Diddy Disciples website. For tips on teaching songs for the first time, see Book 1, p. 215.

Ho - ly Spi-rit, come! Ho - ly Spi-rit, come! Come, come! Spi-rit come! Ho - ly Spi-rit, come!
Ho - ly Spi-rit, come! Come, come! Spi-rit, come! Fire on the ceil-ing! Fire on the floor!
Fire at the win - dow! Fire at the door! The fire of the Spi - rit:
can you see? Ho - .ly Spi - rit, dance in me!

*If you're using the What's in the Box? option (Book 1, p. 221), invite one of the children to open the box. Inside will be a picture of fire.*

What's in the box? *Ask the child to respond*

Today's story is about fire!

To tell our story today, we need to learn a song.

> *You may find this introduction helpful for learning the song together.*
> Let's learn the words 'my turn' *point to self*, 'your turn' *leader's hands out to group*.
>
> *Say the words (without the tune) in the rhythm of the song:*
> The fire of the Spirit! Can you see?
> **The fire of the Spirit! Can you see?**
> Holy Spirit, dance in me!
> **Holy Spirit, dance in me!**

Let's try singing that. *Add the tune*
The fire of the Spirit! Can you see? *Point out*
**The fire of the Spirit! Can you see?** *Point out*
Holy Spirit, dance in me! *Point to self*
**Holy Spirit, dance in me!** *Point to self*

That's the end of the song.
Let's learn the middle words.
Can you say after me
*say in the rhythm of the song:*
Fire on the ceiling! *Point up* Fire on the floor! *Point down*
**Fire on the ceiling!** *Point up* **Fire on the floor!** *Point down*
Fire at the window! *Point to window* Fire at the door! *Point to door*
**Fire at the window!** *Point to window* **Fire at the door!** *Point to door*

Then it's the part we already know.
*Start singing and encourage the children to join in.*
**The fire of the Spirit:** *waving bodies and aids like flames*
**can you see?** *Waving bodies and aids like flames*
**Holy Spirit, dance in me!** *Waving bodies like flames*

Let's try that one more time this time, let's sing:
*Start singing and encourage the children to join in. The children will probably recognize the song by now so the tune here won't need to be taught 'my turn, your turn'.*

**Fire on the ceiling!** *Point up*
**Fire on the floor!** *Point down*
**Fire at the window!** *Point to window*
**Fire at the door!** *Point to door*
**The fire of the Spirit: can you see?** *Point out*
**Holy Spirit, dance in me!** *Point to self*

We're ready to tell our story.

Jesus has gone!
He's gone up and up and up to heaven! *Point up higher and higher*
Let's wave goodbye to Jesus.
*Lead the children in waving goodbye.*
'Goodbye, Jesus!'

Before Jesus went up,
Jesus told his friends to go and wait!
>*If appropriate:* Can anyone remember who they had to wait for?
>*Help the children out if necessary:* The . . . Holy . . . Spirit!

So at the beginning of our story,
the disciples are waiting.
But they're not just waiting.
They're praying!
They're praying, 'Holy Spirit, come!' *Reverse winding action from 'Wind the bobbin up' with hands open: this will be the 'come' action for the song.*

Let's be Jesus' friends, the disciples, and pray:
*Lead the children in singing quietly:*
**Holy Spirit, come!** *'Come' action throughout*
**Holy Spirit, come!**
**Come, come! Spirit, come!**

*Lead the children in looking around.*
Can anyone see the Holy Spirit?
Not yet . . .

Let's keep praying . . .
**Holy Spirit, come!** *'Come' action throughout*
**Holy Spirit, come!**
**Come, come! Spirit, come!**

*Lead the children in looking around.*
Any sign of the Holy Spirit?
*Sigh* Not yet . . .
Let's keep praying . . .

**Holy Spirit, come!** *'Come' action throughout*
**Holy Spirit, come!**
**Come, come! Spirit, come!**

The disciples prayed for nine whole days.
Let's count to 9.
*Lead the children in counting on their fingers.*
1, 2, 3, 4, 5, 6, 7, 8, 9 . . .
That's a long time to pray!

**Holy Spirit, come!** *'Come' action throughout*
**Holy Spirit, come!**
**Come, come! Spirit, come!**

*Lead the children in looking around.*
Is the Holy Spirit here yet?
No! Shall we give up?!
Nothing seems to be happening *sigh*
But it's what Jesus TOLD us to do!
Let's keep praying.

**Holy Spirit, come!** *'Come' action throughout*
**Holy Spirit, come!**
**Come, come! Spirit, come!**
Sssssssssshhhh! What's that?
*Look around and upwards and put hand to your ear.*

*Blow into the air.*
Can you hear that?
There's a sound like wind blowing!
*Blow, and encourage the children to join in blowing.*
Louder . . . *Blow louder* and louder . . . *Blow even louder* . . .
*Then lead the children in banging hands on the floor, louder and louder . . .*

And look! *Point* What's that?
Fire! There's fire everywhere!
Let's show the fire with our bodies:
*Lead the children in swaying your whole body to look like a fiery flame.*

It's waving and swaying everywhere!
Look! The whole room is filled with fire!
*Lead the group in singing:*
**Fire on the ceiling!** *Point up in shock*
**Fire on the floor!** *Point down*
**Fire at the window!** *Point to window in shock*
**Fire at the door!** *Point to door*
**The fire of the Spirit: can you see?** *Point all around*
**Holy Spirit, dance in me!** *Sway like a flame*

And look! *Point to a child in surprise*
Now the fire is dancing on your head!

And your head! *Point to another child*
On all our heads!
*Put hands together above head and wave them side to side to show a flame dancing on your head.*
Let's show the fire dancing on our head.
*Lead the children in the same action.*

The fire danced on the disciples' heads!
I wonder how the disciples are feeling now?
Can you show me with your face?
*Follow the children's suggested expressions.*

Then all of a sudden the fire was gone!
Even the flames on the disciples' heads had gone!
Quick! Let's hide the flames behind our back.
*Lead the children in placing hands behind back.*

Let's sit down for a moment.
*When the group is ready:*
The flames had gone!
But the FIRE hadn't gone away!
The fire had gone INSIDE the disciples! *Trace circle on heart*

All the power and light and dancing
of the fire had gone INSIDE them!
Making them feel strong and not afraid:
full of fire and life!

The fire was the Holy Spirit!
The Holy Spirit had come!
And the disciples weren't afraid or lonely or sad any more,
because the Spirit was inside them!

Shall we tell the story again with our song.
Let's be the disciples, praying and waiting.
*Lead the children in singing:*
**Holy Spirit, come!** *'Come' action throughout*
**Holy Spirit, come!**
**Come, come! Spirit, come!**

*Lead the children in looking around.*
Can anyone see the Holy Spirit?
Not yet . . .
Let's keep praying . . .

**Holy Spirit, come!** *'Come' action throughout*
**Holy Spirit, come!**
**Come, come! Spirit, come!**

*Lead the children in looking around.*
Any sign of the Holy Spirit?
*Sigh* Not yet . . .
Let's keep praying . . .

**Holy Spirit, come!** *'Come' action throughout*
**Holy Spirit, come!**
**Come, come! Spirit, come!**

*Lead the children in looking around.*
Is the Holy Spirit here yet?
No! Shall we give up?!
*Accept children's responses.*

Jesus told us to wait!
Let's keep praying.

**Holy Spirit, come!** *'Come' action throughout*
**Holy Spirit, come!**
**Come, come! Spirit, come!**

Sssssssssh! What's that?
*Look around and upwards and put hand to your ear.*

*Blow into the air.*
Can you hear that?
*Blow, and encourage the children to join in blowing.*
Louder . . . *Blow louder* and louder . . . *Blow even louder . . .*
Then lead the children in banging hands on the floor, louder and louder . . .

And look! *Point* What's that?
*Lead the group in singing:*
**Fire on the ceiling!** *Point up in shock*
**Fire on the floor!** *Point down*
**Fire at the window!** *Point to window in shock*
**Fire at the door!** *Point to door*
**The fire of the Spirit! Can you see?** *Point all around*
**Holy Spirit, dance in me!** *Sway like a flame*

Let's sit down for a moment.
In our story, the Holy Spirit came on the disciples like fire!
The Holy Spirit made them feel strong and not afraid.

I wonder if you ever feel like the Holy Spirit is in you?
Dancing and making you strong?
I wonder if you'd like to pray for the Holy Spirit?
I'm going to pray our song now as a prayer.
If you like, you can join in and ask the Holy Spirit to come inside you.

We can't always SEE the Holy Spirit.
But the Spirit is like God's fire,
dancing around us and inside us.
And if we learn to see with God's eyes, *point to eyes*
we might learn to see it!

Shall we sing our song again.
This time, let's sing it for ourselves.
Let's make Jesus' friends' song into our song.

*Sing quietly and reflectively*
**Holy Spirit, come!** *'Come' action throughout*
**Holy Spirit, come!**
**Come, come! Spirit, come!**
**Holy Spirit, come!**
**Holy Spirit, come!**
**Come, come! Spirit, come . . .**

We can't always SEE the Holy Spirit.
But the Spirit is like God's fire dancing INSIDE us.
I wonder if you can feel the Spirit dancing inside YOU?
*End with a short moment of silence.*
*If appropriate:* Today's the Day of Pentecost!
It's the day that all around the world
we remember the day the Holy Spirit came in fire
and we pray for the Holy Spirit to dance in us!

## Tip

If you use 'This little light of mine to close, you could use these words just before you introduce the song.

> That fire dancing on the heads of Jesus' friends,
> *Show fire dancing on your head*
> is the little light that we sing about:
> the fire and light of the Holy Spirit inside us.
>
> When we're feeling lost or lonely or sad,
> When we don't know what to say to God,
> We can ask the Holy Spirit to come.
> We can ask the Holy Spirit to dance inside us
> and make us strong.
>
> Let's imagine that little light of the Spirit
> That God has lit in us now.
> *Continue with the introduction to the Closing Song.*

# Extra: Trinity Sunday

→ Song: '1, 2, 3, the Trinity!' Words: © Sharon Moughtin-Mumby
→ Tune: © Sharon Moughtin-Mumby. For a taster see the Diddy Disciples website.

## Tip

The Easter season is now over. Churches following the liturgical year may prefer to use 'Holy Spirit, come!' (the Bible Storytelling song from the previous week) as a Gathering Song in the place of 'When all the world was sleeping . . .' If your church would like to do this, start from the recap of the story on p. 197. The following introduction may be helpful:

> In our story last week, the Holy Spirit came like fire!
> Let's remember the story with our song.
> Let's be the disciples praying and waiting . . .

---

This second version of the Trinity song is available for older children or all-age worship. It allows for more development, but is too much for younger children to sing unsupported by an older group. If this version is appropriate for your group, amend the material accordingly.

**1, 2, 3, the Trinity!** *Count on fingers followed by a triangle shape*

**Father, Son and Holy Spirit.** *Cross self or count to 3 again*

**Let us praise the Trinity!** *Hands lifted up*

**God is One and God is Three!** *One hand shows 1, the other 3*

**God is a mystery!** *Hands turned upwards, confused face*

---

*If your group is using the What's in the Box? option (Book 1, p. 221):*
*Invite a child to open the box.*
*Inside is golden fabric or tinfoil (or something similar) that is breaking out of the box as it's too big!*

What's in the box?
*Accept the child's response.*

Look, it doesn't fit! It's too big for our box!

Today we're not going to tell a story!
Today we're going to learn something big!
Can you show me big with your body?
*Lead the children in standing and stretching out with their whole bodies.*
Even bigger! And bigger!
Impossibly big!
Freeze!

Imagine the biggest thing you can imagine!
God is big!
God is bigger than the biggest thing you can imagine.

Let's sit down for a moment.

*When the group is ready:*
God is so big that we can't know all about God.
We can't squeeze God *show hands squeezing*
into our heads or our words.
Sometimes God doesn't make sense. *Shake head*
That means God is a 'mystery'. *Hands out in question*
Can you say 'mystery'?
**Mystery!**
A mystery is something that's too big *stretch out wide with arms*
to understand all of it.

We're going to learn a song today
That's all about God being so big
That God is a mystery!
It's too BIG to make sense. *Shake head*

Our song starts with counting: 1, 2, 3 *Count on fingers*
Then we show a shape with three sides.
Can anyone tell me what shape has three sides?
*Lead the children in showing a triangle with their fingers.*

Let's sing the words 'my turn' *point to self*, 'your turn' *leader's hands out to group*.

1, 2, 3, the Trin-it-y! *Count on fingers followed by a triangle shape*
**1, 2, 3, the Trin-it-y!** *Count on fingers followed by a triangle shape*

> *Either:*
> The Trinity is: *Count to 3 on fingers in time with the words*
> Father, Son and Holy Spirit.
> Let's try that 'my turn' *point to self*, 'your turn' *leader's hands out to group*.
>
> Father, Son and Holy Spirit. *Counting to three in time with the song*
> **Father, Son and Holy Spirit.** *Counting to three in time with the song*
>
> *Or:*
> Then another way of showing the Trinity
> is by drawing a cross on ourselves.
> Father, Son and Holy Spirit. *Cross yourself in time with the song*
> **Father, Son and Holy Spirit.** *Cross yourself in time with the song*

*All groups:*

Let's put that all together.
*Lead the children in singing:*
**1, 2, 3, the Trinity!** *Count on fingers followed by a triangle shape*
**Father, Son and Holy Spirit.** *Cross self or count to 3 again*
**1, 2, 3, the Trinity!** *Count on fingers followed by a triangle shape*

Then this is the bit that's impossible to understand.
God is One: let's show one finger with one hand. *One finger*
AND God is Three! *Three fingers*
Let's show three fingers with our other hand at the same time. *Three fingers*
*Look from one hand to the other, looking confused.*

Let's say that 'my turn' *point to self*, 'your turn' *leader's hands out to group*.

*Look from one hand to the other, looking confused.*
God is One and God is Three! *One hand shows one, the other three*
**God is One and God is Three!** *One hand shows one, the other three*
God is a mystery! *Hands turned upwards, confused face*
**God is a mystery!** *Hands turned upwards, confused face*

Let's try singing that all at once.
*Sing very slowly and clearly, giving the children the chance to keep up with at least the actions.*

**1, 2, 3, the Trinity!** *Count on fingers followed by a triangle shape*
**Father, Son and Holy Spirit.** *Cross self or count to 3 again*
**1, 2, 3, the Trinity!** *Count on fingers followed by a triangle shape*
**God is One and God is Three!** *One hand shows one, the other three*
**God is a mystery!** *Hands turned upwards, confused face*
*Repeat until the children are confident with at least the actions*

Let's show one finger! *Lead the children in showing one finger*
Number 1 is God the Father!
God the Father made the world!
Who can show us an action for 'the world'.
*Choose one of the actions for the group to use, or leave the children free to make their own actions.*
Let's sing 'God the Father made the world!'

**God the Father made the world!** *World action*
**God the Father made the world!** *World action*
**God the Father made the world!** *World action*
*Sing louder at this point to make the words clear to the children, who will otherwise carry on with 'God the Father made the world'.*
**God is One and God is Three!** *One hand shows one, the other three*
**God is a mystery!** *Hands turned upwards, confused face*
*Repeat.*

So we have . . .
*If appropriate see if the children can help you remember.*
Number 1: *Show one finger* God the . . . **Father**

Now let's show two fingers. *Lead the children in showing two fingers*
Number 2 is God the Son.
God the Son is JESUS!
Jesus was born as a baby. *Rock baby in arms*
He died on the cross. *Stretch arms out*
And then he burst from the dark cave. *Crouch down and jump up*
What action shall we use for Jesus?
*Choose one of the actions for the group to use (or another that the children have suggested), or leave the children free to make their own actions.*
Let's sing 'God the Son is Jesus'.

**God the Son is Jesus!** *Jesus action*
**God the Son is Jesus!** *Jesus action*
**God the Son is Jesus!** *Jesus action*
**God is One and God is Three!** *One hand shows one, the other three*
**God is a mystery!** *Hands turned upwards, confused face*
*Repeat.*

So we have . . .
*If appropriate, see if the children can join in at the dots.*
Number 1: *show one finger* God the . . . **Father**
Number 2: *show two fingers* God the . . . **Son**

Now let's show three fingers. *Lead the children in showing three fingers*
Number 3 is God the HOLY SPIRIT!

God the Holy Spirit came like a dove on Jesus.
Can you show me the Spirit coming down like a dove, a bird?
*Lead the children in showing a bird flying down.*
Then the Holy Spirit came like fire on Jesus' friends!
Can you show me the fire of the Holy Spirit?
*Lead the children in swaying their body like flames.*
Now the Holy Spirit lives in you and me! *Point at children then self*
The Holy Spirit makes us strong!
Who can show us STRONG?
What action shall we use for the Holy Spirit?
*Choose one of the actions for the group to use (or another that the children have suggested), or leave the children free to make their own actions.*
Let's sing 'God the Spirit lives in us!'

**God the Spirit lives in us!** *Spirit action*
**God the Spirit lives in us!** *Spirit action*
**God the Spirit lives in us!** *Spirit action*
**God is One and God is Three!** *One hand shows one, the other three*
**God is a mystery!** *Hands turned upwards, confused face*
*Repeat.*

So we have . . .
*If appropriate see if the children can join in at the dots.*
*Show one finger* God the . . . **Father.**
*Show two fingers* God the . . . **Son.**
*Show three fingers* And God the . . . **Holy Spirit!**
Father, Son and Holy Spirit!

So today we celebrate the Trinity!
*If appropriate, see if the children can join in after the dots.*
*One finger* God the . . . **Father** made the . . . **world.**
*Two fingers* God the . . . **Son** is . . . **Jesus.**
*Three fingers* And God the . . . **Spirit**, lives in . . . **us!**
Let's sing our Trinity song again.

**1, 2, 3, the Trinity!** *Count on fingers followed by a triangle shape*
**Father, Son and Holy Spirit.** *Cross self or count to 3 again*
**1, 2, 3, the Trinity!** *Count on fingers followed by a triangle shape*
**God is One and God is Three!** *One hand shows one, the other three*
**God is a mystery!** *Hands turned upwards, confused face*

So today we've learned a big mystery about God.
God is too big . . .
Let's show big again! *Lead the children in showing a big shape with their arms*

God is too big to squash into our thinking. *Squeeze with hands*
Or to squeeze into our words. *Squeeze with hands*
God is a MYSTERY! *Hands turned upwards, confused face*

We're going to sing our Trinity Song two more times to finish.
Let's sing the first one really quietly to God.
Then let's stand up and sing the second time really loudly
to let the whole world know about the Trinity!

*Quietly, seated:*
**1, 2, 3, the Trinity!** *Count on fingers followed by a triangle shape*
**Father, Son and Holy Spirit.** *Cross self or count to 3 again*
**1, 2, 3, the Trinity!** *Count on fingers followed by a triangle shape*
**God is One and God is Three!** *One hand shows one, the other three*
**God is a mystery!** *Hands turned upwards, confused face*

Let's stand up!
*Singing strongly:*
**1, 2, 3, the Trinity!** *Count on fingers followed by a triangle shape*
**Father, Son and Holy Spirit.** *Cross self or count to 3 again*
**1, 2, 3, the Trinity!** *Count on fingers followed by a triangle shape*
**God is One and God is Three!** *One hand shows one, the other three*
**God is a mystery!** *Hands turned upwards, confused face*

# Creative Response starter ideas: Jesus Is Alive! Alleluia! unit

→ **Guide: Book 1, p. 228**

These starter ideas are designed to spark imaginations and open up opportunities for the children to respond creatively in their different ways to the worship and storytelling you've taken part in together.

---

**Tip**

As outlined in the Guide of *Diddy Disciples* Book 1 from p. 228, we've found the following rules of thumb helpful for fostering an environment where children are encouraged to engage personally and openly.

1  Encourage the children to make their own choices.
2  Give the children space to develop their response as they wish.
3  Create space for 'bridge building'.
4  It's the act of responding that matters, not the final result.
5  These responses are 'holy ground'.

---

**Weekly Starter Ideas** relate directly to the Bible Storytelling of each session, including a print-and-go option.

**Sensory Starter Ideas** are designed for sensory explorers, including babies and toddlers. These can remain the same through the whole unit.

**Unit Starter Ideas** are designed to remain relevant throughout the whole unit. Keeping these resources available each week gives children the opportunity to deepen and develop their responses, while making preparation more manageable for leaders.

---

**Tip: Free response area**

In addition to any other resources you provide, keeping a free response area available every week will give the children the opportunity to create anything they wish in response to the story they've told, building their sense of confidence and personal responsibility. In this area you could simply provide blank paper and crayons, pencils, paints or pastels. If you have them, other interesting media (see Book 1, p. 256) will provide even more scope for the children to nurture and strengthen their imaginative skills.

# Weekly Starter Ideas

## Week 1: Jesus is Risen! Alleluia! (Easter Day)

- Invite the children to decorate an Easter egg in their own way. Will their egg be closed or open (they could cut a jagged or straight line across the egg to show its opening)? Will there be a chick inside? Or will it be hollow like the empty tomb? *Provide paper, Easter egg templates (p. 372 or website), scissors, crayons/ pencils/pastels/paints. Optional: collage materials (Book 1, p. 255 or website), glue, glitter, chick templates (p. 379 or website), paper fasteners so the children can create an egg that opens and closes if they wish, with the fastener holding the two sections together at the corner.*

- Invite the children to decorate an Easter card or postcard to send. *Provide folded card, pencils/crayons/ pastels. Optional: postcard template (p. 385 or website), Easter egg template (p. 372 or website), collage materials (Book 1, p. 255), glue.*

- Give the children the opportunity to paint real Easter eggs to take home and eat. *Provide real eggs (boiled [!] that morning and refrigerated), paints, pastels or felt tips.*

- Invite the children to create Easter paper chains to celebrate Easter Day! *Provide strips of yellow/white or Easter-themed paper and glue.*

- See other Easter egg starter ideas from the unit starter ideas on p. 211.

## Week 2: On Easter Day in the Morning

- Invite the children to make a picture or collage of the empty tomb. They may even like to add angels, Jesus' friends or the Risen Jesus there. *Provide the empty tomb template (p. 373 or website), scissors, glue, pencils/crayons/pastels. Optional: paper fasteners (so the stone can open and shut) and collage materials (Book 1, p. 255; newspapers make great collage materials for the tomb).*

- Invite children to make one of the angels from the story. Remember to give them the space to imagine for themselves what angels look like. *Provide angel templates (p. 362 or website), blank paper for those who would like to draw freestyle, pencils/crayons/pastels/paints. Optional: collage materials (Book 1, p. 255), glue.*

- Give the children the opportunity to make their own Easter Garden (see p. 149). *Provide a box or tub from recycling or a paper plate to hold the garden (tubs with lids such as margarine tub or takeaway containers are ideal for easy transportation home), plus a range of materials that could be used to create the garden such as: soil and grass/flower seeds, or green fabric/paper and real or paper flowers (for the garden), a paper cup, yoghurt pot, plant pot, section of an egg tray or eggshells\* (for the cave), a suitably sized stone to seal the cave.*

---

\* Using eggshells creates a wonderful opportunity to make connections between the tomb and Easter eggs but they need to be handled carefully. Before the session, make sure you wash the eggshells thoroughly, then boil or bake them in the oven at 120 °C (250 °F, gas mark ½) for 15–20 minutes to sterilize them.

---

- Invite the children to make an Easter flower collage to celebrate the joy of Easter from magazines. They may even like to decorate a cross with their joyful flowers. *Provide paper/card, flower magazines, glue, scissors. Optional: cross template (p. 370 or website).*

- Give the children the opportunity to decorate Easter Garden cakes to celebrate Easter. *Provide cupcakes (pre-made or bought), green icing and flower sprinkles. Optional: desiccated coconut dyed green to be the grass, marzipan or royal icing that can be shaped into an empty tomb and stone.*

UNIT 4 • JESUS IS ALIVE! ALLELUIA!    JESUS IS ALIVE! ALLELUIA!

Section 3: Creative Response starter ideas

## Week 3:  The Walk to Emmaus

⌕ Invite the children to create finger puppets of Jesus' friends and the 'stranger' to tell the story themselves.  Each child will need at least three finger puppets. *Provide finger puppet templates (p. 375), scissors, pencils/crayons, glue.*

⌕ Give the children the opportunity to spend time kneading and shaping bread dough into a roll to take home, bake and share. *Provide a simple bread dough for the children (use a readymade mix, see Book 1, p. 258 for a recipe, or use your own recipe), a floured container or cling film to take the roll home in, and appropriate instructions for baking the bread. Optional: if you have the facilities, you may even like to bake the bread on site.*

⌕ Invite the children to make an icon of the Risen Jesus *Provide a card rectangle, tinfoil to wrap around the card to create a silver icon background and paper, pencils/crayons/pastels/paints, scissors. Optional: glue, collage materials (Book 1, p. 255), body template (p. 366 or website).*

## Week 4:  The Good Shepherd

⌕ Invite the children to show themselves, or friends/family, as a sheep: as part of a picture or collage, as a  necklace, Easter card, puppet or anything they like. *Provide sheep template (p. 386 or website), pencils/ crayons/pastels, etc. If you have cotton wool, lollipop sticks/straws/pipe cleaners, glue and any other collage materials (Book 1, p. 255), make these available too.*

⌕ Invite the children to make their own shepherd's crook and decorate it. *Provide real sticks, plus coloured wool/ string/pipe cleaners.*

## Week 5:  The Catch of Fishes

⌕ Invite the children to make their own fish. *Provide fish template (p. 377 or website), pencils/crayons/ pastels, etc. If you have collage materials (Book 1, p. 255), make these available too. Optional: add a card handle to a paper plate to make a frying pan, or decorate the fish with finger paints (see Book 1, p. 258 for a recipe for edible finger paints).*

⌕ Give the children the opportunity to build a fire from sticks. Once the fires are ready, you could mime lighting them (1, 2, 3 . . . Tssss *Strike imaginary match*) then sit around the fires, imagining Jesus there cooking fish with you. *Provide a range of sticks.*

⌕ Give a small group of children the opportunity to work together to make a boat to sit in from whatever you have to hand. They may like to create a sea around themselves and a fishing net. They may like to act out fishing from the boat, or they may simply like to get caught up in the act of creating. *Provide a range of open-ended materials: chairs, tables, rugs, blue/white sheets and pillow cases, brush handles, etc.*

⌕ Invite the children to make their own fish from paper plates. Cut a triangle from the edge to the centre of the plate (the hole becomes the mouth and the triangle can be glued to the other end of the fish to become its tail). The fish can then be painted, coloured or collaged. *Provide paper plates, scissors, glue, pencils/crayons/paints/ pastels. Optional: collage materials (Book 1, p. 255).*

⌕ Give the children the opportunity to imagine swimming through the water to find Jesus through one of the water-themed (River Jordan) starter ideas in the John the Baptist unit (p. 96).

## Week 6:  Peter's Story

⌐ Peter is given the keys to God's Kingdom! Peter's given a new start and an important job! Invite the children to make Peter's key (or set of keys) and to decorate them with joyful colours. *Provide key templates (p. 380 or website). Optional: string/wool/pipe cleaners to create a set of keys.*

⌐ Give the children the opportunity to explore the different emotions from the story with face templates. Which part of the story will they choose? When Peter has said, 'No! I do NOT follow Jesus!'; when Jesus gives Peter a new start and says, 'Follow me!'; or another part of the story? Maybe the children would prefer to respond to a moment from their own life with their face picture. *Provide face templates (p. 374 or website), pencils/crayons/pastels/paints.*

⌐ Invite the children to create Jesus' footsteps to follow by drawing around their own or each other's feet. What would they like to do with their footprint(s)? Decorate them? Make them into a necklace or card? *Provide paper, pencils, scissors, pencils/crayons/pastels/paints, plus string and collage materials (Book 1, p. 255) if you have them.*

## Week 7:  Jesus Goes Up!

The story of Ascension Day for the week before Pentecost.

⌐ Invite the children to make an image of the Risen Jesus the last time his friends saw him. You could invite them to attach string to the back so that Jesus can go 'up' from the ground. Some children may even like to create clouds from card, paper plates or an upturned open box, into which they can pull Jesus up. *Provide body template (p. 366), pencils/crayons/pastels, scissors. Optional: paper plate/card/box, string/wool.*

⌐ Invite the children to create a waving hand by drawing around their own hand and cutting it out. They may like to attach their hand to a stick with masking tape, so they can wave goodbye to Jesus with it. *Provide card, pencils, scissors. Optional: lollipop stick/straw/real stick and masking tape.*

⌐ Get ready for the fire of the Spirit at Pentecost by creating fire pictures! Invite the children to make their paintbrushes/fingers 'dance' with fire on paper with swirls and swooshes in reds/yellows/oranges to create images of fire. Ask the children if they're willing to make more than one painting and to leave one behind to be used during the Creative Response next week. *Provide blank paper, different shades of red/yellow/orange paint and paintbrushes (or use fingerpaints, see Book 1, p. 258 for recipe).*

Section 3: Creative Response starter ideas   ⌐ UNIT 4 • JESUS IS ALIVE! ALLELUIA!

207

## Week 8:  Come, Holy Spirit!

⌒ Invite the children to dance with their pencils/crayons/pastels to colour their tongues of fire with fiery colours. The children may even like to attach their flames to a hatband to show the Spirit's fire resting on them. *Provide fire template (p. 376 or website), fire-coloured pencils/crayons/pastels/paints. Optional: hatband (see p. 360) and masking tape, fiery coloured collage materials (Book 1, p. 255) and glue.*

⌒ Invite the children to collage fire. *Provide paper, fiery coloured collage materials, glue.*

⌒ Invite the children to collage a dove shape with fire. They may enjoy attaching red/yellow/orange streamers to it. *Provide bird template (p. 365 or website), fiery coloured collage materials (Book 1, p. 255) glue, scissors. Optional: streamer materials such as red/yellow/orange ribbon/wool/curling ribbon/crepe/ tissue paper.*

⌒ Give the children the opportunity to create Holy Spirit streamers by attaching yellow/orange/red streamers to a real stick. *Provide real sticks (check for sharp points), masking tape, streamer materials such as red/yellow/ orange ribbon/wool/curling ribbon/crepe/tissue paper.*

⌒ Invite younger children to dance like fire with paint on a paper plate (which allows for spillages). *Provide paper plates, red/yellow/orange paints, paintbrushes (or use fingerpaints, Book 1, p. 258).*

⌒Give the children the opportunity to make a fire and wind shaker so they can make the sound of the Spirit rushing into the room. Invite the children to pour dried orange lentils/rice into a transparent bottle with a teaspoon. You could even ask them to feed little twigs in first, for the lentils to run through. Allow plenty of time for this and expect lots of lentils to escape! When the children are ready, they may need help with attaching the lid tightly. The children may like to attach fiery streamers to their bottles. *Provide plastic bottles with secure lids (transparent if possible), dried red lentils/rice. Optional: twigs, streamer materials such as red/yellow/orange ribbon/wool/curling ribbon/crepe/tissue paper.*

⌒ If you made fire pictures last week, invite the children to take one of the pictures (it doesn't need to be their own and you could even contribute more yourself). Ask the children to dance like the fire of the Spirit again, this time using scissors to sway and turn through the fire paintings to create flame shapes. Use the freestyle red/yellow/ orange cuttings that are created by this to create a large-scale fire collage. *Provide: fire paintings (dried), scissors, large roll of paper, glue.*

## Tip

At St Peter's, Walworth, we created an altar frontal inspired by Henri Matisse's cut-outs for Pentecost this way. See the website for pictures.

## Week 9: Trinity Sunday

⌒ Invite the children to make a Trinity banner to celebrate the Trinity. You might like to create individual banners or a large group banner with lots of different pictures representing God the Father, God the Son and God the Holy Spirit. Starter ideas include: draw around your own hand, create something with a piece of plasticine/ball of mud/clay (God the Father, the Maker), a cross or empty cave (God the Son, Jesus), a dove or fire (God the Holy Spirit). However, encourage the children to create their own drawings. How would they like to show God the Father, God the Son and God the Holy Spirit? If you're making individual banners, they might like to glue their pictures to paper or attach them to string. *Provide lots of blank paper, bird template (p. 365 or website), cross template (p. 370 or website), empty tomb template (p. 373 or website), fire template (p. 376 or website), scissors, glue. Optional: string/wool/ribbon, masking tape, large pieces of paper.*

⌒ Invite the children to create Trinity triangles from lollipop sticks to celebrate the Trinity. See if they'd like to attach string to them to create Trinity necklaces or hanging decorations. Before older children construct their triangle, they may like to draw pictures of God the Father, God the Son and God the Holy Spirit on the sticks. Give the children space to explore other shapes (beyond triangles) as images of the Trinity. *Provide lollipop sticks, glue sticks, pencils/felt tips, string.*

⌒ Give the children the opportunity to focus on one Person of the Trinity. Who do they feel most close to? Father, Son or Holy Spirit? Invite them to create a picture of that Person of the Trinity. You may like to share your different responses as a group, ending with the Trinity song while holding your different pictures up in praise of God, Father, Son and Holy Spirit. *Provide lots of blank paper, pencils/pastels/paints/crayons. With very young children, you may like to offer the templates outlined in the first option above as starter ideas to collage or decorate.*

# Sensory Starter Ideas (including for babies and toddlers)

Resources that you could provide for the children to explore for themselves include the following.

- a Jesus figure (we use Joseph from our nativity set);

- child-safe crosses (holding crosses are particularly appropriate);

- an Easter Garden to explore. Note: If your group is using an Easter Garden during your time of saying sorry or prayers, you could leave this and flowers for the children to continue adding their prayers or 'sorries' during the Creative Response time;

- wooden/metal or other child-safe cup and plate or chalice and paten for children to explore and tell the story of Jesus' Last Meal and The Walk to Emmaus (at St Peter's, Walworth, we use wooden egg cups and coasters from Baker Ross; check other online suppliers and craft shops);

- yellow imaginative aids;

- lots of stones for building a dark cave. Check none of these present a choking hazard;

- flowers or pictures/magazines/books of flowers to explore;

- boats, fish and a net if you have one. Check that play with any net is closely supervised by a parent or trained helper;

- board books that tell the story of Jesus' Last Week and Easter;

- playdough and modelling tools to make all sorts of things: the empty cave, eggs, chicks, boats, fish, characters from the stories, or anything that sparks the children's imagination;

- mini fluffy chicks (the kind you get as cake decorations at Easter) in a bottle, so the babies can see them safely, with the lid taped shut;

- plastic eggs that break open;

- old Easter cards with Easter pictures on them;

- chick, sheep or fish jigsaws;

- musical instruments: Easter is a time of joy and celebration!

- sticks to make a fire like the disciples, a child-safe frying pan, fish (plastic/wood/printed). When you've made a fire together, you might like to sit around it, cooking fish and imagining Jesus there with you. I wonder how it feels to be with Jesus?

# Unit Starter Ideas

⌒ Invite the children to make edible Easter egg nests with mini eggs in. Melt chocolate just before the Creative Response and stir well to make sure it's cool to the touch with no hot spots. While the children are waiting, invite them to crush cornflakes in bowls with a spoon. Pour a little melted chocolate into each bowl and ask the children to combine the ingredients. When they're ready, invite them to place spoons of the mixture into cupcake cases, to create a little hollow in the middle, then to place two or three mini eggs in the hollow. Give the children the space to create their own versions of nests or simply to be caught up in the act of creation (and inevitable joyful eating). *Provide facilities to wash hands before and after this activity (!!), cornflakes (or another suitable cereal), cupcake cases, spoons, bowls, melted chocolate.*

⌒ Simnel cakes are traditionally eaten at Easter (sometimes on Mothering Sunday). Give the children the opportunity to decorate either their own mini Simnel-like cake or a large Simnel cake for your church to share with your congregation after the service. To decorate the cakes: spread apricot jam on the top, roll out marzipan, cut out a circle shape from it with circle cutters and place it on the jam layer. Next, roll the marzipan into small balls (traditionally 11) and 'glue' them to the top of the cake using the jam. Give the children space to develop the Simnel cake tradition in their own ways. *Provide a large sponge or fruit cake (or one cupcake per child), marzipan, rolling pins, circle cutters (plate/cup/cutter with a similar circumference to the cake), apricot jam, safe knives or spoons to spread the jam.*

⌒ The Easter stories open up lots of opportunities to explore a range of emotions. Invite the children to cut different expressions out of magazines and to create a collage from them. *Provide newspapers/magazines. Check the headlines are suitable. At St Peter's we often use past copies of our diocesan newspaper or the* Church Times *supplemented with suitable pages from TV magazines (which have plenty of cross/shocked faces).*

⌒ Use one of the other Easter egg starter ideas from Week 1 above.

⌒ Invite the children to make an 'Alleluia! banner' to take home (if they didn't make one on the Sunday before Lent). Give the children the opportunity to write their own 'Alleluia!' in bubble letters or on bunting, or to use the 'Alleluia!' template (website only). Invite them to cut the letters out and then to tape them to a length of string to create a banner. Leave the children the imaginative space to create what they would like with their 'Alleluia!' letters. For example, this isn't the time to worry about spelling! *Provide card, 'Alleluia!' template (website only), pencils/crayons/pastels, scissors, masking tape, string/wool.*

⌒ Easter is a time of joyful celebration! On Easter Day, the bells ring out! Give the children the opportunity to create musical instruments to celebrate. For instance, you could adapt the 'fire and wind shaker' starter idea in Week 8: Pentecost (p. 208) to become an Easter joy shaker, using yellows, golds and whites, instead of fiery colours. Or experiment with other musical instruments: elastic bands stretched over a strong box or tub to create a stringed instrument; paper or cellophane stretched over a strong cardboard cup or tub and secured with an elastic band to create a drum; straws with the end flattened and cut into a 'V'-shaped point to create a buzzing oboe! Give the children space and time to experiment! *Provide elastic bands, strong boxes and tubs, straws, scissors, masking tape, paper (or cellophane if you have it).*

⌒ Invite the children to decorate the Easter stone that rolled away. *Provide smooth stones, felt tips/pastels/paints.*

⌒ Invite the children to make the cross of the Risen Jesus beautiful by decorating it with flowers, or bright colours. *Provide wooden crosses or the cross template (p. 370 or website), pencils/crayons/paints and scissors. If you have collage materials (Book 1, p. 255) or real flowers (such as daisies, buttercups, clover) and glue, make these available too. If you have string or wool, you could see if any children would like to make necklaces or bookmarks with their cross.*

⌒ Give the children the opportunity to draw their own cross of the Risen Jesus with bright colours on black paper (to echo the darkness of Good Friday and the joyful colours of Easter Day). *Provide black paper, bright pastels or chalks.*

⌒ Invite the children to have a go at making a daisy chain or another creation from daisies. *Provide freshly picked daisies or go and pick them together outside. Optional: you could provide wool and plastic needles to support younger children in making a daisy chain. The needle can go through the head of the daisy if the stalk is too tricky.*

**Tip**

At St Peter's, Walworth, we keep last year's Paschal candle to show as an example in Diddy Disciples sessions. We also use it during our baptism workshops!

⌒ If the Paschal/Easter candle is prominent in your church during Easter, you could give the children the opportunity to paint their own design on a candle to make their own Paschal candle. You might like to show them your church's Paschal candle as an example. *Provide candles that are large enough to paint on, paints, paintbrushes.*

⌒ Alternatively, invite the children to decorate a 2D candle template. *Provide candle template (p. 367 or website), pencils/crayons/pastels/paints.*

# UNIT 5
# LET YOUR KINGDOM COME! (GREEN TIME/ ORDINARY TIME BETWEEN JULY AND NOVEMBER)

The Let Your Kingdom Come! unit invites young children to take part in telling some of Jesus' colourful parables about God's Kingdom. There are also lots of opportunities to make connections with the 'Our Father'/ Lord's Prayer, which many young children will be hearing around them or learning themselves. Christians pray 'thy Kingdom come' all the time. But what's God's Kingdom like?

The Green Time units are designed to be used at any time between July and November. Groups are encouraged to use them in the order that makes most sense in their context. Two further Green Time units can be found in Book 1.

## Section 1

# The Building Blocks: Let Your Kingdom Come! unit

Pick and choose from these Building Blocks and their various options to build sessions for your group. Whatever choices you make, we suggest you keep to that pattern for the whole of the unit as this will open up opportunities for the children to participate fully and confidently during your time together.

> **Build your own Diddy Disciples session** (Book 1, p. 6) provides an overview of the Building Blocks and a short introduction to fitting them together, along with examples.
>
> **Guide to the Building Blocks** (Book 1, p. 217) provides a step-by-step guide to each Building Block.

# Welcome

→ **Guide: Book 1, p. 218**

*Welcome your group.*

Let's start by going around the circle
And saying our name out loud.
My name's _____.

*Go around the circle so that every adult and child has the chance to say her or his name (and introduce any dolls, teddies or toys). If any of the children don't want to say their name or aren't able to, you (or a parent or carer) could say it for them and wave.*
It's time to sing our Welcome Song!

## Welcome Song: Option 1

→ **Song: 'The Diddy Disciples welcome song'. Words: © Sharon Moughtin-Mumby**
→ **Tune 'Glory, glory, alleluia!' (traditional). For the music see p. 357, or for a taster see the Diddy Disciples website. For tips on teaching songs for the first time, see Book 1, p. 215.**

*Go around the circle the same way as above. See if you can remember each other's names and insert them into the song.*

**Welcome** *Name 1* **to** *St Peter's\**
**Welcome** *Name 2* **to** *St Peter's\**
**Welcome** *Name 3* **to** *St Peter's\**
**You are welcome in the name of the Lord!**

*\* Insert the name of your church or children's group, or sing 'our worship'.*

## Welcome Song: Option 2

→ **Song: 'You are welcome in the name of the Lord' (traditional)**
→ **Tune: traditional. For the music see p. 360, or for a taster see the Diddy Disciples website. For tips on teaching songs for the first time, see Book 1, p. 215.**

Let's wave with one hand. *Lead waving*
Then with our other hand. *Lead waving*
Then let's choose someone and show God's 'glory'!
*Move arms up and down in front of you with fingers wiggling, palms facing out, towards one person.*
And someone else! *Repeat*
Then let's wave with both hands all around the circle.
*Lead waving.*

We're ready to sing!

**You are welcome in the name of the Lord!**
*Wave with right hand to one person.*
**You are welcome in the name of the Lord!**
*Wave with left hand to another person.*
**I can see all over you, the glory of the Lord!**
*Move arms up and down in front of you with fingers wiggling,
palms facing out, towards one person and then another.*
**You are welcome in the name of the Lord!**
*Wave with both hands all around the circle.*

# Getting Ready to Worship

→ **Guide: Book 1, p. 218**

*Choose one of the following greetings according to which greeting is familiar in your church. (If your church uses a different greeting, you could use that here instead.)*

## Getting Ready to Worship: Option 1

→ Action: the sign of the cross. Words: © Sharon Moughtin-Mumby

*Invite the children to make the sign of the cross slowly with you. As the children become more confident, invite a child to lead the action as the whole group says the words and makes the sign of the cross.*

| | |
|---|---|
| **In my head,** | *touch head* |
| **in my heart,** | *touch chest* |
| **and all around me,** | *touch shoulders one by one* |
| **Jesus is here.** | *open hands in front, facing upwards* |

## Getting Ready to Worship: Option 2

→ Action: 'The Lord be with you' (open hands)

Let's start by clenching our hands together tightly.

*Lead children in clenching fists against your body to show a defensive posture.*

When we close ourselves up like this,
it's hard to let anyone into our heart.
It's hard even to let God into our heart!

When we get ready to worship,
we show that we're open to God and to each other.

*Open your hands out, facing up.*

Can you show me your open hands?
We're ready to let God and each other in!

The Lord be with you.
*Hold hands open to the children.*

**And also with you.**
*Invite the children to open their hands towards you.*

# Introducing the Unit

→ Guide: Book 1, p. 218

## Introducing the Unit: Option 1

*Use 'thy'/'your' with the children according to the version they will hear in your church/at school.*

Jesus told us to pray for God's Kingdom!
After 3, let's say, '*thy/your* Kingdom come' together
**1, 2, 3 . . . *thy/your* Kingdom come!**
And again . . .
**1, 2, 3 . . . *thy/your* Kingdom come!**

Jesus taught us that prayer!
Christians pray '*thy/your* Kingdom come!' all the time!
    *If appropriate:* in the 'Our Father'/Lord's Prayer.
But what's God's Kingdom like? *Hands out in question*
What are we praying for?

God's Kingdom, God's special place,
isn't just up in heaven *Point up*
It isn't just in church. *Shake head*

*Week 1:*
Let me tell you a secret . . .

*Week 2+, if appropriate:*
Can anyone remember our secret?
*Give one of the children the opportunity to convey 'the secret' in his or her own words.*

Sssssssh!
*Whisper* God's Kingdom is coming in the WORLD! *Hands down on the floor*
All around us! *Point around the room*

God's Kingdom is anywhere where we live
by God's special rules of **LOVE**. *Cross arms on chest*
Let's cross our arms on our chest to show love.
*Lead the children in crossing arms on chest.*

*Repeat, encouraging the children to join in after the dots.*
God's Kingdom is anywhere where we live
by God's special rules of . . . *cross arms on chest* **LOVE**.

## Introducing the Unit: Option 2

→ **Words: The Lord's Prayer (use the version that's used in your church or local school)**
→ **Tune (optional for groups who don't know the 'Our Father'): 'Frère Jacques'**

*Use 'thy'/'your' with the children according to the version they will hear in your church/at school.*

Jesus told us to pray for God's Kingdom:
to say, *'thy/your* Kingdom come!'

*Either:*
Let's pray the 'Our Father'/Lord's Prayer together
When we get to *'thy/your* Kingdom come', let's stop!
Let's see if we can do that:

| | |
|---|---|
| **Our Father, who art in heaven,** | **Our Father in heaven,** |
| **hallowed be thy name,** | **hallowed be your name;** |
| **thy Kingdom come . . .** | **your Kingdom come . . .** |

*Or (for very young children):*
Let's sing the prayer Jesus taught us 'my turn' *point to self,* 'your turn' *leader's hands out to group*

*To the tune of 'Frère Jacques':*

| Traditional version | Modern version |
|---|---|
| Our Father | Our Father |
| **Our Father** | **Our Father** |
| Who art in heav'n | I-in heav'n |
| **Who art in heav'n** | **I-in heav'n** |
| Hallowed be thy na-me, | Hallowed be your na-me, |
| **Hallowed be thy na-me,** | **Hallowed be your na-me,** |
| Thy Kingdom come! | Your Kingdom come! |
| **Thy Kingdom come!** | **Your Kingdom come!** |

*All groups:*
Jesus taught us that prayer.
We pray *'thy/your* Kingdom come!' all the time!
But what's God's Kingdom like? *Hands out in question*
What are we praying for?

God's Kingdom, God's special place,
isn't just up in heaven *Point up*
It isn't just in church. *Shake head*

*Week 1:*

Let me tell you a secret . . .

*Week 2+, if appropriate:*

Can anyone remember our secret?

*Give one of the children the opportunity to convey 'the secret' in her or his own words.*

Sssssssh!

*Whisper* God's Kingdom is coming in the WORLD! *Hands down on the floor*

All around us! *Point around the room*

God's Kingdom is anywhere where we live

by God's special rules of **LOVE**. *Cross arms on chest*

Let's cross our arms on our chest to show love.

*Lead the children in crossing arms on chest.*

*Repeat, encouraging the children to join in after the dots.*

God's Kingdom is anywhere where we live

by God's special rules of . . . *Cross arms on chest* **LOVE**.

# Gathering Song

→ Guide: Book 1, p. 219

## Gathering Song: Option 1

→ Song: 'Let your Kingdom come quickly!' *Place version* words: © Sharon Moughtin-Mumby
→ Tune: 'There's a hole in my bucket' (traditional). For a taster see the Diddy Disciples website.

Let's pray for God's Kingdom as Jesus taught us!

*When learning the song for the first time, you may find this material helpful.*

Let's sing 'my turn' *point to self*, 'your turn' *leader's hands out to group*.

Let your Kingdom come quickly *'come' action (see p. 195)*

in *Walworth*, in *Walworth*!* *Point all around*

**Let your Kingdom come quickly:** *'come' action*

**in *Walworth*, in *Walworth*!***

*\*Insert local area/school/church/community/parish.*

Let your Kingdom come quickly! *'Come' action*

Let your *clap hands together in prayer* will be done!

**Let your Kingdom come quickly!** *'Come' action*

**Let your** *clap hands together in prayer* **will be done!**

Let's try that all together:

*If you're using imaginative aids, give them out at this point. You may like to ask the children to create actions that are suitable with the resources you're using.*

**Let your Kingdom come quickly** *'come' action*

**in *Walworth*, in *Walworth*!*** *Point all around*

**Let your Kingdom come quickly!** *'Come' action*

**Let your** *clap hands together in prayer* **will be done!**

*Repeat.*

*When the group is ready:*
We pray for God's Kingdom,
but what's God's Kingdom like? *Hands out in question*
What are we praying for?
I wonder what Jesus will say God's Kingdom is like today?

## Gathering Song: Option 2

→ **Song: 'Let your Kingdom come quickly!'** *Kingdom action version* **words:** © Sharon Moughtin-Mumby
→ **Tune: 'There's a hole in my bucket'** (traditional). **For the music see p. 217, or for a taster see the Diddy Disciples website.**

*This Gathering Song is designed to grow week by week as you explore Jesus' parables about God's Kingdom together. Each week, a new action for 'Kingdom' is introduced, based on the story that you've told the week before. It's designed for groups with at least some regular children who attend weekly/fortnightly. The song shares many of the same words as Option 1, but focuses on the word 'Kingdom' in order to give the children time to create meaningful connections. If you're using the What's in the Box? material (Book 1, p. 221), you may like to place the objects from previous weeks on a focal table to spark the children's memories of the parables you've told together.*

*Week 1:*
Let's pray for God's Kingdom as Jesus taught us!
Let's sing 'my turn' *point to self*, 'your turn' *leader's hands out to group*.

Let your Kingdom come quickly: *'come' action (see p. 195)*
your Kingdom, your Kingdom! *'Come' action*
**Let your Kingdom come quickly:** *'come' action*
**your Kingdom, your Kingdom**! *'Come' action*
Let your Kingdom come quickly! *'Come' action*
Let your *clap hands together in prayer* will be done!
**Let your Kingdom come quickly!** *'Come' action*
**Let your** *clap hands together in prayer* **will be done!**

Let's try that all together.
Let's pray as Jesus taught us!

*If you're using imaginative aids, you may like to give them out at this point, or you may like to leave this for following weeks. You may like to ask the children to create a new action for 'your will be done' that's suitable with the resources you're using.*

**Let your Kingdom come quickly:** *'come' action*
**your Kingdom, your Kingdom**! *'Come' action*
**Let your Kingdom come quickly!** *'Come' action*
**Let your** *clap hands together in prayer* **will be done!**

But what's God's Kingdom like? *Hands out in question*
What are we praying for?

*Weeks 2+:*
Let's pray for God's Kingdom as Jesus taught us!

*If you're using imaginative aids, give them out at this point. You may like to ask the children to create a new action for 'your will be done' that's suitable with the resources you're using.*

But wait a minute, we need an action for God's Kingdom.
Can anyone remember what Jesus said God's Kingdom's like?

*See if the children can remember the parable from the previous week(s). If appropriate, show the children an action or object from the focal table to jog their memories.*

*Accept the children's responses and use that action to sing the song.*

## Tip

In case you also need your memory jogged as leader!

Jesus said, God's Kingdom is:
- a tiny seed that grows and grows into the biggest tree!
- like the biggest party!
- sparkling like treasure!
- growing tall into an amazing harvest!
- turning everything topsy turvy! *Diddy Disciples 'New Start' sign (p. 355)*

*Example:*
*A child suggests 'a party!'*
Who can show me an action for a party?
*Celebrate the children's suggested actions.*

Let's sing our prayer.
This time, whenever we sing 'Kingdom!',
let's show God's Kingdom . . .
like the biggest party! *Party action*

*You may like to sing the song a little slower as the children get used to moving between actions.*
**Let your Kingdom come quickly:** *party action*
**your Kingdom, your Kingdom**! *Party action*
**Let your Kingdom come quickly!** *Party action*
**Let your** *clap hands together in prayer* **will be done!**

*Repeat using the images for God's Kingdom from all the parables you've told together. This song should grow week by week. In the first couple of weeks, you may like to repeat each verse once, but as the number of verses grows (and the children's familiarity with the song) you can sing the song once for each parable.*

*If you're using imaginative aids and need time to collect them up at the end:*
Let's sit down for a moment.
Let's sing our song one last time.
This time, let's sing it as a prayer.
While we pray, *Name* and *Name* will collect your *ribbons*.

*Lead the children in singing quietly. At St Peter's, Walworth, whenever possible, we model prayer as we sing and leave the collecting to the children.*

**Let your Kingdom come quickly:** *'come' action*
**your Kingdom, your Kingdom**! *'Come' action*
**Let your Kingdom come quickly!** *'Come' action*
**Let your** *clap hands together in prayer* **will be done!**

*All groups, end with:*
I wonder what Jesus will say God's Kingdom is like today?

## Gathering Song: Option 3

*Appropriate for groups with older children.*
→ Song: '(Look!) God's Kingdom is coming around us!' Words: © Sharon Moughtin-Mumby
→ Tune: 'My bonny lies over the ocean' (traditional). For a taster see the Diddy Disciples website.

*In Week 1, you may find the following material helpful for teaching the song.*
We're going to learn a song about God's Kingdom.
Let's sing 'my turn' *point to self,* 'your turn' *leader's hands out to group.*

*Singing:*
God's Kingdom is coming around us! *Point around the room*
**God's Kingdom is coming around us!** *Point around the room*
We pray for God's Kingdom to come! *Hands together or outwards in prayer*
**We pray for God's Kingdom to come!** *Hands together or outwards*

Let's sing that together:
**God's Kingdom is coming around us!** *Point around the room*
**We pray for God's Kingdom to come!** *Hands together or outwards*

Then the same words as last time but with a different tune at the end.
Listen carefully at the end!
**God's Kingdom is coming around us!** *Point around the room*
**We pray for God's Kingdom to come!** *Hands together or outwards in prayer*

Let's try that all together from the beginning!
**God's Kingdom is coming around us!** *Point around the room*
**We pray for God's Kingdom to come!** *Hands together or outwards*
**God's Kingdom is coming around us!** *Point around the room*
**We pray for God's Kingdom to come!** *Hands together or outwards*

Now let's sing 'my turn' *point to self,* 'your turn' *leader's hands out to group* again.

And put our hands together to pray with a clap
Amen! *Clap* Amen! *Clap*
We pray *clap* for God's Kingdom to come, to come! *Beckoning gesture*
**Amen!** *Clap* **Amen!** *Clap*
**We pray** *clap* **for God's Kingdom to come, to come!** *Beckoning gesture*

Then:

Amen! *Clap* Amen! *Clap*

We pray *clap* for God's Kingdom to come! *Beckoning gesture*

**Amen!** *Clap* **Amen!** *Clap*

**We pray** *clap* **for God's Kingdom to come!** *Beckoning gesture*

Let's pray for God's Kingdom as Jesus taught us!

*Spoken:* Look!

**God's Kingdom is coming around us!** *Point around the room*

**We pray for God's Kingdom to come!** *Hands together or outwards*

*Spoken:* Look!

**God's Kingdom is coming around us!** *Point around the room*

**We pray for God's Kingdom to come!** *Hands together or outwards*

**Amen!** *Clap* **Amen!** *Clap*

**We pray** *clap* **for God's Kingdom to come, to come!** *Beckoning gesture*

**Amen!** *Clap* **Amen!** *Clap*

**We pray** *clap* **for God's Kingdom to come!** *Beckoning gesture*

*Repeat.*

I wonder what Jesus will say God's Kingdom is like today?

# Getting Ready for Bible Storytelling

→ **Guide: Book 1, p. 221**

## Getting Ready for Bible Storytelling: Option 1

→ **Action: opening your group's box and naming this week's object**
→ **Guide: Book 1, p. 221**

*See the beginning of the weekly storytelling material for ideas of items to place in your box. Invite one of the children to open the box.*

What's in the box? *Invite the child to respond*

## Getting Ready for Bible Storytelling: Option 2

→ **Song: 'Jesus, open up my eyes'. Words: © Sharon Moughtin-Mumby**
→ **Tune: 'Michael, row the boat ashore' (traditional). For the music see p. 359, or for a taster see the Diddy Disciples website. For tips on teaching songs for the first time, see Book 1, p. 215.**

It's time to open the Bible.
Let's get ready!

Let's take our thumb *lead children in showing thumb*
And draw our cross on our eyes, *draw cross*
and our lips, *draw cross*
and our heart. *Draw cross*
Let's ask Jesus to help us get ready to listen out for God!

**Jesus, open up my eyes. Alleluia!**
*Trace a cross between your eyes.*
**Jesus, open up my lips. Alleluia!**
*Trace a cross on your lips.*
**Jesus, open up my heart. Alleluia!**
*Trace a cross on your heart.*
**Jesus, help me hear your voice. Alleluia!**
*Cup your hands behind your ears.*

# Interactive Bible Storytelling

→ **Guide: Book 1, p. 221**

*See the Bible Storytelling material in Section 2 of this unit.*

# Saying Sorry to God

→ **Guide: Book 1, p. 223**

*Invite the children to sit in a circle for a moment of quiet.*
*If appropriate, encourage the children to join in after the dots.*
God's Kingdom is wherever we live by
God's special rules of *cross arms on chest* . . . **love**.
It's time for us to say sorry for the times
we haven't loved like God loves.
It's time to sing our Sorry Song.

## Saying Sorry to God: Option 1

→ **Song: 'The Diddy Disciples sorry song'. Words: © Sharon Moughtin-Mumby**
→ **Tune: © Sharon Moughtin-Mumby. For the music see p. 356, or for a taster see the Diddy Disciples website. For a description of the 'I'm Sorry' and 'New Start' signs, see p. 355 or the website. For tips on teaching songs for the first time, see Book 1, p. 215.**

Let's put our hands on our head.
I wonder if there's anything we've thought this week
that we wish we hadn't thought?

*Lead the children in placing your hands on head, singing:*
**With my hands on my head,**
**I remember the things I've thought today,**
**I remember the things I wish I'd thought a different way.**

**I'm sorry, I'm sorry,** *Diddy Disciples 'I'm Sorry' sign twice (see p. 355)*
**I wish I could start again.** *Diddy Disciples 'New Start' sign (see p. 355)*
**I'm sorry, I'm sorry,** *'I'm Sorry' sign twice*
**I wish I could start again.** *'New Start' sign*

Let's put our hands by our mouths.
I wonder if there's anything we've said this week
that we wish we hadn't said?

*With hands by mouth, singing:*
**With my hands on my mouth,**
**I remember the things I've said today,**
**I remember the things I wish I'd said a different way.**

**I'm sorry, I'm sorry,** *'I'm Sorry' sign twice*
**I wish I could start again.** *'New Start' sign*
**I'm sorry, I'm sorry,** *'I'm Sorry' sign twice*
**I wish I could start again.** *'New Start' sign*

Let's cross our hands on our chest.
I wonder if there's anything we've done this week
that we wish we hadn't done?

*With hands crossed on chest, singing:*
**With my hands on my chest,**
**I remember the things I've done today,**
**I remember the things I wish I'd done a different way.**

**I'm sorry, I'm sorry,** *'I'm Sorry' sign twice*
**I wish I could start again.** *'New Start' sign*
**I'm sorry, I'm sorry,** *'I'm Sorry' sign twice*
**I wish I could start again.** *'New Start' sign*

*Continue with a Saying Sorry Action or move straight to God Gives Us a New Start, below. For Saying Sorry to God: Option 2, see pp. 156–7.*

# Saying Sorry Action

→ **Guide: Book 1, p. 223**

*For alternative actions that can be used during any unit at any time of year, see Saying Sorry Actions: Options 2, 3 and 4 on pp. 40–2 of Book 1.*

## Saying Sorry Action: Option 1

*Place a 'garden' in the centre of the circle. At St Peter's, Walworth, we use a tray with soil or a brown cloth and paper or real flowers, covered with lots of green paper strips to look like weeds). Large groups may like to make sure their garden can be carried around the circle.*

> *If your church follows the liturgical year, you may like to start with the following:*
> In Green Time, everything grows.
> Flowers grow, trees grow and the Church grows!
> We're part of the Church, so we're growing too!

Jesus wants to plant the seed of God's Kingdom in all of us!
Let's close our eyes and imagine
the seed of God's Kingdom growing inside us!

*After a moment:*
Let's open our eyes again.
To help seeds have space to grow,
we need to pull the weeds out.

When we say sorry to God,
it's like we're 'weeding' our heart.
We're pulling all the bad things out
and giving space to the beautiful flowers.

Let's imagine our heart is like this garden.
Let's go around the circle and pull one weed out of the garden
so we can see the beautiful flowers growing beneath.

*As the garden is 'weeded', lead the group in either*
> *Option 1: singing the 'I'm sorry' refrain, or*
> *Option 2: humming the first two lines of the 'We need a new start' song, followed by singing the refrain 'We're sorry, we're sorry. We need a new start'.*

*When the group has finished weeding, ask a child to remove any remaining 'weeds' from the garden.*
Look at our beautiful garden!
Now we can see all the flowers growing.
The Good News is that when we say sorry,
God will always give us a new start!
We can grow beautifully again.
God's Kingdom can grow inside us
Just like our beautiful garden.

After 3, let's shout, 'God gives us a new start!'
**1, 2, 3: God gives us a new start!**

## Saying Sorry Action: Option 2

→ **Action: showing how a seed grows tall with our bodies**

Let's close our eyes for a moment.
Jesus wants to plant the seed of God's Kingdom in all of us!

Let's imagine Jesus coming to us now.
Let's ask Jesus to make our hearts ready.
*Hold a moment of quiet.*

Now let's imagine Jesus planting the seed of
God's Kingdom in our hearts.

*After a moment:*
Let's open our eyes again.
Let's show how a seed grows!
Let's curl up into a ball like a seed.
*Lead the children in curling up into a ball.*

First, we need to put our roots down.
Let's show our roots with our fingers.
*Lead the children in wiggling fingers.*
We need to let our roots grow down deep.
*Lead the children in wiggling fingers down.*
Then after 3, let a little shoot pop up.
**1, 2, 3 . . . Pop!**
*Poke your hands up over your head like a little shoot.*
Then start to grow up tall.
*Gradually stand up, swaying like a growing stalk.*
Taller and taller, onto our tiptoes . . .
*Reach up with pointy hands and on tiptoes.*
Let's turn our faces up towards the sun!
Then let our leaves or branches spread out wide.
*Arms stretch slowly outwards.*

Look at those beautiful plants!
Let's ask for God's Kingdom
to grow even more inside us today.
And let's remember to live by the rules of God's Kingdom
by loving each other.

# God Gives Us a New Start

→ **Guide: Book 1, p. 225**

*Every time of Saying Sorry should end by assuring the children that God gives them a new start. Most Diddy Disciples Saying Sorry Actions already include this promise of a new start. If they don't – or if you have created your own Saying Sorry Action – you should choose from one of the following New Start options, or create your own assurance of forgiveness. You could also choose to move straight from the Sorry Song to God's promise of a new start, without any Saying Sorry Action.*

## New Start Action: Option 1

→ **Action: tracing a cross/smile on each other's forehead**

The Good News is:
God always wants to give us a new start!

Let's turn to the person next to us
and show that God gives us a new start.
Let's take our thumb/finger *show thumb/finger*

224

And draw a cross/smile on that person's forehead
*draw a cross/smile in the air*

> *If your group is drawing a smile, add:*
> to show that God is very happy with us!

Let's say, 'God gives you a new start!'
Then let the other person give you a new start, too!

*When the group has finished showing each other God's new starts:*
Let's use our new start to share God's love this week!

## New Start Action: Option 2

→ **Action: standing up and hugging each other**

The Good News is:
God always wants to give us a new start!

Let's help someone next to us stand up from the floor.
Then let that person help you stand up too!
*Lead the children in helping each other stand up.*

Then let's give each other a hug and say:
'God gives you a new start!'

*When the group has finished showing each other God's new starts:*
Let's use our new start to share God's love this week!

## New Start Action: Option 3

→ **Song: 'God loves to give me a new start!' Words: © Sharon Moughtin-Mumby**
→ **Tune: 'Give me oil in my lamp' (traditional). For the music see p. 357, or for a taster see the Diddy Disciples website. For tips on teaching songs for the first time, see Book 1, p. 215.**

The Good News is:
God always wants to give us a new start!
Let's sing our New Start song together.

**[Yes, my] God loves to give me a new start!** *Trace a smile/cross on own forehead*
**How amazing God's love for me!** *Cross hands on chest*
**[Yes, my] God loves to give me a new start!** *Trace a smile/cross on own forehead*
**How amazing is God's love for me!**

**Sing hosanna! Sing hosanna!** *Wave hands in the air*
**Sing hosanna to the King of Kings!**
*Wave hands in the air followed by crown on head.*
**Sing hosanna! Sing hosanna!** *Wave hands in the air*
**Sing hosanna to the King!**
*Wave hands in the air followed by crown on head.*

# Introduction to Prayers

It's time for us to pray for God's Kingdom to come!

# Prayers for Other People

→ **Guide: Book 1, p. 223 and p. 225**

*Invite the children to sit in a circle in a moment of quiet.*
Let's imagine holding our prayer gently,
*hands together gently in traditional prayer gesture, but cupped so you can imagine a prayer inside*

and then let it go up in prayer to God,
*hands opened upwards to God*

> If you're using Option 1:
> Jesus, *hands together, cupped*
> hear our prayer. *Hands opened upwards to God*
> Let's pray . . .

## Prayers for Other People: Special Option

*You can use this material either in the place of your usual Prayers for Other People, or as the Prayer Action within your usual prayers.*

*Either (for children who already know the Lord's Prayer):*
Let's pray the 'Our Father'/Lord's Prayer together.
When we say, 'your Kingdom come', let's shout that part!
And let's show God's Kingdom . . .

> *Week 1:* growing into the biggest tree! *Tree growing (p. 236)*
> *Week 2:* like the biggest party! *Party action*
> *Week 3:* sparkling like treasure! *Jazz hands*
> *Week 4:* growing tall into an amazing harvest! *Stretch up tall*
> *Week 5:* turning everything topsy turvy! *Diddy Disciples 'New Start' sign (p. 355)*

| | |
|---|---|
| **Our Father, who art in heaven,** | **Our Father in heaven,** |
| **Hallowed be thy name.** | **Hallowed be your name.** |
| **THY KINGDOM COME!** | **YOUR KINGDOM COME!** |
| *This week's Kingdom action* | *This week's Kingdom action* |
| **Thy will be done.** | **Your will be done.** |
| **On earth as it is in heaven.** | **On earth as in heaven.** |
| **Give us this day our daily bread.** | **Give us today our daily bread.** |
| **And forgive us our trespasses,** | **And forgive us our sins,** |
| **As we forgive those who trespass against us.** | **As we forgive those who sin against us.** |
| **And lead us not into temptation** | **And lead us not into temptation** |
| **But deliver us from evil.** | **But deliver us from evil.** |
| **For thine is the Kingdom,** | **For the Kingdom, the power** |
| **The power and the glory,** | **and the glory are yours,** |
| **for ever and ever, Amen.** | **for ever and ever, Amen.** |

*Or (for children who are beginning to learn the Lord's Prayer):*
Let's pray the 'Our Father'/Lord's Prayer together.
When we get to '*thy/your* Kingdom come' let's stop
and let's show God's Kingdom:

> *Week 1:* growing into the biggest tree! *Tree growing*
> *Week 2:* like the biggest party! *Party action*
> *Week 3:* sparkling like treasure! *Jazz hands*
> *Week 4:* growing tall into an amazing harvest! *Stretch up tall*
> *Week 5:* turning everything topsy turvy! *Diddy Disciples 'New Start' sign (p. 355)*

| | |
|---|---|
| **Our Father, who art in heaven,** | **Our Father in heaven,** |
| **Hallowed be thy name;** | **Hallowed be your name;** |
| **Thy Kingdom come . . .** | **Your Kingdom come . . .** |
| *This week's Kingdom action* | *This week's Kingdom action* |

*Or (for very young children):*
*To the tune of 'Frère Jacques' (see Introducing the Unit: Option 2):*
Let's sing the prayer Jesus taught us 'my turn' *point to self*, 'your turn' *leader's hands out to group.*

When we get to '*thy/your* Kingdom come' let's show God's Kingdom:

> *Week 1:* growing into the biggest tree! *Tree growing*
> *Week 2:* like the biggest party! *Party action*

*Week 3:* sparkling like treasure! *Jazz hands*

*Week 4:* growing tall into an amazing harvest! *Stretch up tall*

*Week 5:* turning everything topsy turvy! *'New Start' sign*

| | |
|---|---|
| *Traditional version* | *Modern version* |
| Our Father | Our Father |
| **Our Father** | **Our Father** |
| Who art in heav'n | I-in heav'n |
| **Who art in heav'n** | **I-in heav'n** |
| Hallowed be thy na-me, | Hallowed be your na-me, |
| **Hallowed be thy na-me,** | **Hallowed be your na-me,** |
| Thy Kingdom come! | Your Kingdom come! |
| **Thy Kingdom come!** | **Your Kingdom come!** |
| *This week's Kingdom action* | *This week's Kingdom action* |

## Prayers for Other People: Option 1

→ Song: 'Jesus, hear our prayer!' Words: © Sharon Moughtin-Mumby
→ Tune: 'Brown girl in the ring' (traditional). For the music see p. 358, or for a taster see the Diddy Disciples website. For similar words designed to fit with the alternative tune 'He's got the whole world in his hands', see p. 359.

**For the world:**
*Make a circle shape*
**For the Church:**
*Praying hands*
**For our place, *Walworth*\*:**
*Hands down, moving out in
a semi-circle to show the land around us*
**Lord Jesus, hear our prayer. Amen.**
*Open hands upwards to God*

**Jesus, hear our prayer!**
*Open hands upwards to God*
**Jesus, hear our prayer!**
*Open hands upwards to God*
**Jesus, hear our prayer!**
*Open hands upwards to God*

\* *Insert local area/school/church/community/parish.*

**For the sick and lonely:**
*Fingers showing tears falling
down cheeks*
**For our friends and family:**
**Jesus, hear our prayer!**
*Arms around yourself*
**For ourselves:**
*Both hands on heart*
**Lord Jesus, hear our prayer. Amen.**
*Open hands upwards to God*

**Jesus, hear our prayer!**
*Open hands upwards to God*

*Open hands upwards to God*
**Jesus, hear our prayer!**
*Open hands upwards to God*

Let's close our eyes for a moment.
I wonder if there's someone special
you'd like to pray for?
Let's imagine that person now.

Now, let's imagine Jesus coming to them.
Does Jesus say anything?
Does Jesus do anything?

Let's open our eyes.

*Continue with one of the Prayer Action options outlined below or with the Lord's Prayer as outlined above. Once the Prayer Action has been completed, you may like to use the following verse, to close this time of prayer.*

**Take our prayers:**
*Hands together gently*
**Make them holy:**

**Jesus, hear our prayer!**
*Open hands upwards to God*
**Jesus, hear our prayer!**

| | |
|---|---|
| *Hands together gently* | *Open hands upwards to God* |
| **Make them beautiful:** | **Jesus, hear our prayer!** |
| *Hands together gently* | *Open hands upwards to God* |
| **Lord Jesus, hear our prayer! Amen.** | |
| *Hands together gently, then open hands upwards to God* | |

## Prayers for Other People: Option 2

→ Song: 'The Diddy Disciples little prayers song'. Words: © Sharon Moughtin-Mumby
→ Tune: 'Frère Jacques' (traditional). For the music see p. 356, or for a taster see the Diddy Disciples website. For tips on teaching songs for the first time, see Book 1, p. 215.

*These prayers are especially suited to churches that prefer less traditional prayer forms.*
*Either: choose what you'd like the group to pray for before the session.*
*Or: ask the children at this point if there is anything or anyone that they'd like to pray for.*
*Ask the children to suggest actions for the prayers. You will need two different 'thank you' suggestions and two different 'hear our prayer' suggestions. Try to encourage at least one prayer for other people outside the group.*

*Invite the children to sing after you, repeating your words and their actions. Sometimes it might be almost impossible to fit the child's own words in! It's really valuable to do this where possible, resisting the urge to try and 'neaten' their suggestions. For examples, see p. 17.*

*Having sung your prayers, you could insert a Prayer Action, repeat the process, or move straight on to close with the following (or other words that remain the same each week).*

| | |
|---|---|
| For today, | *Point hands down for 'now'* |
| **For today,** | *Point hands down for 'now'* |
| Thank you, God! | *Open hands upwards to God or hands together in prayer* |
| **Thank you, God!** | *Open hands upwards to God or hands together in prayer* |
| Fo-r your love, | *Cross hands on chest* |
| **Fo-r your love,** | *Cross hands on chest* |
| Thank you, God! | *Open hands upwards to God or hands together in prayer* |
| **Thank you, God!** | *Open hands upwards to God or hands together in prayer* |

## Prayer Action: Option 1

→ Action: praying (part of) the 'Our Father'/Lord's Prayer with an action for 'thy/your Kingdom' that's based on this week's storytelling. See Prayers for Other People: Special Option on p. 226.

## Prayer Action: Option 2

→ **Action: planting seeds and watering them**

*Name* and *Name* are going to bring around these pots of seeds.
If you'd like them to give you a seed,
you could hold your hands out like this.
*Model holding out cupped hands.*

Let's hold our seeds up to God.
*Model holding cupped hands, with seed in, upwards.*
Let's ask God to hear them as a prayer for ourselves
and a special person.

*Hum the tune together, with 'Jesus, hear our prayer' as a refrain until all the children and adults who wish to take seeds have done so.*

God's Kingdom is like a tiny seed!
Our prayers can be part of the Kingdom growing!
As we continue to sing, you might like to sprinkle your seed
onto our garden.

*Hum the tune again as the seeds are planted. Large groups may prefer to ask two older children or an adult to take a garden around the group to collect the sprinkled seeds.*

*When the group is ready:*
As we pray, let's watch beautiful things grow in our garden.

*End this time of prayer with the final verse of the Prayer Song you've chosen.*

## Prayer Action: Option 3

→ **Action: imagining writing party invitations**

God's Kingdom is like a big party!
God has a special party invitation for people who
who are feeling sad or lonely or left out.
Maybe you know someone who's feeling sad?

Let's close our eyes and imagine Jesus
coming to our sad friend and giving them an invitation.

*After a moment:*
Let's open our eyes.

Let's take God's invitation.
*Mime taking an imaginary invitation from 'heaven'*
Let's write the name of a special person on it.
*Lead the children writing the name or mark-making in the air*
Now let's hold the invitation in our hand.
*Lead the children in holding up the imaginary invitation.*

Let's promise to be part of inviting EVERYONE
to God's Big Party this week.
*End this time of prayer with the final verse of the Prayer Song you've chosen.*

## Prayer Action: Option 4

→ **Action: showing how a seed grows tall with our bodies**

Jesus wants plant the seed of God's Kingdom in all of us!
When we pray, it's like we're asking God to water the seed inside us.

Let's close our eyes for a moment.
Let's imagine Jesus coming to us now.
Now let's imagine Jesus watering
the seed of God's Kingdom inside us.
*Hold a moment of quiet.*

Let's open our eyes again.
Let's show how a seed grows when it's been watered!
Let's curl up into a ball like a seed.
*Lead the children in curling up into a ball.*

First, we need to put our roots down.
Let's show our roots with our fingers.
*Lead the children in wiggling fingers.*
We need to let our roots grow down deep.
*Lead the children in wiggling fingers down.*
Then after 3, let a little shoot pop up.
**1, 2, 3 . . . Pop!**
*Poke your hands up over your head like a little shoot.*
Then start to grow up tall.
*Gradually stand up, swaying like a growing stalk.*

Taller and taller, onto our tiptoes . . .
*Reach up with pointy hands and on tiptoes.*
Let's turn our faces up towards the sun!
Then let our leaves or branches spread out wide.
*Arms stretch slowly outwards*

Look at those beautiful plants!
Let's imagine Jesus sprinkling refreshing water
on us now.

Let's ask for God's Kingdom
to grow even more inside us as we pray.

# Thank You, God

→ **Guide: Book 1, p. 227**

## Thank You, God: Option 1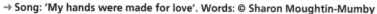

→ **Song: 'My hands were made for love'. Words: © Sharon Moughtin-Mumby**
→ **Tune: 'Hickory, dickory, dock' (traditional). For the music see p. 360, or for a taster see the Diddy Disciples website. For tips on teaching songs for the first time, see Book 1, p. 215.**

*Invite the children to sit in a circle for a moment of quiet.*
It's time to remember all the things we've done this week.
It's time to say 'thank you' to God
for when we've been part of showing God's love.

Let's wiggle our fingers!
I wonder when you've shown love
with your hands this week?

*Wiggle fingers as you sing:*
**My hands were made for love!**
**My hands were made for love!**
**Thank you for the love they've shown.**
**My hands were made for love!**

Let's wiggle our feet!
I wonder when you've shown love
with your feet this week?

*Wiggle feet as you sing:*
**My feet were made for love!**
**My feet were made for love!**
**Thank you for the love they've shown.**
**My feet were made for love!**

Let's put our hands gently on our neck.
Let's sing 'Ahhh!'
**Ahhhhh!**
Can you feel your throat vibrating and dancing with your voice?
I wonder when you've shown love
with your voice this week?

*Hold neck and feel your voice 'dancing' as you sing:*
**My voice was made for love!**
**My voice was made for love!**
**Thank you for the love it's shown.**
**My voice was made for love!**

## Thank you, God: Option 2

→ Song: 'For the love we've shown'. Words: © Sharon Moughtin-Mumby
→ Tune: 'All through the night' (traditional). For the music see p. 357, or for a taster see the Diddy Disciples website. For tips on teaching songs for the first time, see Book 1, p. 215.

*Most suitable for use with children over the age of four.*

*Invite the children to sit in a circle for a moment of quiet.*
It's time to remember all the things we've done this week.
It's time to say 'thank you'
for when we've been part of showing God's love.

> *Either:* Let's wiggle our fingers.
> *Or:* Let's hold up our hands.
> I wonder when you've shown love
> with your hands this week?
>
> *Either:* Let's wiggle our feet.
> *Or:* Let's show our feet.
> I wonder when you've shown love
> with your feet this week?

Let's put our hands gently on our neck.
Let's sing 'Ahhh!'
**Ahhhhh!**
Can you feel your neck vibrating and dancing with your voice?
I wonder when you've shown love
with your voice this week?

Let's sing our 'thank you' song to God
for the times we've been part of sharing God's love.

**For the love we've shown with our hands,**
*hold hands up or wiggle fingers*
**Thank you, God!**
**For the love we've shown with our feet,**
*point to feet or wiggle feet*
**Thank you, God!**
**When we love all those around us,**
*cross hands on chest*
**It's the same as loving Jesus!**
**For the love we've shown with our voice,**
*hands on neck or point to singing mouth*
**Thank you, God!**

# Creative Response

→ Guide: Book 1, p. 228

*See the Creative Response starter ideas in Section 3 of this unit.*

# Sharing God's Peace

→ Guide: Book 1, p. 231

*This Building Block is particularly designed for children's groups that join the adult congregation to share communion but can also be used to end any session or Service of the Word.*

## Sharing God's Peace: Option 1

→ Song: 'I've got peace like a river' (traditional), Isaiah 66.12, NIV
→ Tune: traditional. For a taster see the Diddy Disciples website. For tips on teaching songs for the first time, see Book 1, p. 215.

> *Either: hold one end of the peace cloth (Book 1, p. 231) and ask one of the older children or an adult to hold the other end. Start singing the Peace Song. As the children begin to gather, invite them to join in holding a small section of the cloth, raising and lowering it so it 'flows' like a river as you sing together.*

> *Or: invite the children to sit in a circle in the worship space. Start singing the Peace Song. As the children begin to gather, invite them to join in raising and lowering their hands like the waters of a flowing river.*

**I've got peace like a river,**
**I've got peace like a river,**
**I've got peace like a river in my soul.**
**I've got peace like a river,**
**I've got peace like a river,**
**I've got peace like a river in my soul.**

*As this unit has a strong focus on love, you may like to add the second verse:*

**I've got love like an ocean,**
**I've got love like an ocean,**
**I've got love like an ocean in my soul.**
**I've got love like an ocean,**
**I've got love like an ocean,**
**I've got love like an ocean in my soul.**

*If your group is about to rejoin the adults for communion: when all the children are gathered, continue with the words of the Peace, below.*

## Sharing God's Peace: Option 2

→ Song: 'Peace is flowing like a river' (traditional), Isaiah 66.12, NIV
→ Tune: traditional. For a taster see the Diddy Disciples website. For tips on teaching songs for the first time, see Book 1, p. 215.

> *Either: hold one end of the peace cloth (Book 1, p. 231) and ask one of the older children or an adult to hold the other end. Start singing the Peace Song. As the children begin to gather, invite them to join in holding a small section of the cloth, raising and lowering it so it 'flows' like a river as you sing together.*

> *Or: invite the children to sit in a circle in the worship space. Start singing the Peace Song. As the children begin to gather, invite them to join in raising and lowering their hands like the waters of a flowing river.*

**Peace is flowing like a river,**
**flowing out through you and me.**
**Spreading out into the desert,**
**setting all the captives free.**

*As this unit has a strong focus on love, you may like to add the second verse:*

**Love is flowing like a river,**
**flowing out through you and me.**
**Spreading out into the desert,**
**setting all the captives free.**

*If your group is about to rejoin the adults for communion: when all the children are gathered, continue with the words of the Peace, below.*

## Sharing God's Peace: Option 3

→ Song: 'I've got peace in my fingers'. Words: © 1995 Susan Salidor ASCAP
→ Tune: © 1995 Susan Salidor ASCAP
→ The words and music can be found on the album *Little Voices in My Head* by Susan Salidor © 2003 Peach Head. They can also be found on iTunes or YouTube, or at <www.susansalidor.com>. For tips on teaching songs for the first time, see Book 1, p. 215.

*If your group is about to rejoin the adults for communion: when all the children are gathered, continue with the words of the Peace, below.*

# The Peace

The peace of the Lord be always with you.
*Hold hands open to the children.*
**And also with you.**
*Invite the children to open their hands towards you.*
Let's shake hands or hug each other
and say, 'Peace be with you' *or whatever is said on sharing the Peace in your church*
as a sign of God's peace.

*Lead the children in giving and receiving the Peace. Immediately following this, at St Peter's, Walworth, we lead the children back to join the rest of the congregation to continue our worship with the Eucharistic Prayer.*

# Taking God's Love into the World

→ Guide: Book 1, p. 232
→ Song: 'This little light of mine' (traditional)
→ Tune: traditional. For a taster see the Diddy Disciples website. For tips on teaching songs for the first time, see Book 1, p. 215.

*This Building Block is particularly designed for standalone groups or groups that are held during a Service of the Word. Alternatively, you could use one of the Peace Songs above to end your worship.*

Our time together is coming to an end.
*Invite the children to sit in a circle for a moment of quiet.*
God has lit a little light of love inside all of us.
*Trace a circle on your heart.*
Let's make our finger into a candle.
*Bring your finger from your heart and hold it out.*
Let's be God and light our little light of love together, after 3.
*Lead the children in lighting their finger candle by striking an imaginary match in the air on 3 and pretending to light your finger.*
**1, 2, 3 . . . Tssss!**
Let's imagine God's love shining and dancing like light in us.

*Wave your finger in front of you.*
**This little light of mine, I'm gonna let it shine!**
**This little light of mine, I'm gonna let it shine!**
**This little light of mine, I'm gonna let it shine!**
**Let it shine, let it shine, let it shine!**

*Blow on your finger as if blowing out a candle on 'puff'. Then hold it up high.*
**Won't let no one** *puff* **it out! I'm gonna let it shine!**
**Won't let no one** *puff* **it out! I'm gonna let it shine!**
**Won't let no one** *puff* **it out! I'm gonna let it shine!**
**Let it shine, let it shine, let it shine!**

*Hold your finger behind a cupped hand, then take your cupped hand away*
*to reveal the 'candle' and hold it high!*
**Hide it under a bushel? No! I'm gonna let it shine!**
**Hide it under a bushel? No! I'm gonna let it shine!**

**Hide it under a bushel? No! I'm gonna let it shine!**
**Let it shine, let it shine, let it shine!**

*Lead the children in placing your finger back on your heart.*
Now let's put our little light of love
back in our hearts, where it belongs.
Let's remember to let our little light shine
in all our playing and working today . . .

*If you're building a Service of the Word and this is your final Building Block, you may like to close with a familiar blessing, the Peace and/or one of the following.*

| | | |
|---|---|---|
| *Either:* | Praise the Lord! *Both hands to self* | |
| | **Alleluia!** *Both arms upwards in 'V' shape* | |
| *Or:* | Let us bless the Lord. *Both hands to self* | |
| | **Thanks be to God.** *Both arms upwards in 'V' shape* | |
| *Or:* | And all the people said . . . *both hands to self* | |
| | **Amen!** *Both arms upwards in 'V' shape* | |

*When introducing this call-and-response for the first few times, you may find it helpful to say, for example:*
Now it's 'my turn' *point to self*, 'your turn' *leader's hands out to group*.
When I say, 'Praise the Lord', *both hands to self*
you say, 'Alleluia!' *both arms upwards in 'V' shape*
Praise the Lord! *both hands to self*
**Alleluia!** *both arms upwards in 'V' shape*
*Repeat.*

# Section 2

# The Bible Storytelling material: Let Your Kingdom Come! Unit

## Week 1: The Tiniest Seed

→ **Matthew 13.31–32; Mark 4.30–32; Luke 13.18–19**

*This week's storytelling is shorter to create time for the group to learn the Gathering Song for this new unit.*

> *If your group is using the What's in the Box? option (Book 1, p. 221):*
> *Invite a child to open the box.*
> *Inside is a tiny seed.*
>
> What's in the box?
> *Accept the child's response.*

Jesus said God's Kingdom is like the tiniest seed.
Let's hold out our hands.
*Model to the children holding out cupped hands.*

Let's look at the tiniest seed in our hands.
*Lead the children in peering at an imaginary tiny seed.*
It's so tiny we can't even see it!

Let's pick up that tiny seed with our fingers.
*Lead the children in picking up the tiny seed between finger and thumb.*

Let's plant it gently in the ground
*Lead the children in planting the seed*
and cover it over with soil
*Lead the children in gently moving imaginary soil over the seed.*
All done!

Now let's imagine we're that tiny seed!
Let's curl up like a tiny ball on the floor.
Let's make ourselves as tiny as possible.
*Lead the children in curling up in a ball on the floor (or crouching).*
Let's tuck our knees under and make ourselves tiny!
Even tinier! And tinier!

*When the group is ready:*
Jesus said, God's Kingdom is like the tiniest seed.
A tiny seed that grows!
We're going to grow!

First, we need to put our roots down.
Let's show our roots with our fingers.
*Lead the children in wriggling fingers.*
We need to let our roots grow down deep.
*Lead the children in wriggling fingers down.*
Then after 3, let a little shoot pop up.
1, 2, 3 . . . Pop!
*Poke your hands up over your head like a little shoot.*
Then start to grow up tall.
*Gradually stand up, swaying like a growing stalk.*
Taller and taller, onto our tiptoes . . .
*Reach up with pointy hands and on tiptoes.*
Let's turn our faces up towards the sun!

Jesus said, God's Kingdom
is like a tiny seed that grows into a massive tree!

We're not tall enough yet!
Let's keep growing: up and up on our tiptoes.
*Lead the children in stretching up high.*
Then out and out with our arms stretched as far out as possible.
*Lead the children in stretching arms out.*
Then let's stretch our fingers out as wide as we can
*Lead the children in stretching fingers out*
to make the biggest tree you can possibly be.
And freeze!

Jesus said, God's Kingdom is like the tiniest seed
that grows into the biggest tree . . .
and all of the birds can nest in its branches.

Let's imagine some birds circling up above us in the sky.
Look! *Lead the children in looking upwards still in a tree shape*
There are all sorts of birds:
robins and sparrows and blue tits
and blackbirds and pigeons and eagles.
*Add or exchange names of birds local to your area.*
Now let's imagine the birds flying gently down
and making a nest in our branches on our arms and in our hands.
*Cup hands upwards to make a nest. Lead the children in looking around and imagining birds flying down and nesting.*
All sorts of nests for all sorts of different birds!
What beautiful trees!

*When the group is ready:*
Jesus said God's Kingdom is like the tiniest seed *Hold out palm*
that grows into the biggest tree *Crouch down like a tiny seed and stretch up and outwards in a single motion to show a tree growing. This will become the 'tree growing' action.*
that has room for everyone!

That's what we're praying for in the 'Our Father'/Lord's Prayer!
That God's Kingdom will grow and grow and grow like our trees!

> *Either: if your group used Gathering Song: Option 1*
> Let's sing our prayer for God's Kingdom again!
> As we sing, let's show the tiny seed growing into the biggest tree. *Tree growing action*
> Let's pray for God's Kingdom to come!
> Sssssh! Let's start quietly!
>
> *Lead the group in singing quietly, getting louder and louder as you sing, showing the tree growing throughout.*

**Let your Kingdom come quickly**
**in** *Walworth\**, **in** *Walworth\**!
**Let your Kingdom come quickly!**
**Let your** *clap hands together in prayer* **will be done!**
*\* Replace with the name of your place/parish/school/etc.*

*Or: if your group used Gathering Song: Option 2*
Let's sing our prayer for God's Kingdom again!
Whenever we sing 'your Kingdom',
let's show the tiny seed growing into the biggest tree. *Tree growing action*
Let's pray for God's Kingdom to come!
Sssssh! Let's start quietly!
*Lead the group in singing quietly, getting louder and louder as you sing.*

**Let your Kingdom come quickly,** *tree growing action*
**your Kingdom, your Kingdom**! *Tree growing action*
**Let your Kingdom come quickly!** *Tree growing action*
**Let your** *clap hands together in prayer* **will be done!**

*Or: if your group used Gathering Song: Option 3*
Let's sing our prayer for God's Kingdom again!
Whenever we sing 'God's Kingdom is coming',
let's show the tiny seed growing into the biggest tree. *Tree growing action*

Let's pray for God's Kingdom to come!
Sssssh! Let's start quietly!
*Lead the group in singing quietly, getting louder and louder as you sing.*

*Spoken:* Look!
**God's Kingdom is coming around us!** *Tree growing*
**We pray for God's Kingdom to come!** *Hands together*
*Spoken:* Look!
**God's Kingdom is coming around us!** *Tree growing*
**We pray for God's Kingdom to come!** *Hands together*
*Hands together or outwards*
**Amen!** *Clap* **Amen!** *Clap*
**We pray** *clap* **for God's Kingdom to come, to come!** *Tree growing*
**Amen!** *Clap* **Amen!** *Clap*
**We pray** *clap* **for God's Kingdom to come!** *Tree growing*

*Or: if your group hasn't used a Gathering Song, you may like to end this time of storytelling by praying the Lord's Prayer. The Prayers for Other People Building Block includes this as an option for this unit (p. 226).*

# Week 2: The Biggest Party

→ Luke 14.15–24
→ Song: 'Come and join the party!' Words: © Sharon Moughtin-Mumby
→ Tune: 'Polly, put the kettle on!' (traditional)

Get read-y for the par-ty! Get read-y for the par-ty! Get read-y for the par-ty! There's lots to do!

Come and join the par - ty! Come and join the par - ty! Come and join the par - ty!

Come! Come! Come! Sorr - y, I'm too bu - - sy!

Sorr - y, I'm too bu - - sy! Sorr - y, I'm too bu - sy! Too bu - sy to come!

*If your group is using the What's in the Box? option (Book 1, p. 221):*
*Invite a child to open the box.*
*Inside is a party plate, hat, cup, streamer, balloon or another symbol of a party.*

What's in the box?
*Accept the child's response.*

Jesus said, God's Kingdom is like the BIGGEST party!
Let's get ready for the party!

We're having a party . . .
what do you think we need to do to get ready?

*Invite the children to make suggestions of things we need to do and choose actions for them,.*
*Examples:*
- *Write invitations: 'OK, let's write some invitations!'*
- *Make some party food.*
- *Blow up balloons, etc.*
- *Decorate the party room.*
- *Bake a cake.*

*For each suggestion sing the following song while leading the children in copying the action that the child has chosen. Do this about three times.*

**[Get] ready for the party!**
**[Get] ready for the party!**
**[Get] ready for the party!**
**There's lots to do!**

That was hard work! Everything's ready for the party.
Now we need to let our friends know.
We have three best friends.
Shall we go and tell them?

Let's tell our first best friend that the party's ready!
First we need an action for party.
What can our party action be?
*Choose one of the actions.*

Right. Let's put our party hat on
*lead the children in putting their imaginary hat on*
and let's tell our friend.

**Come and join the party!** *'Come' action (p. 195) followed by party action*
**Come and join the party!** *'Come' action followed by party action*
**Come and join the party!** *'Come' action followed by party action*
**Come! Come! Come!** *'Come' action*

But the first friend said, 'Sorry, I'm too busy'.
*Shake head and look sad.*
Let's be the first friend together, and sing sadly.
We're not going to the party!

*Lead the children in singing sadly to the second verse 'Suki take it off again'.*
**Sorry, I'm too busy!** *Shake head*
**Sorry, I'm too busy!** *Shake head*
**Sorry, I'm too busy!** *Shake head*
**[Too] busy to come!** *Shake head*

Let's take our party hat off.
*Lead the children in taking their imaginary hats off.*
Oh dear! Our friend's not coming to our party!
How are you feeling?
Can you show me?
*Give the children a moment to show their feelings.*

Never mind.
Let's put our party hat back on
*lead the children in putting their imaginary hat on*
and tell our second best friend that the party is ready!

*Lead the children in singing in an upbeat way:*
**Come and join the party!** *'Come' action followed by party action*
**Come and join the party!** *'Come' action followed by party action*
**Come and join the party!** *'Come' action followed by party action*
**Come! Come! Come!** *'Come' action*

But the second friend said, 'Sorry, I'm too busy'.
*Shake head and look sad.*

*Lead the children in singing sadly:*
**Sorry, I'm too busy!** *Shake head*
**Sorry, I'm too busy!** *Shake head*
**Sorry, I'm too busy!** *Shake head*
**Too busy to come!** *Shake head*

Hmmm.
Let's take our party hat off.
*Lead the children in taking their imaginary hats off.*
How are you feeling now?
*Give the children a moment to show their feelings.*

Never mind.
We've still got one best friend left to tell about the party.
Let's put our party hat on and tell our third best friend.
*Lead the children in putting their imaginary hat on.*

*Lead the children in singing in an upbeat way:*
**Come and join the party!** *'Come' action followed by party action*
**Come and join the party!** *'Come' action followed by party action*
**Come and join the party!** *'Come' action followed by party action*
**Come! Come! Come!** *'Come' action*

But what do you think the next friend said?
*Lead the children in singing very sadly:*
**Sorry, I'm too busy!** *Shake head*
**Sorry, I'm too busy!** *Shake head*
**Sorry, I'm too busy!** *Shake head*
**Too busy to come!** *Shake head*

Let's take our party hat off . . .
*Lead the children in taking their imaginary hats off.*
No one's coming to our party!
How are we feeling?
Can you show me with your face?
*Give the children a moment to show their feelings.*

Remember all that work we did to get ready for the party?
What can we do with it now?

In Jesus' story:
the party maker decided to invite EVERYONE to the party.
*Raise voice to be God the party maker:*
Go out to the streets! *Point outwards*
Invite EVERYONE! *'Come' action*
Especially people who aren't normally invited to parties!
Especially people who feel left out!

Let's imagine we're going out in the streets.
Let's stand up.
Let's walk on the spot together.
*Lead the children in walking on the spot.*
Now let's sing really loudly and invite EVERYONE to come,
especially people who feel left out.

*Lead the children in singing loudly:*
**Come and join the party!** *'Come' action*
**Come and join the party!** *'Come' action*
**Come and join the party!** *'Come' action*
**Come! Come! Come!** *'Come' action*
*If necessary, sing again, until the children are singing enthusiastically.*

And lots of people came!
But look! *Point around* There's still room at the party!

So the party maker said:
*Raise voice to be God the party maker:*
'Go out again! *Point out*
Look EVERYWHERE! Under the bushes!
In all the dark corners!
Find EVERYONE!
So my house is full!'

Let's go outside again. *Walk on the spot*
Let's look under the bushes
*Lead the children in bending down and looking.*
And in all the dark corners
*Lead children in shielding eyes with hand and peering.*
Let's shout even louder
so that people feel that they're missing out if they don't come!
And let's keep looking as we sing.

*Lead the children in looking and singing:*
**Come and join the party!** *Bend down and look with 'come' action*
**Come and join the party!** *Shield eyes and peer around with 'come' action*
**Come and join the party!** *Bend down and look with 'come' action*
**Come! Come! Come!** *'Come' action with one hand cupped around mouth*

And they came!
240 The party was the BIGGEST party you've ever seen!

So many people were there: little and big, young and old!
They shared all the food. *Lead the children in sharing action*
Let's eat food together! *Lead the children in eating*
And they celebrated together!
Let's dance at the big party and sing together!

*Lead the children in dancing and singing joyfully:*
**Come and join the party!**
**Come and join the party!**
**Come and join the party!**
**Come! Come! Come!**

Jesus said:
God's Kingdom is like the biggest party,
where EVERYONE'S invited.

*Ask the children to sit down in a moment of quiet and close their eyes.*
EVERYONE is invited to God's Big Party, God's 'Kingdom'.
God has a special invitation
for people who are sometimes left out.
Maybe you know someone who's left out sometimes.
Maybe sometimes you feel left out.
*Leave a moment of quiet.*

*When the group is ready:*
God wants the WHOLE WORLD to be like the big party
where EVERYONE's invited,
where everyone SHARES.

>*Either: if your group hasn't used a Gathering Song*
>Let's sing our song one last time.
>Let's sing the words from the 'Our Father'/Lord's Prayer:
>'Jesus, let *thy/your* Kingdom come!'
>Let's show God's Kingdom
>like a party that's getting bigger and bigger as we sing!
>
>*Lead the children in singing louder and louder:*
>**Jesus, let *thy/your* Kingdom come!**
>**Jesus, let *thy/your* Kingdom come!**
>**Jesus, let *thy/your* Kingdom come!**
>**Come! Come! Come!**
>*Repeat as appropriate.*
>*Leave a moment's silence . . .*
>Amen.
>
>*Or: if your group used Gathering Song: Option 1*
>Let's sing our prayer for God's Kingdom again!
>As we sing, let's show God's Kingdom like the biggest party! *Party action*
>Let's pray for God's Kingdom to come in *Walworth\**!
>
>*Lead the children in the party action throughout.*
>**Let your Kingdom come quickly**
>**in *Walworth\**, in *Walworth\**!**
>**Let your Kingdom come quickly!**
>**Let your** *clap hands together in prayer* **will be done!**
>
>*\* Replace with the name of your place/parish/school/etc.*
>
>*Repeat as appropriate:*
>*Leave a moment's silence . . .*
>Amen.

*Or: if your group used Gathering Song: Option 2*
Let's sing our prayer for God's Kingdom again!
Whenever we sing 'your Kingdom',
let's show the biggest party! *Party action*
Let's pray for God's Kingdom to come!

**Let your Kingdom** *party action* **come quickly:** *'come' action*
**your Kingdom,** *party action* **your Kingdom!** *party action*
**Let your Kingdom** *party action* **come quickly!** *Party action*
**Let your** *clap hands together in prayer* **will be done!**
*Repeat as appropriate:*
*Leave a moment's silence . . .*
**Amen**.

*Or: if your group used Gathering Song: Option 3*
Let's sing our prayer for God's Kingdom again!
Whenever we sing 'God's Kingdom is coming',
let's show the biggest party! *Party action*
Let's pray for God's Kingdom to come!

*Spoken:* Look!
**God's Kingdom is coming around us!** *Party action*
**We pray for God's Kingdom to come!** *Hands together*
*Spoken:* Look!
**God's Kingdom is coming around us!** *Party action*
**We pray for God's Kingdom to come!** *Hands together*
*Hands together or outwards*
**Amen!** *Clap* **Amen!** *Clap*
**We pray for God's Kingdom to come, to come!** *Party action*
**Amen!** *Clap* **Amen!** *Clap*
**We pray for God's Kingdom to come!** *Party action*

*Leave a moment's silence . . .*
Amen.

# Week 3: Hidden Treasure

→ **Matthew 13.44**
→ **Song: 'Dig, dig, dig down deep'. Words: © Sharon Moughtin-Mumby**
→ **Tune: 'B.I.N.G.O.' (traditional). For a taster see the Diddy Disciples website.**

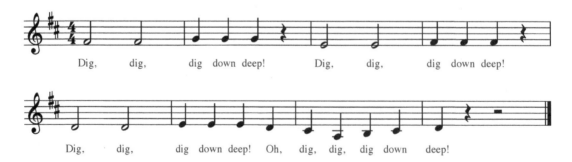

*If your group is using the What's in the Box? option (Book 1, p. 221):*
*Invite a child to open the box.*

*Inside is a spade or a picture of a spade.*

What's in the box?
*Accept the child's response.*

Jesus said: God's Kingdom is like someone digging!
So let's stand up . . .

242

let's put on our wellies . . .
*Lead the children in putting on imaginary wellies.*
Let's pick up a spade.
*Lead the children in picking up an imaginary spade.*
And let's walk on the spot to the field!
*Lead the children in walking on the spot carrying spade.*
Let's sing as we dig!

*The words and tune for this song are so simple, it won't need teaching. Just start singing and the children will join in.*

**Dig, dig, dig down deep!**
**Dig, dig, dig down deep!**
**Dig, dig, dig down deep!**
**Oh, dig, dig, dig down deep!**

Not deep enough! Let's keep going . . .
**Dig, dig, dig down deep!**
**Dig, dig, dig down deep!**
**STOP!** *Interrupt singing*

What's that? Did you hear that? *Hand to ear*
I think our spades just hit something!
*Lead the children in kneeling down before the imaginary hole that's in front of each person.*
It's an old chest!
Can you see your treasure chest in front of you too?
*Encourage them each to find treasure chest in the ground.*

Let's lift our chest out from the hole.
*Lead the children in pulling the chest out from the hole.*
*Grunt* Oh my goodness! It's heavy!

I wonder what's inside?
Shall we open it?
*Lead the children in opening the chest slowly.*
Creeeee-ak!

Look! It's treasure!
*Put hands into the imaginary chest.*
Let's hold it up and look at it!
*Lead children in holding the imaginary treasure high.*
It's shining and sparkling in the light!
*Excitedly:* We've found some treasure!
What are we going to do?!
*Accept responses. If necessary explain the treasure doesn't belong to us – it's not in our field!*

I know! I have an idea!
But first, we need to bury it again!

*Lead the children in miming the following actions:*
Let's put the treasure back in the chest.
Close the treasure chest.
Creeee-ak!
Put it gently back in the hole . . .
Now we need to bury it again.
Let's start digging!

*Lead the children in digging and singing:*
**Dig, dig, dig down deep!**
**Dig, dig, dig down deep!**
**Dig, dig, dig down deep!**
**Oh, dig, dig, dig down deep!**

Phew! That was hard work!
Let's sit down for a moment.

*When the group is ready:*
My idea is, we're going to buy that field!
The field costs ten big bags of money!
Let's count to 10 together . . .

*Lead the children in counting to ten on their fingers:*
**1, 2, 3, 4, 5, 6, 7, 8, 9, 10 . . .**

Now how many bags of money do we have?
*Accept responses.*
*Sound matter of fact:* None! *Shake head*
*Hands up with all fingers down to show zero*

But I have an idea! *Hold finger up*
We're going to sell everything we own!
Absolutely everything!

Put your hands up if you have:
a TV or computer or tablet or phone at home?
*Wait for children to raise their hands.*
Let's sell those!
*Lead the children in miming putting them in a pile in front of you.*
What about fun toys?

Let's sell all our toys! *Add them to the pile*
Who has books at home?
Let's sell all our books! *Add them to the pile*
Our tables and chairs. *Add them to the pile*
Our plates and cups and spoons! *Add them to the pile*
Our beds! *Add them to the pile*
Everything! Let's sell absolutely everything we have!

Let's sing 'Sell, sell everything!'
as we keep putting things
on our pile.

*Lead the children in miming putting everything on the pile as you sing:*
**Sell, sell everything!**
**Sell, sell everything!**
**Sell, sell everything!**
**Oh . . . sell, sell everything!**

Now, how many bags of money did we need?
*Invite a response.*
Let's see how many bags of money we have now.
Let's count on our fingers . . .
*Lead the children in counting to ten on their fingers with excitement.*
**1, 2, 3, 4, 5, 6, 7, 8 . . . 9 . . . 10!**

Hurray! We have enough money!
What do you think we're going to do with our money?
*Invite a response.*

We're going to buy the field!
Let's give the owner the money for the field.
*Lead the children in miming handing the money over.*
The field is ours!
What do you think we're going to do now?
244 *Invite a response.*

We're going to dig up that treasure!
After 3, we're going to get up.
We're going to run on the spot back to the field
as fast as we can . . .
then when I say, 'Freeze!' we're going to freeze!
**1, 2, 3 . . . Run!**
*Lead the children in running on the spot for a few moments.*

And freeze!
*When the group has 'frozen':*
Let's start digging as fast as we can!
*Lead the children in singing very quickly as you dig:*
**Dig, dig, dig down deep!**
**Dig, dig, dig down deep!**
**Dig, dig, dig down deep!**
**Dig! Dig!** *Interrupt digging* **STOP!** *Hand to ear*

Did you hear that? *Hand behind ear*
I think that's the chest again.
*Lead the children in kneeling down.*
Let's take the chest out of the ground.
*Lead the children in pulling a heavy chest out of the ground.*
I really hope the treasure's still there!
We've sold all our things to get it!

Let's open the chest . . .
*Lead the children in opening the chest.*
Creeee-ak!
It's there! The treasure's ours!
*Excitedly:* We're rich!
How does it feel? Can you show me with your face?

Let's sing 'Mine! Mine! It is mine!'
Let's sing and hold our treasure up high in the air.
*Lead the children in singing and swaying and lifting their treasure high.*
**Mine! Mine! It is mine!**
**Mine! Mine! It is mine!**
**Mine! Mine! It is mine!**
**Oh, mine, mine! It is mine!**

Jesus said:
finding God's Kingdom is like finding hidden treasure!
Can you show me how you felt
when you found that treasure?

That's what we're praying for in the 'Our Father'/Lord's Prayer!
We're praying for God's Kingdom to come!
Sparking and shining all around us
like the most beautiful treasure!
What action could we use for sparkling treasure?
*This becomes the 'treasure action'.*

> *Either (if your group hasn't used a Gathering Song):*
> Let's sing our song one last time.
> Let's sing the words from the 'Our Father'/Lord's Prayer:
> 'Let *thy/your* Kingdom come!'
> Let's show God's Kingdom like sparkling treasure as we sing.

*Lead the children in singing louder and louder showing the 'treasure action' throughout.*
**Let** *thy/your* **Kingdom come!**
**Let** *thy/your* **Kingdom come!**
**Let** *thy/your* **Kingdom come!**
**O let** *thy/your* **Kingdom come!**
*Repeat as appropriate.*
*Leave a moment's silence . . .*
Amen.

*Or: if your group used Gathering Song: Option 1*
Let's sing our prayer for God's Kingdom again!
As we sing, let's show let's show the treasure sparkling. *Treasure action*
Let's pray for God's Kingdom to come in *Walworth\**!

*Lead the children in the treasure action throughout.*
**Let your Kingdom come quickly**
**in** *Walworth\**, **in** *Walworth\**!
**Let your Kingdom come quickly!**
**Let your** *clap hands together in prayer* **will be done!**

*\* Replace with the name of your place/parish/school/etc.*

*Repeat as appropriate:*
*Leave a moment's silence . . .*
**Amen.**

*Or: If your group used Gathering Song: Option 2*
Let's sing our prayer for God's Kingdom again!
Whenever we sing 'your Kingdom',
let's show the treasure sparkling. *Treasure action*
Let's pray for God's Kingdom to come!

**Let your Kingdom** *treasure action* **come quickly:** *'come' action*
**your Kingdom,** *treasure action* **your Kingdom!** *Treasure action*
**Let your Kingdom** *treasure action* **come quickly!** *'Come' action*
**Let your** *clap hands together in prayer* **will be done!**
*Repeat as appropriate:*
*Leave a moment's silence . . .*
**Amen.**

*Or: if your group used Gathering Song: Option 3*
Let's sing our prayer for God's Kingdom again!
Whenever we sing 'God's Kingdom is coming',
let's show the treasure sparkling. *Treasure action*
Let's pray for God's Kingdom to come!

*Spoken:* Look!
**God's Kingdom is coming around us!** *Treasure action*
**We pray for God's Kingdom to come!** *Hands together*
*Spoken:* Look!
**God's Kingdom is coming around us!** *Treasure action*
**We pray for God's Kingdom to come!** *Hands together*
*Hands together or outwards:*
**Amen!** *Clap* **Amen!** *Clap*
**We pray** *clap* **for God's Kingdom to come, to come!** *Treasure action*
**Amen!** *Clap* **Amen!** *Clap*
**We pray** *clap* **for God's Kingdom to come!** *Treasure action*

*Leave a moment's silence . . .*
**Amen.**

# Week 4: Let's Sow the Seed!

→ Matthew 13.3–9; Mark 4.3–9; Luke 8.4–8
→ Song: 'Let's sow the seed'. Words: © Sharon Moughtin-Mumby
→ Tune: 'The farmer's in his den' (traditional). For a taster see the Diddy Disciples website.

Let's sow the seed!  Let's sow the seed!  Ee - i - add - i - o  Let's sow the seed!

*If your group is using the What's in the Box? option (Book 1, p. 221):*
*Invite a child to open the box.*
*Inside is a packet or handful of seeds.*

What's in the box?
*Accept the child's response.*

Jesus said, God's Kingdom is like a farmer planting seed.
So today we're going to be farmers.
We're going to have to work hard!
But first . . .
we need to check it's planting time.
Let's see: have the rains come yet.
*Lead the children in looking up to the skies.*
No . . . the rains haven't come yet. *Shake head*
It's not time. We're going to have to wait.

Let's sing 'When will it be time?'
*Don't worry about teaching this song as its tune and shape are so familiar. Just start singing and the children will almost certainly join in.*
**When will it be time?** *Hands out*
**When will it be time?** *Hands out*
**Ee-i-addio**
**When will it be . . .** *Interrupt the singing*

Wait! Look! *Hold hands out to feel the rain*
It's raining!
It's time! We need to get ready!
As soon as the rain's stopped
we need to plant our seed!

Let's get our wellies on! **1, 2 . . .**
*Lead the children in putting wellies on.*
Let's pick up our sack of seed.
*Lead the children in picking up an imaginary sack.*

I hope it grows. *Look concerned*
If it doesn't, we're going to be hungry!
Everyone will be hungry!

Look! *Point upwards*
The rains have stopped!
It's time!
Let's get up and walk on the spot to our field.
*Lead the children in walking.*

We're here! Let's get ready to plant our seed.
We're going to plant our seed by 'sowing' it.
When we sow seed, we don't put it carefully in its own hole.
Look! *Hold up heavy imaginary sack* There's too much of it!

We're going to sprinkle it on the ground like this.
*Demonstrate sowing seed to the children.*

It's time to sow!
*Lead the children in the sowing action as you sing together:*
**Let's sow the seed!**
**Let's sow the seed!**
**Ee-i-addio**
**Let's sow the seed!**

Let's take another big handful of seed and sow even further!
**Let's sow the seed!**
**Let's sow the seed!**
**Ee-i-addio**
**Let's sow the seed!**

And one last time. Even further!
Let's sow the seed as far as we can!
**Let's sow the seed!**
**Let's sow the seed!**
**Ee-i-addio**
**Let's sow the seed!**

Phew! That was hard work.
Let's sit down!
Time to look at what's happened to our seed.
I hope it's growing nicely!
Let's look out of the window.
*Lead the children in opening window shutters and looking out with hand sheltering eyes.*

Oh no! Look! *Point in shock*
The birds are eating our seed!
*Make a bird action with one hand and peck up and down the opposite arm.*
Let's show the birds eating our seed. *Lead children in the action*

Are those seeds going to grow?
*Invite the children to respond and accept their responses.*
No! *Shake head*
Let's sing 'Our seed didn't grow'.

*Lead the children in singing sadly with the birds pecking action while shaking head:*
**Our seed didn't grow!**
**Our seed didn't grow!**
**Ee-i-addio**
**Our seed didn't grow!**

Never mind. Let's take a deep breath.
*Lead the children in taking a deep breath.*
At least the rest of our seed will be growing nicely!
Shall we look out of our window?

*Lead the children in opening window shutters and looking out with hand sheltering eyes.*
Oh dear! Look! *Point sadly to feet*
This seed has fallen on the rock!
It hasn't put its roots down deep enough.
*Shake head and show roots by wriggling fingers.*

No wonder it grew up quickly!
It looked like it was doing so well!
And now look! *Point upwards*

The sun's coming out!

What action can we use for the sun?

*Acknowledge the children's sun actions.*

The sun's burning our seed! *Sun action*

Are those seeds going to grow?

*Invite the children to respond and accept their responses.*

No! *Shake head*

How are you feeling?

All that hard work! And those seeds didn't grow.

*Leave time for the children to show their feelings.*

Let's sing 'Our seed didn't grow'

and show with our voices and bodies how we're feeling!

**Our seed didn't grow!**

**Our seed didn't grow!**

**Ee-i-addio**

**Our seed didn't grow!**

Well, at least there's still some seed left.

That should be growing nicely by now!

Shall we have a look?

*Lead the children in opening window shutters and looking out with hand sheltering eyes.*

Look! Something's growing!

Is it our seed?

Oh no! *Groan with hand on head* It's weeds!

Weeds are growing and choking our plants.

*Place hands together and show weeds twisting up.*

Aarrghh! What are we going to do? *Hands out*

Too late . . . our seeds are dead!

How do we feel now? Can you show me?

*Leave time for the children to show their feelings.*

Let's sing 'Our seed didn't grow' again!

And show how we're feeling.

*Lead the children in singing with the emotion(s) they name while showing the weeds twisting up action.*

**Our seed didn't grow!**

**Our seed didn't grow!**

**Ee-i-addio**

**Our seed didn't grow!**

None of our seed is growing! *Hand on head*

We'll have no crops to make food from!

We're going to be hungry!

How are we feeling? Can you show me?

*Leave time for the children to show their feelings.*

Shall we take one last look

to see if there's any seed left that can grow?

Let's look one last time . . .

*lead the children in looking with hand over eyes*

Wait a minute! Look over there! *Point*

What's that? *Accept responses*

And there! And there! And there!

*Point to different places around the circle.*

It's growing! Our seed is growing! *Joyfully*

That seed fell on good soil! Look!

Let's be our seed growing in the good soil!
Let's curl up into a ball like a seed.
*Lead the children in curling up like a ball.*
First, we need to put our roots down.
Let's show our roots with our fingers.
*Lead the children in wriggling fingers.*

While we thought nothing was growing,
Our seeds were putting their roots down, down, down
deep into the ground!
*Lead the children in wriggling fingers down.*

But now our seeds have started to grow up, up, up!
So we can see them growing!
After 3, let's make a little shoot pop up from the ground.
**1, 2, 3 . . . Pop!**
*Poke your hands up over your head like a little shoot.*

Now let's grow up tall.
*Gradually stand up, swaying like a stalk growing.*
Taller and taller onto our tiptoes.
Let's be wheat swaying in the breeze.
*Lead the children in swaying.*

Look! Our seed has grown!
We're going to have a harvest!
We're going to have food!
We won't go hungry!
How are you feeling?

Let's be the farmer and dance and celebrate!
Our seed is growing tall!
*Lead the children in singing and dancing in celebration.*
**Our seed is growing tall!**
**Our seed is growing tall!**
**Ee-i-addio**
**Our seed is growing tall!**

Hurray! Our seed grew!
Let's sit down for a moment . . .
*Lead the children in sitting down.*

Jesus said:
God's Kingdom is like a farmer sowing seed.
God plants seed in all of us.
In you, in you, in you . . . and in me:
*point around the circle then to yourself*
the seed of God's Kingdom!

If we look with God's eyes . . .
*Use your hands to make 'glasses'.*
Let's all look around with God's eyes . . .
*Lead the children in using hands to make 'glasses'.*
God's Kingdom is like a seed in everyone here.
*Point around the circle.*

Let's close our eyes for a moment.
Let's imagine Jesus coming to us now.
Let's ask Jesus to help us make our hearts ready:
to take away any hard, rocky parts,

any spiky, thorny parts inside us
so that the seed can grow tall in us.

*If you have chosen the Saying Sorry Building Block, you may wish to do this at this point.*
We can do this with our Sorry Song . . .

*This week, the Saying Sorry Action and God Gives Us a New Start could be replaced with the rest of the storytelling below, introduced by:*
The Good News is:
when we say sorry, God loves to give us a new start!
Jesus will make our hearts ready
then plant the seed of God's Kingdom in us.

*All groups continue from here . . .*
[Now] let's imagine Jesus planting a seed in our hearts.
Let's open our eyes!

*Either (if your group hasn't used a Gathering Song):*
Let's sing our song one last time.
Let's sing the words from the 'Our Father'/Lord's Prayer:
'Let *thy/your* Kingdom come!'
Let's show God's Kingdom growing inside us as we sing

*Lead the children in singing louder and louder:*
**Let *thy/your* Kingdom come!**
**Let *thy/your* Kingdom come!**
**Ee-i-addio**
**Let *thy/your* Kingdom come!**
*Repeat as appropriate.*
*Leave a moment's silence . . .*
**Amen.**

*Or: If your group used Gathering Song: Option 1*
Let's sing our prayer for God's Kingdom again!
As we sing, let's show the seed growing inside us.
Let's curl up on the floor and be that seed . . .
Let's pray for God's Kingdom to come in *Walworth*!*

*Lead the children in curling up like a seed, then growing upwards as you sing.*
**Let your Kingdom come quickly**
**in *Walworth*\*, in *Walworth*\*!**
**Let your Kingdom come quickly!**
**Let your** *clap hands together in prayer* **will be done!**

*Repeat as appropriate:*
*Leave a moment's silence . . .*
**Amen.**

\* *Replace with the name of your place/parish/school/etc.*

*Or: if your group used Gathering Song: Option 2*
Let's sing our prayer for God's Kingdom again!
This time, as we sing, let's show the seed growing inside us.
Let's curl up on the floor and be that seed . . .
Let's pray for God's Kingdom to come!

*Lead the children in curling up like a seed, then growing upwards as you sing.*
**Let your Kingdom come quickly:**
**your Kingdom, your Kingdom!**
**Let your Kingdom come quickly!**
**Let your will be done!**
*Repeat as appropriate.*

*Leave a moment's silence . . .*
**Amen.**

*Or: if your group used Gathering Song: Option 2*
Let's sing our prayer for God's Kingdom again!
This time, as we sing, let's show the seed growing inside us.
Let's curl up on the floor and be that seed . . .
Let's pray for God's Kingdom to come!

*Lead the children in curling up like a seed, then growing upwards as you sing.*
*Spoken:* Look!
**God's Kingdom is coming around us!**
**We pray for God's Kingdom to come!**
*Spoken:* Look!
**God's Kingdom is coming around us!**
**We pray for God's Kingdom to come!**
*If you have reached full height by this point, join in the clapping as usual.*
**Amen!** *Clap* **Amen!** *Clap*
**We pray** *clap* **for God's Kingdom to come, to come!** *Growing action*
**Amen!** *Clap* **Amen!** *Clap*
**We pray** *clap* **for God's Kingdom to come!** *Growing action*

*Leave a moment's silence . . .*
**Amen.**

# Week 5: The Last Will Be First!

→ **Matthew 20.1–16**
→ **Song: 'Pick, pick, pick!' Words: © Sharon Moughtin-Mumby**
→ **Tune: 'Hot cross buns' (traditional). For a taster see the Diddy Disciples website.**

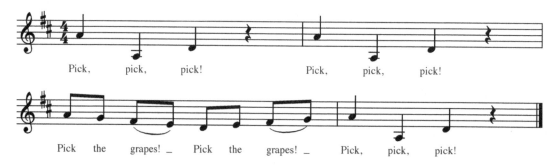

*If you're using the What's in the Box? option (Book 1, p. 221), invite one of the children to open the box. Inside is a bunch of grapes: either real or a picture.*

What's in the box? *Ask the child to respond.*

Jesus said God's Kingdom is like farm workers picking grapes.

There was a farmer who grew grapes . . .
Let's be the farmer!
Let's see how our grapes are doing . . .
*Pick and taste an imaginary grape.*
Mmmm! How are your grapes tasting?
*Lead the children in picking and taste an imaginary grape.*
Yes. I think they'll be ready to pick tomorrow.
Let's go to sleep.
*Lead the children in sleeping. Encourage some snoring.*
Freeze!

The farmer got up really early with the sun.
Let's wake up with the sun.

Let's stretch . . .
*Lead the children in waking and stretching.*
. . . and get up ready to go.
*Lead the children in standing.*

The farmer went to the marketplace.
Let's walk on the spot to the marketplace.
*Lead the children in walking on the spot.*
At the marketplace, there were some workers.
The farmer showed the workers a big coin.
*Show the children an imaginary very large coin.*

He said, 'If you help me pick my grapes
I will give you ONE BIG COIN.' *Show big coin*
Who'd like to work for me?
*Lead the children in putting your hand up.*

The farmer took all the workers with him!
Let's be the workers together.
Can you show me an action for picking grapes?
Remember not to eat them!
Let's sing as we work.
*This song and its words are so repetitive they doesn't need to be taught line by line. Instead, start singing with the actions and the children will gradually begin to join in.*

*Lead the children picking as you sing.*
**Pick, pick, pick!**
**Pick, pick, pick!**
**Pick the grapes!**
**Pick the grapes!**
**Pick, pick, pick!**

The workers worked for three hours!
Who can count to 3 on their fingers?
*Lead the children in counting:* **1, 2, 3 . . .**

But look! There are still lots of grapes to pick!
The farmer went back to the marketplace.
Let's walk to the marketplace.
*Lead the children in walking on the spot.*

There were more workers there.
The farmer said:
'If you help me pick the grapes, *point out*
I'll give you fair pay!' *Point to self*
So the workers went to help pick the grapes.
Now there are more of us. Let's sing together.

*Lead the children in singing and picking.*
**Pick, pick, pick!**
**Pick, pick, pick!**
**Pick the grapes!**
**Pick the grapes!**
**Pick, pick, pick!**

They worked for three more hours!
Can you help me count to 3 on your fingers.
**1, 2, 3 . . .**

But look! There are still lots of grapes to pick!
What do you think the farmer did?
*Accept the children's responses.*
The farmer went back to the marketplace.
'If you help me pick the grapes, *point out*
I'll give you fair pay!' *Point to self*

So the workers went to help pick the grapes.
It's getting really hot now!
Can you show me hot?
Let's sing a bit slower in hot, hot sun.

**Pick, pick, pick!**
**Pick, pick, pick!**
**Pick the grapes!**
STOP! *Interrupt the singing*

There's only one hour left and there are STILL lots of grapes to pick!
They'll be ruined if we don't manage to pick any more!
What do you think the farmer did?
*Accept the children's responses.*

The farmer went back to the marketplace!
There were some workers there
Who'd done NOTHING all day!
What do you think the farmer said?
*Accept the children's responses.*
The farmer said:
'If you help me pick the grapes, *point out*
*Encourage the group to join in after the dots.*
I'll give you . . . **fair pay**!' *Point to self*

So the workers went to the vineyard.
Quick! There's only one hour left!
Let's all get to work and pick really quickly.
*Lead the children in singing twice as fast.*

**Pick, pick, pick!**
**Pick, pick, pick!**
**Pick the grapes!**
*Interrupt the singing:* STOP!

The working day's over.
Let's all sit down.

*When the group is ready:*
It's pay time!
First the farmer called the workers
Who'd worked for just one hour.
*Show one with your fingers.*

Let's be these workers.
We've hardly done any work!
We're bright and full of energy.
How do you look when you feel full of energy!
Can you show me?
*Lead the group in looking energetic.*

The farmer gives us ONE BIG COIN! *Hold up imaginary big coin*
How are we feeling?
Can you show me?

Second, the farmer called the workers who worked for three hours and six hours.
Let's count to 6 on our fingers: **1, 2, 3, 4, 5, 6.**
Let's be the workers who've worked six hours.
We've been working almost all day!
We're hot and tired.
Can you show me hot and tired?
The farmer gives us ONE BIG COIN. *Hold up imaginary big coin*
How are we feeling?
Can you show me?

Then at last the farmer called the first group.
Let's be the first group.
We woke up with the sun and worked hard all day.
For hours and hours and hours.
Nine whole hours!
Let's count to 9 on our fingers.
*Get slower and slower as you count:*
**1, 2, 3, 4, 5, 6, 7 . . . 8 . . . 9!**

We're exhausted!
Really, really, really tired.
Can you show me really tired?
*Lead the group in looking exhausted.*
Even tireder?
We can't even stand up properly!
*Lead the group in drooping.*

What do you think the farmer is going to pay us?
We've worked much, much longer than everyone else!
*Invite the children to make suggestions.*

The farmer gives us . . .
ONE BIG COIN!
Exactly the same as everyone else!
Is that fair?
How are we feeling?
Can you show me?
*Accept the children's responses.*

Well, in our story, the workers who'd worked all day said
'That's not fair!'
Let's all be the hard workers and show our cross face.
*Lead the group in looking cross.*
Now a really, really cross face.
*Lead the group in looking even crosser.*

Let's get up *lead the children in standing* and after 3
let's stamp our foot and shout, 'That's not fair!'
1, 2, 3 . . . **That's not fair!**

Let's try that again, even louder.
1, 2, 3 . . . **That's not fair!**
Freeze!

Let's sit down again.
The farmer said:
*Sound defiant.*
'You said you were happy to work for ONE BIG COIN.
I gave you ONE BIG COIN!
Take it and enjoy it!'

Then Jesus said:
The first will be last. And the last will be first.
Everything's upside down! *Diddy Disciples 'New Start' sign (p. 355)*

Let's say that together:
'my turn' *point to self*, 'your turn' *leader's hands out to group*.

The first will be last. *'New Start' sign*
**The first will be last.** *'New Start' sign*
And the last will be first. *'New Start' sign*
**And the last will be first.** *'New Start' sign*
*Repeat.*

Jesus said God's Kingdom is
a place where everyone's given the same.
Where the first are last and the last are first.
Where everything's turned upside down. *'New Start' sign*

Let's pray that God's topsy turvy Kingdom will COME!

> *Either (if your group hasn't used a Gathering Song):*
> Let's sing our song one last time.
> Let's sing the words from the 'Our Father'/Lord's Prayer:
> 'Come! Come! Come!
> Jesus, let your Kingdom come!'
> Let's show God's Kingdom
> turning everything topsy turvy. *'New Start' sign*
> Let's pray for God's Kingdom!

> *Lead the children in singing louder and louder:*
> **Come! Come! Come!**
> **Come! Come! Come!**
> **Jesus, let your Kingdom come!**
> **Come! Come! Come!**
> *Repeat as appropriate.*
> *Leave a moment of silence.*
> **Amen.**

> *Or: If your group used Gathering Song: Option 1*
> Let's sing our prayer for God's Kingdom again!
> Let's show God's Kingdom
> turning everything topsy turvy. *'New Start' sign*
> Let's pray for God's Kingdom to come in *Walworth*\*!

> *Lead the children in the 'New Start' sign throughout.*
> **Let your Kingdom come quickly**
> **in *Walworth*\*, in *Walworth*\*!**
> **Let your Kingdom come quickly!**
> **Let your** *clap hands together in prayer* **will be done!**

> *Repeat as appropriate.*
> *Leave a moment's silence . . .*
> **Amen.**

*\* Replace with the name of your place/parish/school/etc.*

*Or: If your group used Gathering Song: Option 2*
Let's sing our prayer for God's Kingdom again!
This time, when we sing 'your Kingdom',
let's show God turning everything topsy turvy. *'New Start' sign*
Let's pray for God's Kingdom to come!

**Let your Kingdom** *'New Start' sign* **come quickly:** *'Come' action*
**your Kingdom,** *'New Start' sign* **your Kingdom**! *'New Start' sign*
**Let your Kingdom** *'New Start' sign* **come quickly!** *'Come' action*
**Let your** *clap hands together in prayer* **will be done!**
*Repeat as appropriate:*
*Leave a moment's silence . . .*
**Amen.**

*Or: If your group used Gathering Song: Option 2*
Let's sing our prayer for God's Kingdom again!
This time, when we sing 'your Kingdom',
let's show God turning everything topsy turvy. *'New Start' sign*
Let's pray for God's Kingdom to come!

*Spoken:* Look!
**God's Kingdom is coming around us!** *'New Start' sign*
**We pray for God's Kingdom to come!** *Hands together or outwards*
*Spoken:* Look!
**God's Kingdom is coming around us!** *'New Start' sign*
**We pray for God's Kingdom to come!** *Hands together or outwards*
**Amen!** *Clap* **Amen!** *Clap*
**We pray** *clap* **for God's Kingdom to come, to come!** *'New Start' sign*
**Amen!** *Clap* **Amen!** *Clap*
**We pray** *clap* **for God's Kingdom to come!** *'New Start' sign*
*Leave a moment's silence . . .*
**Amen.**

# Week 6: God's Kingdom Is Here Among Us!

*If your group is using the What's in the Box? option (Book 1, p. 221):*
*Invite a child to open the box.*
*Inside is an example of the kind of thing your group will be making.*

What's in the box?
*Accept the child's response.*

Jesus told lots of stories about God's Kingdom,
but today we're not going to tell a story.

Instead we're going to SHOW what God's Kingdom is about.
We're going to BE PART of bringing God's Kingdom here in *name of place*.
We're going to make _____.

*Either: you could invite the children to make a gift for everyone in your congregation or for their families. This could be anything that you know that the children will enjoy making. Something with a local feel would be particularly appropriate.*

*Or: if you have not done this for The Last will be First! you could invite the children to make a coin-shaped gold medal. Everyone in the church could be given a gold medal for what they have done for the church: even people who never normally come to church. God's Kingdom is where everyone is given the same, no matter how much they do.*

*Or: if your group didn't make invitations as a response to The Biggest Party (or you would like to make more), you could invite the children to make invitations for their friends, family and neighbours to come to church, either for a particular event or for any Sunday. God's Kingdom is a place where everyone is invited.*

*Or: You could make biscuits/fairy cakes or decorate biscuits for everyone in your congregation. It's time for the big party and everyone's invited! After the service, if appropriate, you could even ask an adult to give out some outside church to passers-by who haven't come to church. Or you could invite the children to take some home to give to friends, family and neighbours who don't go to church.*

# Section 3

# Creative Response starter ideas: Let Your Kingdom Come! Unit

→ **Guide: Book 1, p. 228**

These starter ideas are designed to spark imaginations and open up opportunities for the children to respond creatively in their different ways to the worship and storytelling you've taken part in together.

## Tip

As outlined in the Guide of *Diddy Disciples* Book 1 from p. 228, we've found the following rules of thumb helpful for fostering an environment where children are encouraged to engage personally and openly.

1 Encourage the children to make their own choices.
2 Give the children space to develop their response as they wish.
3 Create space for 'bridge building'.
4 It's the act of responding that matters, not the final result.
5 These responses are 'holy ground'.

---

**Weekly Starter Ideas** relate directly to the Bible Storytelling of each session, including a print-and-go option.

**Sensory Starter Ideas** are designed for sensory explorers, including babies and toddlers. These can remain the same through the whole unit.

**Unit Starter Ideas** are designed to remain relevant throughout the whole unit. Keeping these resources available each week gives children the opportunity to deepen and develop their responses, while making preparation more manageable for leaders.

---

## Tip: Free response area

In addition to any other resources you provide, keeping a free response area available every week will give the children the opportunity to create anything they wish in response to the story they've told, building their sense of confidence and personal responsibility. In this area you could simply provide blank paper and crayons, pencils, paints or pastels. If you have them, other interesting media (see Book 1, p. 256) will provide even more scope for the children to nurture and strengthen their imaginative skills.

# Weekly Starter Ideas

## Week 1: The Tiniest Seed

🕊 Invite the children to draw leaves and birds on the big tree. What else could sit in the tree? Or you may even like to provide fingerpaints (either bought or homemade) and felt tips, inviting the children to press fingerprints on the tree, then to add eyes, a beak, even wings and feet to transform their fingerprints into different birds. *Provide bare tree template (p. 364 or website), pencils/crayons/pastels. Optional: fingerpaints (Book 1, p. 258) and felt tip pens.*

🕊 Give the children the opportunity to invent their own bird. What colours will their bird be? What will it be good at? *Provide bird template (p. 365 or website), pencils/crayons/pastels. Optional: collage materials (Book 1, p. 255) if you have them.*

🕊 Give the children the opportunity to decorate a plant pot; then, when they're ready, let them add compost and plant their own seed. You could use sunflower seeds, for instance, which can grow into a tall, tall plant, possibly taller than the child! *Provide plant pots, glue and collage materials, or paper cups, compost, sunflower (or other) seeds.*

## Tip

At St Peter's, Walworth, we use compostable paper cups for our tea and coffee after the Sunday service. These can easily be drawn on with pencils, crayons or pens and come in useful for all sorts of things, including as compostable plant pots!

## Week 2: The Biggest Party

🕊 Invite the children to design their own party invitations to invite someone to God's Big Party. *Provide blank paper plus pencils/crayons. If you can, provide collage materials (Book 1, p. 255) to create plenty of options for the children's imagination.*

🕊 Give the children the opportunity to make a party hat for God's Big Party. *Provide simple coloured hatbands (p. 360) plus pencils/crayons and collage materials (Book 1, p. 255).*

🕊 Invite the children to enter into the part of the story where the party maker gets ready for the party by making party food, decorating (pre-made or bought) fairy cakes or biscuits with icing and sprinkles, making a fruit salad, making chocolate lollipops (fridge required), etc. How would the children like the party food to look?

🕊 You could hold a party like the Biggest Party, with favourite food and drink. You could invite the children to help you get ready for the party by each setting a place at the table. As you enjoy your food and drink, encourage the children to imagine the Biggest Party where no one is left out. *Provide party food and drink, paper plates/napkins and cups for the place setting.*

🕊 'Come and join the party!' Is there a job you could do together for your church to get ready for a big party or event? Could you design invitations/welcome posters?

🕊 Make a giant picture together of God's Big Party where everyone is invited. Invite children to make people to look like themselves and someone else they'd like to invite. *Provide body templates (p. 366 and website), scissors, pencils/pens/crayons, glue and collage materials (Book 1, p. 255) that will encourage diversity and difference among those who are invited.*

🕊 Invite the children to make napkin rings from card and place kitchen roll or napkins/serviettes in them for a church special event or a homeless shelter. How many can each child make? *Provide coloured card, glue, pencils/crayons, kitchen roll or napkins/serviettes.*

🕊 Invite the children to make paper chains for God's Big Party. *Provide coloured strips of paper and glue.*

## Week 3: Hidden Treasure

❧ Invite the children to decorate and fill their own treasure chest to look like God's Kingdom. *Provide treasure chest template (p. 389 or website) plus pencils/crayons/pastels. Optional: sparkly collage, tinfoil, foil shapes, glitter and glue.*

❧ What could you give up for the Kingdom? Invite the children to draw pictures of their favourite toys or to cut pictures of toys and books from old magazines or catalogues to make a collage. They may like to draw or stick these on plain paper, or they may like to draw around their open hand first to show that they're ready to give them up. Jesus says we would give up anything and everything for God's Kingdom! *Provide paper, pens. Optional: magazines with pictures of toys, glue.*

❧ Give the children the opportunity to make treasure such as jewellery or medals. God's Kingdom is like the most amazing treasure! *Provide a range of resources, for example string, tinfoil, snipped straws of different colours, penne pasta (colourfully dyed, if you like: Book 1, p. 257), beads, buttons, foil medal shapes, ribbon. Check that none of the materials presents a choking hazard to children in your group.*

❧ Invite the children to make hidden treasure bottles by filling plastic bottles with sand plus shiny foil shapes (bought or homemade from tinfoil). Ask the children to screw the lid on when they're ready and give them a hand to check it's tightly sealed. Encourage the children to shake the bottles and look inside to find the treasure. When we see with God's eyes we see the treasure of God's Kingdom shining all around us! *Provide transparent bottles, sand (or rice), shiny foil shapes, tinfoil or other 'treasure'.*

❧ Invite the children to collage a person or heart template with sparkly collage or glitter/sparkly foil shapes. When we live by God's special rules of love, we sparkle with the treasure of God's Kingdom. *Provide body templates (p. 366 or website) or large heart templates (p. 382 or website), glue, sparkly collage/glitter/foil shapes.*

## Week 4: Let's Sow the Seed!

❧ Invite the children to draw a seed growing in their heart. *Provide large heart template (p. 382 or website), crayons/pencils/pastels. You could even provide real seeds for the children to use in their pictures (these can be seeds for planting or seeds that you happen to have in the cupboard: whole cumin or coriander, sesame, poppy, mustard, pumpkin seeds, etc.).*

❧ Invite the children to make the farmer who sows the seed. Which part of the story will they show: when the farmer's seed isn't growing? Or when the harvest has come in? *Provide body template (p. 366 or website), crayons/pencils/pastels.*

❧ Give the children the opportunity to 'sow' (sprinkle, not throw!) wildflower seeds in a take-home tray. Invite them to prepare the soil beforehand, removing weeds and stones, etc. *Provide tubs set aside for recycling (with lids is helpful for transportation home), compost, wildflower seeds. At St Peter's we add stones and leaves (e.g. daisy/dandelion/buttercup leaves) to the compost beforehand for the children to remove!*

❧ Give the children the opportunity to witness a plant putting down roots. Invite the children to stuff a transparent cup full of kitchen roll. When they've done this, give them five or six bean seeds and show them how to slide the seeds down the side of the cup, about halfway, so the paper is holding them against the cup. We leave this to the children but tend to check that at least one seed is visible at the end, adding one if necessary! Encourage the children to water the seed when they get home and check it every day. They can watch the bean putting its roots down first before it grows up! *Provide transparent plastic cups, lots of kitchen roll, butter beans or similar. The dried beans provided in the supermarket for cooking work perfectly well and are much more affordable!*

❧ Invite the children to plant cress seeds and to eat the harvest when they've grown! *Provide tubs set aside for recycling (with lids is helpful for transportation home), compost or cotton wool, cress seeds.*

❧ Invite the children to paint a picture of wheat growing, using fork prints or fingerprints to show the wheat grains and lines for the stalks. With younger children, you may like to draw basic stalks beforehand to start them off. *Provide paper, yellow/brown paint, forks (or use finger paint: recipe in Book 1, p. 258).*

❧ If you haven't had a party the week before, you could have one now to celebrate the harvest! Enjoy bread and butter/jam or make wheat bracelets from wheat hoops and string/wool/pipecleaners. Thank God for the harvest! *Remember to check for any food allergies. It's possible to get gluten-free cereal hoops.*

## Week 5: The Last will be First!

❧ Invite the children to design their own One Big Coin for God's Kingdom, where everyone is given the same. What would a coin look like in God's Kingdom? Whose face will be on it? God's? Jesus'? Our own? Or another picture? Remember to give the children space to use their own imagination. *Provide circle template (p. 369 or website), crayons/pencils/pastels/paints. If you have collage materials (Book 1, p. 255, e.g. tinfoil), you could provide these plus glue for younger children.*

❧ The grape-pickers work hard for God's Kingdom. What could you do to bring about God's Kingdom where everyone shares so that everyone has the same? Invite the children to draw around their own hand, then to draw inside it something that they could share with someone else this week. *Provide paper, pencils/crayons/pastels, scissors.*

❧ Give the children the opportunity to make and present medals for everyone who contributes to the group. This will mean one for everyone who is there, as by being there (even late and for the first time!) they have contributed! Encourage the children to swap medals with each other, but some may like to take their own home. *Provide the circle template (p. 369 or website), pencils/crayons/pastels, masking tape, ribbon/string/wool.*

❧ Another opportunity for a party: God's Kingdom is full of parties! Invite the children to share grapes from their harvest. Taste and see that the Lord is good! *Provide grapes cut in half lengthways and make sure the children eat them sitting down and supervised to minimize the risk of choking.*

❧ Invite the children to create their own 'topsy turvy' response that will show how God turns everything upside down. Who or what will they draw to be turned upside down? Give the children space to use their imaginations. Help the children to pierce their picture and then the paper plate (both towards the centre) then fasten them together with a paper fastener. Show the children how their designs can now twizz around, turning 'topsy turvy'. *Provide paper plates, paper fasteners and paper. Optional: body templates (p. 366 or website) for children who'd like to use one. To pierce the pictures and paper plates, you could either use a hole punch or push a pencil through the paper/card into sticky tack/playdough/plasticine/clay.*

❧ The grape-pickers work hard for God's Kingdom. Invite the children to share in the task of cleaning and sorting out resources, sharpening pencils, etc. Or is there another job your group could do for your church/school/community?

# Sensory Starter Ideas (including for babies and toddlers)

You could provide:

- clean watering cans, spades, wellies (we put an old pair in the washing machine), etc. God's Kingdom is like farming and planting and digging;

- 'small world' resources (small plastic figures or wooden/knitted figures): e.g. men, women, children, farmers, tractors, chefs, cooks (see p. 95);

- treasure items in a chest, box or basket: silver, sparkly things, precious-looking items. God's Kingdom is like treasure!

- a sand/rice tray with hidden treasure or (child-safe) coins;

- imaginative aids (like those used for the Gathering Songs from different units) can encourage sensory explorers to explore movement and feelings more openly;

- a range of sparkly jewellery and medals (safe for under threes) for the children to explore with magnifying glasses, notebooks and pens;

- board books of any of the stories from the unit or the 'Our Father'/Lord's Prayer;

- paper or plastic party cups and plates, or a tea party set, to set out God's Big Party;

- a toy kitchen with pots and pans and toy food for party preparation;

- if you're using one of the planting starter ideas from Weeks 1 or 4, ask the children to plant extra pots that can then stay in your group. As the plants grow, invite the children to explore what's happening to the roots, shoots, leaves, etc. Provide rulers, magnifying glasses, scales, pencils, notebooks or paper, or even a microscope if you have access to one.

# Unit Starter Ideas

The Let Your Kingdom Come! unit challenges us to wonder how we can be part of bringing about God's Kingdom in our place, by living by God's special rules of love.

- Invite the children to reflect on God's love spreading and making our hearts beautiful by dripping paint onto coffee filter hearts (or other shapes they may like to cut from the filter paper) and watching what happens. *Provide coffee filters and diluted paint in different colours. See large heart template (p. 382 or website).*

- Give the children the opportunity to make glasses from pipe cleaners or a telescope/binoculars from cardboard rolls. Let's remember to look around us with God's eyes, seeing the signs of God's Kingdom around us. *Provide pipe cleaners and/or masking tape and cardboard rolls (e.g. kitchen roll, cling film, tinfoil, etc.).*

- Invite the children to make crowns for King Jesus, the King of God's Kingdom. What kind of crown would they like to make? What symbols or pictures will be on it? *Provide hatbands (p. 360) and/or crown templates (p. 371 or website), pencils/crayons/pastels plus collage materials (Book 1, p. 255) and glue if you have them.*

# UNIT 6
# GOD'S BEST FRIEND, MOSES (GREEN TIME/ ORDINARY TIME BETWEEN JULY AND NOVEMBER)

> " Thus the LORD used to speak to Moses face to face, as one speaks to a friend. EXODUS 33.11 "

This unit invites children to take part in telling the rich and foundational stories of Moses and the birth of God's people through the Red Sea. Step by step, the Bible Storytelling takes us from slavery in Egypt, through the birth of Moses, his flight to the wilderness, his encounter with God in the Burning Bush and his confrontation of Pharaoh, leading to God's people's dramatic escape from Egypt through the Red Sea.

Towards the end of the unit, there's an opportunity for children to take part in a baptism workshop, which explores the way in which many of our symbols of baptism echo these stories of the escape from Egypt. The stories of Moses also open up all sorts of opportunities for groups to explore strong feelings, such as rage, fury, fear and desolation, and to witness them being taken up by God and transformed into a passion and thirst for justice and God's mission.

The unit's Gathering Song picks up Moses' words in Deuteronomy 5.15: 'Remember that you were a slave in the land of Egypt.' Repeatedly through the Bible, the people of God are called on to remember this foundational experience of slavery and rescue. They – and therefore we (see Book 1, p. 226) – are charged to let it shape our understanding not only of God, who has the power to save, but also of how we are to behave to others, particularly the stranger or the vulnerable among us. See Exodus 13.3, 20.2; Leviticus 25.42, 26.13; Deuteronomy 5.6, 5.15, 6.12, 6.21, 7.8, 8.14, 13.5, 13.10, 16.12, 24.18, 24.22; Joshua 24.17; Judges 6.8; Jeremiah 34.13–14; Micah 6.4.

> The Diddy Disciples portrayal of Pharaoh the consumerist bully, who always wants 'MORE!' is strongly influenced by Walter Brueggemann's book, *Sabbath as Resistance: Saying No to the Culture of Now* (Louisville, Kentucky: Westminster John Knox Press, 2014). This very accessible book is really worth reading (particularly the introduction and first chapter).

> " In Exodus 5, we are given a passionate narrative account of that labor system in which Pharaoh endlessly demands more production . . . Pharaoh is a hard-nosed production manager for whom production schedules are inexhaustible. WALTER BRUEGGEMANN[4] "

The Green Time units are designed to be used at any time between July and November. Groups are encouraged to use them in the order that makes most sense in their context. Two further Green Time units can be found in Book 1.

# Section 1

# The Building Blocks: God's Best Friend, Moses, unit

Pick and choose from these Building Blocks and their various options to build sessions for your group. Whatever choices you make, we suggest you keep to that pattern for the whole of the unit as this will open up opportunities for the children to participate fully and confidently during your time together.

> **Build your own Diddy Disciples session** (Book 1, p. 6) provides an overview of the Building Blocks and a short introduction to fitting them together, along with examples.
>
> **Guide to the Building Blocks** (Book 1, p. 217) provides a step-by-step guide to each Building Block.

# Welcome

→ **Guide: Book 1, p. 218**

*Welcome your group.*

Let's start by going around the circle
And saying our name out loud.
My name's _____.

*Go around the circle so that every adult and child has the chance to say his or her name (and introduce any dolls, teddies or toys). If any of the children don't want to say their name or aren't able to, you (or a parent or carer) could say it for them and wave.*

It's time to sing our Welcome Song!

## Welcome Song: Option 1

→ **Song: 'The Diddy Disciples welcome song'. Words: © Sharon Moughtin-Mumby**
→ **Tune: 'Glory, glory, alleluia!' (traditional). For the music see p. 357, or for a taster see the Diddy Disciples website. For tips on teaching songs for the first time, see Book 1, p. 215.**

*Go around the circle the same way as above. See if you can remember each other's names and insert them into the song.*

**Welcome** *Name 1* **to** *St Peter's\**
**Welcome** *Name 2* **to** *St Peter's\**
**Welcome** *Name 3* **to** *St Peter's\**
**You are welcome in the name of the Lord!**

*\* Insert the name of your church or children's group, or sing 'our worship'.*

## Welcome Song: Option 2

→ **Song: 'You are welcome in the name of the Lord'** (traditional)
→ **Tune:** traditional. For the music see p. 360, or for a taster see the Diddy Disciples website. For tips on teaching songs for the first time, see Book 1, p. 215.

Let's wave with one hand. *Lead waving*
Then with our other hand. *Lead waving*
Then let's choose someone and show God's 'glory'!
*Move arms up and down in front of you with fingers wiggling, palms facing out, towards one person.*
And someone else! *Repeat*
Then let's wave with both hands all around the circle.
*Lead waving.*

We're ready to sing!
**You are welcome in the name of the Lord!**
*Wave with right hand to one person.*
**You are welcome in the name of the Lord!**
*Wave with left hand to another person.*
**I can see all over you, the glory of the Lord!**
*Move arms up and down in front of you with fingers wiggling,*
*palms facing out, towards one person and then another.*
**You are welcome in the name of the Lord!**
*Wave with both hands all around the circle.*

# Getting Ready to Worship

→ **Guide: Book 1, p. 218**

*Choose one of the following greetings according to which greeting is familiar in your church. (If your church uses a different greeting, you could use that here instead.)*

## Getting Ready to Worship: Option 1

→ **Action: the sign of the cross. Words: © Sharon Moughtin-Mumby**

*Invite the children to make the sign of the cross slowly with you. As the children become more confident, invite a child to lead the action as the whole group says the words and makes the sign of the cross.*

| | |
|---|---|
| **In my head,** | *touch head* |
| **in my heart,** | *touch chest* |
| **and all around me,** | *touch shoulders one by one* |
| **Jesus is here.** | *open hands in front, facing upwards* |

## Getting Ready to Worship: Option 2

→ **Action: 'The Lord be with you'** (open hands)

Let's start by clenching our hands together tightly.

*Lead children in clenching fists against your body to show a defensive posture.*

When we close ourselves up like this,
it's hard to let anyone into our heart.
It's hard even to let God into our heart!

When we get ready to worship,
we show that we're open to God and to each other.

*Open your hands out, facing up.*

Can you show me your open hands?
We're ready to let God and each other in!

The Lord be with you.
*Hold hands open to the children.*

**And also with you.**
*Invite the children to open their hands towards you.*

# Introducing the Unit

→ **Guide: Book 1, p. 218**

## Introducing the Unit: Option 1

*Week 1*
Starting this week, we're going to tell
the Bible's stories about God's best friend, Moses.

*Week 2 onwards:*
At the moment,
we're telling stories about God's best friend, Moses.

*All weeks:*
*Invite the children to close their eyes.*
Let's close our eyes for a moment.
Let's imagine we can see our friend
or someone we love right in front of us.
Now imagine that person giving you a big hug!
*If there are parents/carers of babies or toddlers present:*
Parents and carers, can you give your children a big hug!

Let's open our eyes.
How did hugging your friend make you feel?
Can you show me with your face?
*Accept responses.*

God had a best friend! His name was Moses.
Moses made God feel a bit like that.
God LOVED talking with Moses!
We're going to tell one of the stories about
God's friend Moses today.

## Introducing the Unit: Option 2

→ **Focus: the liturgical colour, green**

Who can tell us what colour season we're in now?
*If appropriate* You may have seen it in church.
*Invite a child to respond with the colour.*

Can anyone tell me what colour season we're in now?
At the moment, the Church is in Green Time!
In Green Time, the Church grows like a tree.
We're the Church, so we're going to be growing, too!
When trees grow, first they put their roots down.

Let's show our roots with our fingers.
*Lead the children in wriggling fingers.*
Before trees can grow up. *Point up*
First their roots need to grow down deep, deep, deep!
*Lead the children in wriggling fingers down.*

We're going to put our roots down deep in Green Time
by telling some of the very first stories in the Bible.
The stories of God's best friend, Moses.

*Invite the children to close their eyes.*
Let's close our eyes for a moment.
Let's imagine we can see our friend
or someone we love right in front of us.
Now imagine that person giving you a big hug!
*If there are parents/carers of babies or toddlers present:*
Parents and carers, can you give your children a big hug!

Let's open our eyes.
How did hugging your friend make you feel?
Can you show me with your face?
*Accept responses.*

God had a best friend! His name was Moses.
Moses made God feel a bit like that.
This Green Time, we're telling the Bible's stories
about God's best friend Moses.

# Gathering Song

" Remember that you were a slave in the land of Egypt, and the Lord your God brought you
out from there with a mighty hand and an outstretched arm. DEUTERONOMY 5.15:

Pharaoh said, 'You are lazy, lazy; that is why you say, "Let us go and sacrifice to the Lord." '
EXODUS 5.17 "

→ Guide: Book 1, p. 219
→ Song: 'Remember when we were slaves in Egypt!' Words: © Sharon Moughtin-Mumby
→ Tune: 'The old grey mare' (traditional, also known as the tune for 'I'm in the Lord's army'). For a taster see the Diddy
   Disciples website.

*In Week 1, skip the Gathering Song and go straight to the storytelling, which is longer than usual and introduces many of the ideas and characters from this song.*

*If you're introducing this song for the first time, you may find the following introduction helpful. We find it easier to learn new songs BEFORE giving out imaginative aids!*

We've got a new song to learn.
It's the slaves' song.
Let's sing 'my turn' *point to self*, 'your turn' *leader's hands out to group*.

*Singing:*
Remember when we were slaves in Egypt,
slaves in Egypt, slaves in Egypt.
**Remember when we were slaves in Egypt,**
**slaves in Egypt, slaves in Egypt.**

Then again, but with a different ending.
Listen!
Remember when we were slaves in Egypt,
then God set us free!
**Remember when we were slaves in Egypt,**
**then God set us free!**

Let's try that all together.
*Lead the children in singing:*
**Remember when we were slaves in Egypt,**
**slaves in Egypt, slaves in Egypt,**
**remember when we were slaves in Egypt,**
**then God set us free!**

Then we celebrate!
Let's sing 'my turn' *point to self*, 'your turn' *leader's hands out to group* again.

*As you sing, wave arms in celebration.*
Then God set us free! Then God set us free!
**Then God set us free! Then God set us free!**

Then we go back to the beginning again.
Let's see if you can join in!
**Remember when we were slaves in Egypt,**
**slaves in Egypt, slaves in Egypt,**
**remember when we were slaves in Egypt,**
**then God set us free!**

We're ready!
*Continue with the rest of the material.*

*If you're using imaginative aids, ask two or three children to give them out at this point. Then invite the children to warm up their imaginations by exploring actions for different emotions. Example: Can you show me: happy? sad? excited? scared? angry?*

For our stories about Moses,
we need to go to Egypt.
Egypt had a powerful king called Pharaoh.
Who can show us powerful?
*Lead the children in showing 'powerful'.*

Pharaoh the King was very rich and very powerful.
Show me powerful again!
*Lead the children in showing 'powerful'.*

Pharaoh had some amazing buildings!
Some of the tallest buildings in the world!

Can you show me tall?
*Lead the children in stretching up tall.*
Even taller! Higher and higher!

Pharaoh loved tall buildings!
But he didn't do any of the hard building work! *Shake head*
Pharaoh was a bully!

> *Once the children are familiar with this introduction you might like to ask them:*
> Can anyone tell me who built the buildings?
> *Accept the children's responses and their language.*

The 'slaves' – the poor people – had built the buildings.
Let's be the 'slaves' doing some hard digging work.
Let's stand up.
*Lead the children in standing.*
Time to start digging!

*Speak in a rhythm, digging on each 'dig':*
**Dig, and dig, and dig, and dig . . .**
*Start singing to the rhythm as you continue digging.*

**Remember when we were slaves in Egypt,**
**slaves in Egypt, slaves in Egypt,**
**remember when we were slaves in Egypt . . .**
Freeze!

> *Once the children are familiar with this introduction you might like to ask them:*
> THEN what happened?
> Can anyone remember?
> *Accept the children's responses and their language.*

God sent MOSES to set the slaves free!
The people were so excited and full of joy!
Let's show excited and joyful! *Excited action*

*Lead the group in continuing the song:*
**Then God set us free!** *Excited action*
**Then God set us free!** *Excited action*
**Remember when we were slaves in Egypt,** *Digging action*
**then God set us free!** *Excited action*

It's hot in Egypt! Can you show me hot!
*Lead the children in looking 'hot'.*
The slaves were tired and sad.
Can you show me tired and sad?
*Lead the children in looking 'tired and sad'.*
But they had to keep on building . . .

*Lead the children in singing and digging as if tired and sad.*
**Remember when we were slaves in Egypt,**
**slaves in Egypt, slaves in Egypt,**
**remember when we were slaves in Egypt,**
**then God set us free!** *Excited action*
**Then God set us free!** *Excited action*
**Then God set us free!** *Excited action*
**Remember when we were slaves in Egypt,**
**slaves in Egypt, slaves in Egypt,**
**remember when we were slaves in Egypt,** *digging*
**then God set us free!** *Excited action*

270

The slaves were sore! The slaves were tired!

Can you show me sore and tired?

*Follow the children's 'sore and tired' actions.*

But Pharaoh the Bully shouted:

'LAZY! LAZY! LAZY! I WANT MORE!' *Stamp foot on 'more'*

Let's be Pharaoh and shout:

**'LAZY! LAZY! LAZY! I WANT MORE!'** *Stamp foot on 'more'*

And the slaves had to work twice as fast.

Let's sing our song twice as fast!

Ready . . . go!

*Lead the children in digging and singing at double speed.*

**Remember when we were slaves in Egypt,**

**slaves in Egypt, slaves in Egypt,**

**remember when we were slaves in Egypt,**

**then God set us free!** *Excited action*

**Then God set us free!** *Excited action*

**Then God set us free!** *Excited action*

**Remember when we were slaves in Egypt,**

**slaves in Egypt, slaves in Egypt,**

**remember when we were slaves in Egypt,** *digging*

**then God set us free!** *Excited action*

# Getting Ready for Bible Storytelling

→ **Guide: Book 1, p. 220**

## Getting Ready for Bible Storytelling: Option 1

→ **Action: opening your group's box and naming this week's object**
→ **Guide: Book 1, p. 221**

*See the beginning of the weekly storytelling material for ideas of items to place in your box. Invite one of the children to open the box.*

What's in the box? *Ask the child to respond*

## Getting Ready for Bible Storytelling: Option 2

→ **Song: 'Jesus, open up my eyes'. Words: © Sharon Moughtin-Mumby**
→ **Tune: 'Michael, row the boat ashore' (traditional). For the music see p. 359, or for a taster see the Diddy Disciples website. For tips on teaching songs for the first time, see Book 1, p. 215.**

It's time to open the Bible.

Let's get ready!

Let's take our thumb *lead children in showing thumb*

And draw our cross on our eyes, *draw cross*

and our lips, *draw cross*

and our heart. *Draw cross*

Let's ask Jesus to help us get ready to listen out for God!

**Jesus, open up my eyes. Alleluia!**

*Trace a cross between your eyes.*

**Jesus, open up my lips. Alleluia!**

*Trace a cross on your lips.*

**Jesus, open up my heart. Alleluia!**

*Trace a cross on your heart.*

**Jesus, help me hear your voice. Alleluia!**

*Cup your hands behind your ears.*

# Interactive Bible Storytelling

→ **Guide: Book 1, p. 221**

*See the Bible Storytelling material in Section 2 of this unit.*

# Saying Sorry to God

→ **Guide: Book 1, p. 223**

We're telling stories about God's best friend, Moses.
God wants to be best friends with all of us,
but sometimes we're not a good friend to God.
Sometimes we make God sad by making other people sad.

It's time to say sorry for the times that we haven't been a good friend.
Let's sing our Sorry Song together.

## Sorry Song: Option 1

→ **Song: 'The Diddy Disciples sorry song'. Words: © Sharon Moughtin-Mumby**
→ **Tune: © Sharon Moughtin-Mumby. For the music see p. 356, or for a taster see the Diddy Disciples website. For tips on teaching songs for the first time, see Book 1, p. 215. For a description of the 'I'm Sorry' and 'New Start' signs, see p. 355 or the website.**

Let's sing/say sorry to God with our Sorry Song.
Let's put our hands on our head.
I wonder if there's anything we've thought this week
that we wish we hadn't thought?

*Lead the children in placing your hands on head, singing:*
**With my hands on my head,**
**I remember the things I've thought today,**
**I remember the things I wish I'd thought a different way.**

**I'm sorry, I'm sorry,** *Diddy Disciples 'I'm Sorry' sign twice (see p. 355)*
**I wish I could start again.** *Diddy Disciples 'New Start' sign (see p. 355)*
**I'm sorry, I'm sorry,** *'I'm Sorry' sign twice*
**I wish I could start again.** *'New Start' sign*

Let's put our hands by our mouths.
I wonder if there's anything we've said this week
that we wish we.hadn't said?

*With hands by mouth, singing:*
**With my hands on my mouth,**
**I remember the things I've said today,**
**I remember the things I wish I'd said a different way.**

**I'm sorry, I'm sorry,** *'I'm Sorry' sign twice*
**I wish I could start again.** *'New Start' sign*
**I'm sorry, I'm sorry,** *'I'm Sorry' sign twice*
**I wish I could start again.** *'New Start' sign*

Let's cross our hands on our chest.
I wonder if there's anything we've done this week
that we wish we hadn't done?

*With hands crossed on chest, singing:*
**With my hands on my chest,**
**I remember the things I've done today,**
**I remember the things I wish I'd done a different way.**

**I'm sorry, I'm sorry,** *'I'm Sorry' sign twice*
**I wish I could start again.** *'New Start' sign*
**I'm sorry, I'm sorry,** *'I'm Sorry' sign twice*
**I wish I could start again.** *'New Start' sign*

*Continue with a Saying Sorry Action or move straight to God Gives Us a New Start, below.*

## Sorry Song: Option 2

→ Song: 'We need a new start'. Words: © Sharon Moughtin-Mumby
→ Tune: 'Molly Malone' (traditional). For the music see p. 356, or for a taster see the Diddy Disciples website. For tips on teaching songs for the first time, see Book 1, p. 215. For a description of the 'I'm Sorry' and 'New Start' signs, see p. 355 or the website.

> **Tip**
>
> This song can be sung using 'we're sorry' as indicated, or as 'I'm sorry' adapting the material accordingly.

Let's put our hands on our head.
I wonder if there's anything we've thought this week
that we wish we hadn't thought?

*Lead the children in placing your hands on head, singing:*
**For the things we have thou-ght**
**that we wish we'd not thou-ght,**
**we're sor-ry, we're sor-ry,** *Diddy Disciples 'I'm Sorry' sign twice (see p. 355)*
**we need a new start.** *Diddy Disciples 'New Start' sign (see p. 355)*

Let's put our hands by our mouths.
I wonder if there's anything we've said this week
that we wish we hadn't said?

*With hands by mouth, singing:.*
**For the things we have sa-id**
**that we wish we'd not sa-id,**
**we're sor-ry, we're sor-ry,** *'I'm Sorry' sign twice*
**we need a new start.** *'New Start' sign*

Let's cross our hands on our chest.
I wonder if there's anything we've done this week
that we wish we hadn't done?

*With hands crossed on chest, singing:.*
**For the things we have done**
**that we wish we'd not done,**
**we're sor-ry, we're sor-ry,** *'I'm Sorry' sign twice*
**we need a new start.** *'New Start' sign*

*Continue with a Saying Sorry Action or move straight to God Gives Us a New Start, below.*

# Saying Sorry Action

→ Guide: Book 1, p. 223

*For alternative actions that can be used during any unit at any time of year, see Saying Sorry Actions: Options 2, 3 and 4 on pp. 40–2 of Book 1.*

When Moses grows up, he does something wrong.
Moses tries to hide from everyone in the wilderness.
Sometimes we do wrong things.
We feel like we want to hide.

Let's curl up in a ball now
and pretend we want to hide away from everyone,
hide even from God.
*Lead the children in curling up into a ball or covering face.*

*When the group is ready:*
When Moses was hiding, God came to find him.
God gave Moses a new start.

God wants to come and find us to give us a new start too.
God wants to be our best friend!
Let's pretend that our finger is God's finger!
*Lead the group in holding index finger up.*

Let's count to 3
and tap ourselves on the shoulder with God's finger!
Then let's jump up and shout:
'God gives me a new start!'

**1,** *tap* **2,** *tap* **3** *tap* . . .
*jump up*
**God gives me a new start!**

Now let's turn to someone
and give that person a big hug
to show that God wants to be best friends with them . . .
and let that person give you a hug as well.
*Lead the children in giving and receiving new starts.*

*When the group is ready:*
I wonder how it feels to know that God
wants to be your best friend?
Can you show me?

# God Gives Us a New Start

→ Guide: Book 1, p. 225

*Every time of Saying Sorry should end by assuring the children that God gives them a new start. Most Diddy Disciples Saying Sorry Actions already include this promise of a new start. If they don't – or if you've created your own Saying Sorry Action – you should choose from one of the following New Start options, or create your own assurance of forgiveness. You could also choose to move straight from the Sorry Song to God's promise of a new start, without any Saying Sorry Action.*

## New Start Action: Option 1

→ **Action: tracing a cross/smile on each other's forehead**

The Good News is:
God always wants to give us a new start!

Let's turn to the person next to us
and show that God gives us a new start.
Let's take our thumb/finger *Show thumb/finger*
and draw a cross/smile on that person's forehead *Draw a cross/smile in the air*

> *If your group is drawing a smile, add:*
> to show that God is very happy with us!

Let's say, 'God gives you a new start!'
Then let the other person give you a new start, too!

*When the group has finished showing each other God's new starts:*
Let's use our new start to share God's love this week!

## New Start Action: Option 2

→ **Action: standing up and hugging each other**

The Good News is:
God always wants to give us a new start!

Let's help someone next to us stand up from the floor.
Then let that person help you stand up too!
*Lead the children in helping each other stand up.*

Then let's give each other a hug and say:
'God gives you a new start!'

*When the group has finished showing each other God's new starts:*
Let's use our new start to share God's love this week!

## New Start Action: Option 3

→ **Song: 'God loves to give me a new start!' Words: © Sharon Moughtin-Mumby**
→ **Tune: 'Give me oil in my lamp' (traditional). For the music see p. 357, or for a taster see the Diddy Disciples website. For tips on teaching songs for the first time, see Book 1, p. 215.**

The Good News is:
God always wants to give us a new start!
Let's sing our New Start song together.

**[Yes, my] God loves to give me a new start!** *Trace a smile/cross on own forehead*
**How amazing God's love for me!** *Cross hands on chest*
**[Yes, my] God loves to give me a new start!** *Trace a smile/cross on own forehead*
**How amazing is God's love for me!**

**Sing hosanna! Sing hosanna!** *Wave hands in the air*
**Sing hosanna to the King of Kings!**
*Wave hands in the air followed by crown on head.*
**Sing hosanna! Sing hosanna!** *Wave hands in the air*
**Sing hosanna to the King!**
*Wave hands in the air followed by crown on head.*

# Introduction to Prayers

God heard the slaves when they groaned.
God answered them!
It's time for us to bring our prayers to our friend, God.

# Prayers for Other People

→ **Guide: Book 1, p. 223 and p. 225**

*Invite the children to sit in a circle in a moment of quiet.*
Let's imagine holding our prayer gently,
*hands together gently in traditional prayer gesture, but cupped so you can imagine a prayer inside*
and then let it go up in prayer to God,
*hands opened upwards to God*

> *If you're using Option 1:*
> Jesus, *hands together, cupped*

hear our prayer. *hands opened upwards to God*
Let's pray . . .

## Prayers for Other People: Option 1

→ Song: 'Jesus, hear our prayer!' Words: © Sharon Moughtin-Mumby
→ Tune: 'Brown girl in the ring' (traditional). For the music see p. 358, or for a taster see the Diddy Disciples website. For similar words designed to fit with the alternative tune 'He's got the whole world in his hands', see p. 359. For tips on teaching songs for the first time, see Book 1, p. 215.

| | |
|---|---|
| **For the world:** | **Jesus, hear our prayer!** |
| *Make a circle shape* | *Open hands upwards to God* |
| **For the Church:** | **Jesus, hear our prayer!** |
| *Praying hands* | *Open hands upwards to God* |
| **For our place,** *Walworth*\*: | **Jesus, hear our prayer!** |
| *Hands down moving out in* | *Open hands upwards to God* |
| *a semi-circle to show the land around us* | |
| **Lord Jesus, hear our prayer. Amen.** | |
| *Open hands upwards to God.* | |

\* *Insert local area/school/church/community/parish.*

| | |
|---|---|
| **For the sick and lonely:** | **Jesus, hear our prayer!** |
| *Fingers showing tears falling* | *Open hands upwards to God* |
| *down cheeks* | |
| **For our friends and family:** | **Jesus, hear our prayer!** |
| *Arms around yourself* | *Open hands upwards to God* |
| **For ourselves:** | **Jesus, hear our prayer!** |
| *Both hands on heart* | *Open hands upwards to God* |
| **Lord Jesus, hear our prayer. Amen.** | |
| *Open hands upwards to God.* | |

Let's close our eyes for a moment.
I wonder if there's someone special
you'd like to pray for?
Let's imagine that person now.

Now, let's imagine Jesus coming to them.
Does Jesus say anything?
Does Jesus do anything?

Let's open our eyes.

*Continue with one of the Prayer Action options outlined below. Once the Prayer Action has been completed, you may like to use the following verse, to close this time of prayer.*

| | |
|---|---|
| **Take our prayers:** | **Jesus, hear our prayer!** |
| *Hands together gently* | *Open hands upwards to God* |
| **Make them holy:** | **Jesus, hear our prayer!** |
| *Hands together gently* | *Open hands upwards to God* |
| **Make them beautiful:** | **Jesus, hear our prayer!** |
| *Hands together gently* | *Open hands upwards to God* |
| **Lord Jesus, hear our prayer! Amen.** | |
| *Hands together gently, then open hands upwards to God.* | |

## Prayers for Other People: Option 2

→ Song: 'The Diddy Disciples little prayers song'. Words: © Sharon Moughtin-Mumby
→ Tune: 'Frère Jacques' (traditional). For the music see p. 356, or for a taster see the Diddy Disciples website. For tips on teaching songs for the first time, see Book 1, p. 215.

*These prayers are especially suited to churches that prefer less traditional prayer forms.*

*Either: choose what you'd like the group to pray for before the session.*

*Or: ask the children at this point if there is anything or anyone that they'd like to pray for. Ask them or others to suggest actions. You will need two different 'thank you' suggestions and two different 'hear our prayer' suggestions. Try to encourage at least one prayer for other people outside the group.*

*Invite the children to sing after you, repeating your words and their actions. Sometimes it might be almost impossible to fit the child's own words in! It's really valuable to do this where possible, resisting the urge to try and 'neaten' their suggestions. For examples, see p. 17.*

*Having sung your prayers, you could insert a Prayer Action, repeat the process, or move straight on to close with the following (or other words that remain the same each week).*

| | |
|---|---|
| For today, | *Point hands down for 'now'* |
| **For today,** | *Point hands down for 'now'* |
| Thank you, God! | *Open hands upwards to God or hands together in prayer* |
| **Thank you, God!** | *Open hands upwards to God or hands together in prayer* |
| Fo-r your love, | *Cross hands on chest* |
| **Fo-r your love,** | *Cross hands on chest* |
| Thank you, God! | *Open hands upwards to God or hands together in prayer* |
| **Thank you, God!** | *Open hands upwards to God or hands together in prayer* |

# Prayer Actions

→ **Guide: Book 1, p. 225**

*Continue with one of the Prayer Actions outlined below, or you can use the Prayer Actions: Options 2 and 3 in Book 1, pp. 47–8 at any time of year.*

## Prayer Action: Option 1

→ **Action: taking a sad face and placing it on a cloth**

In our story, the slaves are sad.
They groan.

After 3, let's all groan together like the slaves.
**1, 2, 3,** *groan!*
And again!
**1, 2, 3,** *groan!*
Ssssh! Listen! *Hand behind ear*
God's heard the slaves groaning!
God's going to send Moses to help them.
I wonder if you know someone who's sad at the moment?

*Name* and *Name* are going to bring around a basket of sad faces.
If you like you can take a sad face
and hold it up to God like this. *Model holding one high*
Let's ask God to hear our sad face as a prayer.

*Hum the tune together, with 'Jesus, hear our prayer' as a refrain until all the children and adults who wish to take sad faces have done so.*

God hears us when we groan or cry.
Let's give our friend's sadness to God.
Let's put our sad faces on this cloth in the centre.
Let's ask God to help our sad friend.

Maybe God is asking US to help them?

*Lead the children in singing again as they place their sad faces on a cloth in the centre. Some groups may like to ask two children to go round the circle in opposite ways with trays to collect the faces. The trays can then be placed in the centre of the circle. End this time of prayer with the final verse from the Prayer Song you've chosen.*

## Prayer Action: Option 2

→ **Action: taking water and placing it on face like tears**

In our story, the slaves are sad.
They groan.
After 3, let's all groan together like the slaves.
**1, 2, 3,** *groan!*

Ssssh! Listen! *Hand behind ear*
Go's heard the slaves groaning!
God's going to send Moses to help them!

I wonder if you know someone who's sad at the moment?
*Name* and *Name* are going to bring around a bowl of water.
If you like you can dip your fingers in the water.
You can put water on your cheeks like tears.

Let's remember the people we know who are sad.
Let's ask God to hear their sadness like a prayer.
Let's ask God to help them.

Maybe God is asking US to help them?

*Hum the tune together, with 'Jesus, hear our prayer' as a refrain until all the children and adults who wish to take water and make tears on their face have done so.*

# Thank You, God

→ **Guide: Book 1, p. 227**

## Thank You, God: Option 1

→ **Song: 'My hands were made for love'. Words: © Sharon Moughtin-Mumby**
→ **Tune: 'Hickory, dickory, dock' (traditional). For the music see p. 360, or for a taster see the Diddy Disciples website. For tips on teaching songs for the first time, see Book 1, p. 215.**

*Invite the children to sit in a circle for a moment of quiet.*
It's time to remember all the things we've done this week.
It's time to say 'thank you' to God
for when we've been part of showing God's love.

Let's wiggle our fingers!
I wonder when you've shown love
with your hands this week?

*Wiggle fingers as you sing.*
**My hands were made for love!**
**My hands were made for love!**
**Thank you for the love they've shown.**
**My hands were made for love!**

Let's wiggle our feet!
I wonder when you've shown love
with your feet this week?

*Wiggle feet as you sing.*
**My feet were made for love!**
**My feet were made for love!**
**Thank you for the love they've shown.**
**My feet were made for love!**

Let's put our hands gently on our neck.

Let's sing 'Ahhh!'

**Ahhhhh!**

Can you feel your throat vibrating and dancing with your voice?

I wonder when you've shown love

with your voice this week?

*Hold neck and feel your voice 'dancing' as you sing.*

**My voice was made for love!**

**My voice was made for love!**

**Thank you for the love it's shown.**

**My voice was made for love!**

## Thank you, God: Option 2

→ Song: 'For the love we've shown'. Words: © Sharon Moughtin-Mumby

→ Tune: 'All through the night' (traditional). For the music see p. 357, or for a taster see the Diddy Disciples website. For tips on teaching songs for the first time, see Book 1, p. 215.

*Most suitable for use with children over the age of four.*

*Invite the children to sit in a circle for a moment of quiet.*

It's time to remember all the things we've done this week.

It's time to say 'thank you'

for when we've been part of showing God's love.

*Either:* Let's wiggle our fingers.

*Or:* Let's hold up our hands.

I wonder when you've shown love

with your hands this week?

*Either:* Let's wiggle our feet.

*Or:* Let's show our feet.

I wonder when you've shown love

with your feet this week?

Let's put our hands gently on our neck.

Let's sing 'Ahhh!'

**Ahhhhh!**

Can you feel your neck vibrating and dancing with your voice?

I wonder when you've shown love

with your voice this week?

Let's sing our 'thank you' song to God

For the times we've been part of sharing God's love.

**For the love we've shown with our hands,** *Hold hands up or wiggle fingers*

**Thank you, God!**

**For the love we've shown with our feet,** *Point to feet or wiggle feet*

**Thank you, God!**

**When we love all those around us,** *Cross hands on chest*

**It's the same as loving Jesus!**

**For the love we've shown with our voice,** *Hands on neck or point to singing mouth*

**Thank you, God!**

# Creative Response

→ Guide: Book 1, p. 228

*See the Creative Responses in Section 3 of this unit.*

# Sharing God's Peace

→ **Guide: Book 1, p. 231**

*This Building Block is particularly designed for children's groups that join the adult congregation to share communion but can also be used to end any session or Service of the Word. During Advent and Christmas, you might like to keep to your normal option for Sharing God's Peace.*

## Sharing God's Peace: Option 1

→ **Song: 'I've got peace like a river' (traditional), Isaiah 66.12, NIV**
→ **Tune: traditional. For a taster see the Diddy Disciples website. For tips on teaching songs for the first time, see Book 1, p. 215.**

> *Either: hold one end of the peace cloth (Book 1, p. 231) and ask one of the older children or an adult to hold the other end. Start singing the Peace Song. As the children begin to gather, invite them to join in holding a small section of the cloth, raising and lowering it so it 'flows' like a river as you sing together.*

> *Or: invite the children to sit in a circle in the worship space. Start singing the Peace Song. As the children begin to gather, invite them to join in raising and lowering their hands like the waters of a flowing river.*

**I've got peace like a river,**
**I've got peace like a river,**
**I've got peace like a river in my soul.**
**I've got peace like a river,**
**I've got peace like a river,**
**I've got peace like a river in my soul.**

*If your group is about to rejoin the adults for communion: when all the children are gathered, continue with the words of the Peace, below.*

## Sharing God's Peace: Option 2

→ **Song: 'Peace is flowing like a river' (traditional), Isaiah 66.12, NIV**
→ **Tune: traditional. For a taster see the Diddy Disciples website. For tips on teaching songs for the first time, see Book 1, p. 215.**

> *Either: hold one end of the peace cloth (Book 1, p. 231) and ask one of the older children or an adult to hold the other end. Start singing the Peace Song. As the children begin to gather, invite them to join in holding a small section of the cloth, raising and lowering it so it 'flows' like a river as you sing together.*

> *Or: invite the children to sit in a circle in the worship space. Start singing the Peace Song. As the children begin to gather, invite them to join in raising and lowering their hands like the waters of a flowing river.*

**Peace is flowing like a river,**
**flowing out through you and me.**
**Spreading out into the desert,**
**setting all the captives free.**

*If your group is about to rejoin the adults for communion: when all the children are gathered, continue with the words of the Peace, below.*

## Sharing God's Peace: Option 3

→ **Song: 'I've got peace in my fingers'. Words: © 1995 Susan Salidor ASCAP**
→ **Tune: © 1995 Susan Salidor ASCAP**
→ **The words and music can be found on the album *Little Voices in My Head* by Susan Salidor © 2003 Peach Head. They can also be found on iTunes or YouTube, or at <www.susansalidor.com>. For tips on teaching songs for the first time, see Book 1, p. 215.**

*If your group is about to rejoin the adults for communion: when all the children are gathered, continue with the words of the Peace, below.*

# The Peace

→ 2 Thessalonians 3.16; 1 Peter 5.14

*Once you have finished singing . . .*

The peace of the Lord be always with you.
*Hold hands open to the children.*
**And also with you.**

*Invite the children to open their hands towards you.*
Let's shake hands or hug each other
and say, 'Peace be with you' *or whatever is said on sharing the Peace in your church*
as a sign of God's peace.

*Lead the children in giving and receiving the Peace. Immediately following this, at St Peter's, Walworth, we lead the children back to join the rest of the congregation to continue our worship with the Eucharistic Prayer.*

# Taking God's Love into the World

→ Guide: Book 1, p. 232
→ Song: 'This little light of mine' (traditional)
→ Tune: traditional. For a taster see the Diddy Disciples website. For tips on teaching songs for the first time, see Book 1, p. 215.

*This Building Block is particularly designed for standalone groups or groups that are held during a Service of the Word. Alternatively, you could use one of the Peace Songs above to end your worship.*

Our time together is coming to an end.
*Invite the children to sit in a circle for a moment of quiet.*
God has lit a little light of love inside all of us.
*Trace a circle on your heart.*
Let's make our finger into a candle.
*Bring your finger from your heart and hold it out.*

Let's be God and light our little light of love together, after 3.
*Lead the children in lighting their finger candle by striking an imaginary match in the air on 3 and pretending to light your finger.*
**1, 2, 3 . . . Tssss!**
Let's imagine God's love shining and dancing like light in us.

*Wave your finger in front of you.*
**This little light of mine, I'm gonna let it shine!**
**This little light of mine, I'm gonna let it shine!**
**This little light of mine, I'm gonna let it shine!**
**Let it shine, let it shine, let it shine!**

*Blow on your finger as if blowing out a candle on 'puff'. Then hold it up high.*
**Won't let no one** *puff* **it out! I'm gonna let it shine!**
**Won't let no one** *puff* **it out! I'm gonna let it shine!**
**Won't let no one** *puff* **it out! I'm gonna let it shine!**
**Let it shine, let it shine, let it shine!**

*Hold your finger behind a cupped hand, then take your cupped hand away*
*to reveal the 'candle' and hold it high!*
**Hide it under a bushel? No! I'm gonna let it shine!**
**Hide it under a bushel? No! I'm gonna let it shine!**
**Hide it under a bushel? No! I'm gonna let it shine!**
**Let it shine, let it shine, let it shine!**

*Lead the children in placing your finger back on your heart.*
Now let's put our little light of love

back in our hearts, where it belongs.
Let's remember to let our little light shine
in all our playing and working today . . .

*If you're building a Service of the Word and this is your final Building Block, you may like to close with a familiar blessing, the Peace and/or one of the following. If you're using one of these call-and-responses with your group for the first time, see p. 25 for an introduction.*

*Either:* Praise the Lord! *Both hands to self*

**Alleluia!** *Both arms upwards in 'V' shape*

*Or:* Let us bless the Lord. *Both hands to self*

**Thanks be to God.** *Both arms upwards in 'V' shape*

*Or:* And all the people said . . . *both hands to self*

**Amen!** *Both arms upwards in 'V' shape*

# Section 2

# The Bible Storytelling material: God's Best Friend, Moses, unit

## Week 1: The Baby Pulled from the Water

→ Exodus 1.8—2.10
→ Song: 'The river went up!'. Words: © Sharon Moughtin-Mumby
→ Tune: 'Everywhere we go' (traditional camp song)

The ri - ver went up! ___ The ri - ver went up! ___ The
ri - ver went down! ___ The ri - ver went down!

We're ready to tell our first story about Moses.

> *If your group is using the What's in the Box? option (Book 1, p. 221):*
> *Invite a child to open the box.*
> *Inside is a blue cloth to show the river (e.g. your peace cloth; see Book 1, p. 231) or a picture of a river.*

> What's in the box?
> *Accept the child's response.*

> Today we're going to tell the story about a river.

For our stories about Moses, we're in Egypt.
Egypt is a very hot country.
Can you show me hot?
*Lead the children in fanning yourselves and showing 'hot'.*

A wide river ran down the middle of it.
Let's be the river together.
Let's show our fingers rippling like water.
*Lead the children in wiggling their fingers.*
We need to raise our arms up, up, up high. *Hands up*
And down. *Hands down, fingers still wiggling*
Up . . . and down . . .

Can you sing after me,
'my turn' *point to self*, 'your turn' *leader's hands out to group*?

*Lead the children in singing, fingers wiggling throughout.*
The river went up! *Raise hands up*
**The river went up!** *Raise hands up*
And the river went down! *Lower hands down*
**The river went down!** *Lower hands down*

The river went up! *Raise hands up*
**The river went up!** *Raise hands up*
And the river went down! *Lower hands down*
**The river went down!** *Lower hands down*

And freeze!
Now Egypt had a very powerful king!
Who can show us powerful?
*Lead the children in showing 'powerful'.*
Let's stand up tall and powerful and be Pharaoh the King.
*Lead the children in standing tall and powerful.*

Pharaoh the King was very rich and very powerful.
But our story doesn't start with the powerful person! *Shake head*
It starts with the very poorest people.
Our story starts with the 'slaves'.

Egypt had some amazing buildings!
Let's reach up tall and show the tallest buildings!
Higher and higher!
These amazing buildings were all built by 'slaves'!
Let's be slaves and do some building!
Who can show me building?
*Lead the children in miming building.*

It's 'my turn' *point to self*, 'your turn' *leader's hands out to group* again.

*Lead the children in building as you sing to the same tune:*
We're building a palace!
**We're building a palace!**
We're working all day!
**We're working all day!**
We're building a pyramid!
**We're building a pyramid!**
We're working all night!
**We're working all night!**

Now, Pharaoh the King was a bully.
He loved tall buildings!
But he didn't do any of the hard building work! *Shake head*
Let's stand up tall and be Pharaoh the King again.
*Lead the children in standing tall.*
All Pharaoh did was shout :
'LAZY! LAZY! LAZY! *Point*
I WANT MORE!' *Stamp foot on 'more'*

Let's be Pharaoh and shout that together:
**'LAZY! LAZY! LAZY!** *Point*
**I WANT MORE!'** *Stamp foot on 'more'*

Even louder:
**'LAZY! LAZY! LAZY!** *Point*
**I WANT MORE!'** *Stamp foot on 'more'*

And the slaves had to work twice as fast.
Let's sing our song twice as fast as before.
Ready . . . go!

*Lead the children in singing and building in double time:*
We're building a temple!
**We're building a temple!**
We're working all day!
**We're working all day!**
We're building a city!
**We're building a city!**
We're working all night!
**We're working all night!**

Freeze!
Now someone in Egypt was scared.
Who do you think was scared?
*Accept responses.*

Believe it or not: it was Pharaoh! The bully!
Let's show Pharaoh being scared!
*Lead the children in being scared.*

Pharaoh said, 'There are too many slaves!
They might hurt me!' *Look scared*
Then Pharaoh said . . .
After 3, let's get ready to point together.
1, 2, 3 . . . *point*
*As leader, say Pharaoh's words as the children point:*
'Throw the baby boys in the river!'

Oh my goodness! *Look shocked*
I wonder how the slaves felt?
Can you show me?
*Accept the children's responses.*

Let's sit down for a moment.

*When the group is ready:*
Now, one of the slaves had a baby.
Let's be the slave and hold our baby.
He was lovely!
*Sound shocked:* She didn't want to throw him in the river. *Shake head*

The slave was a Clever Slave!
So she made a basket from river reeds like grass.
Let's be the Clever Slave and weave a basket together.
*Lead the children in weaving for a brief moment.*

Let's put our baby ever so gently into the basket.
*Lead the children in putting the imaginary baby gently in an imaginary basket.*
She put the basket in the reeds by the side of the waters.
*Ask one child to stand up in the centre and be the 'reeds'. Ask the child to hold her or his hands up high, holding the 'basket'.*
*You may like to use a doll as the baby within a real basket or Moses basket at this point, or you can leave this to the children's imaginations.*

That was a clever idea wasn't it!

*Try and bring the humour out:*

The slave put her baby boy in the river like Pharaoh said!

But Pharaoh didn't say anything about baskets! *Shake head*

Let's hope the baby stays safe in the basket!

Now, let's stand up and be the river again.

*Name*, hold that basket high! We don't want the river to get in!

*To the group:* Let's show our wiggly water fingers.

*Lead the children in wiggling fingers.*

Let's start down low . . .

> *If appropriate:*
> But the Nile is a tidal river like the Thames*.
> It goes up and down with the sea's tides.
>
> * *In Walworth, our children are familiar with the River Thames and its different heights. Exchange this with the name of another local river, if relevant.*

Our river's going to go up and down!

I hope the baby will be all right!

*Lead the children in singing.*

The river went up! *Raise hands up high*

**The river went up!** *Raise hands up high*

And the river went down! *Lower hands down*

**And the river went down!** *Lower hands down*

Let's see, is the baby safe?

*Peer over at the baby held high by the child.*

Yes, he looks safe!

The river went up! *Raise hands up*

**The river went up!** *Raise hands up*

And the river went . . .

*Interrupt yourself.*

Wait! Look! Who's that over there!

*Point to the corner of the room.*

That's Pharaoh's daughter, the Princess!

She's getting washed in the river.

Let's sit down and be the Princess getting washed together.

> *To the child holding the real or imaginary basket:*
> You can sit down now too and be the Princess.
> *If the child was holding a real doll/basket, you may like to put it on the focal table or to one side at this point.*

*Lead the children in pretending to wash yourself, humming to yourself.*

Wait a minute! What's that basket?

*Point to the corner of the room.*

*Lead the children in taking an imaginary basket from an imaginary servant.*

Let's all be the Princess taking the basket from the river.

I wonder what's inside?

*Lead the children in opening the basket carefully.*

Oh my goodness!

*Ask the children, to check they're following:*

What's inside the basket?

*Accept the children's responses.*

It's a baby!

Let's take him out.

*Lead the children in holding an imaginary baby up gently.*
Oh, he's lovely!

*To the group:*
Now Pharaoh the Bully was the Princess's dad!
What did Pharaoh say everyone had to do to baby boys?
*Accept the children's responses.*

Pharaoh said, 'Throw the baby boys in the river!'
Shall we throw him in the river?!
*Hold baby close and look shocked* No!
Pharaoh's daughter decided to keep the baby.
*Lead the children in cuddling the baby.*
But the Princess wasn't used to doing any work. *Shake head*
And how much work are babies?
*Accept responses from the children. You may like also to ask parents/carers if relevant!*

Babies are very, VERY hard work.
The Princess needed someone to help her.
Someone who was used to hard work.
She needed a slave!
Can anyone guess which slave ended up
looking after the baby?
*Accept children's responses.*

> This version of the story misses out the part with the baby's sister as it's already a long and complex story with lots of
> characters. However, if the children mention Moses' sister, you could add:
> The baby's sister told the Princess
> SHE knew someone who could help.
> She ran and she brought the Clever Slave!
> The baby's mum!

It was the Clever Slave! The baby's mum!
So the Clever Slave took her baby home.
Let's be the slave and hold our baby close and look clever!
*Lead the children in cuddling the baby and looking clever.*

Let's sit down and hold our baby carefully.
*When the children are ready:*
The baby grew and grew and grew . . .
Let's stand up slowly and show the baby
growing, and growing, and growing . . .

*Lead the children in standing slowly until you're standing tall.*
Until the baby was about as tall as YOU! *Point to the children*
He wasn't a baby any more, he was a boy!

Then the Clever Slave took him by the hand.
Let's be the boy and hold our mummy's hand.
*Lead the children in miming holding our mummy's hand.*

The Clever Slave took the boy to the palace
to live with the Princess.
The boy wasn't a slave any more. He was a prince!
Let's put a crown on our head to show we're a prince!
*Lead the children in miming putting on a crown.*

The Princess gave the little Prince a name:
Moses, which means 'pull'! *(in Hebrew)*
Can you show me an action for pull?
*Lead the children in showing pulling.*

Moses was the baby boy that was PULLED *pull action*
from the river instead of being THROWN IN! *throw action*

Let's show those actions together!
*Lead the children in the actions as you repeat the words:*
Moses was the baby boy that was PULLED *pull action*
from the river instead of being THROWN IN! *throw action*

We'll hear more about Moses,
the baby who was PULLED *pull action* from the river, next week.

# Week 2: Moses in the Wilderness

→ **Exodus 2.11–25**
→ **Song: 'We're building a temple'. Words: © Sharon Moughtin-Mumby**
→ **Tune: 'Everywhere we go' (traditional camp song). For a taster see the Diddy Disciples website.**

If your group is using the What's in the Box? option (Book 1, p. 221), show the children a wilderness tray (p. 86). At St
Peter's, Walworth, we use a tray filled with sand (or brown sugar) with a few rocks and stones placed around so that it looks
desolate. You may like to have a cloth over it, in which case invite a child to remove the cloth at this point.

What do you see? *Invite a child to respond.*

Sand, rocks and sky and nothing else. *Shake head*
This is the 'wilderness'. Today we're going to tell the story
of when Moses did something wrong and ran away to the 'wilderness'.

But to start with . . .

For today's story, we're [STILL] in Egypt.
We're the 'slaves' doing some hard building work!

> *If your group has sung the Gathering Song:*
> We've just been digging!
> Now it's time to do some building!

Let's build and sing 'my turn' *point to self*, 'your turn' *leader's hands out to group.*

*Lead the children in building as you sing.*
We're building a temple!
**We're building a temple!**
We're working all day!
**We're working all day!**
We're building a pyramid!
**We're building a pyramid!**
We're working all night!
**We're working all night!**

The slaves were so tired!
Can you show me tired?
*Lead the children in looking exhausted.*
But Pharaoh the Bully shouted:

288

'LAZY! LAZY! LAZY! I WANT MORE!' *Stamp foot on 'more'*
Let's be Pharaoh and shout:
**'LAZY! LAZY! LAZY! I WANT MORE!'** *Stamp foot on 'more'*

Let's sing our song faster!
*Lead the children in building as you sing twice as fast.*

We're building a city!
**We're building a city!**
We're working all day!
**We're working all day!**
We're building a temple!
**We're building a temple!**
We're working all night!
**We're working all night!**

There was a man called Moses.
Moses lived with Pharaoh in a huge palace.
He didn't have to do any work! *Shake head*
Let's sit down and be Moses.

*When the group is ready:*
Moses' mummy and daddy were slaves.
And his sister and brother were slaves.
But Moses lived in the PALACE with Pharaoh.

Every day Moses watched his family working hard. *Building action*
And looking so tired! *Look tired*
I wonder how Moses felt to see his family working so hard?
Let's all show how you think Moses felt with your face.
*Accept the children's actions and expressions.*

Then one day, one of Pharaoh's helpers
HIT one of the slaves! *Raise hand and look shocked*

That was ENOUGH! *Look angry*
Now Moses was ANGRY!
Can you show me cross?
*Lead the children in looking angry.*
Now show me angry!
Now show me boiling and bursting with anger!
The most angry you've ever been!
*Follow the children in looking furious!*

Moses was FURIOUS!
Moses looked one way.
Let's all look one way . . .
*Lead the children in looking one way.*
Then he looked the other way . . .
*Lead the children in looking the other way.*
Sssssshhhhh! *Finger to lips*
*Whisper:* Then Moses killed Pharaoh's helper.
All the slaves were shocked!
Can you show me shocked!
*Follow the children in looking shocked.*

People started whispering.
Can you whisper, 'Moses! Moses! Moses!'?
*Lead the children in whispering to each other.*
**Moses! Moses! Moses!'**

And Pharaoh heard the whispers. *Hand over ear*
How do you think Pharaoh felt?
*Accept the children's responses.*

Now it was Pharaoh's turn to boil and burst with anger.
Can you show me your angry face again?
*Follow the children's expressions.*
Your furious face?
Pharaoh wanted to KILL Moses!

So Moses ran!
After 3, let's get up and run on the spot together.
1, 2, 3 . . . **Run!**
*Lead the children in running on the spot.*
Moses ran and ran and ran and ran and ran . . .
Faster and faster and faster!
Freeze!

Until Moses reached the wilderness, the desert.
And there . . . he hid!
Let's curl up on the floor and pretend we're hiding!
*Lead the children in curling up and hiding.*
Moses hid from everyone in the wilderness.

Back in Egypt, the slaves were still building.
Get up! It's time to build again!
*If you're lucky, some of the group will groan!*

*Lead the children in building as you sing.*
We're building a temple!
**We're building a temple!**
We're working all day!
**We're working all day!**
We're building a pyramid!
**We're building a pyramid!**
We're working all night!
**We're working all night!**

And slaves GROANED from all the hard work.
After 3, let's all groan.
**1, 2, 3 . . . groan!**
*Hands over face, lead the children in groaning.*
It was a groan that said, 'Help!'
Let's groan again.
**1, 2, 3 . . . groan!**

Sssh! Listen! *Hand behind ear*
God heard that groan!
Let's sit down again.

*When the group is ready:*
Now who do you think God could find
that was STRONG enough to stop Pharaoh?
*Leave just a couple of seconds for this rhetorical question.*

Who could God find that was ANGRY enough to stop Pharaoh?
*This time see if any of the children can guess.*

*If necessary:* Who was really, really angry earlier in our story:
angry enough to kill one of Pharaoh's helpers?
MOSES!

But where's Moses? *Look around the room*
Can anyone remember what Moses is doing at the moment?
*Accept responses from the children.*

Moses is HIDING!
Let's hide behind our hands and show Moses hiding.
*Lead the children in hiding behind hands.*
Moses is hiding far away,
in a place called the 'wilderness'.

> *If your group is using a wilderness tray for What's in the Box?, show it to the children again here. Even if your group doesn't usually use What's in the Box?, you may like to show them a wilderness tray (see p. 86) at this point. If you used a wilderness tray for the stories about Jesus in the wilderness around the beginning of Lent this will introduce hints of Jesus as 'the new Moses' into the storytelling, as in the Gospel of Matthew.*

In the Bible, the wilderness is the place
where people are thrown out when
no one wants them any more.
When they're thrown away:
a bit like we throw away rubbish.

Let's pretend we're throwing rubbish away.
*Lead the children in sitting up and pretending to screw up a piece of paper and throw it away.*
In our story, Moses thought he was rubbish!
He threw himself away like rubbish!
But let me tell you a secret.
*Whisper:* God loves rubbish!

*Normal voice:*
God loves rubbish
because God can do amazing things with rubbish!

God's going to come and find Moses!
Let's be Moses again hiding in the wilderness.
*Lead the children in curling up on the floor.*

*Show finger.*
Let's pretend our finger is God's finger.
*Lead the children in holding up index finger, still curled up on the floor.*

Let's be God and tap three times on Moses's shoulder.
*Lead the children in tapping on their own shoulder as they mime being Moses.*
**1,** *tap* **2,** *tap* **3** *tap . . .*

Let's do that again.
But this time after 3, let's be Moses and jump up!
Let's shout, 'Moses! God gives you a new start!' *Hands cupped around mouth*

Let's get ready to tap with God's finger again . . . *Hold out finger*
*Lead the children in tapping on their own shoulder as they mime being Moses.*

**1,** *tap* **2,** *tap* **3** *tap . . .*
*Lead the children in jumping up.*
**Moses! God gives you a new start!**

God gives Moses a brand new start.
Moses is going to be God's best friend.
Moses is going to do amazing things!
Moses is going to help God set the slaves free!

> *Either:* We'll hear what happens next, next week.
> *End at this point.*

> *Or: continue with the following material.*

Let's sit down again for a moment.

*When the group is ready:*
I wonder whether you ever feel
as if you want to hide from everyone, like Moses?
As if you want to hide from God?
I wonder if you ever feel like you're rubbish because you've done something that's hurt someone?

> *If your group is familiar with a Sorry Song, you could sing this together at this point, returning to tell the rest of the story with the words:*
> When Moses did a wrong thing,
>   he tried to hide from everyone in the wilderness.
> Sometimes when we do wrong things,
>   we feel like we want to hide.

Let's curl up in a ball now
and pretend we want to hide away from everyone,
to hide even from God.
*Lead the children in curling up and hiding.*
When Moses was hiding, God came to find him.
God gave Moses a new start.
And Moses became God's best friend.
Moses did amazing things!

When we're hiding, God wants to come and find us
to give us a new start too.
God wants to be our best friend!
Let's pretend that our finger is God's finger!
*Lead the children in holding up index finger.*
Let's count to 3 and tap ourselves
on the shoulder with God's finger!
Then let's jump up and shout, 'God gives me a new start!'

*Lead the children in tapping on their own shoulder as they mime being Moses.*
**1,** *tap* **2,** *tap* **3** *tap, jump up . . .*
**God gives me a new start!**

Now let's turn to someone
and give that person a big hug
to show that God wants to be best friends with them . . .
and let that person give you a hug as well.
*Lead the children in giving and receiving new starts.*

*When the group is ready:*
I wonder how it feels to know that God wants to be your best friend?
We'll hear more about God's best friend, Moses, next week.

# Week 3: Moses, You Will Set My People Free!

→ Exodus 3.1—4.17
→ Song: 'I'm climbing up the mountain with my sheep!' Words: © Sharon Moughtin-Mumby
→ Tune: 'If you're happy and you know it' (traditional). For a taster see the Diddy Disciples website.

*If your group is using the What's in the Box? option (Book 1, p. 221):*

*Invite a child to open the box.*

*Inside is a picture of fire.*

What's in the box?

*Accept the child's response.*

Today, we're going to tell the story of how Moses met God – in fire!

For our story today, we're STILL in Egypt.

Let's be the slaves working hard.

*Lead the slaves in building.*

We're building a temple!

**We're building a temple!**

We're working all day!

**We're working all day!**

We're building a pyramid!

**We're building a pyramid!**

We're working all night!

**We're working all night!**

The slaves were tired from building!

They groaned. Let's all groan together after 3.

**1, 2, 3,** *groan!*

*Repeat if necessary.*

Someone heard them. *Hand behind ear*

GOD heard them!

God decided to send someone to stop Pharaoh the Bully.

God decided to send MOSES.

But where's Moses?

*Look around the room in confusion.*

Moses is hiding!

Let's hide behind our hands like Moses.

*Lead children in hiding behind hands and peering through fingers.*

Moses had done something wrong!

He was hiding from everyone,

like we hide sometimes.

Moses was hiding on a mountain in the 'wilderness'.

We're going to be Moses.
Let's get up . . .
*Lead the children in standing.*
*Once the group is ready:*
. . . and climb the mountain.

*Lead the children in climbing.*
Climb, and climb, and climb, and climb.
Sssssshhh! Quiet! Let's tiptoe and sing quietly.
We don't want anyone to find us!

*The words and tune for this song are so repetitive, they won't need teaching. Simply start singing and encourage the group to join in.*
*Climb on tiptoes as you sing:*
**I'm climbing up the mountain with my sheep!** [Sssssh!]
*Pause and look around to check no one's following.*
**I'm climbing up the mountain with my sheep!** [Sssssh!]
*Pause and look around to check no one's following.*
**I'm climbing up the mountain, climbing up the mountain,**
*Pause and look around to check no one's following.*
**I'm climbing up the mountain . . .**
*Interrupt yourself.*
Wait! Sssssh! Look! What's that?

*Point to the middle of the circle.*
It's a bush (a little tree) that's on fire!
Let's all kneel down and take a look . . .
*Lead the children in kneeling around the imaginary bush.*

Look! That's strange! *Look confused*
The bush is burning but its leaves are still green!
Shall we be the burning bush together?
*Still kneeling, lead the children in placing palms together and swaying your joined hands side to side like little flames.*

Ssssh! Listen! What's that!
There's a voice coming from the bush!
First, the Voice said, 'Moses!' *Cup hands around mouth to speak God's words*
After 3, let's say, 'Moses!' together.
**1, 2, 3, Moses!** *Cup hands around mouth to speak God's words*

How do you think Moses was feeling?
Can you show me?
*Accept the children's expressions.*

The Voice spoke again:
'I'm God!' *Cup hands around mouth to speak God's words*
Now how do you think Moses was feeling?
Moses hid!
*Lead children in hiding behind hands.*
Let's be Moses and hide again! We're scared!

Now we're going to be God!
Let's kneel up tall.
Can you say God's words after me,
'my turn' *point to self*, 'your turn' *leader's hands out to group*?

I've heard my people's groans. *Hand behind ear*
**I've heard my people's groans.** *Hand behind ear*
Go to Pharaoh! *Point dramatically*
**Go to Pharaoh!** *Point dramatically*

294

Set my people free! *Arms dramatically out in a 'V' shape*
**Set my people free!** *Arms dramatically out in a 'V' shape*

God had seen what Pharaoh the Bully was doing!
What did God want Moses to do?
*Accept the children's responses.*

Let's be the flames of the Burning Bush again.
Let's sing '[Now] Moses, you will set my people free!'

*Lead the children in singing and swaying their arms.*
**[Now] Moses, you will set my people free!**
**[Now] Moses, you will set my people free!**
**[Now] Moses, you will set, [now] Moses, you will set,**
**[Now] Moses, you will set my people free!**
Freeze!

Moses was terrified!
He hid his face again!
Let's hide behind our fingers like Moses.
*Lead the children in hiding and peering through fingers.*
Let's sing in a very small and scared voice:
'Who are you and what is your name?'

**[But] who are you and what is your name?**
**[But] who are you and what is your name?**
**[But] who are you and what . . .**
**[But] who are you and what . . .**
**[But] who are you and what is your name?**

God said, 'I am . . . *Leave the sentence hanging*
*Defiantly:* who I AM!'

That's a funny answer isn't it?
'I am who I am????' *Hands out in question*

Then God spoke again . . .
Let's kneel up tall and be the bush burning even brighter.
Let's show the flames growing and getting bigger!
*Lead the children in singing and swaying their whole bodies.*
**[Now] Moses, you will set my people free!**
**[Now] Moses, you will set my people free!**
**[Now] Moses, you will set, [now] Moses, you will set,**
**[Now] Moses, you will set my people free!**

How do you think Moses is feeling now?
Can you show me?
*Accept the children's expressions.*

Moses said, 'Please don't send me!' *Clasp hands*
'I'm too scared to speak!' *Shake head*
Let's be Moses and shake our head
and sing in our scared voice.
'Please don't send me! I'm too scared to speak!'
*Clasp hands and shake head as you lead the children in singing.*
**[Oh] please don't send me! I'm too scared to speak!**
**[Oh] please don't send me! I'm too scared to speak!**
**[Oh] please don't send me! I'm . . .**
**[Oh] please don't send me! I'm . . .**
**[Oh] please don't send me! I'm too scared to speak!**

But God said again.

Let's sing a little bit louder . . .

Let's stand up and use our whole bodies as flames.

*Lead the children in dancing and singing again.*

**[Now] Moses, you will set my people free!**

**[Now] Moses, you will set my people free!**

**[Now] Moses, you will set, [now] Moses, you will set,**

**[Now] Moses, you will set my people free!**

And whatever Moses said . . .

God said the same thing!

Let's sing God's song one last time.

This time, let's sing really loudly

and dance tall like fire, like we really mean it.

*Lead the children in singing loudly and swaying.*

**[Now] Moses, you will set my people free!**

**[Now] Moses, you will set my people free!**

**[Now] Moses, you will set, [now] Moses, you will set,**

**[Now] Moses, you will set my people free!**

Freeze!

So Moses went to find Pharaoh the Bully!

*If appropriate:* We'll find out what happens when Moses meets Pharaoh next week.

# Week 4: Let My People Go!

→ **Exodus 7.14—12.32**

→ **Song: 'Let my people go!' Words: © Sharon Moughtin-Mumby**

→ **Tune: 'The wheels on the bus' (traditional). For a taster see the Diddy Disciples website.**

*If your group is using the What's in the Box? option (Book 1, p. 221):*

*Invite a child to open the box.*

*Inside is a picture of a hand (either a photo or a cut-out of your own hand).*

What's in the box?

*Accept the child's response.*

Today we're going to tell the story

about when the whole world and everything in it

shouted, 'Stop!' *hand out* to Pharaoh!

For our stories about Moses, we're in Egypt.

Let's be the slaves working hard.

*Lead the slaves in building as you sing:*

We're building a temple!

**We're building a temple!**

We're working all day!

**We're working all day!**

We're building a pyramid!

**We're building a pyramid!**
We're working all night!
**We're working all night!**

The slaves were so tired, they groaned.
After 3, let's groan.
**1, 2, 3,** *groan!*

Ssssh! Listen!
God can hear their groaning!
God's going to stop Pharaoh the Bully!
God has sent Moses!

Let's be Moses and stand in front of Pharaoh.
We're really nervous and shaking and trembling.
Can you show me scared and nervous?
*Lead the children in looking utterly terrified.*
Let's try and stand up straight and tall
even though we're scared.
*Lead the children in trying to stand up but still looking terrified.*

Moses said to Pharaoh, 'God says . . .'
Let's say this 'my turn' *point to self*, 'your turn' *leader's hands out to group*.

"Let my people go!" *Point outwards*
**"Let my people go!"'** *Point outwards*

But Pharaoh the Bully looked at Moses and said:
'my turn' *point to self*, 'your turn' *leader's hands out to group*.
*Raise chin defiantly:* 'No!' *Stamp foot*
**'No!'** *Stamp foot*
'I will NOT let them go!' *Shake head and fold arms*
**'I will NOT let them go!'** *Shake head and fold arms*

So God got everything in the WORLD:
animals, insects, weather, even the water,
to join in shouting, 'STOP!' as loud as they could.
Let's tell the story together.

First, the water shouted, 'Stop!' to Pharaoh.
All the water in Egypt started to smell really bad:
to stink! *Hold nose*
Let's smell the water in the river together. *Sniff*
Eurgh! That stinks! *Hold nose again*
That's how the water shouted, 'Stop!'

*Hold nose with one hand and with 'Stop!' hold the other hand out in a 'stop' sign.*
**The water in Egypt shouts:**
**'Stop! Stop! Stop!**
**Stop! Stop! Stop!**
**Stop! Stop! Stop!'**
**The water in Egypt shouts,**
**'Stop! Stop! Stop!**
**Let my people go!'** *Point strongly*

Pharaoh smelled the water in the Nile.
*Lead the children in taking a little sniff.*
Euurgh! . . . *hold nose*
and said, 'All right! I'll let them go . . .'

The slaves were just about to go . . .

when Pharaoh said,
*raise chin defiantly:* 'Actually . . .'
Can you say after me
'No!' *Stamp foot*
**'No!'** *Stamp foot*
'I will not let them go!' *Shake head and fold arms*
**'I will not let them go!'** *Shake head and fold arms*

Next, the whole land was filled with jumping frogs!
*Use one hand to show a frog hopping up and down the opposite arm.*
How did the frogs shout STOP?
The frogs shouted STOP with a . . . ?
*Encourage the children to provide a sound and action for the frogs and use these to sing the song. Example only: Ribbit.*

**The frogs in Egypt shout,**
*'Ribbit, Ribbit, Ribbit!*
*Ribbit, Ribbit, Ribbit!*
*Ribbit, Ribbit, Ribbit!'*
**The frogs in Egypt shout,**
*'Ribbit, Ribbit, Ribbit!*
**Let my people go!'**

Pharaoh saw frogs EVERYWHERE and said,
'All right! I'll let them go.'
The slaves were just about to go . . .

Then Pharaoh said,
*raise chin defiantly:* 'Actually . . .'
*aside:* What do you think Pharaoh's going to say?
All together! *Lead the children in saying*
**'No!** *Stamp foot*
**I will not let them go!'** *Shake head and fold arms*

Then the land was filled with buzzing flies! *Flap hands by side*
How did the flies shout STOP?
The flies shouted STOP with a . . . ?
*Encourage the children to provide a sound and action for the flies and use these to sing the song. Example only: Bzzz!*

**The flies in Egypt shout,**
*'Bzzz, Bzzz, Bzzz!*
*Bzzz, Bzzz, Bzzz!*
*Bzzz, Bzzz, Bzzz!'*
**The flies in Egypt shout,**
*'Bzzz, Bzzz, Bzzz!*
**Let my people go!'**

Pharaoh saw the buzzing flies and said,
'All right! I'll let them go.'
The slaves were just about to go . . .

Then Pharaoh said,
*raise chin defiantly:* 'Actually . . .'
*lead the children in saying:*
**'No!** *Stamp foot*
**I will not let them go!'** *Shake head and fold arms*

Then the weather joined in!
The land was filled with giant hailstones and thunder.
*Cover head to protect yourself from the weather.*
How did the thunder shout STOP?

The thunder shouted STOP with a . . . ?
*Encourage the children to provide a sound and action for the thunder and use these to sing the song. Example only: Crash!*

**The thunder in Egypt shouts,**
*'Crash, crash, crash!*
*Crash, crash, crash!*
*Crash, crash, crash!'*
**The thunder in Egypt shouts**
*'Crash, crash, crash!*
**Let my people go!'**

Pharaoh saw the hail and heard the thunder and said,
'All right! I'll let them go.'
The slaves were just about to go . . .

Then Pharaoh said,
*raise chin defiantly:* 'Actually . . .'
*lead the children in saying:*
**'No!** *Stamp foot*
**I will not let them go!'** *Shake head and fold arms*

Then the land was filled with locusts –
insects like grasshoppers who ate EVERYTHING that they could see.
The locusts shouted STOP with a MUNCH!
*Open and close both hands like a munching mouth.*

*Lead the children in singing:*
**The locusts in Egypt shout,**
*'Munch, munch, munch!*
*Munch, munch, munch!*
*Munch, munch, munch!'*
**The locusts in Egypt shout,**
*'Munch, munch, munch!*
**Let my people go!'**

Pharaoh saw the locusts and said,
'All right! I'll let them go.'
The slaves were just about to go . . .

When Pharaoh said . . .
*raise chin defiantly:* 'Actually . . .
*lead the children in saying:*
**No!** *Stamp foot*
**I will not let them go!'** *Shake head and fold arms*

And this time, Pharaoh said to Moses,
'Don't ask me again! I will not let them go!'

Let's stand up.
After 3, let's stamp our feet and say:
'No! *Stamp*
I will not let them go!' *Shake head and fold arms*
And this time let's really mean it!

**1, 2, 3 . . .**
**No!** *Stamp*
**I will NOT let them go!** *Shake head and fold arms*

Moses had had enough!
Moses told the slaves to paint a special sign on their door.
Let's paint a sign on our door.
*Lead the children in turning around and painting up high (we don't know what this sign was).*
Then Moses told the slaves to pack.
Let's pack our bags . . .
*Lead the group in miming throwing clothes in a bag.*
And be ready to run!

Let's sit down to hear what happened.
*When the group is ready:*
The last 'Stop!' was a sad and awful 'Stop'.
It's so sad, we won't sing this one. *Shake head*
We'll sit with our arms crossed on our chest and listen quietly.
*Lead the children crossing their arms on their chests.*

Pharaoh the Bully had made people
throw the slaves' baby boys in the river.
It was time for Pharaoh the Bully to understand
what it felt like to have someone hurt your baby boy.

*Quietly and seriously:*
That night,
the oldest boy from every family in Egypt died.
Let's show tears on our faces for those boys.
*Lead the children in running fingers down their faces.*
*Hold a moment of silence.*

*Seriously:*
'You MUST stop bullying!' said God.
'You WILL let my people go!'

At last, Pharaoh the Bully understood.
Let's sing 'At last Pharaoh said:
Go! Go! Go!' *Point hand outwards in anger*

*Sing and point hand outwards in anger with 'Go!'*
**At last Pharaoh said,**
**'Go! Go! Go!**
**Go! Go! Go!**
**Go! Go! Go!'**
**At last Pharaoh said,**
**'Go! Go! Go!'**
*Loudly:* **'GO! GO! GO!'**

And the slaves got up.
After 3, we're going to get up
and run on the spot as fast as we can.

**1, 2, 3 . . . RUN!**
Faster! Faster!
Even faster!
Freeze!

We'll hear what happens to the slaves next time.

# Week 5: The Path through the Red Sea

→ Exodus 12.31–33, 13.17–22, 14.1—15.21
→ Song: 'Come, God's people, walk through the Red Sea!' Words: © Sharon Moughtin-Mumby
→ Tune: 'The old grey mare' (traditional, also known as the tune for 'I'm in the Lord's army'). For a taster see the Diddy Disciples website.

*For this week's storytelling, you may like to use a length of blue fabric for the Red Sea. At St Peter's, Walworth, we use our peace cloth (Book 1, p. 231). We begin the session with this blue fabric draped at the front of our worship space.*

## Tip

Large groups will need to think through carefully how to manage their space for the 'journey' through the Red Sea. At St Peter's, we use the line of chairs we've set out for the adults on one side of the room as an 'island' to walk around in a circle for our journey. If necessary, your group can adapt the material so that the children walk on the spot throughout, but where possible it's worthwhile giving the children the opportunity to go on a physical journey through the 'sea'.

*If your group is using the What's in the Box? option (Book 1, p. 221):*
*Invite a child to open the box.*
*Inside is blue fabric (e.g. the peace cloth) or a picture of the sea.*

What's in the box?
*Accept the child's response.*

Today we're going to tell the great story
of how God made a path through the sea!
God's going to set the slaves free!

[Today] we need to start by learning a new song.

*For groups that have sung, 'Remember when we were slaves in Egypt':*
It has the same tune as our
'Remember when we were slaves in Egypt' song
but different words.

*All groups:*
Let's sing it 'my turn' *point to self*, 'your turn' *leader's hands out to group*.

*Singing:*
Come, God's people,
walk through the Red Sea,
walk through the Red Sea,
walk through the Red Sea!
**Come, God's people,**
**walk through the Red Sea,**
**walk through the Red Sea,**
**walk through the Red Sea!**

'My turn' *point to self* again!
Come, God's people,
walk through the Red Sea,
God has set us free! *Wave hands above head*
**Come, God's people,**
**walk through the Red Sea,**
**God has set us free!** *Wave hands above head*

*For groups that are already familiar with the tune through singing 'Remember when we were slaves in Egypt', you could simply say:*
Then we sing 'God has set us free!' a lot!
And go back to the beginning.
*Continue by leading the children in singing the whole song as below.*

*For groups that are not familiar with the tune, it may be helpful to recap at this point:*
Let's sing that together and add some actions:
**Come, God's people,** *'come' action (p. 195)*
**walk through the Red Sea,** *move arms as if walking*
**walk through the Red Sea,** *move arms as if walking*
**walk through the Red Sea!** *Move arms as if walking*
**Come, God's people,** *'come' action*
**walk through the Red Sea,** *move arms as if walking*
**God has set us free!** *Wave hands above head*

Then we celebrate!
'My turn' *point to self*, 'your turn' *leader's hands out to group* again:

God has set us free, *wave hands above head*
God has set us free! *Wave hands above head*
**God has set us free,** *wave hands above head*
**God has set us free!** *Wave hands above head*

Then we sing the words from the beginning again.

*All groups:*
Let's see if we can sing that all together!

*Lead the children in singing:*
**Come, God's people,** *'come' action*
**walk through the Red Sea,** *move arms as if walking*
**walk through the Red Sea,** *move arms as if walking*
**walk through the Red Sea!** *Move arms as if walking*
**Come, God's people,** *'come' action*
**walk through the Red Sea,** *move arms as if walking*

**God has set us free!** *Wave hands above head*
**God has set us free,** *wave hands above head*
**God has set us free!** *Wave hands above head*

**Come, God's people,** *'come' action*
**walk through the Red Sea,** *move arms as if walking*
**God has set us free!** *Wave hands above head*

*When the children seem familiar with the song (there will be more time to become confident with it later):*
So we've learned our song.
Now we need to practise something.

> The aim is for two children (assisted by adults if necessary) to form an arch for the rest of the
> group to walk under, like in the singing of the nursery rhyme 'Oranges and lemons'. It may help
> to choose taller children so that the group is able to walk through the arch they make.

*Invite two children to come forward.*
*Name* and *Name*,
Can you come and stand here and here.
*Indicate where you'd like them to stand.*

When I say, can you
>        *Either:* lift this blue cloth up as high as you can.
>        *Or:* hold hands and lift them high
to make a tunnel for us to walk through.

Shall we practise that now . . .
Let's sing our song quietly while we practise.
*Lead the children in singing 'Come God's people . . .' quietly as you show the Red Sea children what you'd like them to do with*
*their arms or the blue fabric so they'll be confident later in the story. When those involved have understood, encourage them to sit*
*somewhere appropriate so they're ready for their roles later in the storytelling.*

We're ready to tell our story.
Let's sit down.

*When the group is ready:*
Our story together starts with waiting,
crouched down ready to run.
Can you show me ready to run?
*Lead the children in crouching on the floor.*

We're the slaves in Egypt.
Pharaoh the King has been bullying us
and making us work too hard.
Now Pharaoh's said we can go!
So we're about to run!

After 3, let's get up and run on the spot as fast as we can.
**1, 2, 3 . . .** get up . . . and run!
*Lead the children in running on the spot.*
Faster! Faster!
Even faster!
Freeze!

We've got away from Pharaoh the Bully.
We're free!
No more working!
No more: 'Lazy! Lazy! Lazy! I want MORE!'
How do you feel?
Can you show me?
*Accept the children's expressions.*
But where are we going to go?

Look! *Point*
God sent a pillar of fire
and a huge cloud
to show the slaves where to go!
The slaves followed the pillar of fire!

After 3, let's run on the spot again.
Follow that fire! *Point*
**1, 2, 3** . . . Run!
*Lead the children in running on the spot.*
Faster! Faster!
Even faster!
Freeze!

Ssssshhhh!
What's that? *Hand behind ear*
Look!
*If you're using blue fabric for the sea, point to it. If not, point behind you.*
Oh no! It's the sea! The Red Sea!
*Aside:* That's the name of this sea.
It isn't red! *Shake head* But it's called the Red Sea.

The slaves looked this way . . . *Point*
*Lead children in looking with hand shielding eyes.*
Sea!
The slaves looked that way . . . *Point the other way*
*Lead children in looking with hand shielding eyes.*
Sea!
The slaves looked in front . . . *Point ahead of the group (behind you)*
*Lead children in looking with hand shielding eyes.*
Sea!
The slaves looked behind . . . *Point behind the rest of the group*
*Lead children in looking with hand shielding eyes.*
Aaarrrgh!
It's Pharaoh and all his soldiers and horses!
He's come to get us!
How are you feeling now?
Can you show me?
*Accept the children's expressions.*
Freeze!

Let's all stand back . . .
*Invite the children who will form the Red Sea to come forward.*
*Aside: Name* and *Name,*
can you come and stand in your places and
hold hands/hold the cloth?
But don't lift your hands up yet! When I say!
*When the children are ready continue . . .*

So the slaves saw the Red Sea!
They couldn't get across. *Shake head*
It was too wide and too deep.

And look! *Point behind the group*
Pharaoh's soldiers are going to get us!

The slaves were terrified!
Can you show me terrified!
Very, very, very scared!
*Follow the children's actions.*

Then God spoke!

God told Moses to stand before the sea.

Let's be Moses and stand up tall before the sea . . .

*Lead the children in standing tall and calm.*

God said to Moses, 'Hold up your hand over the sea!'

Let's all hold our hand up.

*Lead the children in holding your palm flat towards the sea.*

The sea began to part!

So there was a path through the middle of the sea!

*Aside to the Red Sea children:*

This is your moment!

Can you make a path through the sea?

*Assist the Red Sea children in making an arch that the group can walk under.*

*When they're ready:*

The sea parted!

God had made a path through the middle of the sea!

The slaves could escape!

It's time for our song!

It's time to walk through the Red Sea.

···········································································

## Tip

Point very clearly where you're going to walk, for the benefit of both children and adults. With a large group it may help to walk quickly around as leader to show the group. Example:

> We're going to go through the sea *point*
> then around the chairs, *point the path you'll follow*
> then back into our places.
> Let's go!

···········································································

*Lead the children through the arch, around in a circle and back to their place as you sing together:*

**Come, God's people,**

**walk through the Red Sea,**

**walk through the Red Sea,**

**walk through the Red Sea!**

**Come, God's people,**

**walk through the Red Sea,**

**God has set us free!** *Wave hands above head*

**God has set us free,** *wave hands above head*

**God has set us free!** *Wave hands above head*

**Come, God's people,**

**walk through the Red Sea,**

**God has set us free!** *Wave hands above head*

*Repeat.*

*When all the children have had the opportunity to walk through the sea and the group is back in the worship space, ask the children to close the sea up again.*

The path through the sea has gone!

Pharaoh's solders can't get us!

How do you feel now you're safe and free!

Can you show me?

*Follow the children in celebrating.*

*Optional:*
That moment when God's people
walk through the Red Sea
is one of the most important moments in the Bible!
Let's do it again!
*Make sure the sea is 'closed'.*

The slaves saw the Red Sea!
*Point to the barrier formed by the children's lowered arms.*
They couldn't get across. *Shake head*
It was too wide and too deep.
And look! *Point behind the group*
Pharaoh's soldiers are going to get us!

Then God told Moses to stand before the sea.
Let's be Moses and stand up tall before the sea . . .
What did God ask Moses to do?
*Invite responses.*

God said, 'Hold up your hand over the sea!'
Let's all hold our hand up. *Palm flat towards the sea*
And the sea began to part!
*Nod to the Red Sea children.*

When they've formed the tunnel . . .
There's the path through the sea!
Let's go!

*Lead the children through the arch, around in a circle and back to their place as you sing together:*
**Come, God's people,**
**walk through the Red Sea,**
**walk through the Red Sea,**
**walk through the Red Sea!**
**Come, God's people,**
**walk through the Red Sea,**
**God has set us free!** *Wave hands above head*

**God has set us free,** *wave hands above head*
**God has set us free!** *Wave hands above head*
**Come, God's people,**
**walk through the Red Sea,**
**God has set us free!** *Wave hands above head*
*Repeat.*

*When all the children have had the opportunity to walk through the sea and the group is back in the worship space, ask the children to close the sea up again.*

The path through the sea has gone!
Pharaoh's soldiers can't get us!
How do you feel now you're safe and free?
Can you show me?
*Follow the children's responses.*

*If your group has used the Gathering Song 'Remember when we were slaves in Egypt' (p. 268), you may like to use the following material:*

Then the slaves danced and sang a song of victory!

Every year, God's people still celebrate crossing the Red Sea.

*If appropriate:*
Jesus celebrated it at the 'Passover' with his friends.

Let's be God's people and celebrate.
Let's sing our 'Remember when we were slaves in Egypt' song
and celebrate.

**Remember when we were slaves in Egypt,** *digging*
**slaves in Egypt, slaves in Egypt,** *digging*
**remember when we were slaves in Egypt,** *digging*
**then God set us free!** *Wave hands above head*
**Then God set us free!** *Wave hands above head*
**Then God set us free!** *Wave hands above head*
**Remember when we were slaves in Egypt,** *digging*
**then God set us free!** *Wave hands above head*

*All groups:*

*Ask the children to sit down quietly in a circle.*
Can you show me how you felt again
when you walked through the sea?
*Accept the children's responses and expressions.*

The slaves became God's people!
They had a new start!

We're part of God's people too!
When we get baptized in water,
we remember the slaves walking through the sea!
And we get a new start as well!

> *If appropriate:* Next week, we'll do some baptizing ourselves
> and remember our story of the slaves in Egypt.

# Extra: Our Baptism

→ Song: 'Come, God's people, walk through the Red Sea!' Words: © Sharon Moughtin-Mumby
→ Tune: 'The old grey mare' (traditional, also known as the tune for 'I'm in the Lord's army'). See p. 301 for music.
→ Song: 'Remember when we were slaves in Egypt'. Words: © Sharon Moughtin-Mumby
→ Tune: 'The old grey mare' (traditional, also known as the tune for 'I'm in the Lord's army'). See p. 268 for music.
→ Song: 'We're building a temple'. Words: © Sharon Moughtin-Mumby
→ Tune: 'Everywhere we go' (traditional camp song). See p. 288 for music.

## Introductory notes

Baptism roleplaying workshops that involve simulating baptism with a doll are becoming increasingly common
in primary schools and churches. Witnessing or taking part in roleplay has been shown to both accelerate and
deepen learning experiences among children (and adults!). The following material is offered as an optional week
for churches, groups or schools who would like to offer a baptism roleplaying workshop to give the children
opportunities to make connections between the Bible stories about baptism that you've been telling together and the
Christian baptisms they see in their place.

Baptism looks different in every church and setting. The following material is based on infant baptism material in
*Common Worship* (both *Christian Initiation* 2006 and *Additional Baptism Texts in Accessible Language* 2015) and BCP 2004
(Church of Ireland). However, please adapt the Diddy Disciples resources freely so your workshop reflects baptism in
your church as closely as possible. It may also be appropriate for your group to omit some sections because of time
limitations.

The words and symbols of baptism are full of meaning! This workshop concentrates solely on the meanings brought
to baptism by the stories of Moses and the crossing of the Red Sea, building on the songs and actions that the
children have learned over the weeks. For an opportunity to explore more meanings of these rich symbols, see

the similar baptism roleplaying workshop in the John the Baptist unit (p. 70). Other Diddy Disciples workshops for baptism (for instance, exploring baptism in the context of the Easter stories and the death and resurrection of Jesus) will become available on the website over time.

> **Tip**
>
> The titles used for the different sections in this workshop match the ones used in *Common Worship* and BCP 2004 so, if you like, you can compare the material easily. Some of the order of the service has been changed for practical reasons (e.g. the Signing with the Cross is before the Prayer over the Water): to bring together the parts of the workshop that will take place at the tables. If you prefer, you can adapt the material to follow *Common Worship*'s order of service.

## Practical notes

At St Peter's, Walworth, we find that we're all shattered at the end of our baptism roleplaying workshops (so be prepared and perhaps find extra helpers!) but everyone who's taken part thinks they're hugely worthwhile for the way in which they make links between the stories and baptism material for churches.

For today's session, you will need:

- a range of baby dolls or figures set out in a line in front of the group: one for each child. For 'babies' we provide a baby doll. For 'adults' we provide a 'small world' figure (see p. 95). We enjoy seeing the range of farmers, police officers, shopkeepers, soldiers, elderly people, etc., who are brought to 'baptism'. If your church does not have infant baptism, you could use adult figures only.

> **Tip**
>
> - We don't give the children access to the dolls/figures until later in the session, as we've found that they can prove really distracting to the children if given out early on. If children have brought toys with them, you could ask them to place them at the end of the line so you can make sure they're reunited for the workshop.
> - As our group is large, we don't give children the choice of exactly which doll/figure they'll 'baptize' (unless they've brought their own) – this would prove too disruptive – but smaller groups may like to do this.

For the baptism demonstration (leader) in the first part of the session:

- a baby doll (or adult figure if your church does not have infant baptism);
- a large, transparent bowl of water;
- a white robe or dress, or a piece of white cloth to act as a robe (if your church dresses baptism candidates in white after baptism);
- a pot of oil (if your church uses oil for the Signing with the Cross).

For the baptism workshop (whole group) in the second part of the session, you will need to set up tables beforehand with:

- a bowl of water for each child. At St Peter's we use a range of bowls including recyclable cartons. We fill them with water beforehand, just deep enough for the children to be able to scoop water out easily;
- a piece of white cloth to act as a robe for each child (if your church dresses baptism candidates in white after baptism);
- access to towels to dry hands and for inevitable spillages;
- two or more pots of oil on each table that the children can easily access (if your church uses oil for the Signing with the Cross and/or anointing).

┌─────────────────────────────────────────────────────────────┐

**Tip**

You may like (or need) to invite children to bring their own dolls or figures to the baptism workshop. If you do invite children to bring a favourite toy, it's important to then honour this invitation (even if the favourite toy turns out to be a teddy or a rabbit, for instance). Psychology suggests that favourite toys can represent much more than the toy itself for many children. The danger of rejecting such a toy as 'not quite right' is that children may then feel rejected themselves. If your group might find this challenging, then it may be best not to make an invitation like this.

└─────────────────────────────────────────────────────────────┘

## Introduction

*If your group has been using the 'Remember when we were slaves in Egypt' Gathering Song, begin with this song and its introductory material as usual.*

> *If your group hasn't been using the Gathering Song, you may like to recap with the following material.*

> We've been telling stories about God's best friend, Moses.
> Today, we're going to go back to Egypt again.
> We're going to be the 'slaves' doing some hard building work!

> Let's build and sing 'my turn' *point to self*, 'your turn' *leader's hands out to group*.

> *Lead the children in building as you sing.*
> We're building a temple!
> **We're building a temple!**
> We're working all day!
> **We're working all day!**
> We're building a pyramid!
> **We're building a pyramid!**
> We're working all night!
> **We're working all night!**

> The slaves were so tired!
> Can you show me tired?
> But Pharaoh the Bully shouted:
> 'LAZY! LAZY! LAZY! I WANT MORE!' *Stamp foot on 'more'*
> Let's be Pharaoh and shout:
> **'LAZY! LAZY! LAZY! I WANT MORE!'** *Stamp foot on 'more'*

*All groups:*
[So] We're the slaves in Egypt. *Point to self and around the group*
Pharaoh the King has been bullying us
and making us work too hard.
But God's about to set us free!
Are you ready?!

God's told us to paint a sign on our door!
So let's stand up.
*Lead the children in standing.*
Let's turn around and paint a sign on our door.
*Lead the children in painting an imaginary sign on the top of the door frame. (We don't know what that sign was.)*
Now we're getting ready to run . . .
Let's crouch down . . . and wait . . .
*Lead the children in crouching for a moment.*

Listen! *Hand behind ear*
Pharaoh's said we can go!
After 3, let's get up and run on the spot as fast as we can.

309

**1, 2, 3** . . . Get up . . . and run!
*Lead the children in running on the spot.*
Faster! Faster!
And freeze!

But look! *Point ahead of the group (behind you)*
Look what's there!
It's the sea!
The Red Sea!

And look! *Point behind the group (in front of you)*
It's Pharaoh and his soldiers coming to get us!
They're going to get us!
The slaves were terrified!
Can you show me very scared and terrified?
*Lead the group in looking terrified.*

God told Moses to hold his hand over the sea.
After 3, let's stand tall and be Moses.
Let's hold our hand over the sea.
*Lead the children in standing tall.*
1, 2, 3!
*Lead the children in holding their hand over the sea.*

The sea began to part!
It made a path through the sea!
Now the slaves could walk through the sea.

> *Either:* let's walk on the spot through the sea.
> We're free!

> *Or, if the children are familiar with the song:*
> Let's sing our song as we walk on the spot through the sea.
> *Lead the children in walking on the spot throughout.*

> **Come, God's people,** *'come' action (p. 195)*
> **walk through the Red Sea,**
> **walk through the Red Sea,**
> **walk through the Red Sea!**
> **Come, God's people,**
> **walk through the Red Sea!**
> **God has set us free!** *Wave hands above head in celebration*

> **God has set us free,** *wave hands above head*
> **God has set us free!** *Wave hands above head*
> **Come, God's people,**
> **walk through the Red Sea,**
> **walk through the Red Sea,**
> **walk through the Red Sea!**
> **Come, God's people,**
> **walk through the Red Sea!**
> **God has set us free!** *Wave hands above head*

*All groups:*
We're free! How does that make you feel!
Can you show me?
*Follow the children's responses.*
Let's sit down for a moment.

*When the group is ready:*

In the Church/as Christians we BAPTIZE people.
We baptize people with WATER.

> *If appropriate:*
> Put your hand up if you've been baptized.

*All groups:*
Put your hand up if you've seen a baptism in our church.

When we baptize people we remember lots of stories.
One of the stories we remember is the story of
the slaves walking through the Red Sea.
That story becomes our story.

When we're baptized
we walk through the Red Sea too!
But we don't have a sea in our church! *Shake head*
It wouldn't fit!
And we don't walk!
Today we're going to show how we baptize in our church.
We're going to 'baptize' one of these friends.
*Indicate dolls and models to be 'baptized'.*

## Presentation of the Candidates

*This section is based on the material from* Common Worship's Additional Baptism Texts in Accessible Language. *If your church uses different words, you may wish to adapt the material accordingly.*

When we baptize someone,
we start by asking an important question.
If someone wants to be baptized,
the answer is, 'I do!' *Thumbs up*
Shall we help our friend answer?
Let's practise saying, 'I do!' *Thumbs up*
*Lead the children in saying:* **I do!** *Thumbs up*

The question is:
Do you want to be baptized?
**I do!** *Thumbs up*

## The Decision

> *If your church lights the Easter Candle visibly during baptisms, you could light a real candle in a safe place or light a battery candle at this point. At St Peter's, Walworth, we use our church's Paschal Candle from the previous year.*
> Now we light a candle. In church, it's a really big candle!
> It's a bit like the pillar of fire
> that the slaves followed when they ran from Pharaoh.
> It shows us the way!

In our stories about Moses,
the slaves were given a choice:
stay in Egypt with Pharaoh the Bully
or follow God.
Can anyone tell me what the slaves chose:
Pharaoh or God?
*Accept responses.*
The slaves chose God!

When we baptize someone,
we ask them to make choices too.

We're going to ask our friends to make four choices
*Show four fingers.*

If they want to be baptized,
They need to choose to follow JESUS.
Jesus is God!

*As leader, go and lead from the opposite end of the room so that the children turn face the other way.*
To ask our questions, I'm going to sit over here.
Can you all turn around to face me?

*When the group is ready, continue:*
Let's help our friends make the choices.
Let's answer for them.

*Hold up one finger.*
Question number 1 is:
will you run away from everything that's BAD? *Move arms in running action*

> *If appropriate:* A bit like the slaves chose to run away
> from Pharaoh the Bully in our stories.

Let's say 'my turn' *point to self,* 'your turn' *leader's hands out to group.*

I'll run away from everything that's BAD. *Move arms in running action*
**I'll run away from everything that's BAD.** *Move arms in running action*

*Hold up two fingers.*
Question number 2 is:
do you choose a new start? *Diddy Disciples 'New Start' sign (see p. 355)*

'My turn' *point to self,* 'your turn' *leader's hands out to group.*
I choose a new start! *'New Start' sign*
**I choose a new start!** *'New Start' sign*

*Hold up three fingers.*
Question number 3 is:
do you TURN to Jesus? *Arms out in cross shape*

Now for this question, after 3,
we're all going to turn to face the opposite way.
We're going to TURN to Jesus.

> *If appropriate:* Look! Can you see the cross on our table/altar?

Are you ready to turn to face that way/the cross?
*Point the way you want the children to turn.*

**1, 2, 3 . . . Turn**
*When everyone in the group has turned, return to your usual place as leader.*

We've TURNED to Jesus.
We've chosen Jesus!

Let's say 'my turn' *point to self,* 'your turn' *leader's hands out to group.*

I TURN to Jesus! *Arms out in cross shape*
**I TURN to Jesus!** *Arms out in cross shape*

And the last question . . .
*Hold up four fingers.*
Question number 4 is:
do you TRUST Jesus? *Arms out in cross shape*

> *If appropriate:*

Moses and the people had to trust God when Pharaoh was chasing them!
It must have been scary!

'My turn' *point to self*, 'your turn' *leader's hands out to group*.

I TRUST Jesus! *Arms out in cross shape*
**I TRUST Jesus!** *Arms out in cross shape*

So we've helped our friends make their choice!
Now we're ready for the WATER,
like the slaves ran to the RED SEA.

## Tip

At St Peter's, Walworth, we move to the font when we're holding the sessions with the school but on Sundays this isn't possible. With the school group, we show the children the font, then put the lid back on and place a transparent bowl filled with water on top of the font. This is partly because the font has baptism water in it and partly so the children can then see the water inside the bowl and the 'baptism' itself more easily.

If you're moving to the font, you could take this opportunity to ask a helper to move the dolls/figures to the baptism tables ready for their 'baptism'. We place dolls on the floor around the tables: one for each bowl. Or figures on top of the tables: one next to each bowl. If some children have brought their own toys, keep these to one side and make sure the children are reunited with them for the workshop.

> *If you're going to show the children the font:*
> But we're not going to run!
> We're going to tiptoe and sing
> 'Come God's people, walk through the Red Sea'
> while we go there.
>
> *Lead the children in singing as you move to the font.*
> *Invite the children to sit around the font.*
> This is a 'font'. It's like a big bowl filled with water.

*All groups:*
*Show the children water in a transparent bowl so everyone can see it.*
This is just ordinary water.
But we say a prayer over the water to make it special.

> *If appropriate:* Let's hold our hands up
> over the water to show our prayer.
> *Lead the children in holding hands up over the water.*

The prayer remembers
how important water is in our Bible stories.
One of the stories is the story of the Red Sea!

Let's remember our story
of walking through the Red Sea with our song.

**Come, God's people,** *'come' action*
**walk through the Red Sea,**
**walk through the Red Sea,**
**walk through the Red Sea!**
**Come, God's people,**
**walk through the Red Sea,**
**God has set us free!** *Wave hands above head in celebration*
*Cut the singing short to save time:*
Let's stop there for the moment!

When we get baptized, the song about the Red Sea
becomes our song!

This water *point to water*
becomes the water of the Red Sea!
But we don't walk through it! *Shake head*
Let's show how we baptize in our church.

## Signing with the Cross

*If your church does not make the sign of the cross here, skip this section and continue at Baptism, below.*

*Pick up the doll that you will demonstrate baptism with.*
First, when we baptize someone,
we draw a special sign on the baby's forehead.

Do you remember when we were slaves
and we were waiting to run fast from Pharaoh the Bully?
We had to paint a special sign on our door.
Let's remember painting a sign on our door now.
*Lead the children in turning around and painting a sign on their door.*

When we baptize someone,
we draw a special sign on that person's forehead.
It's like the sign on the door from our story.
But when we're baptized, it's the sign of the CROSS:
the sign of Jesus. *Hold arms out in cross shape*

> *If your church uses oil for the Signing with the Cross:*
> I'm going to dip my finger/thumb in this oil.
> *Dip finger in oil and show the oily finger/thumb.*

> *If it's the oil of catechumens:*
> This oil is the oil of getting ready and learning.
> It shows that we're getting ready to be baptized.

*All groups:*
I'm going to draw a cross on this baby's forehead.
Can you say the words after me:
'my turn' *point to self*, 'your turn' *leader's hands out to group*?

You belong to Jesus. *Look baby in the eyes*
**You belong to Jesus.**
I sign you with the cross. *Sign cross on forehead*
**I sign you with the cross.**

## Baptism

*Continue from here if your church doesn't make the sign of the cross before the baptism.*

[Now] I'm going to 'baptize' this baby.
Let's see if you can count on your fingers
how many times I pour water.

*Hold the doll like a baby in one arm and look into its eyes.*
Alex, *or another unisex name*
I baptize you in the name of . . . *pause*
the Father, *pour*
and of the Son, *pour*
and of the Holy Spirit. *Pour* Amen.

Can you show me on your fingers
how many times I poured water?
*Accept the children's responses.*

Three times! *Show three fingers*
The three are:
Father, *bend first finger up and down*
Son *bend second finger up and down*
and Holy Spirit. *Bend third finger up and down*

When we're baptized, we show that's what we believe.
Can you show me one finger?
*Lead the children in holding up index finger.*

*When the group is ready:*
Watch this!
*Demonstrate to the children:*
I believe in the Father. Nod, nod, nod. *Nod first finger three times*
Let's try that together.
**I believe in the Father. Nod, nod, nod.** *Nod first finger three times*

Now two fingers.
*Lead the children in holding up two fingers.*
I believe in the Son. **Nod, nod, nod.** *Nod second finger*

Three fingers.
*Lead the children in holding up three fingers.*
I believe in the Holy Spirit. **Nod, nod, nod.** *Nod third finger*

So we pour water THREE times.
Father, Son and Holy Spirit!

> *If your church places a white robe on the newly baptized, you could do this at this point.*
> Then we put a white robe on our friends
> to show they've been 'baptized'.

> *If your church makes the sign of the cross at this point:*
> Now I'm going to draw the sign of the cross
> on the baby's forehead.
> *Demonstrate to the group.*

> *If your church anoints with oil of Chrism:*
> Now we're going to 'anoint' the baby's head with oil.
> This oil is the same oil
> used to sign the Queen with the cross
> when she was made Queen!
> We could say it's 'Royal Oil'.
> Can you say 'Royal Oil'?
> **Royal Oil!**

> The oil reminds us that our baby or adult
> is going to be part of a ROYAL family: God's family!

> I'm going to dip my finger/thumb in this oil.
> *Dip finger in oil and show the oily finger/thumb.*

> *Either:* Now I'm going to rub oil on the baby's head.
> *Or:* Now I'm going to draw a cross on the baby's head with oil.
> *Demonstrate to the group.*

## Baptism Workshop

So you've watched how we baptize in our church.
I think you're ready for our baptism roleplay!
At the tables, there's a bowl of water

> *If you've moved the toys to the tables:*
> and a friend who's ready to be 'baptized'.
> *If the toys are still lined up at the front of the group.*
> On the way, we'll give you a friend to 'baptize'.
> *Get ready to distribute the toys to the children. If any of the children have brought toys, make sure each child is reunited with the right toy!*

Let's go to our table(s) and find a place.
But wait!
Don't touch the water until we're all ready!
Let's sing as we go . . .
Let's tiptoe!
*Lead the children in singing 'Come, God's people, walk through the Red Sea!' as they find a place next to a bowl of water.*

## Roleplay: Signing with the Cross

*As in the demonstration above, if your church does not make the sign of the cross here, skip this section and continue from Roleplay: Baptism, below.*

*When the group is ready:*
Can anyone remember what we did just before we poured water on our friend?
*Encourage the children to join in after the dots:*
We signed our friend with the . . . **cross**!

We're going to make the sign of the cross on our friend's forehead.

> *If you're using oil:*
> Let's dip our finger/thumb in the oil
> and hold it up in the air to show we're ready.
> *Show the children your oily finger/thumb and wait as all the children dip their finger/thumb in oil and hold it up.*

*When the group is ready:*
Let's say the words 'my turn' *point to self*, 'your turn' *leader's hands out to group*.
You belong to Jesus.
**You belong to Jesus.**
I sign you with the cross. *Draw a cross on the doll's forehead*
**I sign you with the cross.** *Draw a cross on the doll's forehead*

## Roleplay: Baptism

Now let me tell you something important!
You can't be baptized without a name!
So let's call our babies and adults 'Alex'. *Or another unisex name*

Now say these words after me
and copy my actions,
'my turn' *point to self*, 'your turn' *leader's hands out to group*.

Alex! *Look into the doll/figure's eyes*
**Alex!**
I baptize you
**I baptize you**
in the name of . . .
**in the name of . . .**

*Aside to the children quietly:* Now let's put our hand in the water ready . . .

*Scoop one:* the Father,

*Scoop one:* **the Father,**

*Scoop two:* and of the Son,

*Scoop two:* **and of the Son,**

*Scoop three:* and of the Holy Spirit.

*Scoop three:* **and of the Holy Spirit.**

Amen!

**Amen!**

> *If your church places a white robe on the newly baptized,*
> Then we put a white robe on our friends
> to show they've been 'baptized'.
> *Lead the children in placing a white robe on their friend.*
>
> *If your church makes the sign of the cross at this point:*
> Now we're going to make the sign of the cross
> on the baby's forehead.
> *Demonstrate to the group.*
>
> *If your church anoints with oil of Chrism:*
> Now we're going to 'anoint' the baby's head with oil
> to show they're part of God's people.
>
> Let's dip our finger/thumb in the oil
> and hold it up in the air to show we're ready.
> *Lead the group in rubbing oil on the toy's head or drawing the sign of the cross.*

## The Welcome

Then we welcome our friends into God's people.
Welcoming our new brothers and sisters
into the church family is really important!

> *Either:*
> Let's sing our Welcome Song to them!
> *If your group uses one of the Welcome Songs, sing your Welcome Song here. If you're using Welcome Song: Option 1, you could sing 'Welcome frie-ends to God's people!' throughout.*
>
> *Or:*
> Let's give them all a big clap!
> *Lead the children in clapping.*

## Opportunity for 'overlearning'

Now, we only ever need to get baptized once
in our whole lives.
But as this is roleplay, shall we do that again?

*Use the same pattern as you used earlier.*

> *If appropriate:*
> Can anyone remember what we did first?
> *Encourage the children to join in after the dots:*
> We signed our friends with the . . . **cross**!
>
> *If you're using oil:*
> Let's dip our finger/thumb in the oil
> and hold it up in the air to show we're ready.
>
> *When the group is ready:*
> Let's say the words 'my turn' *point to self*, 'your turn' *leader's hands out to group.*

*Lead the children in signing cross and saying words:*
You belong to Jesus.
**You belong to Jesus.**
I sign you with the cross.
**I sign you with the cross.**

Let's pretend to baptize our friends!
Alex! *Look into the doll/figure's eyes*
**Alex!**
I baptize you
**I baptize you**
in the name of . . .
**in the name of . . .**

*Aside quietly:* Now let's put our hand in the water ready . . .
*Scoop one:* the Father,
*Scoop one:* **the Father,**
*Scoop two:* and of the Son,
*Scoop two:* **and of the Son,**
*Scoop three:* and of the Holy Spirit.
*Scoop three:* **and of the Holy Spirit.**
Amen!
**Amen!**

*If appropriate:*
Then what do we do?
*Accept children's responses.*

*If your church places a white robe on the newly baptized,*
Then we put a white robe on our friends
to show they've been 'baptized'.
*Lead the children in placing a white robe on their friend.*

*If your church makes the sign of the cross at this point:*
We make the sign of the cross on the baby's forehead.
*Demonstrate to the group.*

*If your church anoints with oil of Chrism:*
We 'anoint' our friend's head with oil.

Let's dip our finger/thumb in the oil
and hold it up in the air to show we're ready.
*Lead the group in rubbing oil on the head or drawing the sign of the cross.*

And let's welcome our friends into God's people.
*Use the same welcome as you did earlier.*

. . . . . . . . . . . . . . . . . . . . . . . . . . . . . . . . . . . . . . . . . . . . . . . . . . . . . . . . . . . . . . . . . . . . .
**Tip**

At St Peter's, Walworth, by the third time, we don't use 'my turn, your turn' but have a go at saying the words together all at the same time: 'You're baptism experts now! You don't need to copy me any more! You can do this yourself!'
. . . . . . . . . . . . . . . . . . . . . . . . . . . . . . . . . . . . . . . . . . . . . . . . . . . . . . . . . . . . . . . . . . . . .

## Roleplay: Giving of a Lighted Candle

*If your group includes children who are likely to want to continue exploring the water, you may find it helpful to say something like: 'Now let's take our friend and take one step back from our tables.'*

*When the group is ready:*

> *If your church gives a candle at the end of the service, show one of the candles you use to the children.*
> The last thing we do in a baptism is give a candle
> to remind our friends to shine like little lights in the world.

> *If appropriate:*
> Look! It's a bit like the pillar of fire
> that the slaves followed out of Egypt!
> It's showing our friends the way!

> Let's hold our friends in one hand
> and make our other finger into a candle/pillar of fire now.
> *Lead the children in holding your finger up in front of you.*

> After 3, I'm going to light your friends' candles.
> Are you ready?
> **1, 2, 3 . . . Tssssss!**
> *Mime striking a match in the air and hold it out towards the children's finger candles to 'light' them.*

*End with a suitable song. For example:*

> *Either (for groups that have used 'Remember when we were slaves in Egypt' as their Gathering Song):*
> Now our friends are part of God's people!
> They're part of the slaves in Egypt that God rescued!
> Let's teach our friends our
> 'Remember when we were slaves in Egypt' song.
> Let's help them learn how to celebrate!

> **Remember when we were slaves in Egypt,** *digging*
> **slaves in Egypt, slaves in Egypt,** *digging*
> **remember when we were slaves in Egypt,** *digging*
> **then God set us free!** *Wave hands above head*
> **Then God set us free!** *Wave hands above head*
> **Then God set us free!** *Wave hands above head*
> **Remember when we were slaves in Egypt,** *digging*
> **then God set us free!** *Wave hands above head*

> *Or:*
> Let's sing to our friends and help them remember to be little lights in the world for God.

> *Lead the children in waving their candle finger in front of their friend.*
> **This little light of mine, I'm gonna let it shine!**
> **This little light of mine, I'm gonna let it shine!**
> **This little light of mine, I'm gonna let it shine!**
> **Let it shine, let it shine, let it shine!**
> *Continue with the rest of the song, if appropriate.*

> *Or: close by singing another song with which the group is familiar, either about living in God's light or about being welcomed into God's family.*

## Tip

If you're planning to have a time of Creative Response (bearing in mind that this session will already have been longer than normal) remember that the tables (and possibly the floor) will be wet from the baptisms so you may need to rethink your space.

# Week 6: When Moses Climbed up the Mountain

→ Exodus 19.16—20.21
→ Song: 'When Moses climbed up the mountain'. Words: © Sharon Moughtin-Mumby
→ Tune: 'The bear climbed over the mountain' (traditional)
→ Song: '1, 2, 3, 4, 5! Love the God who gave you life!' Words: © Sharon Moughtin-Mumby
→ Tune: '1, 2, 3, 4, 5! Once I caught a fish alive!' (traditional). For a taster see the Diddy Disciples website.

*If your group is using the What's in the Box? option (Book 1, p. 221):*

*Invite a child to open the box.*

*Inside is a picture or photograph of a mountain.*

What's in the box?

*Accept the child's response.*

In the Bible, there are lots and lots of stories about Moses.
Today we're going to tell one last story about Moses.
It's the story of when Moses climbed up the mountain.

To tell our story, we need to learn a song.
The words for our song are: 'When Moses climbed up the mountain'.
Let's sing it 'my turn' *point to self*, 'your turn' *leader's hands out to group*.

*Singing:*
When Moses climbed up the mountain,
when Moses climbed up the mountain . . .
**When Moses climbed up the mountain,**
**when Moses climbed up the mountain . . .**

'My turn' *point to self* again:
When Moses climbed up the mountain . . .
*point finger up to show the tune staying up*
. . . then all that we could hear . . .
**When Moses climbed up the mountain . . .**
*point finger up to show the tune staying up*
**then all that we could hear . . .**

Then all that we could hear . . . *point to self*
then all that we could hear . . . *point to self*
**Then all that we could hear . . .** *leader's hands out to group*
**then all that we could hear . . .** *leader's hands out to group*

Then we sing the words from the beginning again.
Let's see if we can sing that all together.

**When Moses climbed up the mountain,**
**when Moses climbed up the mountain,**
**when Moses climbed up the mountain . . .** *point finger up to show the tune staying up*
**then all that we could hear:**
**then all that we could hear,**
**then all that we could hear . . .**

**When Moses climbed up the mountain,**
**when Moses climbed up the mountain,**
**when Moses climbed up the mountain . . .** *point finger up to show the tune staying up*
**. . . then all that we could hear!**

We're ready to tell our story about Moses and the mountain.
We're going to be God's people, the slaves.
We're standing, watching at the bottom of the mountain.
Let's look up and watch Moses going up the mountain.
*Lead the children in looking upwards with hand shielding eyes.*

When Moses climbed up the mountain last time,
he met God in the Burning Bush.

This time, not just the Burning Bush is on fire:
the whole MOUNTAIN's on fire!
Let's pretend the whole mountain in front of us is on fire.
Let's show the flames of the fire!
*Lead the children in waving arms to show fire.*

The mountain's wrapped in smoke and thick cloud.
We can't see ANYTHING! *Shake head*
Let's put our hands over our eyes to show we can't see!
*Lead the children in placing their hands over their eyes.*
We can only HEAR! *Hands behind ears*

Let's sing our song about what we could hear
when Moses climbed up the mountain.

The mountain's burning with fire!

What noise does a fire make?

*Invite the children to make up a sound and an action for fire. Example only: ROAR!*

*Continue with the fire action throughout as you sing:*

**When Moses climbed up the mountain,**

**when Moses climbed up the mountain,**

**when Moses climbed up the mountain . . .**

**then all that we could hear:** *ROAR!*

**then all that we could hear:** *ROAR!*

**then all that we could hear:** *ROAR!*

**When Moses climbed up the mountain,**

**when Moses climbed up the mountain,**

**when Moses climbed up the mountain . . .**

**. . . then all that we could hear!** *ROAR!*

There wasn't just fire on the mountain!

There was an earthquake.

Quick! Let's sit down before the earthquake knocks us over.

*Lead the children in sitting.*

Look! The floor's shaking!

Let's bang on the floor with our hands to make the earth quake!

*Lead the children in banging on floor with hands.*

And FREEZE!

Do you think we can sing our song with that earthquake going on?

Let's try! After 3:

1, 2, 3:

*Lead the children in singing and banging on the floor throughout.*

**When Moses climbed up the mountain,**

**when Moses climbed up the mountain,**

**when Moses climbed up the mountain . . .**

**then all that we could hear:** *banging!*

**then all that we could hear:** *banging!*

**then all that we could hear:** *banging!*

**When Moses climbed up the mountain,**

**when Moses climbed up the mountain,**

**when Moses climbed up the mountain . . .**

**. . . then all that we could hear!** *Banging*

And FREEZE!

Ssshh!

So we can hear FIRE: *ROAR!*

An EARTHQUAKE: *banging hands*

Freeze!

This is getting a bit scary!

And look! Now there's LIGHTNING!

What noise does lightening make?

*Example only: PTCHEW!*

And what action shall we show for lightning?

*Lead the children in showing their action for lightning throughout as you walk on the spot and sing:*

**When Moses climbed up the mountain,**

**when Moses climbed up the mountain,**

**when Moses climbed up the mountain . . .**

**then all that we could hear:** *PTCHEW!*

**then all that we could hear:** *PTCHEW!*
**then all that we could hear:** *PTCHEW!*

**When Moses climbed up the mountain,**
**when Moses climbed up the mountain,**
**when Moses climbed up the mountain . . .**
**. . . then all that we could hear!** *PTCHEW!*

So we can hear FIRE: *ROAR!*
An EARTHQUAKE: *stamping*
Freeze!
LIGHTNING! *PTCHEW!*
And listen!
What's that?
*Make a trumpet sound and action.*

A trumpet?! *Trumpet action*
It's the blast of a trumpet!
Who can show me one big blast on the trumpet!

*Lead the children in miming blasting on the trumpet as you walk on the spot and sing.*
**When Moses climbed up the mountain,**
**when Moses climbed up the mountain,**
**when Moses climbed up the mountain . . .**
**then all that we could hear:** *trumpet blast*
**then all that we could hear:** *trumpet blast*
**then all that we could hear:** *trumpet blast*

**When Moses climbed up the mountain,**
**when Moses climbed up the mountain,**
**when Moses climbed up the mountain . . .**
**. . . then all that we could hear:** *trumpet blast*

Then Moses reached the top of the mountain.
Moses spoke and God answered in THUNDER.
Let's stand up and be God.
Let's answer in thunder!
What noise does thunder make?
*Lead the children in stamping for a few moments.*
And FREEZE!

In the thunder, God gave Moses ten rules.
Let's count to 10 on our fingers.
1, 2, 3, 4, 5, 6, 7, 8, 9, 10.
Ten rules to show how to love God
and how to love each other.

Then Moses came down the mountain.
He had God's ten rules written on flat stones.
We still keep those ten rules today!
They're called the Ten Commandments.

> *If appropriate, you could teach the children the following song:*
> We have a song about God's ten rules.
> Let's learn it 'my turn' *point to self*, 'your turn' *leader's hands out to group.*
>
> 1, 2, 3, 4, 5! *Count on fingers*
> Love the God who gave you life! *Cross arms then point heavenwards*
> **1, 2, 3, 4, 5!** *Count on fingers*
> **Love the God who gave you life!** *Cross arms then point heavenwards*

6, 7, 8, 9, 10! *Count on fingers*
Love each other. Yes! Amen!
*Cross arms, point to each other, then clap hands together on 'Amen'.*
**6, 7, 8, 9, 10!** *Count on fingers*
**Love each other. Yes! Amen!**
*Cross arms, point to each other, then clap hands together on 'Amen'.*

Let's sing that all together!
*Lead the group in singing:*
**1, 2, 3, 4, 5!** *Count on fingers*
**Love the God who gave you life!** *Cross arms then point heavenwards*
**6, 7, 8, 9, 10!** *Count on fingers*
**Love each other. Yes! Amen!**
*Cross arms, point to each other, then clap hands together on 'Amen'.*

*Groups with older children may like to continue:*
Then listen and watch!
This bit has lots of pointing!

*Sing slowly to the same tune as '1, 2, 3, 4, 5':*
Love with your heart *point to heart* and mind *point to head*
and with your soul *wiggle fingers from toes to head*
and with your strength! *Arms flexed to show strength*
**Love with your heart** *point to heart* **and mind** *point to head*
**and with your soul** *wiggle fingers from toes to head*
**and with your strength!** *Arms flexed to show strength*

Then we sing the same words again.
But remember:
this time the tune goes down at the end.

Love with your heart *point to heart* and mind *point to head*
and with your soul *wiggle fingers from toes to head*
and with your strength! *Arms flexed to show strength*
**Love with your heart** *point to heart* **and mind** *point to head*
**and with your soul** *wiggle fingers from toes to head*
**and with your strength!** *Arms flexed to show strength*

Let's try that all together!

**1, 2, 3, 4, 5!** *Count on fingers*
**Love the God who gave you life!** *Cross arms then point heavenwards*
**6, 7, 8, 9, 10!** *Count on fingers*
**Love each other. Yes! Amen!**
*Cross arms, point to each other, then clap hands together on 'Amen'.*

**Love with your heart** *point to heart* **and mind** *point to head*
**and with your soul** *wiggle fingers from toes to head*
**and with your strength!** *Arms flexed to show strength*

**Love with your heart** *point to heart* **and mind** *point to head*
**and with your soul** *wiggle fingers from toes to head*
**and with your strength!** *Arms flexed to show strength*

---

Traditionally, the Ten Commandments are divided into two groups:
■ commandments 1–4 are about loving God;
■ commandments 5–10 are about loving your neighbour.
We've played a little loosely with this to fit the song. The important point remains: the Ten Commandments cover not only our relationship with God, but our relationships with each other.

## Section 3

# Creative Response starter ideas: God's Best Friend, Moses, unit

→ **Guide: Book 1, p. 228**

These starter ideas are designed to spark imaginations and open up opportunities for the children to respond creatively in their different ways to the worship and storytelling you've taken part in together.

> ### Tip
>
> As outlined in the Guide of *Diddy Disciples* Book 1 from p. 228, we've found the following rules of thumb helpful for fostering an environment where children are encouraged to engage personally and openly.
>
> 1 Encourage the children to make their own choices.
> 2 Give the children space to develop their response as they wish.
> 3 Create space for 'bridge building'.
> 4 It's the act of responding that matters, not the final result.
> 5 These responses are 'holy ground'.

**Weekly Starter Ideas** relate directly to the Bible Storytelling of each session, including a print-and-go option.

**Sensory Starter Ideas** are designed for sensory explorers, including babies and toddlers. These can remain the same through the whole unit.

**Unit Starter Ideas** are designed to remain relevant throughout the whole unit. Keeping these resources available each week gives children the opportunity to deepen and develop their responses, while making preparation more manageable for leaders.

> ### Tip: Free response area
>
> In addition to any other resources you provide, keeping a free response area available every week will give the children the opportunity to create anything they wish in response to the story they've told, building their sense of confidence and personal responsibility. In this area you could simply provide blank paper and crayons, pencils, paints or pastels. If you have them, other interesting media (see Book 1, p. 256) will provide even more scope for the children to nurture and strengthen their imaginative skills.

Many of these starter ideas share resonances with the starter ideas from other units. This is deliberate! The aim is to assist children in making connections between stories of Moses and Jesus (we see this all the time in Matthew's Gospel). Offering the same starter ideas for Creative Responses across different units will help the children start to make important connections: 'Haven't we done/seen this before?' Repetition and 'overlearning' can be a hugely valuable form of learning.

# Weekly Starter Ideas

---

### Week 1: The Baby Pulled from the Water

🧒 Give the children the opportunity to make their own baby Moses to take home. What will he look like? Would they like to make a basket to put him in? (See below.) *Provide the baby template (p. 363 or website), pencils/crayons/paints and scissors.*

🧒 Invite the children to make a picture of the Clever Slave. What will she look like? Someone the child knows? *Provide the body template (p. 366 or website), pencils/crayons/paints and scissors. If you have collage materials (Book 1, p. 255) and glue, make these available too.*

🧒 Invite the children to be like the Clever Slave and have a go at weaving a 'plate basket'. Before the session, fold paper plates in half and cut five or six lines into the central circle of the plates to form slits. During the time for Creative Response, invite the children to weave wool or string in and out of the slits to form their own patterns in their own way. *Provide pre-cut paper plates, different coloured wool/string.*

🧒 Invite the children to have a go at weaving a 'cup basket'. Before the session, cut about six equally spaced lines into the rim of a disposable cup down to the base to form slits. During the time for Creative Response, invite the children to weave wool or string in and out of the slits to form their own patterns in their own way. *Provide pre-prepared disposable cups, different coloured wool/string.*

🧒 For starter ideas for the River Nile, see the River Jordan starter ideas in the John the Baptist unit (p. 96).

---

### Week 2: Moses in the Wilderness

🧒 Invite the children to explore feelings and face expressions from the story. Whose face would they like to draw? The slaves (tired/groaning), Pharaoh the Bully shouting, 'I want MORE!', Moses (when he's angry/running for his life), themselves (when they feel as if they want to hide) or someone else? *Provide the face template (p. 374 or website), pencils/crayons/paints and scissors. If you have collage materials (Book 1, p. 255) and glue, make these available too.*

🧒 Give the children the opportunity to make a body template into Pharaoh the Bully. Or perhaps they'd prefer to make Moses, one of the slaves, themselves in the story, or another person that they're aware of at the moment. *Provide body template (p. 366), pencils/crayons/pastels/paints, scissors. Optional: glue and collage materials (Book 1, p. 255) if you have them.*

🧒 Give the children an opportunity to make their own wilderness tray or wilderness picture. See p. 86 and p. 94 for descriptions.

🧒 Invite the children to make a wilderness scene by gluing sand (or brown sugar) and small pebbles to card or paper. All you can see in the wilderness is sand or stones! They might even like to draw Moses hiding in the wilderness.

🧒 Create a giant picture of the Burning Bush over two weeks (similar to the opportunity to create the fire of the Spirit at Pentecost, see p. 208). God is about to meet Moses in fire (next week's story!). Invite the children to make their paintbrushes/fingers 'dance' with fire on paper with swirls and swooshes in reds/yellows/oranges to create images of fire. Ask the children if they're willing to make more than one painting and to leave one behind for next week. *Provide paper, different shades of red/yellow/orange paint and paintbrushes (or use fingerpaints, see Book 1, p. 258 for recipe).*

## Week 3: Moses, You Will Set My People Free!

☝ Invite the children to create their own Burning Bush. How big will the flames be in their picture? *Provide bare tree template (p. 364 and website), green and red/yellow/orange pencils/crayons/pastels. Optional: green and red/orange/yellow crepe/tissue paper, real green leaves (little ones!) or fire-coloured fingerpaints (see recipe in Book 1, p. 258).*

☝ Give the children the opportunity to create a stained glass picture of the Burning Bush by collaging green and fire-coloured tissue paper onto squares or circles of wax/baking paper. Give them freedom to let the fire burn out of control! Encourage the children to take their creations home and attach them to a window to see the light shining through. *Provide wax/baking paper (some pound shops sell ready-cut circles or squares), green and orange/red/yellow tissue paper, glue, scissors.*

☝ If you didn't do this last week: invite the children to create a collage of the Burning Bush on paper. Your group may prefer to make individual collages or a giant group collage. Remember to give the children freedom to let the fire burn out of control! *Provide individual sheets of paper or a large roll of paper, plus green and orange/red/yellow tissue paper, glue, scissors.*

☝ Give the children the opportunity to make a branch from the Burning Bush from real branches. *Provide branches (check for sharp points: it's even better if the leaves are still on!), glue, masking tape, sticky tack, red/orange/yellow tissue or crepe paper.*

☝ If you made fire pictures last week, invite the children to take a fire picture (it doesn't need to be their own and you could provide more created by yourself). Ask the children to dance like the fire again, this time using scissors to sway and turn through the fire paintings to create flame shapes. Use the free-style red/yellow/orange cuttings that are created by this to create a large-scale fire collage of the Burning Bush. *Provide: fire paintings (dried), scissors, a large roll of paper, glue.*

## Week 4: Let My People Go!

☝ Imagine having to pack your case quickly and run! What would the children take with them? Invite them to draw these things in their suitcase. They may remember Joseph, Mary and Jesus, the refugees, having to do something similar in their escape TO Egypt (see Baby Jesus, the Refugee, p. 47). *Provide suitcase template (p. 388 or website).*

☝ This week's story is all about who is king. Pharaoh sees himself as king (with a very impressive crown! see website), but God is King of Kings! Invite the children to design a crown for God. *Provide a choice of simple hatbands (p. 360) and crown templates (p. 371) plus pencils/crayons/pastels/paints. Optional: glue and a range of collage materials, if you have them.*

☝ Invite the children to create a story wheel to take home and remember how the world shouted, 'STOP!' to Pharaoh for God by drawing the smelly water, frogs, flies, hail (and thunder) and locusts on the wheel. In the sixth section, they could draw Pharaoh finally shouting, 'Go!', or a picture of Moses and the slaves finally running in the great escape from Egypt. They might even like to write 'STOP!' on the arrow. As this is a print-and-go resource, groups without paper fasteners to attach the wheel can leave it floating free, for the children to pick up and move around at will. *Provide wheel with arrow template (p. 390 or website), scissors, pencils/crayons/felt tips. Optional: paper fasteners. If you're using these, a hole punch may also come in handy, or show the children how to make a hole by placing clay/plasticine/playdough on the table under the centre of the circle then pressing a pencil/crayon gently into the clay to make a hole.*

☝ Give the children the opportunity to use playdough/clay to create animals, birds, fish and other parts of creation (trees, rivers and seas, weather) to shout, 'Stop!' to Pharaoh the Bully. I wonder who or what the whole of creation might want to shout, 'Stop!' to today? *Provide playdough, clay, plasticine or other modelling resources.*

## Week 5: The Path through the Red Sea

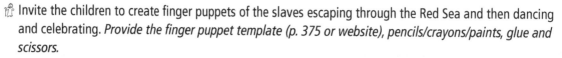

🛠 Invite the children to create finger puppets of the slaves escaping through the Red Sea and then dancing and celebrating. *Provide the finger puppet template (p. 375 or website), pencils/crayons/paints, glue and scissors.*

🛠 Give the children the opportunity to draw their own picture of the people escaping through the Red Sea. *Provide picture frame template (p. 384 or website), pencils/crayons/pastels/paints. Optional: 'Crossing the Red Sea' is the subject of many famous paintings (see website). You could explore two or three of these first with the children, pointing out how each painter has chosen different moments of the story and created a unique work of art. Encourage the children to then create their own unique pictures.*

🛠 Invite the children to create the Red Sea on a paper plate. Will they show the sea open (with the 'wilderness' beneath showing, cf. Psalm 106.9) or closed? Or perhaps even the moment when the waves crash in again and the sand and water are swirled together in chaos? *Provide paper plates and either blue/green and yellow/brown paints, or blue/green and yellow/brown collage materials (Book 1, p. 255), including sand/soil, if you like, and glue.*

🛠 Give the children the opportunity to make their own staff, like Moses. They might even like to use different coloured wools to remember the story. What colour would they use for where the story starts, in Egypt? What colour for the water – the Red Sea – in the middle? Then what colour for FREEDOM and celebrating on the other side? Take care to leave these colours to the children's imaginations. Equally, they may like to do something different with their staff. *Provide sticks and different coloured wools.*

🛠 Invite the children to make their own Moses staff from a lollipop stick, decorating it with pictures from the Moses stories. *Provide wooden lollipop stick and pencils/crayons/pens.*

🛠 Give the children the opportunity to use collage materials to create a Red Sea that opens up. Would they like to draw the slaves walking through the middle, or perhaps themselves? Or would they prefer to collage the sea bed with sand/soil? *Provide yellow/brown paper, scissors, glue and strips of blue paper with the ends curled, or blue/green collage (Book 1, p. 255). Optional: sand/soil to sprinkle for the sea bed.*

🛠 For starter ideas around the Red Sea, see starter ideas for the River Jordan in the John the Baptist unit (p. 96).

## Extra: Our Baptism

🛠 Give the children the opportunity to make a baptism card for their friends. Leave it entirely up to their imaginations. *Provide card plus pencils/paints/pastels/crayons. Optional: blue collage materials (Book 1, p. 255, for water), sand materials (for the sea bed) and glue.*

🛠 Invite the children to design a baptism candle with a picture of the pillar of fire that the slaves followed. *Provide candle template (p. 367 or website), pencils/crayons/pastels/paints. Optional: fiery coloured collage materials (Book 1, p. 255).*

🛠 Give the children the opportunity to design their own baptism font. They may like to use the template as a starter, or to create their own shape. Remind the children to show the water inside! They might like to decorate the font with patterns, with pictures of the slaves crossing the Red Sea or with pictures from the same stories as your church's font. Younger children may like to use collage materials. *Provide font template (p. 378 or website), pencils/crayons/pastels/paints. Optional: glue, scissors, collage materials (Book 1, p. 255).*

🛠 For more starter ideas for baptism, see starter ideas for Our Baptism in the John the Baptist unit (p. 97).

# Sensory Starter Ideas (including for babies and toddlers)

Resources that you might provide include:

- a range of building blocks and other building materials to build like the slaves in Egypt;

- playdough for making and inventing and creating like the slaves in Egypt;

- carpenter's sets or workbenches for the slaves;

- dressing up: Pharaoh's crown, robe, Moses' staff, sacks with holes for sleeves;

- Moses basket and baby;

- sand (or brown sugar) in clear bottles filled to different levels. Tape the lids tight shut!

- water in clear bottles filled to different levels. You could even add glitter/food colouring or both. Tape the lids tight shut!

- a river cloth;

- different sizes of stones and rocks in a box/feely bag/socks. Where Moses went in the wilderness there were only rocks and sand. Make sure these are a suitable size for under threes. If they present a choking hazard place them in a clear bottle and tape the lid tight shut;

- a long roll of paper, taped to the floor, for children and parents to add wavy blue or green lines with chunky crayons;

- a sand and/or water tray if appropriate for your setting;

- a wilderness tray (see p. 86);

- musical instruments: in Exodus 15.20, Miriam sings and dances and plays the timbrel to celebrate the escape through the sea.

# Unit Starter Ideas

🏛 Invite the children to make a story wheel to remember moments from the stories of Moses. For instance, in the six sections they could draw: slaves in Egypt, baby Moses. the Burning Bush, Moses before Pharaoh, the crossing of the Red Sea, the singing and dancing of freedom. *Provide: wheel with arrow template (p. 390), scissors, pencils/crayons/pastels, paper fasteners.*

🏛 Give the children the opportunity to make their own bricks from mud. Invite them to pack mud tightly into ice cube trays. Depending on the mud you've used, these may be ready to turn out straight away or you may need to leave them to dry. Have a go yourself beforehand to find out! If you leave the mud bricks to dry over the week, the children could start building with them next time! *Provide ice cube trays, mud, spoons. If necessary: a little water.*

🏛 Different moments from the stories of Moses and God's people have been the subject of many famous paintings. Explore two or three of these paintings with the children, pointing out how each painter has chosen different moments of the story and created a unique work of art. Encourage the children to then choose which moment they would like to depict and invite them to create their own unique pictures with interesting media. *Provide images of famous paintings to explore (search online or see the website) plus a wide range of interesting media (Book 1, p. 256, or website) for the children to experiment with.*

🏛 Invite the children to make a building picture from square cereal shapes: a pyramid, a temple, a city, a tower or anything the children can imagine. *Provide coloured paper, square cereal shapes, glue. Remember to check for any food allergies. If gluten-free food is necessary, try using gluten-free cereal hoops to build with.*

🏛 In Exodus 15.20, Miriam sings and dances and plays the timbrel to celebrate the escape through the sea. Give the children the opportunity to experiment making musical instruments: elastic bands stretched over a strong box or tub to create a stringed instrument; paper or cellophane stretched over a strong cardboard cup or tub and secured with an elastic band to create a drum; straws with the end flattened and cut into a V-shaped point to create a buzzing oboe! Give the children space and time to experiment! *Provide elastic bands, strong boxes and tubs, scissors, masking tape, straws, paper (or cellophane if you have it).*

# Part 2
# Additional information and resources

# DIDDY DISCIPLES STORYTELLING WITH BABIES AND TODDLERS

At St Peter's, Walworth, we've tended to hold mixed groups for children aged nought to eight because we've found that both the babies and the children over the age of three gain so much from this experience (see Book 1, pp. 3–4). If your group is made up only of babies and toddlers under two and half years, however, you may wish to adapt the session accordingly. For a group like this, I would build a simple baby singing session as follows.

## Welcome

→ **Guide: Book 1, p. 218**

*Welcome your group.*

Let's start by going round the circle
and saying our name out loud.
My name's _____.

*Go round the circle so that every adult and child (and toy) has the chance to say his or her name. If any of the children don't want to say their name or aren't able to, you (or a parent or carer) could say it for them and wave.*

It's time to sing our Welcome Song!

## Welcome Song: Option 1

→ **Song: 'The Diddy Disciples welcome song'. Words: © Sharon Moughtin-Mumby**
→ **Tune: 'Glory, glory, alleluia!' (traditional). For the music see p. 357, or for a taster see the Diddy Disciples website.**

*Go around the circle the same way as above. See if each of you can remember the others' names and insert them into the song.*

**Welcome *Name 1* to *St Peter's* \***
**Welcome *Name 2* to *St Peter's* \***
**Welcome *Name 3* to *St Peter's* \***
**You are welcome in the name of the Lord!**

\* *Insert the name of your church or children's group, or sing 'our worship'.*

## Interactive Bible Storytelling

> ### Tip
>
> Choose a suitable number of songs from the material laid out below (or from other resources) that fit with the theme of the unit you've chosen. Move through these songs in the same order each week. Punctuate the singing with getting ready for the next song by giving out the visual aids or imaginative aids suggested. Keeping the songs the same each week will give the children (and adults) plenty of time to familiarize themselves with the songs and begin to join in actively. You may like to make simple song sheets for each unit, but most of the songs here simply repeat the first line, making it easy to join in.

# Thank You, God

→ Song: 'My hands were made for love'. Words: © Sharon Moughtin-Mumby
→ Tune: 'Hickory, dickory, dock' (traditional). For the music see p. 360, or for a taster see the Diddy Disciples website.

*If you'd like to include a time of prayer to follow the Bible Storytelling, you may find the following material from the 'Thank You, God' Building Block helpful. Having said this, we've found that the Sorry Song (p. 356) and the 'Jesus, hear our prayer!' song (p. 358) are the parts of Diddy Disciples that our youngest babies engage with most.*

*Invite the children to sit in a circle for a moment of quiet.*

It's time to remember all the things we've done this week.
It's time to say 'thank you' to God
for when we've been part of showing God's love.

Let's wiggle our fingers!
I wonder when you've shown love with your hands this week?

*Wiggle fingers as you sing.*
**My hands were made for love!**
**My hands were made for love!**
**Thank you for the love they've shown.**
**My hands were made for love!**

Let's wiggle our feet!
I wonder when you've shown love with your feet this week?

*Wiggle feet as you sing.*
**My feet were made for love!**
**My feet were made for love!**
**Thank you for the love they've shown.**
**My feet were made for love!**

Let's put our hands gently on our neck.
Let's sing 'Ahhh!'
**Ahhhhh!**
Can you feel your throat vibrating and dancing with your voice?
I wonder when you've shown love
with your voice this week?

*Hold neck and feel your voice 'dancing' as you sing.*
**My voice was made for love!**
**My voice was made for love!**
**Thank you for the love it's shown.**
**My voice was made for love!**

## Feast

*Eat, drink and sit together as a sign of what God's Kingdom looks like (Luke 14.15–24). This may be a simple snack (for instance, a drink and pieces of fruit or a biscuit). Aim to provide for everyone, including adults. You may instead prefer to hold your feast after your closing song.*

# Closing Song

→ Song: 'I've got peace like a river' (traditional), Isaiah 66.12, NIV
→ Tune: traditional. For a taster see the Diddy Disciples website.
→ See Guide, Book 1, p. 231

> *Either: invite the children each to hold a small section of the peace cloth (Book 1, p. 231), helped by adults, and to raise and lower it so it 'flows' like a river as you sing.*
> *Or: invite the children to lie beneath the peace cloth as two adults wave it over their heads.*

*Or: if you don't have a peace cloth, invite the group to join in raising and lowering their hands like the waters of a flowing river as you sing.*

**I've got peace like a river,**
**I've got peace like a river,**
**I've got peace like a river in my soul.**
**I've got peace like a river,**
**I've got peace like a river,**
**I've got peace like a river in my soul.**

# Jesus, Light of the World! (Epiphany): storytelling with babies and toddlers

*In the weeks after Christmas, you may like to continue celebrating the birth of Jesus in your group, especially if your church follows the seasons of the church year. Light of the World (Epiphany)-themed songs for babies and toddlers, including songs about the Magi/Three Kings/Wise Men can be found on pp. 250–3 of Book 1. You may also like to add Song 1, below. Alternatively, you may like to move to the John the Baptist unit in the weeks before Lent (see p. 336).*

## Introducing the Unit

Baby Jesus is here!
Baby Jesus is the Light of the World, shining bright. *Jazz hands*
Let's show jazz hands for Jesus' light. *Lead the group in jazz hands*
It's time to celebrate!

*You may like to place a Baby Jesus doll in a manger/Moses basket/cardboard box in the centre of the circle. If the children like playing with Baby Jesus, you might like to have more than one doll ready!*

## Song 1: 'We are marching in the Light of God'

→ **Tune and words: traditional. For the music see p. 7, or for a taster see the Diddy Disciples website.**

Our song's all about Jesus' light shining.
It's about how everything we do is in 'the light of God'.

**We are waking** *stretching action* **in the light of God,**
**we are waking** *stretching action* **in the light of God!**
**We are waking** *stretching action* **in the light of God,**
**we are waking** *stretching action* **in the light of God!**
*Interrupt the song:* Breakfast time!
**We are eating,** *eating action* **we are eating, oh!** *Jazz hands*
**We are eating** *eating action* **in the light of God!**
**We are eating,** *eating action* **we are eating, oh!** *Jazz hands*
**We are eating** *eating action* **in the light of God!**

*Repeat with different actions, changing actions halfway through the song. You may like to ask children or parents/carers what they will be doing that day to help make connections between this time of worship and the rest of each baby/toddler's day. For examples, see p. 8.*

*You may like to end with this final verse, sung quietly.*

**We are resting in the light of God,** *resting action*
**we are resting in the light of God!** *Resting action*
**We are resting in the light of God,** *resting action*
**we are resting in the light of God!** *Resting action*
*Interrupt:* Sleepy time! Ssssh! *Lead the babies and toddlers in settling down to sleep*
**We are sleeping, we are sleeping, ssssh!**
**We are sleeping in the light of God!**
**We are sleeping, we are sleeping, ssssh!**
**We are sleeping in the light of God!**

# John the Baptist: storytelling with babies and toddlers

*This unit is particularly appropriate for groups who would like to explore baptism. It can be held in the weeks between Christmas and Lent, or at any time of the year.*

## Introducing the Unit

We're telling stories about John the Baptist!

> *If there are toddlers present:*
> John wore clothes made from camel hair!
> Let's put our camel-hair coat on!
> *Lead the group in putting on a coat and scratching.*
> It's very itchy!
>
> John's job was to get the world ready for God!
> John called out, 'Get ready!' *Cup hands around mouth*
>
> After 3, let's shout, 'Get ready!'
> 1, 2, 3 . . . **Get ready!** *Cup hands around mouth*

## Song 1: 'Get ready for our God!'

→ **Words: © Sharon Moughtin-Mumby**
→ **Tune: 'She'll be coming round the mountain' (traditional). For the music see p. 56, or for a taster see the Diddy Disciples website.**

*If your group has imaginative aids (Book 1, p. 256), you may like to use them for this song. Either choose some actions yourself, leave the group to wave their imaginative aids as they wish or invite the toddlers/parents/carers to invent actions for the song.*

Let's sing our song about getting ready for God.

**Get ready, get ready for our God!** *Get ready action*
**Get ready, get ready for our God!** *Get ready action*
**It's time for a new start, time for a new start!** *Diddy Disciples 'New Start' sign (p. 355)*
**Get ready, get ready for our God!** *Get ready action*
*Repeat.*

## Song 2: 'Wash me in the river'

→ **Words: © Sharon Moughtin-Mumby**
→ **Music: 'Alive, alive-o': the chorus to the traditional Irish song 'Molly Malone'. For the music see p. 54, or for a taster see the Diddy Disciples website.**

People heard John shouting 'Get ready!'
and they came!

> *You may like to give out 'small world' people (see p. 95) to any toddlers at this point, or place them in the middle of the circle, expecting some to be taken.*

But they didn't feel ready to meet with God. *Shake head*
They asked John to wash them in the river.
Let's sing the people's song together.

**Wash me in the river,** *Diddy Disciples 'I'm Sorry' sign (p. 355)*
**wash me in the river.** *'I'm Sorry' sign*
**O wash me, o wash me,** *'I'm Sorry' sign twice*
**I need a new start!** *Diddy Disciples 'New Start' sign (p. 355)*
*Repeat as appropriate.*

336

# Song 3: 'Down, down, down into the water'

→ Words: © Sharon Moughtin-Mumby
→ Tune: 'Glory, glory, alleluia!' (traditional). For a taster see the Diddy Disciples website.

John the Baptist shouted, 'Get ready!' *Cup hands round mouth*
and the people came. *Point to the 'small world' people if you're using them.*
John helped the people get ready for God.
He washed them in the river!

> *Either:* Let's wiggle our fingers to show the water!
> *Lead the group in wiggling fingers.*
> *Or: place a long piece of blue fabric on the floor (e.g. a peace cloth, Book 1, p. 231).*
> *Or: place a water tray containing a little water in the centre of the circle.*

Let's show the people going down into the water!

> *If you're showing a river with your fingers, lead the children in crouching down slowly as you sing each line, while holding your nose.*
> *If you're using a piece of blue fabric, lead the toddlers in showing the 'small world' people going 'down' onto the fabric as you sing each line.*
> *If you're using a water tray, lead the toddlers in making the 'small world' people go down under the water as you sing each line.*

**Down, down, down into the water,**
**down, down, down into the water,**
**down, down, down into the water,**
**God gives you a new start!**

*Repeat as above, this time emphasizing the 'up' motion out of the water with each line.*

**Up, up, up out of the water,**
**up, up, up out of the water,**
**up, up, up out of the water,**
**God gives you a new start!**
*Repeat as appropriate.*

Then one day, Jesus came to the river!
Let's show John baptizing Jesus.

*As before, lead the children in showing Jesus going down into the water with your bodies or with 'small world' people.*
**Down, down, down into the water,**
**down, down, down into the water,**
**down, down, down into the water . . .**
*until the group are familiar with the change of words for Jesus' baptism*
Freeze!

But Jesus didn't need a new start! *Shake head*
A voice came from heaven:
*Sing to the last line of the song.*
**'I love you! You're my child!'**

Let's sing the story of Jesus' baptism again!

Down, down, down into the water,
down, down, down into the water,
down, down, down into the water . . .
'I love you! You're my child!'

Up, up, up out of the water,
up, up, up out of the water,
up, up, up out of the water,
'I love you! You're my child!'

*Either continue with the following to sing about baptism in your place or move on to the next song.*
Jesus was baptized.
When we follow Jesus, we get baptized too.
Let's show someone being baptized in our church.

> *If you've been showing a river with your fingers, this time mime holding a baby in one arm and pouring water over its head, or mime pouring water over an adult's head.*
> *If you've been using a piece of blue fabric and 'small world' people, lead the toddlers in miming scooping water up from the river with one hand and 'pouring' it over the head of one of the figures.*
> *If you're using a water tray, lead the toddlers in using your hand to pour water over the head of one of the figures.*
> *If your church has baptism by full immersion, repeat the 'Down, down, down' and 'Up, up, up' verses, ending with your choice of final line.*

Pour, pour, pour with the water,
pour, pour, pour with the water,
pour, pour, pour with the water,
*Choose from the following last lines, according to what is most relevant to your setting:*
> . . . 'I love you! You're my child!' *Cross on forehead or dove flying down*
> . . . to follow Jesus Christ! *Walk on spot*
> . . . God gives you a new start! *Cross on forehead or another suitable action*
> . . . now you belong to God! *Cross on forehead or another suitable action*

*Repeat as appropriate.*

## Songs 4 and 5: 'The Diddy Disciples welcome song' and 'You are welcome in the name of the Lord'

→ 'The Diddy Disciples welcome song': words: © Sharon Moughtin-Mumby
→ Tune: 'Glory, glory, Alleluia!' (traditional). For the music see p. 357, or for a taster see the Diddy Disciples website.
→ 'You are welcome in the name of the Lord': words and music traditional. For the music see p. 360, or for a taster see the Diddy Disciples website.

When we baptize people,
we welcome them into God's family *or:* the church family.

> *Either:*
> Let's sing a welcome song to them!
> Let's wave as we sing.
>
> *Lead the toddlers and parents/carers in waving and singing:*
> Welcome frie-ends to God's fam'ly!
> Welcome frie-ends to God's fam'ly!
> Welcome frie-ends to God's fami'ly!
> You are welcome in the name of the Lord!
>
> *Or:*
> Let's sing a welcome song to them!
> Let's wave with one hand. *Lead waving*
> Then with our other hand. *Lead waving*
> Then let's show God's 'glory' in them!
> *Move arms up and down in front of you with fingers wiggling, palms facing out, towards one person then another.*

Then let's wave with both hands.
*Lead waving.*
We're ready to sing!

**You are welcome in the name of the Lord!**
*Wave with right hand.*
**You are welcome in the name of the Lord!**
*Wave with left hand.*
**I can see all over you, the glory of the Lord!**
*Move arms up and down in front of you with fingers wiggling,*
*palms facing out, towards one person and then another.*
**You are welcome in the name of the Lord!**
*Wave with both hands all around the circle.*

## Song 6: 'I am going to follow Jesus'

*This song will reappear within the Journey to the Cross (Lent) unit that comes straight after this John the Baptist unit. It can therefore provide some helpful continuity.*

→ **Words:** © Sharon Moughtin-Mumby
→ **Tune:** 'Bobby Shaftoe' (traditional). For the music see p. 72, or for a taster see the Diddy Disciples website.

When we get baptized, we promise to follow Jesus.
Let's sing a song about following Jesus.
Let's march on the spot:
*Lead the children in march in time to the beat:*
1, 2, 3, 4! 1, 2, 3, 4!

*Continue marching as you sing:*
**I am going to follow Jesus,**
**I am going to follow Jesus,**
**I am going to follow Jesus,**
**follow, follow Jesus!**

*If your group has imaginative aids, you may like to distribute them at this point.*
Let's practise following Jesus!
*Name* is going to be Jesus!
*To the toddler or baby's parent/carer:*
'Jesus!' Can you show us an action?
Let's all copy what 'Jesus' does.
Let's 'follow Jesus'.

*Continue 'following' the child's action as you sing:*
**I am going to follow Jesus,**
**I am going to follow Jesus,**
**I am going to follow Jesus,**
**follow, follow Jesus!**

## Songs 7 and 8: 'This little light of mine' and 'We are marching in the light of God'

*Singing a song about light is particularly relevant for groups from churches which give out candles at the end of their baptism service.*

→ **'This little light of mine':** words and tune traditional. For a taster see the Diddy Disciples website. For more verses that are suitable for young children to sing, see p. 24.
→ **'We are marching in the light of God':** words and tune traditional. For the music see p. 7, or for a taster see the Diddy Disciples website.

When we baptize someone, we give them a candle.
*If appropriate, show one of the candles you use to the group.*
Like this!

We tell our friends to shine like little lights in the world for Jesus.

Let's make our finger into a candle now.

*Lead the children in holding your finger up in front of you.*

After 3, I'm going to light your candles.

Are you ready?

**1, 2, 3 . . . Tssssss!**

*Mime striking a match in the air and hold it out towards the children's finger candles to 'light' them.*

> *Either:*
>
> Let's sing about shining our light in the world!
>
> *Lead the children in waving their candle finger in front of their friend.*
>
> **This little light of mine, I'm gonna let it shine!**
>
> **This little light of mine, I'm gonna let it shine!**
>
> **This little light of mine, I'm gonna let it shine!**
>
> **Let it shine, let it shine, let it shine!**
>
> *Continue with the rest of the song, if appropriate (see p. 24).*
>
> *Or:*
>
> Let's march on the spot and sing about God's light!
>
> **We are marching in the light of God,**
>
> **we are marching in the light of God!**
>
> **We are marching in the light of God,**
>
> **we are marching in the light of God!**
>
> **We are marching, we are marching, oh!**
>
> **We are marching in the light of God!**
>
> **We are marching, we are marching, oh!**
>
> **We are marching in the light of God!**
>
> *Or: the extended version of 'We are marching in the light of God' from the material for the weeks after Christmas (see p. 7).*
>
> Let's sing about how everything we do 'is in the light of God!'

# The Journey to the Cross (Lent): storytelling with babies and toddlers

## Introducing the Unit

*Week 1:* This week we're starting on a journey with Jesus:

*All other weeks:* We're on a journey with Jesus:

*You may like to show the group a cross.*

the journey to the cross.

## Song 1: 'I am going to follow Jesus'

→ **Words: © Sharon Moughtin-Mumby**

→ **Tune: 'Bobby Shaftoe' (traditional). For the music see p. 72, or for a taster see the Diddy Disciples website.**

Our song is all about following Jesus.

Let's get ready to follow Jesus.

> *Either:* Let's get up and march on the spot.
>
> *Or: lead the parents/carers in lying their babies in front of them and gently moving their babies' legs to the beat.*

1, 2, 3, 4! 1, 2, 3, 4!

*Continue 'marching' as you sing:*

**I am going to follow Jesus,**

**I am going to follow Jesus,**

**I am going to follow Jesus,
follow, follow Jesus!**

*If you have imaginative aids, you may like to distribute them at this point.*
Let's practise following Jesus!
*Choose one of the toddlers/babies to be 'Jesus'.*
*Name* is going to be Jesus!
*To the toddler or parent/carer:* 'Jesus!' Can you show us an action?'
Let's all copy what 'Jesus' does.
Let's 'follow Jesus'.

*Continue 'following' the toddler/baby's actions as you sing:*
**I am going to follow Jesus,
I am going to follow Jesus,
I am going to follow Jesus,
follow, follow Jesus!**

*Invite another toddler/baby to be 'Jesus' and repeat as appropriate.*
*When the group is ready to finish:*
In Lent, we follow Jesus!
> *If you're using a cross, show it to the group again at this point.*
We follow Jesus to the cross.

## Song 2: 'Jesus came riding on a donkey'

→ Words: © Sharon Moughtin-Mumby
→ Tune: 'Sing hosanna' (traditional). For the music see p. 121. For a taster see the Diddy Disciples website.

*For this song, you may like to distribute branches, leaves, green imaginative aids (or a mixture). Check that whatever you distribute is child-safe (and not toxic). You might like to try singing the song while moving around the room.*

Let's sing our song about the day Jesus went to the big city, Jerusalem!
Let's follow Jesus with our song!

**Jesus came riding on a donkey** *hold reins and jig up and down*
**and the people all danced and sang!** *Wave hands above head*
**They threw down their cloaks before him** *'Glory of the Lord' sign (see p. 5)*
**and waved gre-en palm leaves in their hands!** *Wave hands above head*
**Sing hosanna! Sing hosanna!** *Wave hands above head*
**Sing hosanna** *wave hands* **to the King of Kings!** *Crown action twice*
**Sing hosanna! Sing hosanna!**
**Sing hosanna** *wave hands above head* **to the King!** *Crown action*
*Repeat.*

## Song 3: 'When the king says . . .'

→ Words: © Sharon Moughtin-Mumby
→ Tune: 'If you're happy and you know it!'. For a taster see the Diddy Disciples website.
→ Words: © Sharon Moughtin-Mumby
→ Tune: 'Bobby Shaftoe' (traditional). For the music see p 72, or for a taster see the Diddy Disciples website.

Jesus is the King! *Crown action*
The King of Kings! *Crown action twice*
Let's practise being servants and kings!

*Invite a child to be 'king' and place a real or imaginary crown on her or his head. Ask the child what she or he would like the group to do (sweep the floor, jump, draw, etc.). If appropriate make a suggestion. Then lead the rest of the group in being the servants.*

We're King *Name*'s servants, we have to do as the king says!
*Lead the children in miming and singing.*

**When the king says '___!'**
**We will ____!**

When the king says '___!'
We will ____!
When the king says '___!'
When the king says '___!'
When the king says '___!'
We will ____!

*Choose another child to be 'king' and repeat with different actions as appropriate.*

Jesus is the King! *Crown action*
The King of Kings! *Crown action twice*
What will King Jesus ask us to do?

King Jesus did something very surprising!
He knelt down and washed his friends' feet! *Mime washing*
Kings don't kneel on the floor! *Crown action and shake head*
Kings don't wash feet! *Crown action and shake head*
But King Jesus did!

*Lead the group in miming washing feet as you sing together new words to Song 1: 'I am going to follow Jesus'. For the music see p. 72.*
Washing, washing, washing feet,
washing, washing, washing feet,
washing, washing, washing feet,
washing, washing feet.

*Lead the group in miming drying feet as you sing together:*
Drying, drying, drying feet,
drying, drying, drying feet,
drying, drying, drying feet,
drying, drying feet.

Then King Jesus said:
'You . . .' *point around the group*
'must be SERVANTS like me!'

So let's kneel down and wash each other's feet.
*You may even like to try using real water for one or more weeks. For tips on holding a real footwashing, see p. 133.*

*Lead the children in 'washing feet' as they sing:*
Washing, washing, washing feet,
washing, washing, washing feet,
washing, washing, washing feet,
washing, washing feet.

I am going to serve like Jesus,
I am going to serve like Jesus,
I am going to serve like Jesus,
serve like, serve like Jesus.

> *If you're using actual water, you may like to extend the song with the following:*
> I am going to follow Jesus,
> I am going to follow Jesus,
> I am going to follow Jesus,
> follow, follow Jesus!

Now let's dry our friend's feet.
*Lead the children in singing as they wash feet.*
Drying, drying, drying feet,
drying, drying, drying feet,
drying, drying, drying feet,
drying, drying feet.

I am going to serve like Jesus,
I am going to serve like Jesus,
I am going to serve like Jesus,
serve like, serve like Jesus.

> *If you're using actual water, you may like to extend the song with the following:*
> **I am going to follow Jesus,**
> **I am going to follow Jesus,**
> **I am going to follow Jesus,**
> **follow, follow Jesus!**

## Poem: 'Do this to remember me'

→ **Words: © Sharon Moughtin-Mumby**

*You may like to tell the story of the Last Supper to end your time together. For this you will need bread and grape juice. See p. 139 for more details and the 'Do this to remember me' poem.*

# Jesus Is Alive! Alleluia! storytelling with babies and toddlers

## Introducing the Unit

> *If you have an Easter Garden (see p. 149), show it to the children.*
> Can anyone tell me what this is?
> *Accept children's responses and ways of naming the garden.*
> This is our Easter Garden with the dark cave in the middle.

We're telling the stories of what happened
when Jesus burst from the 'tomb', the dark cave.

## Song 1: 'He is risen, risen, risen!'

→ **Words: © Sharon Moughtin-Mumby**
→ **Tune: 'Wide awake' © Mollie Russell-Smith and Geoffrey Russell-Smith, also known as 'The dingle, dangle scarecrow'. It is now published by EMI Harmonies Ltd. For the music see p. 170, or for a taster see the Diddy Disciples website.**

Let's tell the story of Easter Day with our song.
*If there are toddlers in the group, encourage them to follow you in the actions.*

On Good Friday, Jesus died on the cross. *Stretch arms out*
His friends took Jesus' body down from the cross. *Mime holding Jesus' body gently*
They put it gently into the dark cave *mime placing Jesus' body in the cave*
and rolled the stone across. *Mime rolling a large stone across*

They went home feeling very, very, very sad.
Nothing happened for one whole night and day after that.
But then the night after, something amazing happened!
Let's sing our song about the dark cave!

*Lead the children in curling up on the floor or crouching to sing:*
**When all the world was sleeping**
**and the sun had gone to bed . . .**
**up jumped Lord Jesus** *jump up with hands in the air*
**and this is what he said:** *hands out, palms up*

**'I am risen, risen, risen,** *wave hands high in the air*
**I have won us a new start!** *Diddy Disciples 'New Start' sign (p. 355) over head*
**I am risen, risen, risen,** *wave hands high in the air*
**I have won us a new start!'** *'New Start' sign over head*
*Repeat.*

## Song 2: 'On Easter Day in the morning'

→ Words: © Sharon Moughtin-Mumby
→ Tune: 'I saw three ships come sailing in' (traditional). For the music see p. 174, or for a taster see the Diddy Disciples website.

Jesus is alive! But no one knows yet!
Let's sing our song about when Jesus' friends found out!

*Lead the toddlers in tiptoeing on the spot and singing quietly and sadly. Invite any parents/carers with babies to 'cycle' their babies legs as if walking.*

**Tiptoe, tiptoe to the tomb,**
**on Easter Day, on Easter Day.**
**Tiptoe, tiptoe to the tomb,**
**on Easter Day in the morning.**

*Lead the toddlers in the winding action from 'Wind the bobbin up' as you sing. Invite any parents/carers with babies to wind their babies' arms around for them.*

**Look! The stone is rolled away**
**on Easter Day, on Easter Day.**
**Look! The stone is rolled away**
**on Easter Day, on Easter Day.**

*Lead the group in singing in amazement and pointing, or flapping wings like angels.*

**Look! Two angels in the cave!**
**On Easter Day, on Easter Day!**
**Look! Two angels in the cave!**
**On Easter Day in the morning.**

We've got to tell someone!
After 3, let's show running with our arms. *Move arms quickly as if running*
*Invite any parents/carers with babies to 'cycle' their babies' legs a little faster.*
1, 2, 3 . . . Run!

*Lead the group in singing faster and making a running motion.*

**Run and run to tell our friends**
**on Easter Day, on Easter Day!**
**Run and run to tell our friends**
**On Easter Day in the morning!**

*Excitedly:*
Look! *Point* There's Peter and John!
And do you know what Peter and John did? *Rhetorical question*
They ran!

*Lead the group in singing even faster and making a running motion with their arms.*

**Run and run and run and run**
**on Easter Day, on Easter Day!**
**Run and run and run and run**
**on Easter Day in the morning!**

*Lead the group in looking around in amazement as you point and sing.*

**Look! The cave is e-empty,**
**on Easter Day, on Easter Day!**
**Look! The cave is e-empty,**
**on Easter Day in the morning!**

*Gasp* Jesus is RISEN!
Jesus IS ALIVE!

*If appropriate:*
Let's shout our special Easter shout of joy.

Alleluia! Christ is risen!

**He is risen indeed! Alleluia**!

## Song 3: 'Back in Galilee'

→ Words: © Sharon Moughtin-Mumby
→ Tune: 'Row, row, row your boat' (traditional). For the music see p. 184, or for a taster see the Diddy Disciples website.

Let's tell another story about Jesus after he burst from the dark cave!

For this story, we need to get into our boats!

*Lead the toddlers in sitting on the floor. Encourage parents/carers to get ready to make a rowing action with their baby as they would for the traditional nursery rhyme 'Row, row, row your boat'.*

**Row, row, row the boat,** *rowing action*

**back in Galilee.** *Rowing action*

**Throw the net then pull it in . . .** *net out, then in*

**What can we see?** *Mime looking in the nets*

Let's have a look! *Lead the children in looking in the imaginary nets*
What have we caught? Nothing! *Shake head*

*Repeat this singing and looking three times.*
Oh no! Have we forgotten how to fish?

Wait! Look! Who's that?
A stranger was standing far away on the beach.
The stranger said: *hands cupped around mouth*
'Throw your net on the OTHER SIDE of the boat!' *Point*

**Row, row, row the boat,** *rowing action*

**back in Galilee.** *Rowing action*

**Throw the net then pull it in . . .** *net out, then in*

**What can we see?** *Mime looking in the nets*

Let's have a look! *Lead the group in looking in the imaginary nets*
The net's full of fish! Look at all the fish!

I know who the stranger is!
It's Jesus! Jesus is alive!

> *If appropriate:*
> Let's shout our special Easter shout of joy.
> Alleluia! Christ is risen!
> **He is risen indeed! Alleluia**!

## Song 4: 'The good shepherd song'

→ Words: © Sharon Moughtin-Mumby
→ Tune: 'Mary had a little lamb' (traditional). For the music see Book 1, p. 64, or for a taster see the Diddy Disciples website.

During Easter, churches all over the world tell a story that Jesus told
about sheep and a shepherd.
Shall we tell the story with our song?
*Continue with the material on p. 235 of Book 1.*

## Song 5: 'Go! And wait for the Holy Spirit!'

→ Words: © Sharon Moughtin-Mumby
→ Tune: 'London Bridge is falling down' (traditional). For the music see p. 191, or for a taster see the Diddy Disciples website.

Let's sing our song about the day Jesus went UP *point up* to heaven.
Our song starts with climbing! Let's go!

*Lead any toddlers in climbing on the spot. Encourage any parents/carers with babies to lift their babies up for each line of the song.*

**Climb the hi-ill, 1, 2, 3!**

**1, 2, 3! 1, 2, 3!** *Climb the hill together*

**Climb the hi-ill, 1, 2, 3!**

**Alleluia!** *'V' shape in the air*

Then Jesus said:

**'Go and wait for the Holy Spirit,** *point*

**the Holy Spirit, the Holy Spirit!** *Point*

**Go and wait for the Holy Spirit.'** *Point*

**Alleluia!** *'V' shape in the air*

When the Holy Spirit comes, it will be in fire! *Sway arms and body to show flames.*

**The Holy Spirit** *fire action* **will make you strong,** *strong action*

**make you strong, make you strong!** *Strong action*

**The Holy Spirit** *fire action* **will make you strong!** *Strong action*

**Alleluia!** *Hands upwards*

Look! *Point upwards*

*Lead any toddlers in pointing up as you sing. Encourage any parents/carers with babies to lift their babies up for each line of the song.*

**Look! Jesus is going up,** *point upwards*

**going up, going up!** *Point upwards*

**Look! Jesus is going up!** *Point upwards*

**Alleluia!** *'V' shape in the air*

Jesus is going! Let's wave goodbye to Jesus.

**Wave goodbye to Je-e-sus!** *Wave*

**Je-e-sus, Je-e-sus!** *Wave*

**Wave goodbye to Je-e-sus!** *Wave*

**Alleluia!** *'V' shape in the air*

Jesus has gone! What shall we do now?

*Lead the group straight into singing with the same actions as before.*

**Go and wait for the Holy Spirit,** *point*

**the Holy Spirit,** *point* **the Holy Spirit!** *Point*

**Go and wait for the Holy Spirit!** *Point*

**Alleluia!** *'V' shape in the air.*

**The Holy Spirit** *fire action* **will make us strong,** *strong action*

**make us strong, make us strong!** *Strong action*

**The Holy Spirit** *fire action* **will make us strong!** *Strong action*

**Alleluia!** *Hands upwards*

## Song 6: 'Holy Spirit, come!'

→ **Words: © Sharon Moughtin-Mumby**

→ **Tune: 'Wind the bobbin up' (traditional). For the music see p. 194. For a taster see the Diddy Disciples website.**

Let's sing our song about the day the Holy Spirit came!

At the beginning of our song, Jesus' friends are waiting . . .

and praying.

*Lead the group in singing quietly:*

**Holy Spirit, come!** *'Come' action (p. 195) throughout*

**Holy Spirit, come!**

**Come, come! Spirit, come!**

*Lead the group in looking around.*

Can anyone see the Holy Spirit?

Not yet . . .

Let's keep praying . . .

**Holy Spirit, come!** *'Come' action throughout*

**Holy Spirit, come!**

**Come, come! Spirit, come!**

*Blow into the air.*

Can you hear that?

*Blow and encourage the group to join in blowing.*

Louder . . . *blow louder* and louder . . . *blow even louder*

*Then, if appropriate, lead the toddlers in banging hands on the floor, louder and louder.*

And look! *Point* What's that?

*Lead the group in singing:*

**Fire on the ceiling!** *Point up in shock*

**Fire on the floor!** *Point down*

**Fire at the window!** *Point to window in shock*

**Fire at the door!** *Point to door*

**The fire of the Spirit: can you see?** *Point all around*

**Holy Spirit, dance in me!** *Sway like a flame*

# Let Your Kingdom Come! storytelling with babies and toddlers

## Introducing the Unit: Option 1

*Use 'thy'/'your' with the children according to the version they will hear around them.*

Jesus told us to pray '*thy/your* Kingdom come'.

After 3, let's say '*thy/your* Kingdom come' together

**1, 2, 3 . . . *thy/your* Kingdom come!**

And again . . .

**1, 2, 3 . . . *thy/your* Kingdom come!**

## Song 1: 'Let your Kingdom come quickly!'

→ **Words:** Place version © Sharon Moughtin-Mumby
→ **Tune:** 'There's a hole in my bucket' (traditional). For the music see p. 217. For a taster see the Diddy Disciples website.

Let's pray as Jesus taught us!

**Let your Kingdom come quickly** *'come' action.*

**in *Walworth*, in *Walworth*\*!** *Point all around*

**Let your Kingdom come quickly!** *'Come' action.*

**Let your** *clap hands together in prayer* **will be done!**

*Repeat.*

We pray for God's Kingdom,

but what's God's Kingdom like? *Hands out in question*

What are we praying for?

## Song 2: 'Come and join the party!'

→ **Words:** © Sharon Moughtin-Mumby
→ **Tune:** 'Polly, put the kettle on!' (traditional). For the music see p. 237, or for a taster see the Diddy Disciples website.

*You may like to pull one or more party hats out of a box/bag to show to the children.*

> *If appropriate:* Let's put our party hat on
>
> *Lead the children in putting imaginary or real party hats on.*

Jesus said, God's Kingdom is like the BIGGEST party!
Let's get ready for the party!

What do you think we need to do to get ready?

*Invite the group to make suggestions of things we need to do and choose an actions for it. For each suggestion sing the following song while leading the group an appropriate action.*
**[Get] ready for the party!**
**[Get] ready for the party!**
**[Get] ready for the party!**
**There's lots to do!**

That was hard work! Everything's ready!
Let's tell our friends.

**Come and join the party!** *'Come' action (p. 195) followed by an action for party*
**Come and join the party!** *'Come' action followed by an action for party*
**Come and join the party!** *'Come' action followed by an action for party*
**Come! Come! Come!** *'Come' action*

But our friend said . . .

*Lead the group in singing sadly to the second verse, 'Suki, take it off again'.*
**Sorry, I'm too busy!** *Shake head*
**Sorry, I'm too busy!** *Shake head*
**Sorry, I'm too busy!** *Shake head*
**[Too] busy to come!** *Shake head*

*Repeat the invitation and decline for two more friends:*
Never mind, let's invite another friend . . .
**Come and join the party . . .**

*When the third friend has declined:*
No one's coming to our party!
Remember all that work we did to get ready?
What can we do with it now?

In Jesus' story,
the party maker decided to invite EVERYONE to the party.
Let's sing really loudly and invite EVERYONE to come,

*Lead the group in singing loudly:*
**Come and join the party!** *'Come' action*
**Come and join the party!** *'Come' action*
**Come and join the party!** *'Come' action*
**Come! Come! Come!** *'Come' action*
And lots of people came!

The party was the BIGGEST party you've ever seen!
Everyone celebrated together!
Let's dance at the big party and sing!
*Lead the group in dancing and singing joyfully 'Come and join the party!' one more time to end.*

Jesus said:
God's Kingdom is like the biggest party,
where EVERYONE'S invited.

# Song 3: 'Dig, dig, dig down deep'

→ Words: © Sharon Moughtin-Mumby
→ Tune: 'B.I.N.G.O.' (traditional). For the music see p. 242. For a taster see the Diddy Disciples website.

What else is God's Kingdom like?
*You may like to pull a spade out of a box/bag to show to the children.*
Jesus said: God's Kingdom is like someone digging!

*Lead the group in miming digging with an imaginary spade.*
**Dig, dig, dig down deep!**
**Dig, dig, dig down deep!**
**Dig, dig, dig down deep!**
**Oh, dig, dig, dig down deep!**

*Show the group a box of 'treasure'.*
Look! It's treasure!
But it's not ours!
I know I have an idea!
Let's bury it again.

**Dig, dig, dig down deep!**
**Dig, dig, dig down deep!**
**Dig, dig, dig down deep!**
**Oh, dig, dig, dig down deep!**

We're going to buy that field!
Let's sell everything we have!
Let's put all our toys and books in a big pile and sell them!

*Lead the group n in miming putting everything on the pile as you sing.*
**Sell, sell everything!**
**Sell, sell everything!**
**Sell, sell everything!**
**O . . . sell, sell everything!**

We've got enough money!
Hurray! Let's buy the field.
And dig up the treasure!

*Lead the children in singing very quickly as you dig.*
**Dig, dig, dig down deep!**
**Dig, dig, dig down deep!**
**Dig, dig, dig down deep!**
**Oh, dig, dig, dig down deep!**

*Show the group the box of 'treasure'.*
Look! It's treasure!
The treasure's ours!

*Excitedly:* We're rich!
*Lead the children in singing and waving hands in the air or making 'twinkle' hands to show the treasure sparkling.*
**Mine! Mine! It is mine!**
**Mine! Mine! It is mine!**
**Mine! Mine! It is mine!**
**Oh, mine, mine! It is mine!**

Jesus said:
finding God's Kingdom is like finding hidden treasure!

## Song 4: 'Let's sow the seed'

→ Words: © Sharon Moughtin-Mumby
→ Tune: 'The farmer's in his den' (traditional). For the music see p. 247. For a taster see the Diddy Disciples website.

What else is God's Kingdom like?
*You may like to pull wellies out of a box/bag to show to the children.*

Jesus said: God's Kingdom is like a farmer planting.
Let's get our wellies on! **1, 2 . . .**
*Lead the children in putting imaginary wellies on.*

> *If there are toddlers in the group, you may like to give out empty paper bags as pretend seed packets.*

Let's take a packet of seed.
Let's sprinkle it on the ground like this.
*Demonstrate sowing seed to the group.*

*Lead the toddlers in the sowing action as you sing together. Encourage any parents/carers with babies to show the seed falling like rain with their hands.*
**Let's sow the seed!**
**Let's sow the seed!**
**Ee-i-addio**
**Let's sow the seed!**

I hope our seed grows nicely!
Oh no! Look! Birds are eating our seed!
*Make a bird action with one hand and peck up and down the opposite arm.*

*Sing sadly with the bird action.*
**Our seed didn't grow!**
**Our seed didn't grow!**
**Ee-i-addio**
**Our seed didn't grow!**

Never mind! Let's see if the rest of our seed is growing nicely!
Oh no! Look! The sun's burning our seed! *Jazz hands for sun*

*Sing sadly with the sun action.*
**Our seed didn't grow!**
**Our seed didn't grow!**
**Ee-i-addio**
**Our seed didn't grow!**

Never mind! Let's see if the rest of our seed is growing nicely!
Oh no! Look! Weeds are growing and choking our plants.
*Place hands together and show weeds twisting up.*

*Sing sadly with the weeds action.*
**Our seed didn't grow!**
**Our seed didn't grow!**
**Ee-i-addio**
**Our seed didn't grow!**

Wait a minute! Look over there! *Point*
And there! And there! And there!
*Point to different places around the circle.*
It's growing! Our seed is growing! *Joyfully*

Let's be the farmer and dance and celebrate!
Our seed is growing tall!
*Lead the group in singing and dancing in celebration.*
**Our seed is growing tall!**

**Our seed is growing tall!**
**Ee-i-addio**
**Our seed is growing tall!**

Jesus said:
God's Kingdom is like a farmer sowing seed!

## Song 5: The Lord's Prayer

→ **Tune: 'Frère Jacques' (traditional)**

*Use 'thy'/'your' according to the version the children will hear around them.*

Let's end by praying for God's Kingdom.
Let's sing the prayer Jesus taught us:
'my turn' *point to self*, 'your turn' *leader's hands out to group*

*Traditional version*
Our Father
**Our Father**
Who art in heav'n
**Who art in heav'n**
Hallowed be thy na-me,
**Hallowed be thy na-me,**
Thy Kingdom come!
**Thy Kingdom come!**
**Your Kingdom come**

*Modern version*
Our Father
**Our Father**
I-in heav'n
**I-in heav'n**
Hallowed be your na-me,
**Hallowed be your na-me,**
Your Kingdom come!

# God's Best Friend, Moses: storytelling with babies and toddlers

## Introducing the Unit: Option 1

God had a best friend called Moses.
Parents and carers, can you give your children a big hug!

*To everyone:*
How did hugging make you feel?
Can you show me with your face? *Accept any responses*

Moses made God feel a bit like that.
Moses was God's best friend!
Let's tell the Bible's stories about God's best friend, Moses.

For our stories about Moses, we need to go to Egypt.

## Song 1: 'We're building a temple'

→ **Words: © Sharon Moughtin-Mumby**
→ **Tune: 'Everywhere we go' (traditional camp song). For the music see p. 288, or for a taster see the Diddy Disciples website.**

*For this song, you may like to pull one or two building blocks from a bag/box to show the children. Not too many or they may get distracted!*

Pharaoh the King loved tall buildings!
But Pharaoh didn't do any of the hard building work! *Shake head*
The 'slaves' – the poor people – had built the buildings.
Let's sing our song about the slaves building.

*Lead the group in singing and building.*
We're building a palace!
**We're building a palace!**
We're working all day!
**We're working all day!**
We're building a pyramid!
**We're building a pyramid!**
We're working all night!
**We're working all night!**
*Repeat.*

The slaves were tired!
But Pharaoh the Bully shouted:
'LAZY! LAZY! LAZY! I WANT MORE!' *Stamp foot on 'more'*

> *If appropriate:*
> Let's be Pharaoh and shout:
> **'LAZY! LAZY! LAZY! I WANT MORE!'** *Stamp foot on 'more'*

Let's sing our song twice as fast!
*Lead the children in singing and building in double time.*

## Song 2: '[Now] Moses, you will set my people free!'

→ **Words:** © Sharon Moughtin-Mumby
→ **Tune:** 'If you're happy and you know it' (traditional). For music see p. 293, or for a taster see the Diddy Disciples website.

The slaves were tired from building!
God decided to send Moses to help.
Let's sing our song about the day Moses met God.

> *At this point, you may like to pull a picture of the Burning Bush from a bag.*
> It's the story of the Burning Bush!

*Either mime climbing on the spot or make a mountain with one arm and show a finger person climbing up it with the other.*
**I'm climbing up the mountain with my sheep!**
**I'm climbing up the mountain with my sheep!**
**I'm climbing up the mountain, climbing up the mountain,**
**I'm climbing up the mountain with my sheep!**

Look! What's that? *Point to picture of bush, or imaginary bush*
That bush is burning!
And sssh! Listen! *Hand behind ear* I can hear a voice!

*Lead toddlers in swaying their whole bodies or parents/carers in swaying hands in front of the babies to show flames.*
**[Now] Moses, you will set my people free!**
**[Now] Moses, you will set my people free!**
**[Now] Moses, you will set, [now] Moses, you will set,**
**[Now] Moses, you will set my people free!**

*Lead the group in peering through fingers as you sing in a scared voice.*
**[But] who are you and what is your name?**
**[But] who are you and what is your name?**
**[But] who are you and what . . .**
**[But] who are you and what . . .**
**[But] who are you and what is your name?**

*Lead toddlers in swaying their whole bodies or parents/carers in swaying hands to show flames in front of the babies.*
**[Now] Moses, you will set my people free!**
**[Now] Moses, you will set my people free!**
**[Now] Moses, you will set, [now] Moses, you will set,**
**[Now] Moses, you will set my people free!**

*Lead the group in clasping hands and shaking head as you lead the children in singing.*

**[Oh] please don't send me! I'm too scared to speak!**
**[Oh] please don't send me! I'm too scared to speak!**
**[Oh] please don't send me! I'm . . .**
**[Oh] please don't send me! I'm . . .**
**[Oh] please don't send me! I'm too scared to speak!**

But God said . . .

*Lead toddlers in swaying their whole bodies or parents/carers in swaying hands in front of the babies to show flames.*

**[Now] Moses, you will set my people free!**
**[Now] Moses, you will set my people free!**
**[Now] Moses, you will set, [now] Moses, you will set,**
**[Now] Moses, you will set my people free!**

So Moses went to tell Pharaoh to 'STOP!' *Hand out.*

# Song 3: 'Let my people go!'

→ Words: © Sharon Moughtin-Mumby
→ Tune: 'The wheels on the bus' (traditional). For the music see p. 296, or for a taster see the Diddy Disciples website.

*This is a shortened version of the song for baby and toddler groups. For the full version, see p. 296.*

Let's sing our song about when the whole world
and everything in it
shouted, 'Stop!' *hand out* to Pharaoh!

*For each verse, you may like to pull an object or picture from a bag/box (or invite the children to do so: the order is not so important).*

**The water in Egypt shouts,**
**'Stop! Stop! Stop!**
**Stop! Stop! Stop!**
**Stop! Stop! Stop!'**
**The water in Egypt shouts,**
**'Stop! Stop! Stop!**
**Let my people go!'** *Point strongly*

**The frogs in Egypt shout,**
**'Ribbit, ribbit, ribbit,**
**ribbit, ribbit, ribbit,**
**ribbit, ribbit, ribbit!'**
**The frogs in Egypt shout,**
**'Ribbit, ribbit, ribbit!**
**'Let my people go!'** *Point strongly*

*Continue with:*
- *flies (bend elbows against body and hold out hands to make tiny wings to flap);*
- *hail and thunder (lead the group in banging on the floor);*
- *locusts (make a mouth from your hand: 'Munch, munch, munch!').*

*To end:*
Then one dark night,
Pharaoh had had enough.
Pharaoh said: Go! Go! Go!' *Point hand outwards in anger*

**At last Pharaoh said,**
**'Go! Go! Go!** *Point three times*
**Go! Go! Go!** *Point three times*
**Go! Go! Go!'** *Point three times*
**At last Pharaoh said,**

'**Go! Go! Go!** *Point three times*
**GO! GO! GO!'** *Point three times*

And the slaves got up and ran!

## Song 4: 'Come, God's people, walk through the Red Sea!'

→ **Words:** © Sharon Moughtin-Mumby
→ **Tune:** 'The old grey mare' (traditional), also known as the tune for 'I'm in the Lord's army'. For music see p. 301, or for a
   taster see the Diddy Disciples website.

*For this song, you may like to use a length of blue fabric for the Red Sea (at St Peter's, Walworth, we use our peace cloth; see Book
1, p. 231). If you're using fabric, you could pull it out of a bag/box at this point.*

To help the slaves escape from Egypt,
God made a path through the sea!
Let's sing our song about the path through the sea!
When the slaves walked through,
they became God's people!

*If you're using blue fabric to show the sea, make a 'tunnel' from the fabric for the group to walk through, either asking two adults
to hold up the cloth or draping it over furniture (clothes pegs can help). Lead the children through the arch, around in a circle and
back to their place as you sing together.*
*If you're singing the song with babies only and would prefer to stay in your places, you could invite the parents/carers to lie their
babies in front of them, then make a walking motion with two fingers above the babies as you sing the walking lines.*

**Come, God's people,**
**walk through the Red Sea,**
**walk through the Red Sea,**
**walk through the Red Sea!**
**Come, God's people,**
**walk through the Red Sea,**

**God has set us free!** *Wave hands above head*
**God has set us free,** *wave hands above head*
**God has set us free!** *Wave hands above head*
**Come, God's people,**
**walk through the Red Sea,**
**God has set us free!** *Wave hands above head*
*Repeat.*

## Song 5: 'Remember when we were slaves in Egypt'

→ **Words:** © Sharon Moughtin-Mumby
→ **Tune:** 'The old grey mare' (traditional), also known as the tune for 'I'm in the Lord's army'. For music see p. 268, or for a
   taster see the Diddy Disciples website.

*For this song, you may like to pull musical instruments out of a bag/box for the babies and toddlers to use. Exodus says that the
slaves of Egypt sang with timbrels!*

Then the slaves danced and sang a song of victory!
Let's sing our 'Remember when we were slaves in Egypt' song
and celebrate!

*Lead the group in digging and singing (to the same tune as Song 4).*
**Remember when we were slaves in Egypt,**
**slaves in Egypt, slaves in Egypt,**
**remember when we were slaves in Egypt,**
**then God set us free!** *Excited action*
**Then God set us free!** *Excited action*
**Remember when we were slaves in Egypt,** *digging action*
**then God set us free!** *Excited action*
*Repeat.*

# DIDDY DISCIPLES RESOURCES

## Signs for the Sorry Song

The 'I'm Sorry' and 'New Start' signs from the Sorry Song are among the very few Diddy Disciples songs and actions that are fixed. It's worth learning these well from the first time you use the Sorry Song, as they become important in a number of units. Videos of both signs can be found on the website next to the Sorry Song Building Block in any of the units.

### The Diddy Disciples 'I'm Sorry' sign

Start with your hands lightly crossed in front of your forehead, then move them in opposing arcs downwards towards your chest and round in opposing circles, and back just in front of your forehead. The opposing circular motion is the 'I'm Sorry' sign. It's designed to convey sadness as well as calling to mind splashing our face with water. There are also echoes of an 'X' shape in the sign to show that we know we've got something 'wrong'.

### Tip

This description is not designed to be used within the group – we would simply make the sign in front of the children and encourage them to imitate it. If at all possible, go to the website to see this sign in practice – it's far easier to do than to describe!

### The Diddy Disciples 'New Start' sign

The 'New Start' sign can best be described as the 'winding' action from the nursery rhyme 'Wind the bobbin up'. Repeatedly rotate your arms around each other in front of your body.

### Tip

Groups with large numbers of children may find it helpful to choose Saying Sorry options or actions where all the children can respond at the same time (such as growing like a seed together), rather than actions where turn-taking is required (such as pulling a 'weed' from a 'garden'). Where actions suggest that the children place a symbol (for instance, crumpled paper) in the centre of the circle, larger groups may find it easier to ask a child or adult to carry a tray or bowl around the circle so the children can place their paper without leaving the circle. You may even like to use two trays going opposite ways. At St Peter's, Walworth, we have found that we have had to continually adapt as our group has grown in number, working out new ways of actively involving all those present in this time of prayer.

# Music resources

Music from the Diddy Disciples Building Blocks in alphabetical order:

**'The Diddy Disciples little prayers song'** Words © Sharon Moughtin-Mumby
From the 'Prayers for Other People' Building Block, Option 2
Tune: 'Frère Jacques' (traditional)

**'The Diddy Disciples sorry song'** Words © Sharon Moughtin-Mumby
From the 'Saying Sorry to God' Building Block, Option 1
Tune: © Sharon Moughtin-Mumby

**'We need a new start'** Words © Sharon Moughtin-Mumby

From the 'Saying Sorry to God' Building Block, Option 2

Tune: Molly Malone (traditional)

For the things we have thought _____ that we wish we'd not thought, _____ we're sor - ry, __ we're sor - ry. __ We need a new start!

**'The Diddy Disciples welcome song'** Words © Sharon Moughtin-Mumby

From the 'Welcome' Building Block, Option 1

Tune: 'Glory, glory, alleluia' (traditional)

Wel - come Name 1 to St Pe - ter's. Wel - come Name 2 to St Pe - ter's. Wel - come Name 3 to St Pe - ter's. You are wel-come in the name of the Lord!

**'For the love we've shown'** Words © Sharon Moughtin-Mumby

From the 'Thank You, God' Building Block, Option 2

Tune: 'All through the night' (traditional)

For the love we've shown with our hands, thank you, God! For the love we've shown with our feet, thank you, God! When we love all those a - round us, it's the same as lov - ing Je - sus. For the love we've shown with our voice, thank you, God!

**'God loves to give me a new start!'** Words © Sharon Moughtin-Mumby
From the 'Saying Sorry to God' Building Block, New Start Action, Option 4
Tune: 'Give me oil in my lamp' (traditional)

Yes, my God loves to give me a new start! How a-ma-zing God's love for me! Yes, my God loves to give me a new start! How a-ma-zing is God's love for me! Sing ho-sa-nna! Sing ho-san-na! Sing ho-san-na to the King of kings! Sing ho-sa-nna! Sing ho-san-na! Sing ho-san-na to the King!

**'Jesus, hear our prayer!'** Words © Sharon Moughtin-Mumby
From the 'Prayers for Other People' Building Block, Option 1
Tune: 'Brown girl in the ring' (traditional)

For the world: Je-sus, hear our prayer. For the Church: Je-sus, hear our prayer. For our place, Wal-worth*: Je-sus, hear our prayer. Lord Je-sus, hear our prayer, A-men.

For the sick and lone-ly: Je-sus, hear our prayer. For our friends and fam-i-ly: Je-sus, hear our prayer. For our-selves: Je-sus, hear our prayer. Lord Je-sus, hear our prayer, A-men.

Take our prayers: Je-sus, hear our prayer. Make them ho-ly: Je-sus, hear our prayer. Make them beau-ti-ful: Je-sus, hear our prayer. Lord Je-sus, hear our prayer, A-men.

**'Jesus, hear our prayer!'** Words © Sharon Moughtin-Mumby **Alternative tune**
From the 'Prayers for Other People' Building Block, Option 1
Tune: 'He's got the whole world in his hands' (traditional)

For the world and all peo-ple: hear our prayer. _ For all Chris-tians in all pla-ces: hear our prayer. _ For the place that we live in: hear our prayer. _ Lord _ Je - sus, hear our prayer. __ For the sick and the lone - ly: hear our prayer. _ For our friends and our fam' - ly: hear our prayer. _ For _ me and my life: _ hear our prayer. _ Lord _ Je - sus, hear our prayer. __ Je-sus, take our prayers: _ hear our prayer. _ Je-sus, make them ho - ly: hear our prayer. _ Je - sus, make them love - ly: hear our prayer. _ Lord __ Je - sus, hear our prayer. __

**'Jesus, open up my eyes'** Words © Sharon Moughtin-Mumby
From the 'Getting Ready for Bible Storytelling' Building Block, Option 2
Tune: 'Michael, row the boat ashore' (traditional)

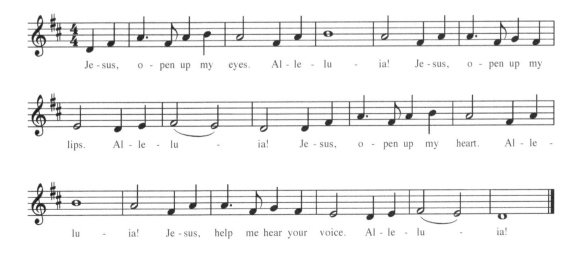

Je - sus, o - pen up my eyes. Al - le - lu - ia! Je - sus, o - pen up my lips. Al - le - lu - ia! Je - sus, o - pen up my heart. Al - le - lu - ia! Je - sus, help me hear your voice. Al - le - lu - ia!

**'My hands were made for love'** Words © Sharon Moughtin-Mumby
From the 'Thank You, God' Building Block, Option 1
Tune: 'HIckory, dickory dock' (traditional)

My hands were made _ for love. My hands were made _ for love.

Thank you for the love they've shown! My hands were made _ for love.

**'You are welcome in the name of the Lord!'** (traditional)
From the 'Welcome' Building Block, Option 2
Tune: traditional

You are wel-come in the name of the Lord! You are

wel-come in the name of the Lord I can see all ov-er you the

glor - y of the Lord, You are wel-come in the name of the Lord!

# Instructions for the hatband

1 Fold a sheet of A4 paper in half or thirds lengthways.
2 Open it out and then cut into strips along the folds.
3 Tape or glue the ends together to the required length.

# Photocopiable templates

The templates on the following pages are for use with the Creative Response starter ideas at the end of each unit.
They are listed here.

## Instructions for the crown template

1  Cut along zigzag line.
2  Tape the two halves together with 1 cm overlap so that you have one long strip.
3  Put the strip round your head so that you can measure where to tape the ends.
4  Tape the ends together to make a crown.

## Instructions for the finger puppet template

1  Cut the finger puppets out along the thick lines.
2  Fold the flaps along the dotted lines, folding away from you.
3  Again folding away from you, fold the puppet in the middle where the arrow is.
4  Tape the flaps to the other half of the puppet.

## Instructions for the lantern template

1  *Optional.* If you want to decorate the lantern, you need to do so before folding and cutting it.
2  Fold along the dotted line. Fold away from you so that the solid lines are on the outside.
3  Starting at the fold, cut along the solid lines, being careful not to cut into the white space at the edge of the paper.
4  Open the paper out. Curl the paper into a cylinder shape with the short edges touching, making sure the fold sticks outwards rather than inwards. Tape or glue the short edges together.
5  *Optional.* To make a handle, cut a strip of paper and glue or tape each end to the top of the lantern.

Joy (8) drew this angel. What can you make from it? Or would you like to draw your own? *An alternative angel template is available in Book 1 (p. 283).*

Zoe M.-M. (8) drew this baby wrapped in cloth. What can you make from it? Or would you like to draw your own?

Joy (8) drew this tree. What can you do with it? Or would you like to draw your own?

Joy (9) drew this bird. What can you make from it? Or would you like to draw your own?

Julia (6) drew these bodies. What can you make from them? Or would you like to draw your own? *A larger body template is available in Book 1 (p. 264).*

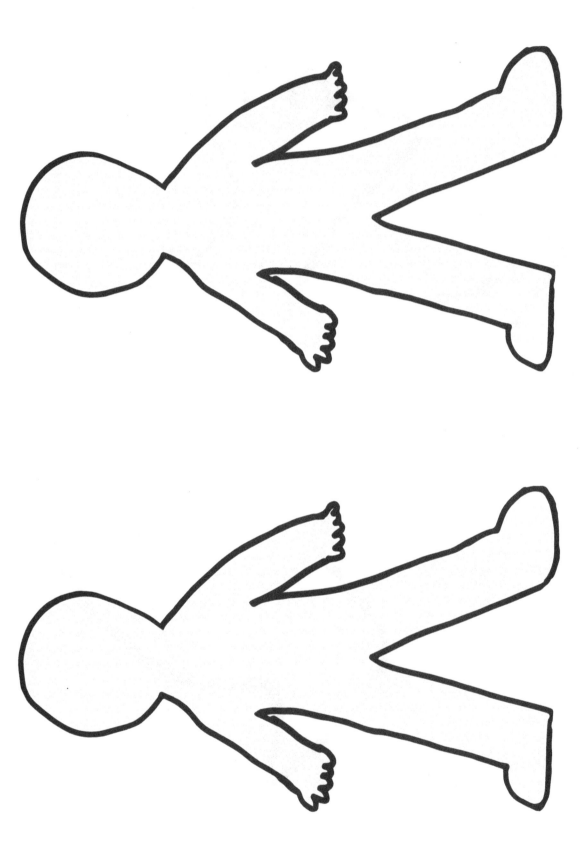

Diddy Disciples actively encourages peer-led learning by children. All our templates are created by Diddy Disciples children or child-leaders. Copyright © Sharon Moughtin-Mumby 2017. *Diddy Disciples Book 2: January to August: Worship and storytelling resources for babies, toddlers and young children.*

Julia (6) drew this candle. What can you make from it? Or would you like to draw your own? *Alternative tall candles are available in Book 1 (p. 269).*

Sarah (7) drew this chalice. Would you like to decorate it? Or would you like to draw your own? *An alternative chalice is available in Book 1 (p. 280).*

Abigail (6) drew around a plate to make this circle. What can you make from it? Or would you like to draw your own?

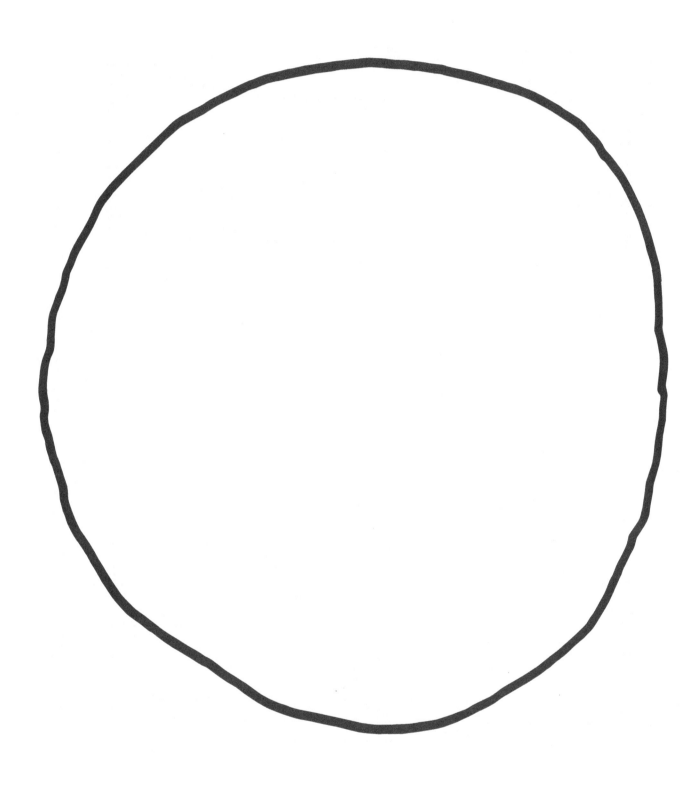

Zayden (6) drew these crosses. What can you make from them? Or would you like to draw your own? *A larger cross template is available in Book 1 (p. 281).*

Philip (6) drew this zigzag line. Can you cut down it to make a crown?

Zayden (6) drew this egg shape. What can you make from it? Or would you like to draw your own?

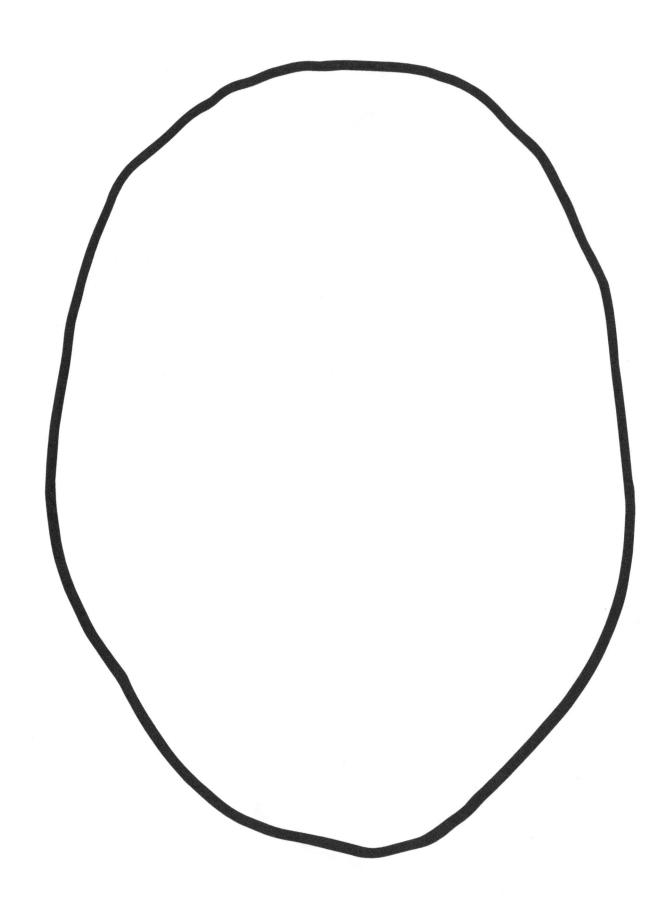

Abigail (6) drew this Easter tomb. What will you do with it? Or would you like to draw your own?

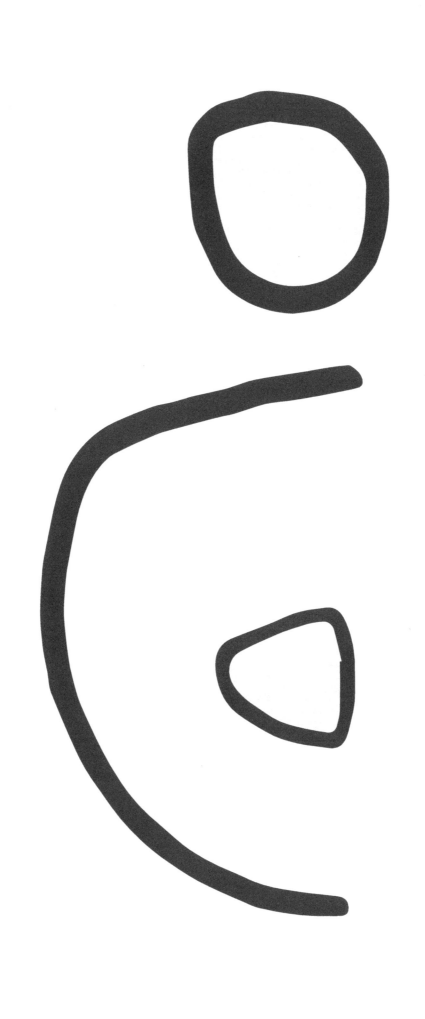

Diddy Disciples actively encourages peer-led learning by children. All our templates are created by Diddy Disciples children or child-leaders. Copyright © Sharon Moughtin-Mumby 2017. *Diddy Disciples Book 2: January to August: Worship and storytelling resources for babies, toddlers and young children.*

Kayleigh (7) drew this face. What can you make from it? Or would you like to draw your own? *Another face template is available in Book 1 (p. 267).*

Isabella (7) drew these finger puppets. Would you like to make them into people? Or would you like to make your own?

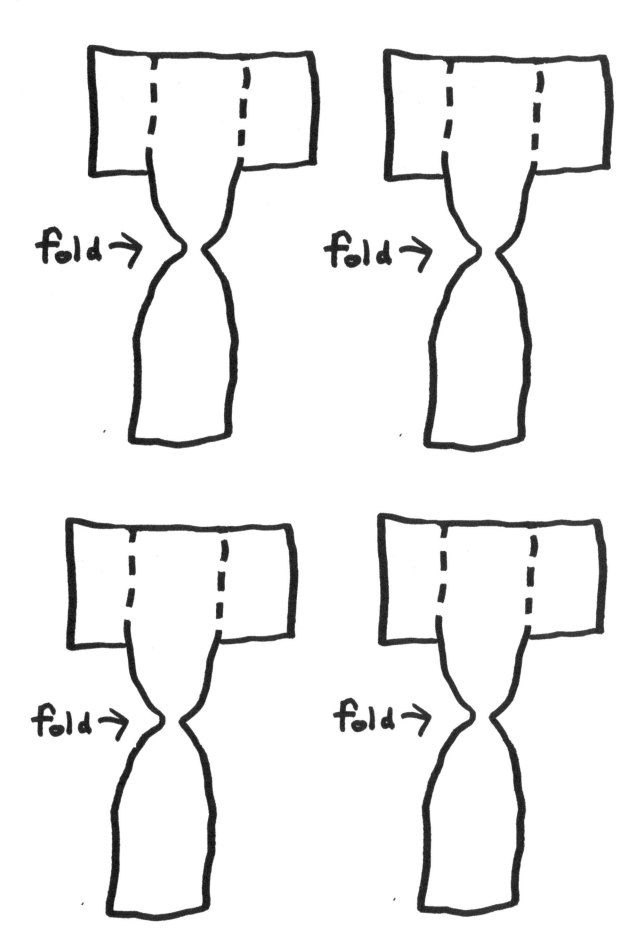

Sultan (7) drew this fire. What can you make with it? Or would you like to draw your own?

Lily (7) drew this fish. What can you make with it? Or would you like to draw your own?

Elijah (7) drew this font. What will you do with it? Or would you like to draw your own?

Isla (6) drew this hen and chicks. What will you make from them? Or would you like to draw your own?

Zoe G. (7) and Joy (8) drew these keys. What will you make from them? Or would you like to draw your own?

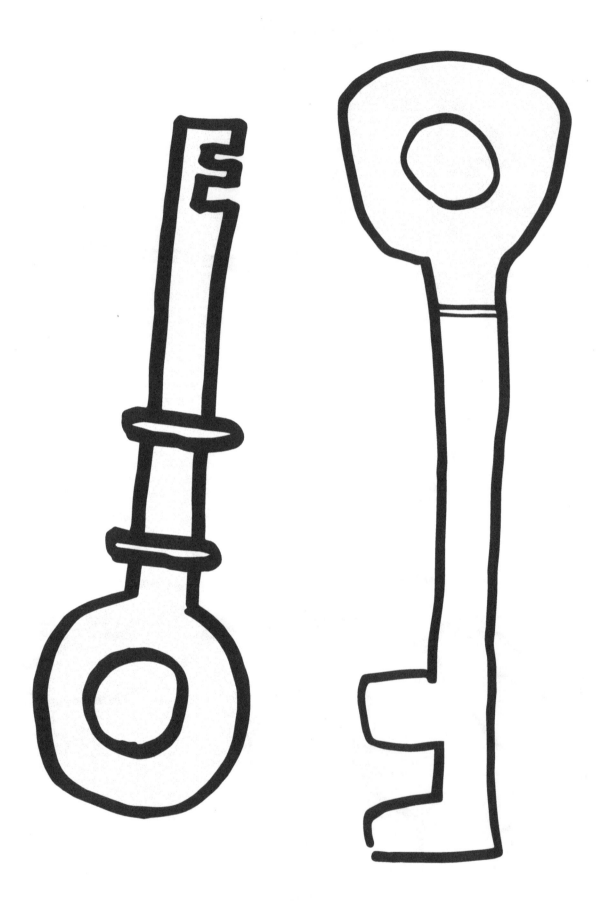

Anastasia (9) created this template for you to make a lantern. Or would you like to make your own? *See p. 361 for instructions.*

fold ↑

Amy (6) drew this heart. What can you make from it? Or would you like to draw your own? *An alternative heart shape is available in Book 1 (p. 270)*.

Michelle (7) drew this palm leaf. What will you make from it? Or would you like to draw your own?

Amy (6) drew this picture frame. What can you draw in it? Or would you like to make your own? *An alternative picture frame is available in Book 1 (p. 275).*

Anastasia (8) drew this postcard. What can you write or draw on it? Or would you like to draw your own?

Diddy Disciples actively encourages peer-led learning by children. All our templates are created by Diddy Disciples children or child-leaders. Copyright © Sharon Moughtin-Mumby 2017. *Diddy Disciples Book 2: January to August: Worship and storytelling resources for babies, toddlers and young children.*

Anastasia (8) drew this sheep. What can you make from it? Or would you like to draw your own?

Kayleigh (7) drew round a star shape to make this star. What can you make from it? Or would you like to draw your own? *An alternative star shape is available in Book 1 (p. 282).*

Amelia (7) created this suitcase. What will you pack inside it? Or would you like to draw your own?

Anastasia (9) drew this treasure chest. What will you make from it? Or would you like to draw your own?

Fold →

Harry (7) drew around a circle shape to make this chart and Amelia (6) drew the arrow. What can you make with it? Or would you like to draw your own?

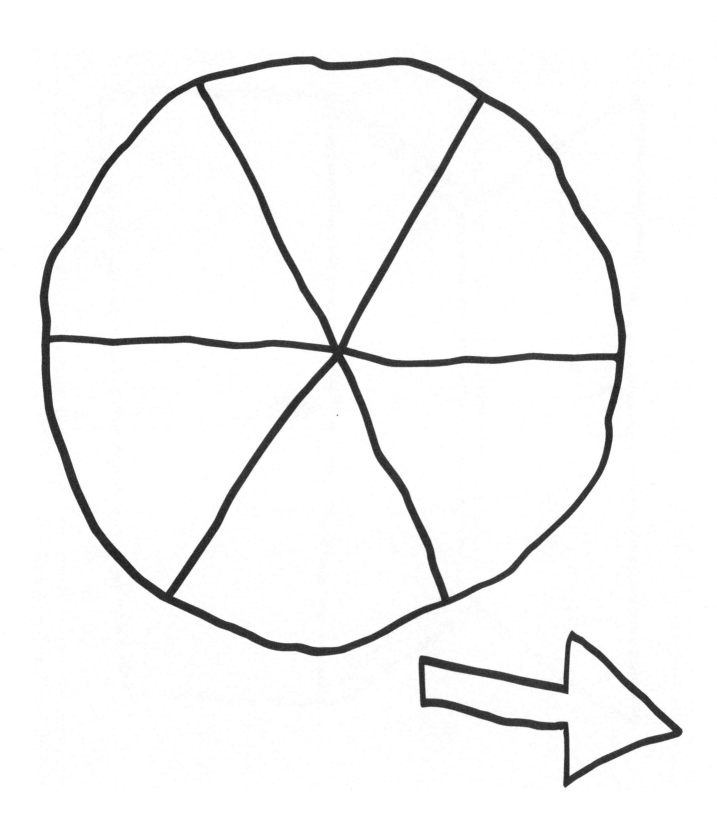

# NOTES

1 From the Church of England website at <https://www.churchofengland.org/prayer-worship/topical-prayers/a-prayer-for-the-refugee-crisis.aspx> (accessed 26 July 2017). Taken from The Church of England Topical Prayers: A Prayer for the Refugee Crisis, © The Archbishops' Council, 2017, and reproduced by permission. All rights reserved. <copyright@churchofengland.org>.

2 Philip Yancey, *What's So Amazing about Grace?* (Zondervan: Grand Rapids, Michigan, 1997), p. 71: 'Grace means there is nothing we can do to make God love us more . . . And grace means there is nothing we can do to make God love us less . . . Grace means that God already loves us as much as an infinite God can possibly love.'

3 Rowan Williams, broadcast Tuesday 18 October 2005 on *The Terry Wogan Show*, BBC Radio 2.

4 Walter Brueggemann, *Sabbath as Resistance: Saying no to the culture of now* (Westminster John Knox Press: Louisville, Kentucky, 2014), p. 3.